GLOBAL EXCHANGE
Reading and Writing in a World Context

Ann Watters

Stanford University

PEARSON

Prentice
Hall

Upper Saddle River, New Jersey 07458

Library of Congress Cataloging-in-Publication Data

Watters, Ann.
  Global exchange : reading and writing in a world context / Ann Watters.
    p. cm.
  ISBN 0-13-048762-7
  1. College readers. 2. English language--Rhetoric--Problems, exercises, etc.
3. International cooperation--Problems, exercises, etc. 4. International relations—
Problems, exercises, etc. 5. Report writin—Problems, exercises, etc. 6. Globalization—
Problems, exercises, etc. 7. Readers—International cooperation. 8. Readers—
International relations. 9. Readers--Globalization. I. Title.

  PE1417.W285 2005
  808'.0427--dc22

                                                                          2004005936

Editor-in-Chief (Editorial): Leah Jewell
Senior Acquisitions Editor: Corey Good
Editorial Assistant: Steve Kyritz
Production Liaison: Joanne Hakim
Executive Marketing Manager:
  Brandy Dawson
Marketing Assistant: Alison Peck
Assistant Manufacturing Manager:
  Mary Ann Gloriande
Cover Art Director: Jayne Conte
Cover Design: Bruce Kenselaar
Cover Illustration/Photo: David Ridley/
  SIS, Inc.
Director, Image Resource Center:
  Melinda Reo

Manager, Rights and Permissions:
  Zina Arabia
Manager, Visual Research: Beth Brenzel
Manager, Cover Visual Research &
  Permissions: Karen Sanatar
Image Permission Coordinator:
  Frances Toepfer
Photo Researcher: Kathy Ringrose
Permissions Specialist: The Permissions
  Group
Composition/Full-Service Project
  Management: John Shannon/
  Pine Tree Composition, Inc.
Printer/Binder: Phoenix Book Tech Park

Credits and acknowledgments borrowed from other sources and reproduced, with permission, in this textbook appear on page 501–502.

Pearson Education LTD., London
Pearson Education Singapore, Pte. Ltd
Pearson Education, Canada, Ltd
Pearson Education–Japan
Pearson Education Australia PTY, Limited

Pearson Education North Asia Ltd
Pearson Educación de Mexico, S.A. de C.V.
Pearson Education Malaysia, Pte. Ltd
Pearson Education, Upper Saddle River,
  New Jersey

10 9 8 7 6 5 4 3 2 1
ISBN 0-13-048762-7

CONTENTS

CHAPTER 4   ISSUES IN GLOBALIZATION   187

CHAPTER 5   WOMEN AND SOCIETY   265

CHAPTER 6   ONE WORLD HEALTH
AND THE ENVIRONMENT   331

PREFACE

In memory of my Irish brother-in-law, Norbert Alfred "Norm" Tracy,
whose formidable skills in argumentation inspired me
to study rhetoric in self-defense. Slán go fóill.

Global Exchange: Reading and Writing in a World Context is a first-year composition reader drawing from diverse genres and cultural traditions. This book is designed to help students expand their perspectives from mainstream American viewpoints and media to include perspectives from other regions, traditions, and cultures. The book aims to use the resources of the Internet as well as the texts and images provided in the book to help accomplish these goals. It includes an introductory chapter devoted to instruction in critical reading and writing, seven thematic chapters on international and global issues, and an appendix with source materials and additional Web sites.

PEDAGOGICAL APPARATUS

Chapter One gives an overview of reading and writing processes, with attention to issues in international and visual rhetoric. It offers guidance in analyzing texts and images; outlines an Aristotelian model for analyzing texts and images; and provides instruction in prewriting, drafting, and revising, as well as suggestions for integrating outside research into essays. It includes several student essays. This chapter includes a description of community service writing and recommendations for implementing service learning experience into a course with a global theme as well as suggestions for collaboration and peer group work.

In addition to the rhetorical discussions in Chapter One, each of the thematic chapters includes an introduction to the chapter theme. For each selection within the chapter, introductory notes provide context and background; to guide students' exploration of the selections, questions for discussion and suggestions for writing and research follow each text or image. At the end of each chapter, questions on the connections between selections enable students to integrate their knowledge of the texts and images both within that chapter and across chapters. End-of-chapter assignments offer suggestions for more expansive research and writing assignments as well as opportunities for service learning and peer collaboration. Finally, selected Web sites are listed to provide opportunities to explore in depth some of the issues raised in the chapter. As noted in the introduction, this book is designed to engage students in the process of reading and analyzing texts and images from diverse sources, and the Web sites included will assist this process.

READINGS AND IMAGES

Chapters Two through Eight are thematically oriented chapters that focus on readings and images for study and discussion. Chapter Two, "America: Perspectives at Home and Abroad," moves from images of America early in its political and social history to reflections on its place in the current global context. Chapter Three, "Crossing Cultures," focuses on the international context including but also moving beyond the United States; it emphasizes beliefs and values as well as divergent views of intercultural exchange. Chapter Four, "Issues in Globalization," examines crosscurrents on a global scale, from divergent world views to integrated economies across nations. Chapter Five, "Women and Society", focuses on a particular theme within and across cultures, drawing both on traditional views and on creative and innovative ways in which women contribute to their communities. Chapter Six, "One World: Health and the Environment", examines two concerns that require worldwide cooperation: global health and the global environment. SARS and the prospects of bioterrorism have pushed international cooperation on health issues to a new level with the realization that epidemics are, as one writer notes, "only a plane ride away." Chapter Seven, "Conflict: Images of the Other", focuses on the ways in which we create an idea and an image of the enemy; this chapter integrates both primary and secondary sources to help us understand the ways in which enemies and conflicts evolve. Chapter Eight, "A Post–9/11 World", explores the events of 9 11 and their context, as well as related topics such as living with terrorism. An appendix includes resources and background selections to provide historical or cultural context for some of the text's themes and selections.

ACKNOWLEDGMENTS

At Prentice Hall, thanks go to Corey Good for his interest and faith in this project and his unfailing support and good humor. Thanks also to Steve Kyritz, Brandy Dawson, Allison Peck, and to John Shannon. Heidi Madison provided invaluable contributions as director of photography.

At Stanford, many thanks go to Susan Wyle and Ardel Thomas for feedback on the manuscript and for professional and personal support throughout the process. Thanks also to Andrea Lunsford and Marvin Diogenes for their interest in the global course theme and to Joyce Moser, Ron Rebholz, Wendy Goldberg, and my other PWR colleagues for their supportive presence and friendship as well as to Christina Huerta and Rania Hegazi for their administrative support. Numerous students provided feedback on materials and assignments as well as sample papers that are included in this book; they continue to inspire me with their intellectual curiosity and their diligence. Notable were research assistants Arjun Rustagi, Sudi West, and Alex Bradford. Additional research and computer wizardry were provided by Andrew Watters and Mike Watters, and Michael Pollatsek offered breadth and depth in his knowledge of art history. Malgorzata Schaefer of Stanford University Libraries was also supportive.

At the Hoover Institution Archives at Stanford, Elena Danielson, Carole Leadenham, and Cissie Hill were remarkably knowledgeable and wonderful colleagues; many thanks for their generous and continued support in locating and obtaining materials for this book.

Among family and friends, Tom Watters was unfailingly supportive throughout the process. Susan Cohn and Laurie Spencer were generous with feedback and support, as were the rest of the Tahoe gang and the Coffee group. Heidi Madison, Alexandra Matthews, and Jean Sarris provided excellent contributions to the project from photo research and direction to wisdom and strong coffee. In addition to inspiring acute stress disorder from previous editing, Pat Miles provided a supportive presence throughout this process.

I also extend my gratitude to the reviewers whose feedback helped to shape and improve this book: Susan McDermott, Hudson Valley Community College; Candace Montoya, University of Oregon; Chitralekha Duttagupta, Arizona State University; William Griffin, St. Charles Community College; Jennifer Palmgren, Saint Paul's College; Robert G. Roth, Middlesex County College; Jane Hammons, University of California at Berkeley; Dan Malachuk, Daniel Webster College; Kim Stanley, McPherson College; and Susan Nash, University of Oklahoma.

Ann Watters
Stanford University

1

INTRODUCTION

READING ACROSS INTERNATIONAL CULTURES

Students in our post–9/11 era probably need little convincing that it may be valuable to learn more about international perspectives. A premise of this textbook is that in the present day, we can benefit from having a clearer understanding of our international context, of non-US perspectives. Between the initial proposal and the publication of this book, the US presidency was disputed, the 9/11 attacks occurred, bin Laden became a household name, and the US and Coalition forces went to war in Iraq and considered options in Liberia. In the United States, France's opposition to war with Iraq prompted a backlash against the French, from "Freedom Fries" to boycotts of travel and commerce. Aung San Suu Kyi, opposition and pro-democratic leader of Myanmar (formerly Burma; see her essay in Chapter Three), was released from house arrest and later rearrested. Iranian students began public protests. A new leader for the Palestinians emerged and hopes for peace between Israelis and Palestinians surfaced and retreated. Anthrax emerged as a critical threat, to be replaced by SARS. The U.S.A. PATRIOT Act emerged as another type of threat to civil liberties, or as a necessary tool to fight terrorism, depending on one's point of view.

To reflect critically on the events of our times, we will benefit from moving beyond our traditional means of obtaining information and exchanging ideas. Scholar and writer Edward Said (pronounced Sigh-eed'), discussing a concept of C. Wright Mills, outlines a "cultural apparatus," or a system that conveys information, culture, even perceptions and experience. It includes the media through which we experience the world and form our opinions and beliefs. Using this textbook involves both working within that cultural apparatus—after all, we do receive information through our written, broadcast, and Internet media—and moving beyond it by increasing our awareness of this system and by finding ways to integrate perceptions and opinions from international cultures and contexts.

This text aims to accomplish these goals through three approaches. First, we will study materials from international contexts. We will examine texts and images using critical thinking skills and, as appropriate, utilizing Aristotle's model of assessing appeals to ethos, pathos, and logos. Many of the discussion questions will focus on these appeals. As we use this approach we need to remain mindful that it is from a Western tradition and consider to what degree it can be universally applied. Second, we will take advantage of our global Internet to obtain and interact with texts from many perspectives and contexts. Often, due to language constraints, we will be looking at texts from other cultures that appear in translation, but we will also make use of translation engines and visual materials that help us experience other cultures more directly. Finally, the Appendix at the end of this book includes source readings or materials on Precedents and Traditions; these selections convey some of the assumptions and values of cultures in which they are prominent.

As scholar Deborah Tannen notes in her recent book, *The Argument Culture,* American media, among others, tend to line up opposing views in an effort to "be fair" and hear from "the other side." Is it Palestine's land or Israel's? Are they terrorists or freedom fighters? Too often, though, highly complex, difficult questions and issues are compressed, flattened, and oversimplified by being presented as a pro–con, either–or proposition. This problem is prominent in "sound bite" broadcast programs, but even a text such as this one, which strives to move beyond all-or-none approaches, has limits in how much it can present. To address this concern, this text will encourage you, both in core assignments outlined later and in chapter questions and assignments, to take the discussion outward, to pursue more information and other viewpoints. You can do so by using outlets and resources outside the mainstream, outside your "cultural apparatus." Such resources include the Internet, starting with the sites included later, chapter assignments in this text and on the companion Web site; discussion groups; and other international media such as newspapers and television or radio broadcasts that can expand your perceptions and challenge your ideas.

Recommended Core Assignments for Reading and Writing in a Global Context

Although Americans have had access to international newspapers and some foreign broadcasts for some years, with the expansion of the Internet and the World Wide Web, we now have access to an abundance of international news sites, discussion sites, and special interest sites. Numerous sites are available in a number of languages, and those that are not can usually be viewed with a translation engine from one of the large portals or search engine sites.

The first recommended core assignment for reading and writing in a global context is that for the duration of this course, you select and follow a non-US Web site. If you are not fluent in a language other than English or cannot obtain a non-English site in translation, consider following the BBC site, or a Canadian, Australian, Irish, or other primarily English-language site. Although not necessarily highly divergent from mainstream American cultures, these sites can provide alternatives to the mainstream US presses that tend toward homogenous reporting. Even sites purporting to be international in scope, such as CNN, are nevertheless rooted in American interests and values. So consider following a Web site that represents a markedly different view from your culture of origin and from mainstream US society.

In addition to following a non-US Web site or news source, consider following and then participating in a discussion group with international participants. In this assignment you will become a participant-observer; you will put forth and test your own ideas and ability to communicate across cultures, and at the same time you can assess how others make their arguments and attempt to persuade others of their point of view.

Analyzing Persuasion across Cultures

Both universal and context-specific elements pervade communication, particularly persuasive communication. Analyzing the issues that so often provoke argument—such as gender; management of land, power, and water; or the role of values in government—can provide perspective on both common denominators and differences. Culture entails the common memories, customs, experiences, and worldview of a group or society. In attempting to understand how different cultures persuade and what assumptions and references are involved in their communication, students may find it helpful to familiarize themselves with relevant historical materials. For example, to understand the political heat President George W. Bush took for using the word "crusade" in a speech post–9/11, it helps to know the history of the Crusades, a series of battles in the Middle Ages fought by Christians against Muslims in the Holy Lands. Consider researching the topic from multiple points of view; for example, consult both *The Oxford Illustrated History of the Crusades* (Riley-Smith, 1995) and *The Crusades through Arab Eyes* (Amin Maalouf, 1984). Another term that has caused intercultural misunderstandings is "martyr." Some Christians who respect and perhaps even venerate martyrs of the early Christian church are appalled by Islamist suicide bombers.

You may not be able to discern the subtler elements of culture, and no matter how much you review historical accounts or even cultural readings, you will not have the worldview of someone who grew up in the culture. Nevertheless, becoming informed about core cultural values and assumptions can help you to communicate with others, to convey your intent as accurately and persuasively as possible, and at the same time to understand clearly the messages you receive.

A goal in reading a range of materials on a particular theme is finding ways in which strategies of persuasion differ or remain universal. For example, appeals to God and to God's authority can be utilized on both sides of a conflict, as we observe in the Bush and bin Laden texts in Chapter Eight. At the same time, the assumptions—about values, about logic—that support arguments may depend on the time and place and means, or the context, of the argument. For example, the US Supreme Court and an ayatollah in an Islamic state can both be cited as authorities, but the appeal will be effective only to audiences for whom that authority is accepted and persuasive.

Despite some universals, different cultures may approach structuring exposition and argument in different ways. Some societies, notably American and many other Western cultures, derive their approach to argument from Greek roots, as noted earlier. They tend to assert points directly and then support them with evidence. American academic institutions generally value this approach and expect that student papers will assert a thesis directly and early in the essay and support it in the body of the essay. In the past several decades, linguists and other scholars have paid attention to what they call "contrastive rhetoric," or intercultural differences in communication. They note, for example, that some cultures avoid the direct statement of thesis and instead provide evidence and assert ideas and let the reader draw the inference. Some writers from other cultures approach a point, veer away, then come back to the point; others gradually move closer to the core point throughout the essay and end the essay with the thesis/conclusion. Some cultures, notably Native American cultures, use narrative more prominently than others. In terms of structure, even sentence style may differ, with some cultures valuing parallel structures whereas others prefer subordination, with amplifying dependent clauses supporting one main point.

In approaching texts from other cultures, then, you may find it useful to be mindful that writers may use divergent approaches in some elements of exposition and persuasion. International businesspersons, whose success relies on cultivating a high level of intercultural understanding, have noted that much of persuasion across cultures relies on individual variables, such as personality, rather than on cultural variables. If this premise is true, you also will be able to use your own responses to texts and arguments to help you understand how readers or viewers from other cultures might respond.

A limitation of a textbook of this kind is that many of the non-US texts will have been translated or will have been written in English by international writers. Furthermore, many writers and leaders from Eastern or Middle Eastern cultures, such as Aung San Suu Kyi and Edward Said, were themselves educated or have resided in Western countries, particularly in Britain and the United States. As persuasive images from other cultures will suggest, however, strategies of persuasion and appeals to values and authority, emotions, and logic are still prominent. Internet searches can supply many examples of persuasive photographs, cartoons, and other images that convey a point but lose less in translation. If you do research texts in other languages, some translation engines such as Alta Vista's Babel Fish will provide a basic sense of content.

Analyzing Texts and Images

Although readers will naturally read and respond to texts in view of their own cultures, ideas, values, and experiences, we can nevertheless strive to understand, analyze, and interpret texts and images from other societies and regions. The selections and exercises in this book are designed to help you understand the assumptions and values that may underlie your own arguments and to become more aware of the beliefs, claims, and arguments originating in non-US cultures.

One approach to analyzing other texts, described in *The Rhetoric of Aristotle,* entails assessing persuasion in terms of appeals to ethos, pathos, and logos. This model can help determine how speakers, writers, or artists make their points by appealing to ethos, or the beliefs and values they have in common with their audiences; pathos, or emotions; and logic, or reasons and examples.

Appeals to ethos include invoking religious beliefs or deities to emphasize shared values and to lend authority to one's own position or argument. Whether it means ending a speech with "God bless America" or peppering a speech with "Praise Allah," the underlying premise is the same: The speaker assumes that the audience will accept the authority of the higher power and that referencing the higher power in the speech will lend credibility to the speaker and invoke a set of values and beliefs rooted in that culture. The extent to which this authority is observed, and the ways in which it interacts with other appeals, may vary considerably by audience. When the Germans invaded Poland in September 1939, Polish musician and patriot Ignacy Jan Paderewski asked Mahatma Gandhi, known for his efforts toward peace and justice through nonviolent resistance in India and elsewhere, to speak out against the German invasion. In the letter that follows, Mahatma Gandhi replies to Paderewski's request:

(HOOVER INSTITUTION ARCHIVES)

What is your sense of the power and authority Paderewski attributes to Gandhi in asking for his help? What sense of Gandhi do you get from this brief reply to Paderewski. What is your sense of his authority and credibility? In what ways could moral authority help in combating an invasion with tanks and bombs? To whom would his authority be persuasive?

Appeals to pathos call upon the emotions, passions, and feelings of the audience. Aristotle noted that engaging the whole person, including emotions, is strategic in persuasion, and for good or ill, emotions are often evoked in attempts to move people to action. Emotional appeals may overlap with religious beliefs—uniting Arab Muslims against the United States by identifying the military presence in the sacred places of Mecca and Medina, for example; or they may overlap with moral outrage, as in President Bush's speech uniting Americans and allies against "the evildoers." A photograph of a baby dressed as a suicide bomber evokes quite strong emotions, though the conclusion drawn from this appeal will, again, vary by audience.

Appeals to logos, or logic, entail forming the logical structure of an argument, such as providing examples to support an inference and invoking general principles that are then applied to specific cases. The two general categories of logical argumentation are known as induction and deduction. Inductive reasoning, or the scientific method, involves observing a number of specific cases and then drawing a conclusion from those cases. For example, if people from another country were criticizing US policy, pointing out American military interventions in Vietnam, Grenada, Panama, Kuwait, and Afghanistan, they might draw an inference that the United States is hawkish and militaristic. An American who does not share such a view might question this conclusion and point out that in most cases US assistance was requested by the foreign power, and furthermore, the aid was offered to restore the rightful government of the region in question; thus the assertions of imperialism are invalid.

Deductive reasoning takes a general principle and applies it to specific cases. If a deductive argument were spelled out, it might sound something like this: "Britain and America always stand together in times of international crisis. The Iraq situation is an international crisis. Therefore Britain and America will stand together in the Iraq crisis." Such an argument will more often be stated in a more compact format: "Britain and America have always stood together as allies and will do so in Iraq." Deductive reasoning holds as long as the claims or premises on which it is based are valid and the reasoning from premises to conclusion is sound. In analyzing this argument, we might dispute whether the situation in Iraq constitutes an international crisis or whether America and Britain have always stood together in international crises; for example, America did not immediately jump to Britain's side in the Falkland Islands conflict, and America has engaged in international conflicts without significant participation from Britain.

Whether or not the author explicitly states a thesis, in your analysis you should determine the core point and then assess whether this thesis or claim is supported by the evidence offered. In analyzing the logic of an argument, you will need to consider if the reasoning is flawed or if there are errors in logic.

These errors, known as logical fallacies, are sometimes obvious but often can be detected only upon careful analysis. Some of the more common logical fallacies are as follows:

> *Either–Or Fallacy, or False Dilemma:* In this fallacy the author states that there are only two choices. For example, when a politician claims that "you are with us or against us," he or she presumes that no possibility exists for a neutral third party, a disinterested bystander.
>
> *Hasty Generalization:* In this case the author draws a broad conclusion from too few examples or too little data; this fallacy figures prominently in stereotyping, a process evident in visual propaganda.
>
> *Ad Hominem:* This fallacy translates literally as "to the man" and means attacking the person rather than the argument he or she is making. If Yasser Arafat makes a proposal for a Middle East peace plan and opponents say, "This plan is poorly conceived and unworkable—after all, it was written by a terrorist," they are attacking the man and not the plan.
>
> *Post hoc ergo propter hoc:* This phrase literally translates as "after this, therefore because of this"; the post hoc fallacy confuses correlation with causation. Because A precedes B does not mean that A caused B. The 9/11 attacks occurred before the anthrax attacks, but that does not mean they caused the anthrax attacks or that the same entity was responsible for both.
>
> *Non Sequitur:* this term translates as "it does not follow" and is often used to refer to a lapse in logic. This fallacy is frequently evident in advertising; for example, advertisers juxtapose a product with an image of an appealing lifestyle and suggest to viewers that the two are connected.

An Approach to Analyzing Texts

Analysis of a text involves identifying the basic parts of the text and determining the ways in which those elements interact to produce the text's effect. Developing a systematic approach to analysis can help critical readers to organize their analysis. Consider the following approach:

> What is the purpose of the text? What is its context—the occasion, author, audience, location, and time?
>
> What is the point, theme, concept, or main idea the author develops?
>
> What is the supporting evidence? What is the quality of the evidence presented? Is it representative? Credible? Acceptable based on the authority of the writer or documented appropriately? Does it support the thesis or claim being asserted?
>
> Examine the logic and shape of the argument. What is the pattern of assertion and support: top-down, with main point and then evidence? Or does the author make general remarks, move into more specific information, and then assert the thesis as conclusion? Are significant opposing points refuted or conceded? Are there unsupported assertions?
>
> How does the language contribute to the argument? Is it clear and appropriate for the intended audience? Do some terms need clarification? Is the language highly connotative or emotionally charged? Does the language patronize the audience?

After developing a thorough analysis, you are ready either to contribute to class discussion of a text or to write an essay developing your analysis. If you are responding to an essay assignment, you may want to focus on a specific aspect or set of elements in the text you are analyzing, depending on the specific assignment and the length of the paper you plan to develop. For example, you may want to focus on religious metaphors, connotative language, or types of evidence in the text. This focused essay, like any essay analyzing a text, will need to develop a main point or thesis rather than simply report the analysis of the various elements. You may find it helpful to see how another student wrote in responding to this type of assignment. Ashlee Lynn's analysis of President Bush's post–9/11 address, which integrates some outside research, is included in the section "Integrating Outside Sources" later in this chapter.

Analyzing Visual Arguments

Although we often think of contemporary cultures as being more image-driven than previous societies, in fact visual arguments are many centuries old. In the eleventh century, the Bayeux Tapestry, the needlework rendering of the Battle of Hastings, relayed the story of the Norman Conquest, but clearly from the point of view of the victors, the Normans. The tapestry, through its emphasis on a Briton's broken oath and on the obligation of loyalty to William, demonstrates the ways in which point of view and selection of evidence can support an argumentative agenda.

Interpretation of images depends on the context—the place, time, audience, and circumstances. Analyzing images entails considering not only universal appeals but also any culture-specific information insofar as you can determine it. For example, the color red is highly significant in several cultures, with some overlap and some distinct meaning. As scholar Victoria Bonnell points out in *Iconography of Power,* the color red appeared in Russian religious icons, used for images of holiness and reference. When Bolshevik poster artists use red in rendering designs of the workers, the color develops the theme and argument about the role of the worker in the communist state because it evokes past historical and cultural associations.

Consider this image of Burmese Opposition leader Aung San Suu Kyi:

(AP/WORLD WIDE PHOTO)

Examine the elements of this photograph—the speaker and the image behind her. Without knowing the context of the image, what are your hypotheses about the setting for the photograph?

As you read about Aung San Suu Kyi in the introductory note in Chapter 3, you can find additional information to help you understand the rhetorical appeals of this photograph. The speaker in this photograph, Aung San Suu Kyi, is leader of the democratic opposition to the regime currently in power in Burma, which the regime has renamed Myanmar. The image behind her is that of her father, national liberation leader General Aung San. The juxtaposition of her image with his larger image behind her appeals to authority by positioning her as his political and philosophical heir.

Consider the following visual argument found at the entrance to a home:

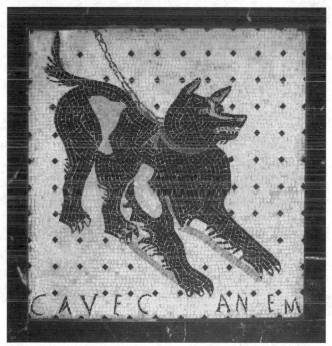

(DR. ANN WATTERS)

You don't need to read Latin to get the point of a big dog showing its teeth at the home's entrance, but if you do, the phrase Cave Canem, or Beware of Dog, reinforces the point and is reinforced by the image. The image evokes the emotional appeal of fear: The dog is not a toy poodle or friendly pug; it is a large black guard dog, such as a German shepherd. A leash is visible, suggesting that the dog is under the control of its owner. The dog is large relative to the space and the size of the accompanying text; white teeth contrast with the dog's dark color.

Even without knowing the social and cultural intricacies of ancient Pompeii, still, we can analyze this image by assessing its persuasive appeals. The argument appeals to emotion by invoking fear, with the image of a large dog with teeth bared. It appeals to values by invoking both the authority of the owner (who holds the leash) and values regarding private property or personal space. And it appeals to logic through inference: If you trespass you will face serious consequences.

Centuries later, and thousands of miles away, the following image appears:

(ANDREW G. WATTERS)

This contemporary version was found in an American suburb. The message, "If you come in uninvited you may be greeted by a large dog and suffer the consequences," clearly spans the ages and crosses cultures.

Analysis of an Image

Important questions when analyzing visual images, from Web sites to posters, include the following:

Who is the intended audience? Why was the image created? Who is the author? Is the source an institution (i.e., government, commercial institution)? An informal group? An individual? What was the author's goal?

What is the context of the image—the source, the medium, the purpose, the audience? What do you know of its culture of origin? Is it intended for that audience or for additional audiences with different cultures, languages, assumptions, and values?

What are the elements or parts—is it image only or image plus text? What is the relationship between image and text in size, position, meaning? Are some figures dominant and some subordinate? Is the author making a particular point by juxtaposing some elements? Is your attention directed to certain areas of the image or away from others? What colors are evident and what might be their significance?

When assessing Web sites, also consider the following:

> *Authority:* Who is the author? on what basis does the author claim authority? Does an individual or an organization take responsibility for the Web site? Does a university, credible government authority, or respected organization support the site? Is the site updated regularly?
> *Evidence:* Does the author offer evidence to support claims made? Can the evidence be located or verified independently elsewhere?
> *Design:* How are the appearance and design of the site? Are they professional or do they seem more amateurish? Is text clear, appropriate, correct? Are images clear and appropriate to theme and content?
> *Connections:* Does the site offer links to other sites? If so, what is the overall quality of those sites?

Case Study: Analyzing an Image.

Chris Babson's assignment in his first-quarter writing class was to select an image and analyze its persuasive appeals. He found a persuasive satire on a Nike advertisement and then assessed the satire's persuasive strategies.

A Call to Action

In the late 1990s, Nike began a revolutionary advertising campaign for a new line of running shoes and clothing. The series of advertisements centered on the portrayal of striking images of athletes determined to succeed and driven, apparently, by the stellar Nike products they wore. Although the advertisements emphasized the resolve and fortitude of both sexes, they were directed primarily at aspiring females in search of recognition and

(*ADBUSTERS* MAGAZINE)

respect in a male-dominated world. Soon after the launch of the Nike series, Adbusters, an environmentally and socially conscious advertising agency, began a similar campaign to raise awareness about Nike products and their origin. Adbusters developed a series of posters depicting what they assert is the harsh reality faced by underpaid workers in Nike's Indonesian factories. In one such ad, an anonymous author questions the materialistic nature of modern society, implicating this society in the exploitation of the Third World by corporate America (*http://adbusters.org/spoofads/fashion/nike/*). The author effectively implements text and visual emphasis, realism, and organization to elicit an emotional response from the audience and then channels this sympathy into resentment toward Nike.

The textual aspect of the poster attempts to gain the sympathy of the audience through confrontational diction and organization. Initially, the author presents the audience with a scenario characteristic of Nike advertisements where the reader temporarily lives the life of the protagonist of the story. This poster, however, quickly deviates from the form and subject of the Nike advertisements that it imitates. Whereas Nike commercials generally plunge their audience into a world where athletes accept suffering as a sacrifice for success, this advertisement lures its audience into the harsh reality of an Indonesian worker, devoid of comfort and hope. The use of the second person throughout the text portion of the poster adds a confrontational tone and further involves the audience: "You" are running, "You" want a raise, "You" are overworked, "You" have no workers' rights. The text confronts the reader with dilemmas that characterize everyday life for Indonesian workers. When they "ask for a raise," they "disappear." The similarity between the American audience and the workers is further noted in the third line: The Indonesian workers, just as the audience, strive "to be all (they) can be." Unfortunately, the image suggests, these workers cannot accomplish this American ideal due to oppression by companies like Nike who underpay them.

The orientation and organization of the text further emphasize the hopelessness of the situation. The passage has a distinctive meter imposed by the division of sentences from line to line. "You're running / . . . but it's not easy / when you / work / sixty hours a week." The pace increases and becomes more frenzied as the worker's struggle to survive becomes more desperate: "Sixty hours a week / making sneakers in an / Indonesian factory / and your friends / disappear." Furthermore, this pacing involves the reader in the worker's plight, adding an element of excitement to the poster. After involving the audience in such a manner, the pace and the tone of the advertisement shift abruptly.

The speed of presentation that was once facilitated by a smaller font size slows due to an overemphasis on the phrase "so think." The audience emerges from the fast-paced scenario to encounter a solution. According to the author, the reader must "think globally" about the effect of buying Nike products instead of considering how these products enhance one's looks or per-

formance. Wearing Nike is not "so cool" anymore. Now aware of
the hardships of Indonesian workers, the reader has a humanitarian obligation to aid them in some manner. In this case, the
option presented to the audience is to reconsider the importance
of purchasing Nike products. Is having brand-name running
shoes as important as objecting to the injustice in Nike factories
overseas? The audience now realizes that by purchasing Nike
products it endorses this inhumane activity. As intended, the author has planted a seed of doubt and objection toward Nike in
the audience that cannot be ignored. This seed is further cultivated through visual contrast and emphasis in the poster.

Just as the text of the poster served to involve the audience
through confrontational second-person narration, the visual aspect of the poster involves the audience by provoking an emotional response to both striking contrast and evocative imagery.
The prevailing image of the poster is an Indonesian woman who
appears to be running. Ironically, although she apparently works
at one of the Nike shoe factories in question, she wears no shoes.
Nike advertisements depict solitary runners in search of com-
pletion and strength, but this poster displays a similar runner
with an entirely different purpose. The runner here flees a hopeless reality where she cannot provide for her child, represented
by the baby-like figure in her arms, or herself. If she cannot afford sufficient clothing, how can she afford sufficient food and
shelter? Her blank and placid stare confronts the audience with
a hopeless situation that it cannot directly affect but cannot ignore. The eyes of the woman peer at the reader and plea for
help. In addition, the perspective from which the audience views
her indicates the severity of the problem in Indonesia. Her size
and, correspondingly, the size of her people's problems, have
grown too large.

The poster leaves the audience with the shadow of a weary
giant on its conscience, encouraging action to improve the situation. While her fading black and white image still remains fresh
in the minds of the audience, a solution emerges. The audience
should "think globally" about Nike and whether it should continue to buy Nike products. The size of the text and the contrast
between its coloration and the rest of the poster further highlight
the author's point. The correlation between blood and Nike is
suggested as the red coloration of the text is identical to that of
the Nike swoosh. This red color emphasizes a deeper message:
The blood of Indonesian factory workers, it argues, now rests on
the hands, or feet, of those who buy Nike shoes.

Overall, the poster argues its point about the plight of Indonesian workers by offering imagery and text to inform the au-

dience of the hardships faced by these workers. After emerging from this experience with sympathy and understanding, the audience sees a possible solution, a way in which it can help improve the lives of Indonesian workers. The readers must reconsider the effects of their actions and change accordingly. As the audience sees in the background of the poster, the image representing all Indonesian factory workers is fading to gray under injustice and hopelessness. If the audience acts correctly, according to this view, it can bring spirit and hope back into lives that are fading away.

Step back and analyze the process Babson used to develop his analysis and his essay. What thesis does he assert? How does he support that thesis? How are topic ideas and paragraphs structured? How effective are transitions? Does the evidence he offers from the image support the assertions he makes?

LEARNING THROUGH WRITING
AND THE WRITING PROCESS

Most of the writing assignments in this textbook focus on writing argumentative or analytical essays, with or without outside research. These types of writing are not dichotomous, either–or categories, however; just about any type of writing you will do in college, and beyond, will make use of varying degrees of persuasive strategies. If we plot out the levels of persuasiveness in different types of writing, the continuum might look something like this:

←――→

lab report business report analytical/expository essay argumentative essay Op Ed debate

For example, a lab report is seemingly so objective that passive voice language is encouraged (i.e., "The experiment was conducted under sterile conditions, using a 100-milliliter Calorimeter. . . ."). However, you are still making appeals to ethos in following the dictates and values of the scientific method and the academic world. You want the reader to know that you followed procedures carefully and recorded your results accurately. An analytical, expository essay asserts a point of view—a claim or thesis—and then supports that thesis with evidence, examples, or reasoning to support its claim. Although it doesn't have a strong agenda or "ax to grind," its goal is to prove a case and it often will benefit from considering alternative approaches, views, or interpretations. Analytical essays are expository in nature; they take apart and examine texts or images, assess how these texts or images work, and develop a core point or thesis supported by the analysis. They use examples from the object of study to support their view and may also integrate secondary material to support the analysis. You may have written similar essays in literature classes, in which you are asked to analyze the structure or language of a poem or the plot of a short story. In the analytical essay assignments in this textbook, you will more often be asked to analyze the persuasive strategies of a text or image or the evidence of a researched essay.

An expository essay is still persuasive in that its goal is to make a point and then support it well to persuade the reader to accept its conclusions. An argumentative essay has more of an edge to it—it proposes a certain point of view or course of action and it considers a response to opposing views—with concession, refutation, or a combination of the two. The writer often utilizes outside research to add credibility and authority to his or her argument and conclusions. As noted earlier, academic essays often entail a direct structure, with an assertion first and then support. Sometimes, however, especially in the case of highly controversial topics, writers can maintain the open mind and interest of the reader by deferring assertion of the thesis statement until the conclusion of the essay, after the writer has had a chance to make the argument, offer evidence, and dispatch opposing views with refutation or concession.

Guidelines for Analytical Essays

You will first need to select a subject for analysis and develop a hypothesis. Choose a subject with enough content and interest to support your analysis and to enable you to develop a thoughtful thesis statement that asserts a point about the subject. A compelling text, an advertisement, editorial cartoon, poster, or Web site that combines text and image in persuasive and thought-provoking ways can engage your interest as well as your readers'. Many assignments in this text will suggest options for analytical essays. Many of the texts and images included here are good prospects for analysis, and every chapter suggests Web sites on the general topic that provide additional material for study.

The Writing Process

In the last two decades educators at all levels have come to view writing as a process of prewriting, writing, and revising; you are likely already familiar with this model of writing instruction. Because prewriting strategies are so useful in developing essays, they are briefly reviewed here.

Prewriting.   Your instructor may assign you a topic, prompt, image, or text to which you will respond. If so, you still need to understand the parameters of the assignment—length, type of essay, use of secondary sources, timeline, and the like. If you have not been assigned a topic for your essay, you could try some of the following exercises to help you decide on a topic of interest to you that is engaging and challenging enough to keep you interested and to help you develop your skills and knowledge base.

Classic prewriting activities include brainstorming, systematic questioning, free writing, and clustering or mapping. In a brainstorming exercise, you list or jot down the different ideas, images, or phrases that come to mind as you think about the topic you have selected. For example, in writing about a persuasive image, such as an advertisement or a Web site photograph accompanying an article, you could write down your immediate reactions to the image, questions, and other thoughts that the image triggers for you. You could write at random or you could start with one area, such as descriptive details, then move to analysis of any text in the image; alternatively, you could brainstorm, focusing in turn on appeals to ethos, pathos, or logos. Some writers find it helpful to do a systematic review, such as responding to the journalistic questions, "Who? What? When? Where? Why? How?" You can apply these basic questions to your topic and note the various responses. For example, "Who?" could apply to the author/artist or to anyone captured in the image.

Free writing involves writing uncritically about a topic without letting your internal critic censor what you might write. This activity is particularly useful if you find yourself prone to writer's block and unable to accumulate much material without deleting or erasing your ideas as soon as they appear. Some writers take this technique a step further and, using a computer, write with the screen dimmed or the monitor turned off so that they can get their ideas out even more freely; a disadvantage is the abundance of typos that accompany this approach. Nevertheless, it is an excellent strategy to try if you feel stuck, uninspired, or blocked from expressing your ideas about the topic. Just be sure that you have opened a document file before starting so you are sure to be recording your writing.

In clustering, or mapping, you put the topic or idea in the middle of a page and map out responses, queries, connections, or related ideas to the primary topic, drawing lines out from the original prompt and then from responses to each other, often enclosing the responses in circles or bubbles. This approach often helps those who feel that they benefit from a more spatial, visual orientation to the topic and to connections between ideas.

A combination of those exercises that work well for you can help you move from envisioning your initial topic or prompt to developing material about it that helps you think through the topic and accumulate material—ideas, assertions, examples—to use in developing your draft. Often you can do short bursts of prewriting; review what you have written; and then take the useful responses, more specific topics, or images and examples and do a second, and then a third, pass through the exercises, developing progressively more material, looking for themes and patterns to emerge, and drawing connections between points, perhaps grouping assertions and examples by subtopic or more focused areas within the topic. Some writers use highlighters in different colors to "sort" the material they accumulate by topic.

After reviewing the prewriting material developed through these exercises; circling or highlighting useful and interesting phrases, sentences, images; and looking for an overall theme or pattern, see if you can develop a dominant main idea or tentative thesis. See if you can group parts of the material you developed under subtopics of the main idea. You may need to go back and do more prewriting to develop additional material or subtopics, generate examples, or develop the examples you do have. Then, write out a working thesis statement and try a working outline of the main points you have accumulated so far. Look for gaps, repetition, or overlap in the outline and refine what you have. Again, revisit the original prompt, text, or image to see if you can develop additional material, fill in the gaps, or clarify points that overlap. Compare the working outline you have with the material you previously sorted with a highlighter or grouped by topic, and then include any additional material developed through the most recent prewriting work. Try to line up the topic points in the order that seems most reader-friendly and logical; discuss *what* before you discuss *why* if that will help your reader follow you. For example, explain the content of a propaganda poster before you analyze the ways in which the various elements work together to form an argument. Consider whether you could discuss contradictory points first, as you go, or after you have made your initial points.

Drafting.   With a working thesis, a brief working outline, and the material supporting your topic points or key ideas supporting the thesis, try to draft out, topic by topic and paragraph by paragraph, the body of your essay. Often, writers jump right into the body of the essay and work out the introduction later. Of course you can start with your introduction if you prefer, but sometimes it's a stumbling point and best left until you've worked out the bulk of the essay.

An introduction generally helps you and your reader get in step, or get on the same wavelength. It provides background or a context for your thesis and discussion; it evokes interest in the topic; and responds to the reader's implied question, "Why should I read this essay?" Most often, you will find it useful to place your thesis at the end of the introduction, because at that point you have provided context for the reader and can use the thesis to launch the body of the essay that supports it.

If you are writing an essay that may reach an international audience—for example, if you will be posting it on the Web—you will need to pay particular attention to the assumptions, values, and biases underlying your assertions. You will need to think carefully about what information your readers already know, what they will accept as given, and what they will challenge or want to see supported with evidence. You may need to state your assumptions or clarify the context more than you would in an audience composed of classmates and an instructor in a traditional classroom. Also, you will want to step back and consider the language you use and the point of view you are taking. For example, you may want to be more careful about expressions such as "Our Bill of Rights guarantees the right to free speech" in favor of "The US Bill of Rights, First Amendment, provides certain protections for free speech. . . ." Your introduction may be a place to indicate point of view and overall assumptions about your topic, but you will need to be mindful of your audience throughout the essay.

When concluding your essay, think not only about the ways in which it can provide a sense of closure, but also a sense of progress in discussing the topic; in short papers, then, a simple summary of the points discussed may seem a bit repetitive. You could consider putting the topic in a larger context, you could mention implications of your discussion or topic, or you could leave the reader with a thought-provoking question or image. At the same time, avoid opening up new topics for discussion at this stage, because you do want to establish closure.

At any point in the drafting phase, from composing your working thesis to developing your core points to the first full draft, consider getting peer feedback to give you a sense of audience and to help you shape your essay appropriately for a reader. Often peer exchange workshops, whether in or out of class, are an excellent way to obtain feedback and also to sharpen your own critical skills by offering feedback to others.

Revising. After putting your draft aside for as much time as you can allow, preferably at least a day, review it by re-reading the thesis and topic ideas guiding each paragraph or section. Do they still work together? Do the topic points adequately develop the thesis? Does the thesis sentence encompass everything you want to discuss in the paper? If not, you need to adjust the thesis or adjust the topic points and body of the essay, because they must work together to form a coherent or unified essay. Then review the essay, paragraph by paragraph, for unity and adequate development within each paragraph. Next, review the whole essay for logic, transitions, and flow. Finally, consider sentences, word choice, grammar, and punctuation, making revisions for clear and concise sentences and for precise word choice as well as corrections of basic grammar and mechanics. Then, have a peer, a classmate, or a friend review the essay and give you feedback. Revise and refine your essay at least once more, proofread it for any typing errors or other issues, and make sure the format corresponds to the class specifications before submitting it.

Integrating Outside Sources

In developing your essay you will need to assess the assignment to determine if you should analyze the text or image with your own knowledge and perspective or if you should integrate outside sources and authority. For example, the assignment might be to write a brief two- to three-page analysis of an advertisement or propaganda poster. You could analyze the text or image, writing out your notes from the analysis, and after reviewing your notes, identify and develop a focus. For example, you could examine the logical fallacies in an advertisement or evaluate the emotional appeals in a piece of propaganda. Then, you could refine and develop your thesis statement, supporting it with evidence or examples from your subject. Chris Babson's essay earlier in this chapter is an example of such an essay. His assignment was to select a persuasive image or text and analyze it based on his own reactions and response to the image. He developed his essay without using additional sources.

For a more in-depth or lengthy assignment you could integrate background readings into your analysis. For example, you could integrate material from Sam Keen's discussion of religious aspects of enemy-making in your analysis of Mark Twain's "The War Prayer."

In a sense, the second type of analytical essay just described is a researched essay in that you have integrated a secondary source such as Keen into your discussion of a primary source—your website, advertisement, poster, or other primary material.

For a more in-depth or lengthy research project on the theme of this course, you would need to identify a topic you want to research in some detail. As a starting point, you could consider reviewing the end-of-chapter assignments for a chapter that interests you. Another way to guide your topic selection might be to determine if a community writing or service learning option exists where your research could benefit a community organization or nonprofit group. You could also consider topics that you want to learn more about, or topics you may be considering for more specialized work later in your college work or in your career. Local environmental or public health advocacy groups, for example, may be interested in your research of local policy, environmental, or political issues (e.g., local recycling efforts or land use). If you are interested in medicine, you could research local efforts for educating people about childhood vaccination programs.

An important and underrated aspect of developing a researched essay is first developing a research question. This question will drive your research and help you focus your topic while at the same time helping you to maintain an open mind about the information you find. After your instructor has provided you with any specifics or parameters you need to follow, try to identify a question to which you genuinely would like to find some answers. Get some feedback from peers and your instructor to help you determine if the scope and approach of the question are feasible for the time and resources available to you.

As you read in the topic area of your research question, you will gradually be able to develop a hypothesis, or a tentative response to your question. Keep track of your sources with a computer program, on note cards, in loose leaf notebooks that allow you to move text around, or some other organizational strategy that works for you. Consider file folders or pocket folders to contain articles, reprints, or loose clippings and notes. It is crucial to track your sources accurately and correctly so that you can document your sources, give credit where it is due, and appeal to authority by incorporating appropriate evidence into your paper.

Your instructor will work with you in identifying sources for your research. In most cases you should start with an overview of your topic by utilizing general reference sources in the library and online. As you become more well versed in your subject area, you will refine the hypothesis, narrow your search, and redouble your efforts in searching for specific information to develop the topic. Books will generally provide the most breadth on your topic unless it is quite current, like an ongoing political situation or a technical topic like "blogging," or Web-logging. Periodicals such as journals, by virtue of regular and ongoing publication, likely have the most current information on a topic. Journals may be either in print or online; in some cases journals are published in both forms. Be sure to determine the authority of the periodicals you use, particularly online journals. Determine who the sponsoring organization is and what the review process is. For example, does a university or professional society sponsor the site? Are the articles published subject to review by peers in the field?

As you read and take notes you will develop support for your hypothesis and gradually develop your thesis statement. You will benefit from roughing out the divisions of your topic in a working outline, and then sorting your notes by section. Some writers find it helpful to list the sources or authors under each outline point and then go back to their notes to flesh out these sections. Effective writing is thesis-driven at the level of the essay and topic-driven at the level of the paragraph. After sorting out the basic outline, consider turning topic headings into topic sentence headings; you will have a much clearer idea of the flow and structure of your argument if you push yourself toward predication, or changing from phrases to complete sentences that assert your main point in each section or paragraph.

After determining the main sections and lining up the evidence, you are ready to start drafting. Use your thesis statement and outline and work in a way that is effective for you. For many writers, starting to draft or fill in one section at a time is less daunting and more effective than trying to write it start to finish. Breaking the task into components, and making sure you have allowed sufficient time to stop and think about your work, will make for a smoother process and a better final product.

Get feedback at all stages of the process, from research question, hypothesis, and thesis to outline to draft. You may want to exchange drafts with peers at the various stages, meet with your instructor, or get help from a campus writing resource. Consider having one specific reader help you in the final stages to check your documentation. Check with your instructor about whether to document your essay in Modern Language Association (MLA), American Psychological Association (APA), or some other documentation style. And determine whether you will submit paper copy, computer copy, or both. If you submit a copy online, you may be able to add hypertext or links to the document.

Student writer Ashlee Lynn wrote an essay analyzing presidential rhetoric at a time of crisis. Part of that larger research project involved examining President George W. Bush's address to Congress and the nation after the 9/11 attacks. She found it helpful to integrate several outside sources, including a thorough overview of political communication, specific peer-reviewed articles, and a documentary film. Her essay on this specific speech follows; the text of Bush's speech is in Chapter Eight.

Presidential Rhetoric in a Time of Crisis: Bush and 9/11

The September 11, 2001, attack on American's home soil presented President George W. Bush with an urgent and difficult rhetorical situation. Americans were overwhelmed by pictures of planes crashing, people jumping out of collapsing buildings, and rescue workers trying to find victims. People came together in grief and anger over the devastating loss of life resulting from the terrorist hijackings and attacks against the World Trade Center and the Pentagon. The catastrophes of September 11, as well as the heroic rescue efforts that followed, have formed the first truly collective memory of the twenty-first century. As the American public remained devastated and confused, President George W. Bush gave a speech on September 20 intended to unite Americans and other nations against terrorism. Bush's speech was successful because he made use of many different persuasive appeals to rally support for the war against terrorism. Although Bush incorporates logical and emotional appeals in his speech, he relies predominantly on the persuasive power of his appeals to Americans' values and beliefs.

Bush's initial statements in his address emphasize core American values in asserting that the state of the union can be seen through the human response to September 11. He utilizes anaphora in his repetition of the phrase "we have seen" to focus on the fundamental ideals Americans illustrated in their responses to September 11. He uses key words such as "courage" and "endurance" to show the specific ideals embodied by Americans who struggled to overtake terrorists on the airplanes or to rescue victims at Ground Zero. By describing these positive actions in the wake of such a disaster, Bush elicits identification with the American cause. He bolsters patriotism as he explains that "the entire world has seen for itself the state of the union, and it is strong." The tone of the speech then shifts as he speaks of the present danger and claims the country has been "called to defend freedom." Bush's incorporation of the fundamental ideal of freedom both aligns listeners with his cause and turns them against those who attack this ideal. Bush's rhetoric is filled with group pronouns such as "we" and "our" that serve to separate Americans and their "enemies." Bill Jersey's film *Faces of the Enemy* addresses this dichotomization and explains how it plays an integral role in defining an enemy. This "us versus them" mentality is an important mindset to create before entering a war.

Bush's appeals to logic and his careful diction allow him to establish parameters for appropriate and inappropriate behaviors. He repeatedly begins his statements with the phrase "America/ we will not forget" as he gives examples of countries showing American kindness and sympathy. It is important that he praise the compassionate actions of America's allies to contrast them with the cruel actions of America's enemies. He presents the facts by listing numbers of citizens of different nations that were killed: "dozens of Pakistanis, more than 130 Israelis. . . ." This logical appeal presents further evidence as to the horror of the bloodshed on September 11. Bush begins his description of the enemy by mentioning the date, thus giving the event a somewhat historical perspective. He uses highly connotative diction, referring to the terrorists as "enemies of freedom," which appeals to ethos. Thus his presentation is not unbiased, for he uses phrases with negative connotations. He paints the terrorists as not just enemies of Americans but rather as enemies of the much larger concept of freedom. His language becomes increasingly persuasive as he comments on how there "have been wars on foreign soil," but "not at the center of a great city on a peaceful morning." He taps into every individual's fears by emphasizing the fact that the attack was on home soil.

Through his persuasive language, Bush continues to define the enemy in his description of the evidence that the government has gathered about the al Qaeda terrorist network. Although he appeals to logic throughout this presentation of facts, his clinical language is studded with persuasive elements. He speaks of the horrors of the terrorists' directive that "commands them to kill Christians and Jews, to kill all Americans and make no distinctions among military and civilians, including women and children." Although saying "all Americans" encompasses women and children, Bush's mention of these two highly sympathetic categories of Americans appeals to emotions. In his description of the strict rules imposed on Afghanis at home, Bush shows how the leadership of al Qaeda and the Taliban regime curtail freedom. These examples of women being prohibited to attend school and individuals being jailed for owning televisions appeal to values and beliefs and cause the audience to reject this system because it contradicts Americans' underlying beliefs in freedom and equality. These descriptions of the al Qaeda and Taliban regime could be viewed as propaganda, for Bush presents information about them with the intent of furthering his cause and damaging their cause. In this situation, however, the use of what might be characterized as propaganda is necessary and acceptable, because as Jaques Ellul describes in *Propaganda: The Formation of Men's Attitudes,* it is through propaganda that governments can transform individuals into a strong group unified by a common cause. To successfully combat terrorism, Bush needed to create a united group that would support the antiterrorism cause and his use of propaganda was extremely effective.

After characterizing the Taliban, Bush proceeds to present a series of demands directed at the Taliban, and through his delivery he appeals to values and beliefs as well as to logic. Bush's requests are direct and commanding; he thus establishes his authority and in doing so appeals to the audience members' sense of ethics. Because Bush presents himself as a credible speaker, the audience is open to what he has to say. Bush dehumanizes the enemy by using words such as "they" and "the Taliban." He focuses on the groups who are the "enemy of America" rather than individuals. As outlined in the film *Faces of the Enemy,* this dehumanization process makes it easier to kill the enemy in times of war. Bush's demands build to a climax where he introduces the idea of absolute victory: "It will not end until every terrorist group of global reach has been found, stopped, and defeated." Because he has primed the audience, this assertive statement is not abrasive but rather a natural progression from his previous ideas. In his explanation of why terrorists hate Americans, he once again appeals to people's underlying beliefs. By saying the terrorists hate democracy and freedom, he shows how they go against Americans' fundamental beliefs and thus persuades the audience to follow his suggested actions. He uses deduction in his comparison of terrorists to Fascists and Nazis by first presenting the general idea of murderous ideologies and then citing specific examples. This comparison also appeals to emotions because he directs the same feelings of horror and fear people felt about the Nazis toward the terrorists.

Switching the focus of his speech, Bush begins preparing the American public for a different type of war. In one of the most memorable lines of the speech Bush says, "Either you are with us, or you are with the terrorists." This powerful statement appeals to values and beliefs as well as to emotions because people don't want to be associated with the terrorists and their values. It is a logical fallacy, however, because it is possible to be against Bush's proposed actions without being "with the terrorists." Nevertheless, as Bruce Miroff explains in his discussion of political spectacles, the president's primary goal is to formulate meaning for the American people(). Thus, although it is illogical to claim that all Americans who do not support Bush's actions are "with the terrorists," Bush uses his presidential authority to make the meaning of this assertion seem feasible. The same persuasive strategies are at work where Bush says, "This is the fight of all who believe in progress and pluralism, tolerance and freedom." Most Americans would like to consider themselves a part of that "all" and are thereby part of the fight. Bush then appeals to emotion in saying that people should continue to live their lives and hug their children. This suggestion lightens the tone of his speech and allows him to connect with the audience on a more personal level. Bush once again utilizes anaphora in his repetition of the phrase, "We will come together. . . ." Here the unity in his prose mirrors the unity he speaks of in his content. In a final effort to rally support for action, Bush appeals to individuals' underlying beliefs by explaining how America is "determined and strong" and how "the great hope of every time" depends on it. He concludes on a positive note by using "struggle for freedom and security" as a euphemism for war and assuring Americans of the rightness of their cause. Throughout his entire speech, Bush's appeals to values and beliefs as well as his use of other rhetorical strategies facilitate his characterization of the enemy and allow him to gain support for the war against terrorism.

Depending on the situation surrounding a particular national crisis, presidents need to fulfill varying public demands through their rhetoric. Because the crisis situation Bush faced seemed to violate fundamental American ideals, it was appropriate that he appealed primarily to values and beliefs in his speech. In his discussion of rhetorical depiction, Michael Osborn notes that "the master rhetorician will build rhetorical depictions carefully, citing evidence that lends substance and authenticity to an image, using stylistic techniques that provide its sense of living presence" (80). President George W. Bush carefully built his "rhetorical depiction" in a manner that not only portrayed the event with authenticity, but also persuaded the American public to share his view and support his response.

Works Cited

Ellul, Jaques. *Propaganda: The Formation of Men's Attitudes, 1965.* Trans. Konrad Kellen and Jean Lerner. New York: Vintage Books, 1973.

Jersey, Bill, prod. and dir. *Faces of the Enemy.* Ed. and co-dir. Jeffrey Friedman. A Quest production for the Catticaus Corporation, 1987.

Miroff, Bruce. "The Presidency and the Public: Leadership as Spectacle." *The Presidency and the Political System,* 6th ed. Ed. Michael Nelson. Washington, DC: CQ Press, a Division of Congressional Quarterly, Inc., 2000.

Osborn, Michael. "Rhetorical Depiction." *Form, Genre, and the Study of Political Discourse.* Eds. Herbert W. Simons and Aram A. Aghazarian. Columbia, South Carolina: University of South Carolina Press, 1986.

SERVICE LEARNING AND COMMUNITY WRITING

One way to develop effective writing strategies and style is to write for an audience beyond the classroom and the academy. Although part of your learning at college will need to entail developing your ability to write in academic contexts, to convey your mastery of a topic or contribute to knowledge in the subject area, many campuses allow for a service learning option through which you contribute service as part of your academic work. Often referred to as community writing, service learning in composition courses generally falls into two categories: first, doing direct service to nonprofit organizations by writing documents, such as informational flyers, press releases, brochures, and other written materials; and second, doing volunteer work in such agencies or organizations and writing about the experience as part of your course work. In the second case, your writing could take the form of journals or reflections on your community service, narrative essays, a collection of oral histories, letters to the editor, or opinion pieces. You could also consider doing research in an area of interest to local groups and contributing documented summaries of your research findings to such groups.

A number of nonprofit groups may be interested both in help with Web sites and in your developing materials that could be posted on the organization's Web sites. They may also find helpful a collection of links in their area of service or interest. You could develop educational materials—for an agency or for local schools—informing them about the agency's work. You may be able to develop a PowerPoint presentation for conveying the agency's mission or goals to other local groups or to the public.

Community Writing in a Global Context

Several options can work for community writing with a global theme. For years the watchword of community involvement was t. ink globally, act locally. Global problems often require numerous small steps to resolve them; environmental problems and health issues are key examples. Some groups of students have become involved with planning and publicizing campus and local events for Earth Day. Another choice is to become involved with local chapters of international groups such as the International Red Cross or UNICEF. Direct service would involve ongoing or fixed-term community service projects in the community. Other potential local agencies may include schools at various levels, public libraries, city and country governments, health services agencies, community mental health, groups working to abate hunger and homelessness, public health groups educating the public about communicable diseases or child welfare, and the like. To write on behalf of organizations, you could consider writing materials that inform the public or spread the word about events or services. You could consider working with recent arrivals or international students; you may also find cultural and international interest groups that welcome your involvement.

If you have a community service center on your campus, talk with your instructor about how to make contact and set up an orientation or informational session. Your center will have listings of agencies that want students to get involved or need help. Your instructor will work with you on which placements are appropriate for your course, which sorts of assignments will be acceptable for your course work, and whether you will be able to structure your community writing to do projects in groups or as individuals.

COLLABORATIONS

Many of the discussion questions and assignments in this text, both end-of-reading and end-of-chapter, have options for peer work. Collaboration, which reflects a goal of this text's approach in fostering interaction and communication, can promote learning and writing at all stages of the writing process.

In a sense, class discussion is a basic form of collaboration. Class discussion can include traditional open discussion, discussion guided by specific questions, panels and debate style formats, small group discussions that then report back to the class, and peer discussion-leading and presentations to the rest of the class. Peer groups or pairs can collaborate to develop and produce PowerPoint presentations if the technology is available on your campus; alternatively, you can consider developing a Web page with contributions from various groups or class members posted. The instructor or your campus may be able to maintain the Web page as part of ongoing course reserves. In addition to class discussion, you may be able to participate in online discussions not only among classmates but also beyond the classroom and campus. One option is collaborating on discussion and on written projects with students from other colleges. Your instructor may be able to facilitate such a joint venture or you may be able to link up through discussion forums or special interest sites.

INTRODUCTION TO THE READINGS: CHAPTER THEMES, SELECTIONS, AND ASSIGNMENTS

This text includes a number of themes that should provide starting points for analysis and reflection. They are not designed to appear comprehensive but rather to provoke thinking about both specific and global issues and about universal principles and local manifestations of them. The selections include images and texts for discussion. Each selection or set of selections is followed by Questions for Discussion and Writing. At the end of each chapter are Connections, or questions designed to evoke connections, interactions, and integration between selections within and across chapters. Each chapter also includes End-of-Chapter writing assignments, with many focusing on research opportunities and assignments for longer papers.

The chapters themselves connect and interact thematically as well as rhetorically; they encompass core issues concerning global exchange and interaction such as cultures and values, gender and society, images of the enemy, globalization, health, and the environment.

Chapter Two, "America: Perceptions at Home and Abroad," opens with perspectives on America's earliest identity and moves to reflections on intercultural issues within America and from abroad. Unlike some of the pat answers recently offered by American politicians (e.g., that others hold America in contempt because "they hate our freedom") these selections, which include non-US views, provide some opportunities to step back from a dominant culture view and consider America from a broader context.

Chapter Three, "Crossing Cultures," expands the discussion from America to an international context. It offers readings and images examining values and beliefs within diverse cultures. In this chapter, authors focus on processes of conflict, change, and in some cases adaptation to outside pressures. Some concerns involve fears of cultural contamination, whether in language or value systems. Other intercultural exchanges occur when they can be co opted by the state—as the case of rock music in Iran illustrates.

Chapter Four, "Issues in Globalization," examines the tensions between economic, political, and social systems on a global level. In some cases the conflict is characterized as being between radically different world views—a western capitalistic, secular view and a traditional, religion-based belief system, a view asserted by Samuel Huntington. This dichotomous view, however, is not accepted by all commentators, including scholar Edward Said, who directly responds to Huntington's thesis. This chapter includes perspectives on globalization, or the process of integrating economies across nations and cultures.

Chapter Five, "Women and Society," provides visual representations, scholarly articles, and contemporary accounts about women's issues across international cultures. It draws on traditions and on current questions as women in different countries find their way in societies that do not always support their efforts to contribute. When we examine the eighteenth-century British etching "Keep within Compass," we see that some of the same assumptions about appropriate behavior for women are still invoked in the twenty-first century. Themes in this chapter include discussions of woman as the other, analysis of gender roles and power, and proposals for increasing women's role in nation building.

Chapter Six, "One World: Health and Environment," focuses on two major themes requiring global cooperation—global environment and public health. Is international cooperation possible given the specific and often divergent interests of each society? Do more developed societies understand the degree to which it is in their best interest to deal with health and environmental issues on a global scale? The SARS outbreak of 2003 provides a critical example of the importance of international cooperation in responding to potentially devastating health crises.

Chapter Seven, "Conflict: Images of the Other," focuses on the ways in which we create images of an enemy. We examine primary source examples in text and image as well as secondary source materials that provide a framework for understanding the ways in which people form an image of the other. The chapter includes images from Europe and from international popular culture.

Chapter Eight, "A Post–9/11 World," focuses on the events of 9/11, their precursors, and their aftermath, as well as broader concerns such as defining terrorism and living with its collateral damage. This chapter provides divergent, international points of view regarding this series of events, with selections by Salman Rushdie and Thomas Friedman, as well as Iranian and American political cartoonists. It includes speeches by central participants such as President George Bush and Osama bin Laden and work by writers trying to grapple with the implications of these attacks while at the same time maintaining their efforts to think critically about one of the defining moments of their lives.

The Appendix, "Precedents and Traditions," presents resources for texts that convey core values and beliefs and focuses on the ways in which societies design lessons, examples, or rules for human behavior, including text and Internet sources for various cultures' holy books—the Bible, the Koran, the writings of Buddha, and philosophical selections from Aristotle and Confucius, key influences on Western and Eastern societies and values. Also included are selections on culture, politics, and economics, including the Puritan Ethic, writings from Marx, a number of declarations of democratic principles, and principles of passive resistance.

AMERICA: PERCEPTIONS AT HOME AND ABROAD

INTRODUCTION

America began as a political and social entity following a revolution in which it saw itself as the underdog fending off an oppressive colonial power. In the nineteenth century, as the land of opportunity, America welcomed immigrants from around the world; by the mid-twentieth century, Americans had died liberating Europe and saw themselves as poised to save the world from Communism. From the vantage point of a place like the American Cemetery in Normandy, France, for example, one is struck by the profound sacrifice of generations of Americans to "fight the good fight" on behalf of humanity.

In recent years Americans have increasingly confronted views from within their own society, as well as from other nations, that are at odds with how they perceive themselves and their motives. Some Americans, and many in other countries, hold a mirror up to the United States and show Americans an image they often do not recognize. Nations from central Europe to the Arab Middle East may embrace some aspects of American culture but also feel invaded by the worst of it. Following the dissolution of the Soviet Union, the United States is no longer perceived as the better of two choices; currently the sole remaining superpower, America seems more often the target of hostility, a topic discussed by Sam Keen in Chapter Seven. Further, Americans are coming to terms with a political history that includes supporting repressive regimes, although as Dinesh D'Souza asserts in this chapter, these regimes, too, were generally the lesser of two evils from America's perspective. Nevertheless, these choices have haunted past and present relations between America and the world. They also make for some paradoxical relationships and shifting perceptions—for example, from Russia as enemy and Mujahideen, or freedom fighter, as friend, to Russia as ally and Mujahideen as mortal enemy.

This chapter approaches the topic of America from the standpoint of diverse voices within American society and from those beyond. The selections include images, a poem, academic essays, and essays designed for the interested generalist. Points of view are diverse and include arguments by Americans whose stance is squarely within the American mainstream, Americans who attempt to step back and see America as other societies do, and international authors who approach America from their own historical and political contexts. Regardless of the medium or the stance, each selection makes a point and conveys a perspective about America; each contributes to a sense of complexity about America's view of itself and its position in the world. These selections also connect with those in other chapters, particularly those concerning America's cultural influence in Chapter Three, the images of friends and enemies to be discussed in Chapter Seven, and reactions to 9/11 in Chapter Eight.

The content of these selections ranges from discussions of America's aspirations and self-assessment, to historical perceptions from abroad, to reflections of America's sometimes controversial role in what has been termed the New World Order. We move from America's early survival as a social and political entity to the hopes of fulfilling America's promise in the twentieth century and the sobering challenges of the twenty-first century.

We begin this chapter with Benjamin Franklin's woodcut, "Join, or Die," reportedly the first American political cartoon. Presenting a dichotomous view, Franklin argues for unity among the states in the face of a common foe, with death the only outcome without unity. This alliance of divergent elements into a political entity for mutual benefit and self-interest remains a compelling metaphor for *e pluribus unum,* out of many, one; the next selection revisits the vision of America's founders from a twenty-first-century perspective. In an introduction to his book *The American Soul,* philosopher Jacob Needleman argues for revisiting fundamental ideas and values that engendered America and that have subsequently influenced the world; he explores a vision of early America, one unified not only by self-interest but also by serving the common good.

The next two selections offer divergent visual images of America. The first seems to suggest that America has not lived up to the early promise and potential derived from the ancient wisdom and founding principles that Needleman discusses; the second suggests a more idealized view. Margaret Bourke-White's startling photograph, "There's No Way Like the American Way," offers a view that sharply contrasts divergent experiences of Americans. Bourke-White's photograph demonstrates the power of photography to assert a point of view rather than merely to report. We then turn to representations of America during times of conflict. In wartime, national identity is often simplified, solidified, and reinforced, and in the world wars of the twentieth century we see visual representations of how Americans saw themselves and how the Allies saw America. The set of war era posters included next demonstrates perceptions from within and outside America and suggests the context in which many Americans and allies of a certain age formed their views of America as defenders rather than oppressors. First, the World War I era poster, "The Ships are Coming," casts America in a familiar and comfortable role. The World War II poster, "The War's Not Over 'til Our Last Man is Free," highlights the sacrifice of American POWs and draws on values of hard work and fair play for the home front. The two posters that follow, "Free Holland Welcomes the Soldiers of the Allies" and (in Russian) "We Will Raise the Flag of Victory over Berlin," promote positive views of America by European and Soviet allies of the World War II era.

Some twenty-five years after Bourke-White's photograph was published, with little progress in racial equality evident, the American Civil Rights Movement became active in pursuing social, legal, and economic equality. Arrested during political action in Birmingham, Alabama, Martin Luther King, Jr. wrote his "Letter from a Birmingham Jail" to respond to questions about using nonviolent resistance and direct action to achieve a more just society, asserting that "injustice anywhere is a threat to justice everywhere." Even those who may appear to have achieved a greater measure of social, economic, or political equality continue to struggle, particularly with stereotypes that erode equality for all. In the next selection, ethnic studies scholar Ronald Takaki addresses the issues of the model minority, suggesting that myths of Asian superiority harm not only other minorities but Asians as well.

The political activism of King and the Civil Rights Movement continues today in the Hawaiian Sovereignty Movement, through which native Hawaiians and their political supporters have taken up the question of justice for Hawaiians and suggested that assimilation is not only undesirable, but also impossible. In their article "The Native Hawaiian Today," Michael Kioni Dudley and Keoni Kealoha Agard argue that the Hawaiians are too integrated with the land and the ancient ways of their culture to adopt modern, Western values and practices. Without the rights to their land, rapidly being absorbed by resort development, their culture will not survive. The history of America's takeover of Hawaii remains a painful story, and the authors argue that it is the native people who continue to suffer for it.

In a selection from her acclaimed work *Borderlands*, Gloria Anzaldua explores the meaning and symbolism of borderlands, especially as the word relates to those who live in the border region between Mexico and the United States, who must "be a crossroads" to survive.

Addressing America's position in the world, writer Dinesh D'Souza suggests a more positive view of America's relationships with other societies. In his essay "In Praise of American Empire," D'Souza responds to critiques of American power and asserts, "America is the most magnanimous of all imperial powers that have ever existed." But as has become sometimes painfully clear since the post–World War II era, perspectives on America from abroad have shifted. When Americans today step back from their own media and cultural apparatus, they are sometimes perplexed at others' perceptions of American cultures, values, and intentions. Often portraying the United States as oblivious, arrogant, or self-absorbed—and that is among friends—the foreign media confront Americans with a different picture than the one Americans would construct themselves. In the next selection, the cartoon "America's World," published by the British periodical *The Economist,* pokes fun at America's self-perception as well as those of America's allies.

Perceptions from abroad are also the theme of the next two articles. In a scholarly essay first appearing in *Journal of Palestine Studies,* Pascal Boniface, European professor and think tank director, asserts that the United States is increasingly one-sided in its foreign policy, as a result of its position as the only superpower and also because of its perceived sense of moral superiority. In this essay, entitled "Reflections on America as a World Power from a European View," the author asserts that Europe tends to pursue a consultative, dialogic model, but America tends to go its own way, a strategy that not only will lessen its prestige and appeal, but also will prove less effective. Critics of US policy would argue that the second Gulf War, "Operation Iraq: Freedom," demonstrates exactly this approach; at the same time, some pro-war politicians characterized this "go it alone" approach as a virtue.

The selections in this chapter may at times be difficult to digest as we step away from our "cultural apparatus" and examine America from alternative perspectives. But a core theme of this textbook is that such a process is essential in moving toward an understanding of America's role in the global context. At the end of this chapter are discussion questions that explore the connections among the readings as well as writing assignments and Web sites that may help you to deepen and broaden your understanding of America and the world.

Join, or Die

BENJAMIN FRANKLIN

Benjamin Franklin (1706–1790) was an American printer, author, inventor, and statesman. At an early age, he became an apprentice to his brother, a printer, and in 1723 went to Philadelphia where he later published *Poor Richard's Almanac.* Franklin was the delegate from Pennsylvania when seven colonies sent representatives to negotiate with the Iroquois Nation. *Join, or Die,* published in 1754 and considered the first American cartoon, was Franklin's contribution to the debate about unity among the colonies as the French and Indian War approached, with a theme of a government for common defense. To make his point, Franklin develops the metaphor of a myth familiar to his audience, that a cut-up snake reassembled before sundown will come back to life. Contemporary editorial and political cartoons echo this early example of political persuasion.

(ATWATER KENT MUSEUM OF PHILADELPHIA)

QUESTIONS FOR DISCUSSION AND WRITING

1. Sort out the premises and conclusion of this cartoon. What is the argument? What alternatives may be left out of the argument? Do you think the cartoon would have been effective if a third choice were acknowledged?
2. What do you make of the analogy to a snake? How does knowing the mythology around a snake (see introductory note) affect the persuasiveness of this argument?
3. In groups or pairs, draft a cartoon with the topic of a contemporary political or social issue. In class, explain your design and why you drew what you did.
4. Research the history of political cartoons. Consider focusing on American cartoons during the "golden age of cartooning" in the late nineteenth century. If you can find back issues of American magazines such as *Puck* you will find numerous and often full-color examples.

Our America

JACOB NEEDLEMAN

Jacob Needleman, philosopher and author, is a professor of philosophy at San Francisco State University. His books include *A Little Book on Love* (1996), *Time and the Soul* (reprinted 2003), *Money and the Meaning of Life* (1994), *The Heart of Philosophy* (1982), and *Lost Christianity* (1980). In addition to his teaching and writing, he serves as a consultant in the fields of psychology, education, medical ethics, philanthropy, and business, and has been featured on Bill Moyers' acclaimed PBS series *A World of Ideas*. His newest book, *American Soul: Rediscovering the Wisdom of the Founders* (2002), in which the following selection was published, is Needleman's effort to "remythologize" America's founders and founding principles.

America was once the hope of the world. But what kind of hope? More than the hope of material prosperity, although that was part of it; and more than the promise of equality and liberty, although that, too, was an important part of it. And more than safety and security, precious as these things are. The deeper hope of America was its vision of what humanity is and can become—individually and in community. It was through that vision that all the material and social promise of America took its fire and light and its voice that called to men and women within its own borders and throughout the world. America was once a great idea, and it is such ideas that move the world, that open the possibility of meaning in human life.

It has been said that any question can lead to truth if it is an aching question. For one person it may be the question of life after death, for another the problem of suffering, the causes of war and injustice. Or it may be something more personal and immediate—a profound ethical dilemma, a problem involving the whole direction of one's life. An aching question, a question that is not just a matter of curiosity or a fleeting burst of emotion, cannot be answered with old thought. Possessed by such a question, one is hungry for ideas of a very different order than the familiar categories that usually accompany us throughout our lives. One is both hungry and, at the same time, more discriminating, less susceptible to credulity and suggestibility. The intelligence of the heart begins to call to us in our sleep.

For many of us, such is now the question of the meaning of America. But it is also an elusive question. If we consider America only as a nation, that is, as a man-made construction, then it is hard to feel any ultimacy about the problem of America. Nations, as such, come and go: Persia, Rome, Byzantium have all sunk into the ocean of time. All the empires and national states of the past have come and gone in what seems like the twinkling of an eye, though in their time each appeared to itself and to the world as strong and real and enduring. And, of course, our era has witnessed the stunning disintegration of vast collectivities: the Third Reich, the Soviet Union, the political organization of Eastern Europe. Even the idea itself of "nation" may be disappearing or transmuting into what has been termed a "global web" of financial instrumentalities, electronic communication, and advanced technological consumerism.

All my life I had been unable to understand or sympathize 5 with people who seemed so passionately concerned about the preservation or enhancement of America. It had often seemed to me hypocrisy, a mask that covered the all-too-human fears for one's personal safety or comfort, sometimes mixed with the kind of self-righteousness that had turned me away from the religions of church and synagogue. But I was even more troubled by people who attacked America and who were always arguing about hidden conspiracies, intentional injustices that were built into "the system," and so forth. Why, I wondered, were they not just as concerned about the human condition itself? And about their own incomprehensible mortal life on earth? They made me feel that I was selfish to have such questions burning in me.

And so, I was astonished and strangely joyous when I finally turned directly to studying the history of America and found almost everywhere that the men and women who carved out the ideals of America were driven by the same transcendent questions that had always been my own as well. I began to see that for many of these men and women America meant the struggle for conditions of life under which these ultimate questions could be freely pursued.

This glimpse of the motive of the Founders was at first very fleeting and insubstantial. Time and again this perception of mine was overwhelmed by the "authority" of the accepted views about everything pertaining to America. Historical knowledge and theory, political and economic opinions about the meaning of past and present events—the old as well as the latest views about America—covered over that glimpse into the origin of the American experiment. Even the accepted views about the religious motivations of the Founders clouded the issue—in fact, these commonly accepted views were the most distracting of all. They equated the religious impulses of our forefathers with the religion I knew from my own childhood, a religion that was simply dull and oppressive.

A New Beginning

America is the fact, the symbol, and the promise of a new beginning. And in human life, in our lives as they are, this possibility is among the most sacred aspects of existence. All that is old and already formed can continue to live only if it allows within itself the conditions for a new beginning. Life itself is the mysterious, incomprehensible blending of the new and the old, of what already is and what is coming into being. The question of America is there: If America loses the meaning of its existence and if, in fact, America is now the dominant cultural influence in the world, then what will become of the world? The question of America leads all of us directly into the question of the purpose and destiny of human life itself in this era.

America and the Teachings of Wisdom

The World of Ideas and the Disease of Materialism

Our world, so we see and hear on all sides, is drowning in materialism, commercialism, consumerism. But the problem is not really there. What we ordinarily speak of as materialism is a result, not a cause. The root of materialism is a poverty of ideas about the inner and the outer world. Less and less does our contemporary culture have, or even seek, commerce with great ideas, and it is that lack that is weakening the human spirit. This is the essence of materialism. Materialism is a disease of the mind starved for ideas.

Throughout history ideas of a certain kind and nature have been disseminated into the life of humanity in order to help human beings understand and feel the possibility of the deep inner change that would enable them to serve the purpose for which they were created, namely, to act in the world as conscious, individual instruments of God, the ultimate principle of reality and value. Ideas of this kind are formulated in order to have a specific range of action on the human psyche: to touch the heart as well as the intellect; to shock us into questioning our present understanding; to point us to the greatness around us in nature and the universe, and the potential greatness slumbering within ourselves; to open our eyes to the real needs of our neighbor; to confront us with our own profound ignorance and our criminal fears and egoism; to show us that we are not here for ourselves alone, but as necessary particles of divine love.

These are the contours of the ancient wisdom, considered as ideas embodied in religious and philosophical doctrines, works of sacred art, literature and music and, in a very fundamental way, in indications of practical methods by which a man or woman can work, as it is said, to become what he or she really is. Without feeling the full range of such ideas, or sensing even a modest, but pure, trace of them, we are bound to turn for meaning to the lawfully existing instinctive impulses within ourselves toward physical pleasure (impulses which are meant to serve and not lead) and to the artificially induced illusions of what the ancient wisdom calls pride or the ego with its attendant fears, hatred and servility, as well as to the ego's exploitation of the intellect in the form of a swollen overestimation of disconnected logic and purely mental knowing. *This* is the root of materialism, the cultural neurosis of an era that believes that only the external senses show us the real world and that only physical or social comfort is worth striving for. Simply put, the neurosis of materialism leads us to despair. Despair because the impulse of hope, which is implanted in human nature as part of our unique consciousness, finds nothing in the world or in our concept of ourselves that carries the mark of indubitable, enduring truth and goodness, those two ultimate principles toward which that impulse of hope is meant to lead us.

But no idea exists alone. Great ideas are always part of a living system of ideas, all of which are necessary for the full understanding of any one of them. When we speak of the idea of America, we are speaking of many interconnected ethical ideas, both metaphysical ideas that deal with ultimate reality, and ethical and social ideas, which *all together* offered hope to the world. The idea of America, with all that it contained within it about the moral law, nature, God, and the human soul, once reflected to some extent the timeless, ancient wisdom that has guided human life since the dawn of history. America was a new and original expression, in the form of a social and political experiment, of ideas that have always been part of what may be called the great web of Truth. Explicitly and implicitly, the idea of America has resonated with this ancient, timeless wisdom and has allowed something of its power to touch the heart and mind of humanity. It is necessary to recover this resonance, this relationship, however tenuous and partial, between the teachings of wisdom and the idea of America.

What are these "teachings of wisdom"? The fact of the matter is that it is possible to discern a profound commonality at the heart and root of all the major religions and spiritual philosophies of the world. Differing in outer expression and emphasis, these age-old traditions are nourished by a single hidden current of interconnected ideas—like so many ancient trees of varied form and foliage watered by the same underground stream.

Between Two Worlds

Within this vast body of teachings about man in the universal world, several elements stand out as critical for our understanding of the idea of America. One of the most central of these elements is the idea of man as a being who exists between two worlds—an inner world of great spiritual vision and power, and an outer world of material realities and constraint. Both worlds call to us, and as long as we live, we are obliged to give each its due. Our task, our place in the scheme of creation, is to become conscious instruments of action on earth under the aegis of divine law and love. But, in order to fulfill this role, we must work to transcend the sense of self-identity that society thrusts upon us and that prevents us from recognizing our own inner self and its power to serve the good. In this ancient teaching, freedom is understood not as the license to obey one's desires but as obedient submission to a deep inner law; independence is understood as the discovery of one's own authentic self, which—although it may seem paradoxical—is also a mirror of the common cosmic Selfhood; equality is understood as every human being's right to seek the truth and to be allowed to give his or her light to the common welfare.

The idea of man's two natures, along with some of its ethical implications, was dramatically expressed in the teaching known as Stoicism, which flourished in the early Roman Empire and which served as inspiration to Washington, Adams, Jefferson, and many other of the Founding Fathers of America.[1] The most politically powerful man of his time, the Emperor Marcus Aurelius, and one of the least powerful, the freed slave Epictetus, who was a mentor to the Emperor, both adhered to the Stoic philosophy. In this teaching, a human being is viewed as a being whose individual mind is meant to reflect and manifest the same all-universal and all-beneficent consciousness that creates and maintains the cosmos. At the same time, we are made to live for a finite time in a mortal body and are obliged by the true power of reason (which includes cosmic love) to care for our neighbor

15

and to answer the moral requirements of family, society, and culture—all of which are also part of the universal scheme. Although our inner nature is cosmic, our finite life is on earth; our duties are to both the immortal presence within and, while we live on earth, to our temporary role in the social order. Our task is simultaneous inner freedom and full outer engagement. In the words of Epictetus:

> It is difficult [and necessary] to unite and combine these qualities—the diligence of a man who devotes himself to material things, and the constancy of one who disregards them [i.e., who is not attached to them—yet not impossible. Otherwise, it would be impossible to be happy.[2]

And in the words of the Emperor Marcus Aurelius, speaking of the need to accept the desires and sufferings attendant upon being obliged to live in a mortal body on earth and the simultaneous duty to act according to the dictates of one's own inner God: "Nothing will happen to me which is not in conformity with the Nature of the All. [But] it depends on me to do nothing which is contrary to my god and my *daimon* [inner spirit]."[3]

The Inner Meaning of Democracy

As for the idea of democracy, the Founding Fathers—Washington, Jefferson, Franklin, and others—never conceived of it solely as an external form of government. The meaning of democracy was always rooted in a vision of human nature as both fallen and perfectible—inwardly fallen and inwardly perfectible. To a significant extent, democracy in its specifically American form was created to allow men and women to seek their own higher principle within themselves. Without that inner meaning, democracy becomes, as Plato and Aristotle pointed out 2,500 years ago, a celebration of disorder and superficiality.

All the rights guaranteed by the Constitution were based on a vision of human nature that calls us to be responsible beings—responsible to something within ourselves that is higher than the all-too-human desires for personal gain and satisfaction; higher than the dictates of the purely theoretical or logical mind; higher than instinctive loyalties to family and tribe.

This higher reality within the self was called many things—reason, conscience, Nature's God. When this idea is left out, or treated as though its meaning were obvious, then the ideals of independence and liberty lose their power and truth. They become mere names that mask the ever-present tendency of nations and groups and individuals to seek only their own external and short-term advantages.

Great ideas, ideas that meaningfully reflect something of the world's ancient tradition of wisdom, have the power to bind people together and to bring unity under a goal and a vision that are stronger and deeper than all personal, short-term gain. This is the mark of great ideas: they unify people and they also act to *unify the disparate parts of the human being;* they speak of a social order that is possible *on the basis of an ordering within the individual self.* The idea of America once had something of this power of unification. [20]

Notes

1. See especially Carl J. Richard, *The Founders and the Classics.* Cambridge: Harvard University Press, 1994.
2. Epictetus, *The Discourses of Epictetus.* Trans. P. E. Matheson, book 2, ch. 5 (brackets mine). Ed. Whitney Oates, *The Stoic and Epicurean Philosophers.* New York: Modern Library, 1940, 288.
3. Marcus Aurelius, *Meditations 5.10.* Trans. Pierre Hadot in Pierre Hadot, The Inner Citadel. (Cambridge: Harvard University Press, 1998), 130.

QUESTIONS FOR DISCUSSION AND WRITING

1. In the author's view, what is the core "aching question" he identifies with regard to America? How does he differentiate between America as a nation and as an idea?
2. How does Needleman connect the meaning of America with the fate of the rest of the world? What can we learn about what the idea of America means to non-Americans?
3. How does Needleman explain the problem of materialism? What are its causes? How does connection with a more spiritual side, with a world of ideas, offer a hopeful vision?
4. Comment on the personal voice, or sense of the author, and his relationship to his audience. How do his choices in

words, sentence structure, and examples contribute voice in the selection?

5. Write a response to this selection in which you summarize the author's explanation of an inner and outer world and then discuss how this concept relates to American democracy and to ancient wisdom.

There's No Way Like
the American Way

MARGARET BOURKE-WHITE

Photojournalist Margaret Bourke-White (1904–1971) covered major news stories for *Life* magazine when that publication was home to the world's best photographers. In addition to her work documenting the Great Depression, she is famous for her photographs of the invasion of Russia in World War II and the liberation of concentration camps at the end of the war in Europe. This 1937 photograph, taken in Depression-era America, captures an ironic juxtaposition of the cheerful billboard advertisement and a line at an emergency relief station after an Ohio flood killed hundreds and left thousands homeless.

(MARGARET BOURKE-WHITE; GETTY IMAGES/TIME LIFE PICTURES)

QUESTIONS FOR DISCUSSION AND WRITING

1. According to the billboard, what constitutes "the American Way"? Does the photographer appear to share this view?

2. Break down the elements of the image and discuss each element's contribution to the effectiveness of the image. What assertions is each part of this photograph expressing? Consider the billboard, the line of people in front of it, and the juxtaposition of the two. The line stretches beyond both ends of the photograph. What effect does this composition have on the argument? The line of people in the photograph was actually a relief line following a flood. How does this information affect your interpretation of the photograph?

3. Write out the argument you believe this photograph makes. Then, write an essay analyzing the photograph and its argument. Be sure to consider point of view, irony, claims and support, and appeals to ethos.

4. Research images and stories of the Great Depression, considering photographs, newspapers, magazines, and reports and stories. Consider interviewing older persons who lived through this time period and determining if their perceptions and memories are consistent with the other information you find.

Images of America in Wartime: World War I and II

Posters developed as a means of communication in the late nineteenth and early twentieth centuries and persist to the present day. Designed to publicize or advertise, they ranged from simple and forthright messages to much more subtle displays. In an era preceding widespread modern communicative media such as film, radio, and television, quickly and cheaply mass-produced posters could establish a new campaign or reinforce existing messages. Some themes, such as support of the war effort through war bonds, could have the same basic message but use different strategies to reach diverse audiences. Because those audiences would likely view a displayed poster quickly, as passersby in a public place, the poster would have to capture attention and make its point, or its argument, quickly and perhaps even dramatically.

The four posters included here range from two for the home front, appealing to American values and self-concept, to two produced by Allies. "The Ships Are Coming," a 1918 poster for the home front in the United States, was one in a series designed to demonstrate the power of the industrial sector and utilizes the traditional symbol for America, the eagle. A more somber 1944 wartime poster follows, using appeals to values and beliefs to bring the war home to Americans far from the front. A third World War II era poster, "Free Holland Welcomes the Soldiers of the Allies," produced in Great Britain, was printed in 1944 but not posted until the Netherlands was liberated in 1945. The fourth poster, in Russian, reads, "We Will Raise the Flag of Victory over Berlin," and was produced in Russia in 1944. In these last two posters, we see some of the political elements in the alliances through the more subtle design elements, such as placement of the flags according to who sponsors or produces the poster.

These posters, and others, are from the impressive collection of the Hoover Institution Archives. Numerous posters can also be accessed online, at sites such as the National Archives and Records Administration of the United States and the Northwestern University Web site.

(HOOVER INSTITUTION ARCHIVES)

**FREE HOLLAND WELCOMES
THE SOLDIERS OF THE ALLIES.**

Great Britain. 1944. (HOOVER INSTITUTION
ARCHIVES)

**WE WILL RAISE THE FLAG
OF VICTORY OVER BERLIN.**

U.S.S.R. 1944. (HOOVER INSTITUTION
ARCHIVES)

QUESTIONS FOR DISCUSSION AND WRITING

1. First, examine the two characterizations of the United States in "The Ships Are Coming" and "The War's Not Over." What types of persuasive appeals do they use? What are the postive and negative connotations and persuasive tactics used? What values do they evoke?

2. From these American posters, what do you infer about America's self-perception in these two wars?

3. Examine the British poster "Free Holland" and the Soviet poster "We Will Raise the Flag." What do the objects that are included and their positioning suggest about the image of cooperation these posters were trying to promote? Consider the forces marching through Berlin's Brandenburg Gate, the position of the three flags over the gate, and the countenance of the soldiers.

4. Using these posters or researching additional examples, examine the ways in which America or American soldiers are characterized in propaganda posters during wartime and develop your findings in an analytical essay.

Letter from a Birmingham Jail

MARTIN LUTHER KING, JR.

Martin Luther King, Jr. (1929–1968), leader of the American nonviolent civil rights movement, was a Baptist preacher from a family of preachers. He became a public figure in his twenties when he led a bus boycott in Montgomery, Alabama. King was the main organizer of sit-ins and marches in segregated southern towns and cities, particularly Birmingham, Alabama. While leading a demonstration he was arrested, and responding to a public statement from eight clergymen arguing against the organized demonstrations, he wrote the essay that follows. King responds both to the clergy and to critics at large in this letter, laying out the premises and context of nonviolent resistance and drawing from the Bible, Mahatma Gandhi, and Henry David Thoreau in the process. King received the Nobel Peace Prize in 1964 and was assassinated in Memphis, Tennessee, in 1968.

April 16, 1963

My Dear Fellow Clergymen:

While confined here in the Birmingham city jail, I came across your recent statement calling my present activities "unwise and untimely." Seldom do I pause to answer criticisms of my work and ideas. If I sought to answer all the criticisms that cross my desk, my secretaries would have little time for anything other than such correspondence in the course of the day, and I would have no time for constructive work. But since I feel that you are men of genuine good will and that your criticisms are sincerely set forth, I want to try to answer your statement in what I hope will be patient and reasonable terms.

I think I should indicate why I am here in Birmingham, since you have been influenced by the view which argues against "outsiders coming in." I have the honor of serving as president of the Southern Christian Leadership Conference, an organization operating in every southern state, with headquarters in Atlanta, Georgia. We have some eighty-five affiliated organizations across the South, and one of them is the Alabama Christian Movement for Human Rights. Frequently we share staff, educational, and financial resources with our affiliates. Several months ago the affiliate here in Birmingham asked us to be on call to engage in a nonviolent direct-action program if such were deemed necessary. We readily consented, and when the hour came we lived up to our promise. So I, along with several members of my staff, am here because I was invited here. I am here because I have organizational ties here.

But more basically, I am in Birmingham because injustice is here. Just as the prophets of the eighth century B.C. left their villages and carried their "thus saith the Lord" far beyond the boundaries of their home towns, and just as the Apostle Paul left his village of Tarsus and carried the gospel of Jesus Christ to the far corners of the Greco-Roman world, so am I compelled to carry the gospel of freedom beyond my own home town. Like Paul, I must constantly respond to the Macedonian call for aid.

Moreover, I am cognizant of the interrelatedness of all communities and states. I cannot sit idly by in Atlanta and not be concerned about what happens in Birmingham. Injustice anywhere is a threat to justice everywhere. We are caught in an inescapable network of mutuality, tied in a single garment of destiny. Whatever affects one directly, affects all indirectly. Never again can we afford to live with the narrow, provincial "outside agitator" idea. Anyone who lives inside the United States can never be considered an outsider anywhere within its bounds.

You deplore the demonstrations taking place in Birmingham. But your statement, I am sorry to say, fails to express a similar concern for the conditions that brought about the demonstrations. I am sure that none of you would want to rest content with the superficial kind of social analysis that deals merely with effects and does not grapple with underlying causes. It is unfortunate that demonstrations are taking place in Birmingham, but it is even more unfortunate that the city's white power structure left the Negro community with no alternative.

In any nonviolent campaign there are four basic steps: collection of the facts to determine whether injustices exist, negotiation, self-purification, and direct action. We have gone through all these steps in Birmingham. There can be no gainsaying the fact that racial injustice engulfs this community. Birmingham is probably the most thoroughly segregated city in the United States. Its ugly record of brutality is widely known. Negroes have experienced grossly unjust treatment in the courts. There have been more unsolved bombings of Negro homes and churches in Birmingham than in any other city in the nation. These are the hard, brutal facts of the case. On the basis of these conditions,

Negro leaders sought to negotiate with the city fathers. But the latter consistently refused to engage in good-faith negotiation.

Then, last September, came the opportunity to talk with leaders of Birmingham's economic community. In the course of the negotiations, certain promises were made by the merchants—for example, to remove the stores' humiliating racial signs. On the basis of these promises, the Reverend Fred Shuttlesworth and the leaders of the Alabama Christian Movement for Human Rights agreed to a moratorium on all demonstrations. As the weeks and months went by, we realized that we were the victims of a broken promise. A few signs, briefly removed, returned; the others remained.

As in so many past experiences, our hopes had been blasted, and the shadow of deep disappointment settled upon us. We had no alternative except to prepare for direct action, whereby we would present our very bodies as a means of laying our case before the conscience of the local and the national community. Mindful of the difficulties involved, we decided to undertake a process of self-purification. We began a series of workshops on nonviolence, and we repeatedly asked ourselves: "Are you able to accept blows without retaliating?" "'Are you able to endure the ordeal of jail?" We decided to schedule our direct-action program for the Easter season, realizing that except for Christmas, this is the main shopping period of the year. Knowing that a strong economic-withdrawal program would be the by-product of direct action, we felt that this would be the best time to bring pressure to bear on the merchants for the needed change.

Then it occurred to us that Birmingham's mayoral election was coming up in March, and we speedily decided to postpone action until after election day. When we discovered that the Commissioner of Public Safety, Eugene "Bull" Connor, had piled up enough votes to be in the run-off, we decided again to postpone action until the day after the run-off so that the demonstrations could not be used to cloud the issues. Like many others, we waited to see Mr. Connor defeated, and to this end we endured postponement after postponement. Having aided in this community need, we felt that our direct-action program could be delayed no longer.

You may well ask: "Why direct action? Why sit-ins, marches, and so forth? Isn't negotiation a better path?" You are quite right in calling for negotiation. Indeed, this is the very purpose of direct action. Nonviolent direct action seeks to create such a crisis and foster such a tension that a community which has constantly refused to negotiate is forced to confront the issue. It seeks so to dramatize the issue that it can no longer be ignored.

10

My citing the creation of tension as part of the work of the nonviolent-resister may sound rather shocking. But I must confess that I am not afraid of the word "tension." I have earnestly opposed violent tension, but there is a type of constructive, non-violent tension which is necessary for growth. Just as Socrates felt that it was necessary to create a tension in the mind so that individuals could rise from the bondage of myths and half-truths to the unfettered realm of creative analysis and objective appraisal, so must we see the need for nonviolent gadflies to create the kind of tension in society that will help men rise from the dark depths of prejudice and racism to the majestic heights of understanding and brotherhood.

The purpose of our direct-action program is to create a situation so crisis-packed that it will inevitably open the door to negotiation. I therefore concur with you in your call for negotiation. Too long has our beloved Southland been bogged down in a tragic effort to live in monologue rather than dialogue.

One of the basic points in your statement is that the action that I and my associates have taken in Birmingham is untimely. Some have asked: "Why didn't you give the new city administration time to act?" The only answer that I can give to this query is that the new Birmingham administration must be prodded about as much as the outgoing one before it will act. We are sadly mistaken if we feel that the election of Albert Boutwell as mayor will bring the millennium to Birmingham. While Mr. Boutwell is a much more gentle person than Mr. Connor, they are both segregationists, dedicated to maintenance of the status quo. I have hope that Mr. Boutwell will be reasonable enough to see the futility of massive resistance to desegregation. But he will not see this without pressure from devotees of civil rights. My friends, I must say to you that we have not made a single gain in civil rights without determined legal and nonviolent pressure. Lamentably, it is an historical fact that privileged groups seldom give up their privileges voluntarily. Individuals may see the moral light and voluntarily give up their unjust posture; but, as Reinhold Niebuhr has reminded us, groups tend to be more immoral than individuals.

We know through painful experience that freedom is never voluntarily given by the oppressor; it must be demanded by the oppressed. Frankly, I have yet to engage in a direct-action campaign that was "well timed" in the view of those who have not suffered unduly from the disease of segregation. For years now I have heard the word "Wait!" It rings in the ear of every Negro with piercing familiarity. This "Wait" has almost always meant

WOMAN GETTING INTO A TAXI

(BEHROUZ MEHRI)

Please see the headnote and discussion questions for this image on pages 113–115.

THREE AFGHAN MOTHERS AT A VACCINATION CLINIC

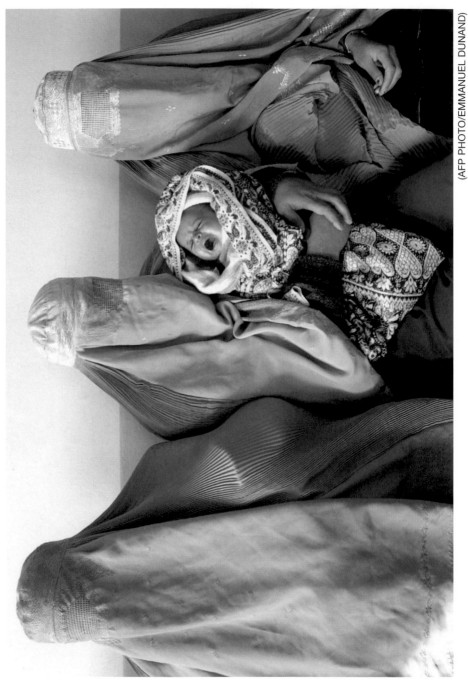

Please see the headnote and discussion questions for this image on pages 113–115.

"SELF-PORTRAIT WITH CROPPED HAIR,"
BY FRIDA KAHLO

Please see the headnote and discussion questions for this image on pages 272–273.

"THE BROKEN COLUMN," BY FRIDA KAHLO

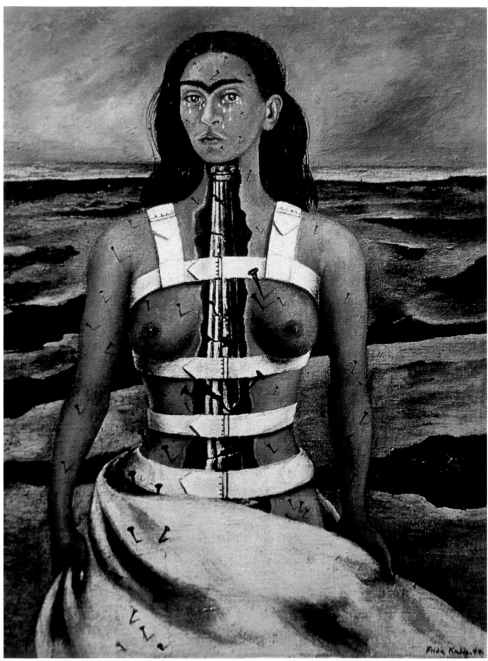

(INSTITUTO NACIONAL DE BELLAS ARTES INBA—MEXICO)

Please see the headnote and discussion questions for this image on pages 272–273.

HIGH-RESOLUTION VIEW
OF DEFORESTATION IN AMAZONIA

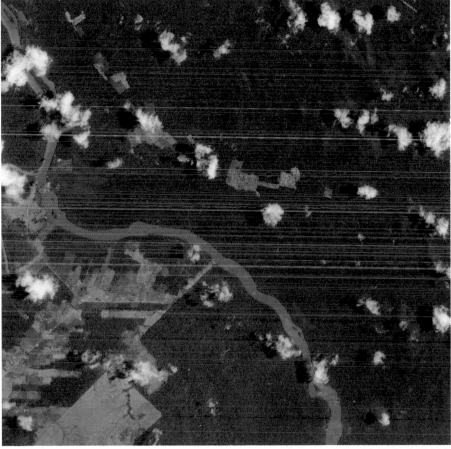

(ROBERT SIMMON/NASA)

Please see the headnote and discussion questions for this image on pages 391–394.

DEFORESTATION IN BRAZIL

(NASA/GODDARD SPACE FLIGHT CENTER)

Please see the headnote and discussion questions for this image on pages 391–394.

ANTI-ORANGE MARCHES MURAL

(WJ ROLSTON)

Please see the headnote and discussion questions for this image on pages 430–434.

C–7

(WJ ROLSTON)

Please see the headnote and discussion questions for this image on pages 430–434.

"Never." We must come to see, with one of our distinguished jurists, that "justice too long delayed is justice denied."

We have waited for more than 340 years for our constitutional God-given rights. The nations of Asia and Africa are moving with jetlike speed toward gaining political independence, but we still creep at horse-and-buggy pace toward gaining a cup of coffee at a lunch counter. Perhaps it is easy for those who have never felt the stinging darts of segregation to say, "Wait." But when you have seen vicious mobs lynch your mothers and fathers at will and drown your sisters and brothers at whim; when you have seen hate-filled policemen curse, kick, and even kill your black brothers and sisters; when you see the vast majority of your twenty million Negro brothers smothering in an airtight cage of poverty in the midst of an affluent society; when you suddenly find your tongue twisted and your speech stammering as you seek to explain to your six-year-old daughter why she can't go to the public amusement park that has just been advertised on television, and see tears welling up in her eyes when she is told that Funtown is closed to colored children, and see ominous clouds of inferiority beginning to form in her little mental sky, and see her beginning to distort her personality by developing an unconscious bitterness toward white people; when you have to concoct an answer for a five-year-old son who is asking: "Daddy, why do white people treat colored people so mean?"; when you take a cross-country drive and find it necessary to sleep night after night in the uncomfortable corners of your automobile because no motel will accept you; when you are humiliated day in and day out by nagging signs reading "white" and "colored"; when your first name becomes "nigger," your middle name becomes "boy" (however old you are), and your last name becomes "John," and your wife and mother are never given the respected title "Mrs."; when you are harried by day and haunted by night by the fact that you are a Negro, living constantly at tiptoe stance, never quite knowing what to expect next, and are plagued with inner fears and outer resentments; when you are forever fighting a degenerating sense of "nobodiness"—then you will understand why we find it difficult to wait. There comes a time when the cup of endurance runs over, and men are no longer willing to be plunged into the abyss of despair. I hope, sirs, you can understand our legitimate and unavoidable impatience.

You express a great deal of anxiety over our willingness to break laws. This is certainly a legitimate concern. Since we so diligently urge people to obey the Supreme Court's decision of 1954 outlawing segregation in the public schools, at first glance

15

it may seem rather paradoxical for us consciously to break laws. One may well ask: "How can you advocate breaking some laws and obeying others?" The answer lies in the fact that there are two types of laws: just and unjust. I would be the first to advocate obeying just laws. One has not only a legal but a moral responsibility to obey just laws. Conversely, one has a moral responsibility to disobey unjust laws. I would agree with St. Augustine that "an unjust law is no law at all."

Now, what is the difference between the two? How does one determine whether a law is just or unjust? A just law is a man-made code that squares with the moral law or the law of God. An unjust law is a code that is out of harmony with the moral law. To put it in the terms of St. Thomas Aquinas: An unjust law is a human law that is not rooted in eternal law and natural law. Any law that uplifts human personality is just. Any law that degrades human personality is unjust. All segregation statutes are unjust because segregation distorts the soul and damages the personality. It gives the segregator a false sense of superiority and the segregated a false sense of inferiority. Segregation, to use the terminology of the Jewish philosopher Martin Buber, substitutes an "I-it" relationship for an "I-thou" relationship and ends up relegating persons to the status of things. Hence, segregation is not only politically, economically, and sociologically unsound, it is morally wrong and sinful. Paul Tillich has said that sin is separation. Is not segregation an existential expression of man's tragic separation, his awful estrangement, his terrible sinfulness? Thus it is that I can urge men to obey the 1954 decision of the Supreme Court, for it is morally right; and I can urge them to disobey segregation ordinances, for they are morally wrong.

Let us consider a more concrete example of just and unjust laws. An unjust law is a code that a numerical or power majority group compels a minority group to obey but does not make binding on itself. This is *difference* made legal. By the same token, a just law is a code that a majority compels a minority to follow and that it is willing to follow itself. This is *sameness* made legal.

Let me give another explanation. A law is unjust if it is inflicted on a minority that, as a result of being denied the right to vote, had no part in enacting or devising the law. Who can say that the legislature of Alabama which set up that state's segregation laws was democratically elected? Throughout Alabama all sorts of devious methods are used to prevent Negroes from becoming registered voters, and there are some counties in which, even though Negroes constitute a majority of the population, not a single Negro is registered. Can any law enacted under such circumstances be considered democratically structured?

Sometimes a law is just on its face and unjust in its application. For instance, I have been arrested on a charge of parading without a permit. Now, there is nothing wrong in having an ordinance which requires a permit for a parade. But such an ordinance becomes unjust when it is used to maintain segregation and to deny citizens the First-Amendment privilege of peaceful assembly and protest.

I hope you are able to see the distinction I am trying to point out. In no sense do I advocate evading or defying the law, as would the rabid segregationist. That would lead to anarchy. One who breaks an unjust law must do so openly, lovingly, and with a willingness to accept the penalty. I submit that an individual who breaks a law that conscience tells him is unjust, and who willingly accepts the penalty of imprisonment in order to arouse the conscience of the community over its injustice, is in reality expressing the highest respect for law. 20

Of course, there is nothing new about this kind of civil disobedience. It was evidenced sublimely in the refusal of Shadrach, Meshach, and Abednego to obey the laws of Nebuchadnezzar, on the ground that a higher moral law was at stake. It was practiced superbly by the early Christians, who were willing to face hungry lions and the excruciating pain of chopping blocks rather than submit to certain unjust laws of the Roman Empire. To a degree, academic freedom is a reality today because Socrates practiced civil disobedience. In our own nation, the Boston Tea Party represented a massive act of civil disobedience.

We should never forget that everything Adolf Hitler did in Germany was "legal" and everything the Hungarian freedom fighters did in Hungary was "illegal." It was "illegal" to aid and comfort a Jew in Hitler's Germany. Even so, I am sure that, had I lived in Germany at the time, I would have aided and comforted my Jewish brothers. If today I lived in a Communist country where certain principles dear to the Christian faith are suppressed I would openly advocate disobeying that country's antireligious laws.

I must make two honest confessions to you, my Christian and Jewish brothers. First, I must confess that over the past few years I have been gravely disappointed with the white moderate. I have almost reached the regrettable conclusion that the Negro's great stumbling block in his stride toward freedom is not the White Citizen's Counciler or the Ku Klux Klanner, but the white moderate, who is more devoted to "order" than to justice; who prefers a negative peace which is the presence of tension to a positive peace which is the presence of justice; who constantly says: "I agree with you in the goal you seek, but I cannot agree with your methods of direct action"; who paternalistically believes he can set the timetable for another man's freedom; who lives by a mythical concept of time and who constantly advises the Negro to wait for a "more convenient season." Shallow understanding from people of good will is more frustrating than absolute misunderstanding from people of ill will. Lukewarm acceptance is much more bewildering than outright rejection.

I had hoped that the white moderate would understand that law and order exist for the purpose of establishing justice and that when they fail in this purpose they become the dangerously structured dams that block the flow of social progress. I had hoped that the white moderate would understand that the present tension in the South is a necessary phase of the transition from an obnoxious negative peace, in which the Negro passively accepted his unjust plight, to a substantive and positive peace, in which all men will respect the dignity and worth of human personality. Actually, we who engage in nonviolent direct action are not the creators of tension. We merely bring to the surface the hidden tension that is already alive. We bring it out in the open, where it can be seen and dealt with. Like a boil that can never be cured so long as it is covered up but must be opened with all its ugliness to the natural medicines of air and light, injustice must be exposed, with all the tension its exposure creates, to the light of human conscience and the air of national opinion before it can be cured.

In your statement you assert that our actions, even though peaceful, must be condemned because they precipitate violence. But is this a logical assertion? Isn't this like condemning a robbed man because his possession of money precipitated the evil act of robbery? Isn't this like condemning Socrates because his unswerving commitment to truth and his philosophical inquiries precipitated the act by the misguided populace in which they made him drink hemlock? Isn't this like condemning Jesus because his unique God-consciousness and never-ceasing devotion to God's will precipitated the evil act of crucifixion? We must come to see that, as the federal courts have consistently affirmed, it is wrong to urge an individual to cease his efforts to gain his basic constitutional rights because the quest may precipitate violence. Society must protect the robbed and punish the robber.

I had also hoped that the white moderate would reject the myth concerning time in relation to the struggle for freedom. I have just received a letter from a white brother in Texas. He writes: "All Christians know that the colored people will receive equal rights eventually, but it is possible that you are in too great a religious hurry. It has taken Christianity almost two thousand years to accomplish what it has. The teachings of Christ take time to come to earth." Such an attitude stems from a tragic misconception of time, from the strangely irrational notion that there is something in the very flow of time that will inevitably cure all ills. Actually, time itself is neutral; it can be used either destructively or constructively. More and more I feel that the people of ill will have used time much more effectively than have the people of good will. We will have to repent in this generation not merely for the hateful words and actions of the bad people but for the appalling silence of the good people. Human progress never rolls in on wheels of inevitability; it comes through the tireless efforts of men willing to be co-workers with God, and without this hard work, time itself becomes an ally of the forces of social stagnation. We must use time creatively, in the knowledge that the time is always ripe to do right. Now is the time to make real the promise of democracy and transform our pending national elegy into a creative psalm of brotherhood. Now is the time to lift our national policy from the quicksand of racial injustice to the solid rock of human dignity.

You speak of our activity in Birmingham as extreme. At first I was rather disappointed that fellow clergymen would see my nonviolent efforts as those of an extremist. I began thinking about the fact that I stand in the middle of two opposing forces in the Negro community. One is a force of complacency, made up in part of Negroes who, as a result of long years of oppression, are so drained of self-respect and a sense of "somebodiness" that they have adjusted to segregation; and in part of a few middle-class Negroes who, because of a degree of academic and economic security and because in some ways they profit by segregation, have become insensitive to the problems of the masses. The other force is one of bitterness and hatred, and it comes perilously close to advocating violence. It is expressed in the various black nationalists groups that are springing up across the nation, the largest and best-known being Elijah Muhammad's Muslim movement. Nourished by the Negro's frustration over the continued existence of racial discrimination, this movement is made up of people who have lost faith in America, who have absolutely repudiated Christianity, and who have concluded that the white man is an incorrigible "devil."

I have tried to stand between these two forces, saying that we need emulate neither the "do-nothingism" of the complacent nor the hatred and despair of the black nationalist. For there is the more excellent way of love and nonviolent protest. I am grateful to God that, through the influence of the Negro church, the way of nonviolence became an integral part of our struggle.

If this philosophy had not emerged, by now many streets of the South would, I am convinced, be flowing with blood. And I am further convinced that if our white brothers dismiss as "rabble-rousers" and "outside agitators" those of us who employ nonviolent direct action, and if they refuse to support our nonviolent efforts, millions of the Negroes will, out of frustration and despair, seek solace and security in black-nationalist ideologies—a development that would inevitably lead to a frightening racial nightmare.

Oppressed people cannot remain oppressed forever. The yearning for freedom eventually manifests itself, and that is what has happened to the American Negro. Something within has reminded him of his birthright of freedom, and something without has reminded him that it can be gained. Consciously or unconsciously, he has been caught up by the *Zeitgeist*, and with his black brothers of Africa and his brown and yellow brothers of Asia, South America and the Caribbean, the United States Negro is moving with a sense of great urgency toward the promised land of racial justice. If one recognizes this vital urge that has engulfed the Negro community, one should readily understand why public demonstrations are taking place. The Negro has many pent-up resentments and latent frustrations, and he must release them. So let him march; let him make prayer pilgrimages to the city hall; let him go on freedom rides—and try to understand why he must do so. If his repressed emotions are not released in nonviolent ways, they will seek expression through violence; this is not a threat but a fact of history. So I have not said to my people: "Get rid of your discontent." Rather, I have tried to say that this normal and healthy discontent can be channeled into the creative outlet of nonviolent direct action. And now this approach is being termed extremist.

But though I was initially disappointed at being categorized as an extremist, as I continued to think about the matter I gradually gained a measure of satisfaction from the label. Was not Jesus an extremist for love: "Love your enemies, bless them that curse you, do good to them that hate you, and pray for them which despitefully use you, and persecute you." Was not Amos an extremist for justice: "Let justice roll down like waters and righteousness like an ever-flowing stream." Was not Paul an extremist for the Christian gospel: "I bear in my body the makers of the Lord Jesus." Was not Martin Luther an extremist: "Here I stand; I cannot do otherwise, so help me God." And John Bunyan: "I will stay in jail to the end of my days before I make a butchery of my conscience." And Abraham Lincoln: "This nation cannot survive half slave and half free." And Thomas Jefferson: "We hold these truths to be self-evident, that all men are created equal. . . ." So the question is not whether we will be extremists, but what kind of extremists we will be. Will we be extremists for hate or for love? Will we be extremists for the preservation of injustice or for the extension of justice? In that dramatic scene on Calvary's hill three men were crucified. We must never forget that all three were crucified for the same crime—the crime of extremism. Two were extremists for immorality, and thus fell below their environment. The other, Jesus Christ, was an extremist for love, truth, and goodness, and thereby rose above his environment. Perhaps the South, the nation, and the world are in dire need of creative extremists.

I had hoped that the white moderate would see this need. Perhaps I was too optimistic; perhaps I expected too much. I suppose I should have realized that few members of the oppressor race can understand the deep groans and passionate yearnings of the oppressed race, and still fewer have the vision to see that injustice must be rooted out by strong, persistent, and determined action. I am thankful, however, that some of our white brothers in the South have grasped the meaning of this social revolution and committed themselves to it. They are still all too few in quantity, but they are big in quality. Some—such as Ralph McGill, Lillian Smith, Harry Golden, James McBride Dabbs, Ann Braden, and Sarah Patton Boyle—have written about our struggle in eloquent and prophetic terms. Others have marched with us down nameless streets of the South. They have languished in filthy, roach-infested jails, suffering the abuse and brutality of policemen who view them as "dirty nigger-lovers." Unlike so many of their moderate brothers and sisters, they have recognized the urgency of the moment and sensed the need for powerful "action" antidotes to combat the disease of segregation.

Let me take note of my other major disappointment. I have been so greatly disappointed with the white church and its leadership. Of course, there are some notable exceptions. I am not unmindful of the fact that each of you has taken some significant stands on this issue. I commend you, Reverend Stallings, for your Christian stand on this past Sunday, in welcoming Negroes to your worship service on a non-segregated basis. I commend the Catholic leaders of this state for integrating Spring Hill College several years ago.

But despite these notable exceptions, I must honestly reiterate that I have been disappointed with the church. I do not say this as one of those negative critics who can always find something wrong with the church. I say this as a minister of the gospel, who loves the church; who was nurtured in its bosom; who has been sustained by its spiritual blessings and who will remain true to it as long as the cord of life shall lengthen.

When I was suddenly catapulted into the leadership of the bus protest in Montgomery, Alabama, a few years ago, I felt we would be supported by the white church. I felt that the white ministers, priests, and rabbis of the South would be among our strongest allies. Instead, some have been outright opponents, refusing to understand the freedom movement and misrepresenting its leaders; all too many others have been more cautious than courageous and have remained silent behind the anesthetizing security of stained-glass windows.

In spite of my shattered dreams, I came to Birmingham with the hope that the white religious leadership of this community would see the justice of our cause and, with deep moral concern, would serve as the channel through which our just grievances could reach the power structure. I had hoped that each of you would understand. But again I have been disappointed.

I have heard numerous southern religious leaders admonish their worshipers to comply with a desegregation decision because it is the law, but I have longed to hear white ministers declare: "Follow this decree because integration is morally right and because the Negro is your brother." In the midst of blatant injustices inflicted upon the Negro, I have watched white churchmen stand on the sideline and mouth pious irrelevancies and sanctimonious trivialities. In the midst of a mighty struggle to rid our nation of racial and economic injustice, I have heard many ministers say: "Those are social issues, with which the gospel has no real concern." And I have watched many churches commit themselves to a completely otherworldly religion which makes a strange, un-Biblical distinction between body and soul, between the sacred and the secular.

I have traveled the length and breadth of Alabama, Mississippi, and all the other southern states. On sweltering summer days and crisp autumn mornings I have looked at the South's beautiful churches with their lofty spires pointing heavenward. I have beheld the impressive outlines of her massive religious-education buildings. Over and over I have found myself asking: "What kind of people worship here? Who is their God? Where were their voices when the lips of Governor Barnett dripped with words of interposition and nullification? Where were they when Governor Wallace gave a clarion call for defiance and hatred? Where were their voices of support when bruised and weary Negro men and women decided to rise from the dark dungeons of complacency to the bright hills of creative protest?"

Yes, these questions are still in my mind. In deep disappointment I have wept over the laxity of the church. But be assured that my tears have been tears of love. There can be no deep disappointment where there is not deep love. Yes, I love the church. How could I do otherwise? I am in the rather unique position of being the son, the grandson, and the great-grandson of preachers. Yes, I see the church as the body of Christ. But, oh! How we have blemished and scarred that body through social neglect and through fear of being nonconformists.

There was a time when the church was very powerful—in the time when the early Christians rejoiced at being deemed worthy to suffer for what they believed. In those days the church was not merely a thermometer that recorded the ideas and principles of popular opinion; it was a thermostat that transformed the mores of society. Whenever the early Christians entered a town, the people in power became disturbed and immediately sought to convict the Christians for being "disturbers of the peace" and "outside agitators." But the Christians pressed on, in the conviction that they were "a colony of heaven," called to obey God rather than man. Small in number, they were big in commitment. They were too God-intoxicated to be "astronomically intimidated." By their effort and example they brought an end to such ancient evils as infanticide and gladiatorial contests.

Things are different now. So often the contemporary church is a weak, ineffectual voice with an uncertain sound. So often it is an archdefender of the status quo. Far from being disturbed by the presence of the church, the power structure of the average community is consoled by the church's silent—and often even vocal—sanction of things as they are.

But the judgment of God is upon the church as never before. If today's church does not recapture the sacrificial spirit of the early church, it will lose its authenticity, forfeit the loyalty of millions, and be dismissed as an irrelevant social club with no meaning for the twentieth century. Every day I meet young people whose disappointment with the church has turned into outright disgust.

Perhaps I have once again been too optimistic. Is organized religion too inextricably bound to the status quo to save our nation and the world? Perhaps I must turn my faith to the inner spiritual church, the church within the church, as the true *ekklesia* and the hope of the world. But again I am thankful to God that some noble souls from the ranks of organized religion have broken loose from the paralyzing chains of conformity and joined us as active partners in the struggle for freedom. They have left their secure congregations and walked the streets of Albany, Georgia, with us. They have gone down the highways of the South on tortuous rides for freedom. Yes, they have gone to jail with us. Some have been dismissed from their churches, have lost the support of their bishops and fellow ministers. But they have acted in the faith that right defeated is stronger than evil triumphant. Their witness has been the spiritual salt that has preserved the true meaning of the gospel in these troubled times. They have carved a tunnel of hope through the dark mountain of disappointment.

I hope the church as a whole will meet the challenge of this decisive hour. But even if the church does not come to the aid of justice, I have no despair about the future. I have no fear about the outcome of our struggle in Birmingham, even if our motives are at present misunderstood. We will reach the goal of freedom in Birmingham and all over the nation, because the goal of America is freedom. Abused and scorned though we may be, our destiny is tied up with America's destiny. Before the pilgrims landed at Plymouth, we were here. Before the pen of Jefferson etched the majestic words of the Declaration of Independence across the pages of history, we were here. For more than two centuries our forebears labored in this country without wages; they made cotton king; they built the homes of their masters while suffering gross injustice and shameful humiliation—and yet out of a bottomless vitality they continued to thrive and develop. If the inexpressible cruelties of slavery could not stop us, the opposition we now face will surely fail. We will win our freedom because the sacred heritage of our nation and the eternal will of God are embodied in our echoing demands.

Before closing I feel impelled to mention one other point in your statement that has troubled me profoundly. You warmly commended the Birmingham police force for keeping "order" and "preventing violence." I doubt that you would have so warmly commended the police force if you had seen its dogs sinking their teeth into unarmed, nonviolent Negroes. I doubt that you would so quickly commend the policemen if you were to observe their ugly and inhumane treatment of Negroes here in the city jail; if you were to watch them push and curse old Negro women and young Negro girls; if you were to see them slap and kick old Negro men and young boys; if you to observe them, as they did on two occasions, refuse to give us good because we wanted to sing our grace together. I cannot join you in your praise of the Birmingham police department.

It is true that police have exercised a degree of discipline in handling the demonstrators. In this sense they have conducted themselves rather "nonviolently" in public. But for what purpose? To preserve the evil system of segregation. Over the past few years I have consistently preached that nonviolence demands that the means we use must be as pure as the ends we seek. I have tried to make clear that it is wrong to use immoral means to attain moral ends. But now I must affirm that it is just as wrong, or perhaps even more so, to use moral means to preserve immoral ends. Perhaps Mr. Connor and his policemen have been rather nonviolent in public, as was Chief Pritchett in Albany, Georgia, but they have used the moral means of nonviolence to maintain the immoral end of racial injustice. As T.S. Eliot has said: "The last temptation is the greatest treason: to do the right deed for the wrong reason."

I wish you had commended the Negro sit-inners and demonstrators of Birmingham for their sublime courage, their willingness to suffer, and their amazing discipline in the midst of great provocation. One day the South will recognize its real heroes. They will be the James Merediths, with the noble sense of purpose that enables them to face jeering and hostile mobs, and with the agonizing loneliness that characterizes the life of the pioneer. They will be old, oppressed, battered Negro women, symbolized in a seventy-two-year-old woman in Montgomery, Alabama, who rose up with a sense of dignity and with her people decided not to ride segregated buses, and who responded with ungrammatical profundity to one who inquired about her weariness: "My feets is tired, but my soul is at rest." They will be the young high school and college students, the young ministers of the gospel and a host of their elders, courageously and nonviolently sitting in at lunch counters and willingly going to jail for conscience sake. One day the South will know that when these disinherited children of God sat down at lunch counters, they were in reality standing up for what is best in the American dream and for the most sacred values in our Judaeo-Christian heritage, thereby bringing our nation back to those great wells of democracy which were dug deep by the founding fathers in their formulation of the Constitution and the Declaration of Independence.

Never before have I written so long a letter. I'm afraid it is much too long to take your precious time. I can assure you that it would have been much shorter if I had been writing from a comfortable desk, but what else can one do when he is alone in a narrow jail cell, other than write long letters, think long thoughts, and pray long prayers?

If I have said anything in this letter that overstates the truth and indicates an unreasonable impatience, I beg you to forgive me. If I have said anything that understates the truth and indicates my having a patience that allows me to settle for anything less than brotherhood, I beg God to forgive me.

I hope this letter finds you strong in faith. I also hope that circumstances will soon make it possible for me to meet each of you, not as an integrationist or a civil-rights leader but as a fellow clergyman and a Christian brother. Let us all hope that the dark clouds of racial prejudice will soon pass away and the deep fog of misunderstanding will be lifted from our fear-drenched communities, and in some not-too-distant tomorrow the radiant stars of love and brotherhood will shine over our great nation with all their scintillating beauty.

Yours for the cause of Peace and Brotherhood.

MARTIN LUTHER KING, JR.

QUESTIONS FOR DISCUSSION AND WRITING

1. What is your response to King's argument? Do you feel most affected intellectually, emotionally, or a combination? What do you think contributed to your response?

2. Outline King's basic argument and supporting points. Which points rest on ethics and values that you would characterize as American? Which rest on beliefs or values that seem to be more global or universal in scope?

3. Discuss King's argument about just and unjust laws. How does he define each? How does he support his definition? How would you respond to King's argument?

4. Why do you think the clergy to whom King was responding were so concerned about King's work in Birmingham? How do you think they would have responded to this letter?

5. Consider the concept of the "outside agitator," or someone from outside a community who works with local activists to support direct action. What is your response to this concept and to King's argument that he is not an outsider with regard to the Birmingham activities? Would you extend the argument across international boundaries? Where would you draw the line?

6. Research a concept from this letter, such as the just law or nonviolent resistance. You could begin your research with some of the works King refers to, such as the writings of Gandhi, and with sources included in this book's Appendix.

The Harmful Myth
of Asian Superiority

RONALD TAKAKI

Ronald Takaki, the grandson of Hawaiian plantation workers, is professor of ethnic studies at the University of California at Berkeley, where he received his Ph.D. in American history in 1967. His numerous and well-respected publications include *Iron Cages: Race and Culture in 19th Century America* (1979); *Pau Hana: Plantation Life and Labor in Hawaii* (1983); *Strangers from a Different Shore: A History of Asian Americans* (1989); *A Different Mirror: A History of Multicultural America* (1993); and *Hiroshima: Why America Dropped the Atomic Bomb* (1995). He also edited *Double Victory: A Multicultural History of America in World War II* (2000) and *Debating Diversity: Clashing Perspectives on Race and Ethnicity in America* (Third Edition, 2002). In the essay that follows, published in the *New York Times* in 1990, Takaki addresses what is sometimes termed the "model minority" issue and the detrimental effects of even "positive" stereotyping.

Asian Americans have been described in the media as "excessively, even provocatively" successful in gaining admission to universities. Asian American shopkeepers have been congratulated, as well as criticized, for their ubiquity and entrepreneurial effectiveness.

If Asian Americans can make it, many politicians and pundits ask, why can't African Americans? Such comparisons pit minorities against each other and generate African American resentment toward Asian Americans. The victims are blamed for their plight, rather than racism and an economy that has made many young African American workers superfluous.

The celebration of Asian Americans has obscured reality. For example, figures on the high earnings of Asian Americans relative to Caucasians are misleading. Most Asian Americans live in California, Hawaii, and New York—states with higher incomes and higher costs of living than the national average.

Even Japanese Americans, often touted for their upward mobility, have not reached equality. While Japanese American men in California earned an average income comparable to Caucasian men in 1980, they did so only by acquiring more education and working more hours.

Comparing family incomes is even more deceptive. Some   5
Asian American groups do have higher family incomes than Caucasians. But they have more workers per family.

The "model minority" image homogenizes Asian Americans
and hides their differences. For example, while thousands of
Vietnamese American young people attend universities, others
are on the streets. They live in motels and hang out in pool halls
in places like East Los Angeles; some join gangs.

Twenty-five percent of the people in New York City's Chinatown lived below the poverty level in 1980, compared with 17
percent of the city's population. Some 60 percent of the workers
in the Chinatowns of Los Angeles and San Francisco are crowded
into low-paying jobs in garment factories and restaurants.

"Most immigrants coming into Chinatown with a language
barrier cannot go outside this confined area into the mainstream
of American industry," a Chinese immigrant said. "Before, I was
a painter in Hong Kong, but I can't do it here. I got no license, no
education. I want a living; so it's dishwasher, janitor, or cook."

Hmong and Mien refugees from Laos have unemployment
rates that reach as high as 80 percent. A 1987 California study
showed that three out of ten Southeast Asian refugee families
had been on welfare for four to ten years.

Although college-educated Asian Americans are entering   10
the professions and earning good salaries, many hit the "glass
ceiling"—the barrier through which high management positions
can be seen but not reached. In 1988, only 8 percent of Asian
Americans were "officials" and "managers," compared with 12
percent for all groups.

Finally, the triumph of Korean immigrants has been exaggerated. In 1988, Koreans in the New York metropolitan area
earned only 68 percent of the median income of non-Asians.
More than three-quarters of Korean greengrocers, those so-called
paragons of bootstrap entrepreneurialism, came to America with
a college education. Engineers, teachers, or administrators while
in Korea, they became shopkeepers after their arrival. For many
of them, the greengrocery represents dashed dreams, a step
downward in status.

For all their hard work and long hours, most Korean shopkeepers do not actually earn very much: $17,000 to $35,000 a
year, usually representing the income from the labor of an entire family.

But most Korean immigrants do not become shopkeepers.
Instead, many find themselves trapped as clerks in grocery
stores, service workers in restaurants, seamstresses in garment
factories, and janitors in hotels.

Most Asian Americans know their "success" is largely a myth. They also see how the celebration of Asian Americans as a "model minority" perpetuates their inequality and exacerbates relations between them and African Americans.

QUESTIONS FOR DISCUSSION AND WRITING

1. Examine the structure of this essay. How does the title predict the essay's stance and approach? How do the first two paragraphs set up the structure that follows? Where and how does the author assert his thesis? And how does he support that thesis?

2. Which logical appeals are prominent in this essay? Do you find that the author relies on both reasons and examples to support his assertions? Do you find any appeals to ethos or logos? If so, identify them and explain what they contribute to the argument.

3. Takaki asserts points early in the essay and then responds, setting up his essay as essentially a refutation. What are the pros and cons of this strategy?

4. Takaki published this essay in 1990. Do you sense that since that time his view has become more widespread or at least more widely discussed?

5. Write a letter responding to Takaki either arguing with his view or agreeing with his thesis, but supporting your view with different evidence or appeals than Takaki uses.

6. Write an essay about a harmful social or cultural myth, following the model Takaki uses—pose the myth or stereotype and then refute it.

The Native Hawaiian Today

MICHAEL KIONI DUDLEY, PH.D.

Michael Kioni Dudley taught at Chaminade University in Honolulu and at the University of Hawaii. His doctoral research focused on ancient Hawaiian culture. Dudley is considered a scholar-activist in Hawaiian educational issues; his other writing has included a guest editorial on this topic in the *Honolulu Star-Bulletin* in 1986 and *A Hawaiian Nation: Man, Gods, and Nature* (1990).

KEONI KEALOHA AGARD

Keoni Kealoha Agard graduated from Kamehameha schools (1969), Chaminade University (1973), and the School of Law at the University of Hawaii (1978). He was deputy attorney general for the state of Hawaii and was a staff attorney for the Native Hawaiian Legal Corporation. A native Hawaiian attorney, he has served as an advocate for native Hawaiians, and his private practice focuses on native Hawaiian issues including land claims.

The article that follows is drawn from their book *A Call for Hawaiian Sovereignty,* previously published in 1990 under the title *A Hawaiian Nation II: A Call for Hawaiian Sovereignty,* and most recently published in 1993 in a Centennial Commemoration Edition, 1893-1993, marking the anniversary of the overthrow of the Hawaiian Nation in 1893. This book contributed notably to the Hawaiian Sovereignty movement.

To complete the picture of why the native Hawaiian is calling for sovereignty, consider the plight of the Hawaiian today.[1]

Even though there are some Hawaiians who are outstanding scholars, doctors, lawyers, politicians, and businessmen, Hawaiians as a people simply are not making it in modern American society. As a group, they hold the lowest paying jobs in the state. They have the greatest number on welfare. They have the worst housing, if they have housing at all.[2]

Hawaiians rank first with most Western diseases for which records are kept: they have the highest death rate from heart diseases, from stroke, from lung cancer, breast cancer, cancer of the stomach, of the esophagus, of the uterus, and of the pancreas. They have the highest infant mortality rate. And they are first with diabetes, hypertension, and kidney failure.

All of this adds up: the native Hawaiians have the shortest life expectancy of all the peoples in the islands.

There are other areas where Hawaiians aren't making it: they have the highest school drop-out rate. And small as they are in percentage of the state's total population, they far outnumber other nationalities in the jails. In the courts Hawaiians who have held land since the *mahele** have lost thousands of acres to American corporations in "adverse possession" cases. By executive and legislative fiat they have again and again been driven from areas where they have tried to live a traditional, subsistence lifestyle. Modern American society is actually pitted against them.

Where can they turn? Nowhere. Hawaiians rank first in suicide. Their future should lie with their young men. Yet the highest suicide rate in the state is for young Hawaiian men, ages eighteen to thirty-four. There is no place to turn.

As a whole, native Hawaiians clearly are not making it in modern American society. To deny that is to hide one's head in the sand. It is time to deal with this fact squarely, and to find out why.

Those Hawaiians who have "succeeded" are generally from families that have actively sought to become Americanized. Those who have not "succeeded" seem, in various ways, to have resisted Americanization.

One reason those resisting have done so is probably because of a subconscious survival need. The melting pot ideal may be fine for continental America. And it may be fine for foreigners coming to these islands to become Americans. But when Italian Americans or Japanese Americans, for example, lose themselves in American society, there are still Italians and Japanese in the homeland to preserve the national culture. There is no other homeland where Hawaiians are preserving their national culture. This is their only home. As Hawaiians mix in with others, Hawaiian culture, Hawaiian identity, and the Hawaiians as a people, become extinct. Those Hawaiians who resist Americanization know this deep in their being. Their resistance is for survival itself. Hawaiians are a very endangered species living in their one and only habitat.

But there is more to their resistance than this. They resist because they truly don't fit in modern Western society. They would not have major problems on every front if they did fit. They are

5

10

*land division—editor's note

different from Westerners and from Asians, truly different. They are island people whom thousands of years of cultural evolution have formed to interrelate with the land and the sea and other people in a special way in order to assure their survival.

Hawaiians sense differently. They feel the wind differently. They relate to land and sea as family and experience a bond with them which is unknown to Westerners. They have different inner clocks and deal with time differently. They have different priorities in life. They have different strengths. They have different ideas of right and wrong. They get "chicken skin" when they sense a spiritual presence rather than when they feel cold. The list of differences goes on and on. These deep, distinguishing differences are ingrained characteristics selectively acquired and developed over generations for island dwelling.

But while traits such as those just mentioned have prepared Hawaiians excellently for island life, they have also made them extremely vulnerable in modern Western society. Hawaiians need the opportunity and the space to reappropriate, and to revitalize, the culture which they developed over their two thousand years in these islands. That culture was carefully honed to meet their specific needs, to protect them, to allow them to survive and flourish in their environment, and to give them direction for advancing into the future. Cut off from their culture, they suffer and perish, as they do today.

Their Own Lands—A Survival Need

"To survive, the Hawaiian race must have large areas of their ancestral lands returned to them. **To survive,** they must have the space—separate from outsiders—to re-experience the islands and their relationship with them in the same way their ancestors did." **"To survive"** is a serious claim. On what reasoning is such a claim based?

The question of Hawaiian racial survival may be discussed in the context of evolutionary survival of the fittest. This discussion presumes that evolution is a fact, and that "survival of the fittest" is one of its driving forces. It also presumes that man shares with animals beneath him many of their ways of dealing with reality, among them ways they have developed to achieve the survival of the fittest. Let us examine this further.

Public television in recent years has presented numerous 15 shows on plant and animal life. One of the most interesting topics they have explored has been the mating rituals of animals. One particularly beautiful episode showed two male peacocks prancing before a prospective mate. Male peacocks have beautiful body feathers, but their tail feathers are probably unmatched for beauty in the bird world. The two males fanned out their stunning feathers and strutted around, striking this pose and that pose, and squawking at each other in obvious derision. Eventually, the female chose one over the other and went off with him to mate.

This is what survival of the fittest at its most basic level is all about. Throughout the animal world we find that males and females have arenas of competition to "show their stuff," attempting to prove to prospective partners that they are the best mate for producing the offspring most fit for survival.

This "survival of the fittest" thrust is found at the basis of many human actions and decisions. But since in humans the drive acts primarily on the subconscious level, people are not aware that many of their actions are directed by their need to produce offspring able to adapt to future situations so that the human species will survive.

Humans have many arenas of competition. Often they compete in arenas from which the other sex is entirely excluded. These are fending competitions, practices where they learn their strengths and their weaknesses, sometimes not even realizing that they are competing. But through their activities they slowly establish their position of respect among the peers of their own sex. Those who are superior win the right to be deferred to by those less worthy when beauties of the opposite sex approach. A teenage boy, for instance, may think, "I'm not worthy of her. She will go for him," and leave her for those who have proven themselves better in various areas of competition.

Arenas of competition in the Western world might be the high school football field or basketball court. They might be competitions for the honor roll, for being the drum major or majorette in the band, for the lead in a play, for membership on the debate team, for class president or student body president. Because there are a number of areas in which a species must excel if it is to survive, there are varied arenas for boys or girls with different personalities and different strengths to compete and to prove themselves in order to eventually attract and win the mate whom they choose.

But the arenas of competition in Westerner culture are much different from those in Hawaiian culture. Centuries ago the new belief that nature was "unaware," and incapable of interrelating with man, influenced Western man to distance himself from the world of nature surrounding him. Centuries ago also, the Industrial Revolution took the people who would lead and influence society off the farm and further out of touch with nature. The arenas of competition Westerners slowly devised as proving grounds to demonstrate "fitness" came to be far divorced from nature, and took on radically new and different forms: knowing how to program a computer, overhaul a car's transmission, and correctly punctuate a letter—all signify "the fit." So do having the latest model car and latest fashions in clothes, never being guilty of gaffes in table etiquette, and never wearing a white tie to a black-tie affair. Keeping up with the Joneses is a multi-faceted competition that permeates American society at every level.

Islanders have not shared the changes Europeans and Americans have gone through. In the world view they developed in ancient days, islanders were participants along with the surrounding world of nature in a conscious, interrelating, familial community. As Hawaiian society developed its areas of competition over the centuries, this world view directed selection of the arenas. Hawaiians of old had their "grand arenas" for showing their prowess—the great competititive games of the *Makahiki* celebrations, riddling matches, chant competitions, and *hula* performances, all were grand demonstrations of their physical abilities, their skill or cleverness, or their intellectual acumen. But most of their arenas were closer to the earth and sea, and were much more subtle. The Hawaiian's competition often was a contest with the conscious natural world around him. The fisherman competed with the sea, competed with the fish, with the man-eating shark, and with sudden squalls at sea. Diving down thirty or more feet on a breath of air to lay net or to fish by hand for lobsters in holes on the side of the reef, the Hawaiian was competing, one on one, in a way unknown to continentals. The diver related with the sea, and was at home in the sea. He trusted his gods to protect him, and he depended on his family relationships with the sea and its creatures. If he was family to the sharks, he relied on those related closely to him to protect him. He proved himself every day by coming back alive, or even better, alive and with food in his net. Farmers and other peoples of the land also had their arenas. All the arenas, like the people, were closely tied to nature.

Since the time of Captain Cook, people coming to the islands have transplanted their competitive Western activities here. This has been fine for them, but as the years have passed, and as newcomers have become predominant, they have attempted to impose their culture and their arenas of competition on the Hawaiians. It has not worked.

Instead of realizing that there is nothing at all inside the Hawaiian fisherman, for instance, which would make him in any way whatsoever want to wear a business suit and compete in the stock market, many Westerners seem to insist on just that. One finds an intolerance towards those whose goals do not include living in modern housing, driving new cars, having huge bank accounts, speaking perfect English, and involving themselves in the rush of American society and business. Such a cavalier attitude is found in sentiments such as "Hawaiians would be better off if they took on the American way. This is the modern day, and when Hawaiians catch on and do things our way, they'll be better off."

If people went into the Midwest and made the same proclamations about Midwest farmers, they would be laughed at. No one would consider taking all the people off the farms in the midwest, and changing their lifestyles, their goals, and their realms of competition. Yet many advocate exactly that for the Hawaiians. What is the difference?

Is it that the farmers living "their" different lifestyle perform a service for Americans, and the Hawaiians do not? If that is the case, have Westerners come to the point of facilitating the survival or extinction of a race based on its perceived immediate usefulness?

25

Certainly it is not desirable to have fewer rather than more distinctive cultures. The greater the variation within a species, the greater the opportunities for further evolution. Variation is the raw material of evolution. The loss of a race—with its physical and mental traits, its philosophy and approach to life, and its traditional lore learned and developed over centuries—is a tragic loss for all mankind. We must preserve the variants. Without them, the future evolution of mankind is limited in its possibilities. For the sake of mankind itself, the Hawaiian race and the Hawaiian culture must be preserved.

To return to our initial topic, arenas of competition are vitally essential for evolutionary advance. Without competition, mankind, at the apex of evolution, cannot choose the best mate, and evolution cannot further progress. Yet it is at this most basic level of existence that Hawaiians are encountering their most fundamental problems.

The Hawaiians' most basic arenas of competition are intertwined with their communal relationship to the land and the sea and the rest of surrounding nature. When Hawaiians were taken from their lands and their traditional ways, when cities were built around them, when their culture was disdained and they were put into Westerners' schools and taught Western values and thought in place of their own—in all these ways Hawaiians were separated from traditional arenas for their competitive "survival of the fittest" rituals. For many, separation from traditional competitions shattered their striving for any goals at all. Today many Hawaiians simply don't compete. The inside drives, for centuries accustomed to work themselves out in certain ways, still surge within. But they are subconscious drives; they are blind by themselves. And the conscious mind is not geared to give them new direction. New arenas have not replaced the traditional ones. Because of this, the Hawaiians' drives to compete and demonstrate fitness and worth are confused, thwarted, and frustrated.

Many young Hawaiians lack goal orientation, lack competition. This is true. But that does not mean these youngsters are lazy. Rather, they do not have a clear view of where they should go, what they should do, what is expected of them. They aren't at home in the Westerner's fields of competition.

In a world where only the fittest survive, every people must have arenas for rituals of competition. If Hawaiians are to have theirs, they must have their lands and seas, and their traditional relationship with them. They must reclaim and revitalize those traditional competitions that evolved over centuries, so that their youth can take them up again, and so that the fittest offspring will emerge. Denied these basic conditions, they cannot survive. 30

A Note on Resort Developments

It should be noted that the problem of opposing arenas of competition is one aspect of the conflict between Hawaiians and developers. At this writing Hawaiians are protesting three major resort developments in the islands. All three are huge complexes planned for remote parts of the islands. In each case a developer has come in and bought a large section of sea-front land with plans to build a huge resort. People have protested because they don't want their country lifestyle changed. They don't want new people, new houses, more cars, sailboats, motor boats, water skis, jet skis, horses, tourist buses, new stores and tourist traps, and all the support businesses that surround a resort hotel.

The local people do not understand why they should accept a complete change of their life and of the surrounding environment, just because men with no relationship to the land, who are strangers from other areas or from other countries, want to make a fortune for themselves by building an unneeded hotel on a beautiful, uncluttered natural landscape. Also at stake, although not consciously recognized, are the country people's arenas of competition which are inextricably intertwined with their relationship to the sea, the land, and the sky. These arenas of competition are a basic survival need, and Hawaiians can't allow the hotel development without suffering this loss which will ultimately destroy their race. The developer, on the other hand, who subconsciously sees the building of his resort as a personal "proof" that he is among the fittest, does not understand their resistance. He sees forcing his will on others as further proof of his prowess. Rather than deny his manhood by just going away, he goes to court to enforce his will.

It must stop. If it doesn't, there will be no unspoiled beaches and old villages left in the state. Hawai'i is so small. Its distinctive character and lifestyle—its local color—are so fragile. It is being overrun so fast. In another generation, life in Hawai'i will be little different from life in any of southern California's sprawling suburbs. The Hawaiian race, the pure blood, the culture, all will be beyond recapture.

At Cook's arrival there were roughly 1,000,000 pure blooded Hawaiians living in the islands. Today there are a mere 8,244.[3] That is 992,000 fewer people, a decrease of more than 99%. Today there is not even one pure-blood Hawaiian for every one hundred in pre-Cook times. The Hawaiian race has not just been decimated—it has been almost completely obliterated. Paralleling what has happened to the race, in the years since annexation to America, Hawaiian culture has also been systematically destroyed. Now developers are attacking the last remnants of Hawaiian existence, the country areas of Hawai'i. If there is any hope for Hawaiians to continue "as Hawaiians," it must lie in their ability to reidentify with their roots and to develop a "modern Hawaiianness" on that foundation. With the vestiges of Hawaiian roots found in the quiet, country valleys and seashores that developers are eyeing as "get-away" resorts for wealthy American tourists, and with the American system supporting the entrepreneur and whatever may be his latest scheme to make bucks, what hope is there?

It really must be asked, "Is what is happening to the Hawaiian people America's form of genocide?"

Notes

1. Much of this chapter is a rewriting of a guest editorial by Michael Kioni Dudley, "A Native Hawaiian Nation," published in *The Honolulu Star-Bulletin,* November 15, 1986.
2. Statistics for this chapter have been gathered from numerous places by co-author Dudley for the editorial mentioned in footnote 1.

Many are also mentioned in the Action Alert. "OHA Moves to Break the Ceded Lands (5f) Trust," published by Ka Lahui in August, 1988. Many are also mentioned in the article "Native Hawaiian Illhealth: Hope for a Painful Paradox in 'Paradise,'" by Richard Kekuni Blaisdell, M.D., in the 1987 "Progress Edition" of the *Honolulu Star Bulletin*.

3. The Hawai'i State Department of Health "1986 Survey: Methods and Procedures, Health Surveillance Survey" lists 8,244 Hawaiians with 100% Hawaiian blood.

QUESTIONS FOR DISCUSSION AND WRITING

1. The introduction offers evidence to support the inference that Hawaiians are not "making it in modern American society." Do you find the evidence persuasive? Are you prepared to hear the rest of the authors' argument? Describe the tone and stance of the essay.

2. The authors argue that Hawaiians resist Americanization not only because to accept it is to lose Hawaiian culture, but also because they "don't fit in modern Western society." Which assertion do you find most convincing? What appeals do the authors use to support these assertions?

3. The authors spend a considerable part of the text making the case for the relationship between Hawaiian natives and the land of Hawaii. Discuss the ways in which, according to the authors, Hawaiians and their land interact with each other to form a unique culture. Why is the relationship of Hawaiians to the land so critical to the authors' argument?

4. Analyze the argument of this selection. Evaluate core premises, types of evidence, structure of argument, and appeals to ethos.

5. Research Hawaiian culture, the impact of Western influence and tourism on the Hawaiian Islands, Asian tourism, the military presence in Hawaii, resort development, or some other element of life in Hawaii.

To Live in the Borderlands means you

GLORIA ANZALDUA

Gloria Anzaldua was born in 1942 in Jesus Maria of the Valley, Texas. She earned a BA from Pan-American University and an MA from the University of Texas at Austin; she did postgraduate work at the University of California at Santa Cruz. Anzaldua has received numerous awards including the American Book Award, the fiction award from National Endowment for the Arts, the 1991 Lesbian Rights Award, and the Sappho Award of Distinction in 1992.

Her book *Borderlands/La Frontera: The New Mestiza* (1987), which combines Spanish and English poetry, memoir, and historical analysis, was chosen as one of the 38 Best Books of 1987 by the *Literary Journal*. In addition to the acclaimed *Borderlands*, from which the following selection was excerpted, and a novel, *La Prieta* (1997), Anzaldua has co-edited *This Bridge Called My Back: Writings by Radical Women of Color* (1981); *This Way Daybreak Comes* (1986); and *Making Face, Making Soul/Haciendo Caras: Creative and Critical Perspectives by Women of Color* (1989). She has also published children's literature, including *Prietita Has a Friend* (1991), *Friends from the Other Side—Amigos del Otro Lado* (1995), and *Prietita y La Llorona* (1996).

To Live in the Borderlands means you

are neither *hispana india negra española*
ni gabacha, eres mestiza, mulata,[1] half-breed
caught in the crossfire between camps
while carrying all five races on your back
not knowing which side to turn to, run from;

To live in the Borderlands means knowing
that the *india in you,* betrayed for 500 years,
is no longer speaking to you,
that *mexicanas* call you *rajetas,*[2]
that denying the Anglo inside you
is as bad as having denied the Indian or Black;

---

[1] Hispanic Indian Spanish nor anglo, you are *mestiza* (Indian/white), *mulata* (black/white).
[2] Someone who betrays her culture.

Cuando vives en la frontera[3]
people walk through you, the wind steals your voice,
you're a *burra, buey,*[4] scapegoat,
forerunner of a new race,
half and half—both woman and man, neither—
a new gender;

To live in the Borderlands means to
put *chile* in the borscht,
eat whole wheat *tortillas,*
speak Tex-Mex with a Brooklyn accent;
be stopped by *la migra*[5] at the border checkpoints;

Living in the Borderlands means you fight hard to   5
resist the gold elixer beckoning from the bottle,
the pull of the gun barrel,
the rope crushing the hollow of your throat;

In the Borderlands
you are the battleground
where enemies are kin to each other;
you are at home, a stranger,
the border disputes have been settled
the volley of shots have shattered the truce
you are wounded, lost in action
dead, fighting back;

To live in the Borderlands means
the mill with the razor white teeth wants to shred off
your olive-red skin, crush out the kernel, your heart
pound you pinch you roll you out
smelling like white bread but dead;

To survive the Borderlands
you must live *sin fronteras*[6]
be a crossroads.

---

[3]When you live on the border.
[4]Ass, ox.
[5]The Immigration Service.
[6]Without borders.

QUESTIONS FOR DISCUSSION AND WRITING

1. Read the poem aloud. Share with classmates or write out your first impressions. What does it mean to you, and how do you respond to it intellectually and emotionally? What role do you think your culture of origin, geographical location, gender, or other personal characteristics play in your response? How do repetition, examples, and images contribute to your impressions?

2. How is living in the borderlands both literal and metaphorical? Which meaning seems to prevail in the poem?

3. What image or word captures the author's theme of borders, crossfire, and crossroads? For example, is it a paradox? Tension? Double exposure?

4. Write a reflection on the ways in which you feel at a border or crossroads, using a similar structure, such as a repeated paragraph opener modeled on the opening line of each stanza.

5. Write an essay analyzing some aspect of the poem, such as word choice, structure, or imagery, and explain what that element contributes to your overall impression and interpretation of the poem.

In Praise of American Empire

DINESH D'SOUZA

Dinesh D'Souza (1961–) is a self-identified conservative and an American of Eastern Indian descent whose works focus on controversial areas such as race relations and ethnic identity. He graduated Phi Beta Kappa from Dartmouth College in 1983 and served as senior domestic policy analyst in the White House from 1987 to 1988, during the Reagan administration. He is currently a fellow at the Hoover Institution in Palo Alto, California. D'Souza most recently published *What's So Great about America* (2002) and has also published *Illiberal Education* (1991), *The End of Racism* (1995), *Ronald Reagan: How an Ordinary Man Became an Extraordinary Leader* (1997), and *The Virtue of Prosperity: Finding Values in an Age of Techno-Affluence* (2000). D'Souza contends in *The End of Racism* that the liberal idea of institutionalized racial discrimination is primarily fiction, spurring rebuke from leaders of the contemporary civil rights movement. The following essay (2002), in the spirit of his recent book on America, is far from the alarmist views of America as empire—asserting, instead, that "If this be the workings of empire, then let us have more of it."

America has become an empire, a fact that Americans are reluctant to admit and that critics of America regard with great alarm. Since the end of the Cold War, America exercises an unparalleled and largely unrivaled influence throughout the world. No other nation has ever enjoyed such economic, political, cultural, and military superiority. Consequently the critics of America, both at home and abroad, are right to worry about how American power is being used.

The critics charge that America is no different from other large and rapacious empires that have trampled across the continents in previous centuries. Within the universities, intellectuals speak of American policies as "neo-imperialist" because they promote the goals of empire while eschewing the term. America talks about lofty ideals, the critics say, but in reality it pursues its naked self-interest. In the Gulf War, for example, America's leaders asserted that they were fighting for human rights but in truth they were fighting to protect American access to oil. The critics point to longtime American support for dictators like Somoza in Nicaragua, Pinochet in Chile, the Shah in Iran, and Marcos in the Philippines as evidence that Americans don't really care about the democratic ideals they give lip service to. Even now America supports unelected regimes in Pakistan, Egypt, and Saudi Arabia. No wonder, the critics say, that so many people around the world are anti-American and some even resort to terrorism in order to lash out against the imperial exercise of American power.

Are the critics right? They are correct to note the extent of American influence, but wrong to suggest that America is no different from colonial powers like the British, the French, and the Spanish that once dominated the world. Those empires—like the Islamic empire, the Mongol empire, and the Chinese empire—were sustained primarily by force. The British, for example, ruled my native country of India with some 100,000 troops.

American domination is different in that it is not primarily sustained by force. This is not to deny that there are American bases in the Middle East and the Far East, or that America has the military capacity to intervene just about anywhere in the world. The real power of America, however, extends far beyond its military capabilities. Walk into a hotel in Barbados or Bombay and the bellhop is whistling the theme song from "Titanic." African boys in remote villages can be spotted wearing baseball caps. Millions of people from all over the globe want to move to America. Countless people are drawn to American technology, American freedom, the American way of life. Some critics, especially from Europe, sneer that these aspirations are short-sighted, and perhaps they are right. People may be wrong to want the American lifestyle, and may not foresee its disadvantages, but at least they are seeking it voluntarily.

What about the occasions, though, when America does exercise its military power? Here we can hardly deny the critics' allegation that America acts to promote its self-interest. Even so, Americans can feel immensely proud of how often their country has served their interests while simultaneously promoting noble ideals and the welfare of others. Yes, America fought the Gulf War in part to protect its oil interests, but it also fought to liberate the Kuwaitis from Iraqi invasion.

But what about long-lasting US backing for Latin American, Asian, and Middle Eastern dictators like Somoza, Marcos, Pinochet, and the Shah? It should be noted that, in each of these cases, the United States eventually turned against the dictatorial regime and actively aided in its ouster. In Chile and the

Philippines, the outcome was favorable: the Pinochet and Marcos regimes were replaced by democratic governments that have so far endured. In Nicaragua and Iran, however, one form of tyranny promptly gave way to another. Somoza was replaced by the Sandinistas, who suspended civil liberties and established a Marxist-style dictatorship, and the Shah of Iran was replaced by a harsh theocracy presided over by the Ayatollah Khomeini.

These outcomes help to highlight a crucial principle of foreign policy: the principle of the lesser evil. This means that one should not pursue a thing that seems good if it is likely to result in something worse. A second implication of this doctrine is that one is usually justified in allying with a bad guy in order to oppose a regime that is even worse. The classic example of this occurred during World War II: the United States allied with a very bad man, Stalin, in order to defeat someone who posed a greater threat at the time, Hitler.

Once the principle of the lesser evil is taken into account, then many American actions in terms of supporting tin-pot dictators like Marcos and Pinochet become defensible. These were measures taken to fight the cold war. If one accepts what is today an almost universal consensus that the Soviet Union was indeed an "evil empire," then the United States was right to attach more importance to the fact that Marcos and Pinochet were anti-Soviet than to the fact that they were autocratic thugs.

But now the Cold War is over, so why does America support despotic regimes like those of Musbaraff in Pakistan, Mubarak in Egypt, and the royal family in Saudi Arabia? Once again, we must apply the principle of the lesser evil and examine the practical alternative to those regimes. Unfortunately there do not seem to be viable liberal, democratic parties in the Middle East. The alternative to Mubarak and the Saudi royal family appears to be Islamic fundamentalists of the bin Laden stripe. Faced with the choice between "uncompromising medievals" and "corrupt moderns," America has no choice but to side with the corrupt moderns.

Empires have to make hard choices, but even if one disagrees with American actions in a given case, one should not miss the larger context. America is the most magnanimous of all imperial powers that have ever existed. After leveling Japan and Germany during World War II, the United States rebuilt those countries. For the most part, America is an abstaining superpower. It shows no real interest in conquering and subjugating the rest of the world, even though it can. On occasion the United States intervenes in Grenada or Haiti or Bosnia, but it never stays to rule those countries. Moreover, when America does get into a

10

war, it is supremely careful to avoid targeting civilians and to minimize collateral damage. Even as American bombs destroyed the infrastructure of the Taliban regime, American planes dropped rations of food to avert hardship and starvation of Afghan civilians. What other country does such things?

Jeane Kirkpatrick once said that "Americans need to face the truth about themselves, no matter how pleasant it is." The reason that many Americans don't feel this way is that they judge themselves by a higher standard than they judge anyone else. Thus if the Chinese, the Arabs, or the sub-Saharan Africans slaughter ten thousand of their own people, the world utters a collective sigh and resumes its normal business. By contrast, if America, in the middle of a war, accidentally bombs a school or a hospital and kills two hundred civilians, there is an immediate uproar and an investigation is launched. What all this demonstrates, of course, is America's evident moral superiority. If this be the workings of empire, let us have more of it.

QUESTIONS FOR DISCUSSION AND WRITING

1. D'Souza begins the essay by acknowledging America's power in the world, conceding that critics have reason to worry, and then outlining the opposition arguments suggesting America is no different from "other large and rapacious empires" of the past. Is this strategy of setting up his opposition and then refuting the arguments effective? Why might the author have chosen this arrangement? D'Souza's paragraphs also generally begin with an opposing point and then respond to that point. How effective do you find this organizational strategy? Which of these opposing points is most effectively refuted? Which refutation do you think is least convincing?

2. Do you think D'Souza accurately summarizes the arguments he plans to refute? Why do you think he attributes some of the arguments to intellectuals? Does he bring up all of the primary opposing arguments?

3. D'Souza describes a foreign policy of the lesser evil. Does this principle seem logical? Do you find his supporting examples appropriate?

4. D'Souza cites a choice between "uncompromising medievals" and "corrupt moderns" and asserts that "America

has no choice but to side with the corrupt moderns." Does he prove this case, or could this assertion be a false dilemma? Is there any middle ground with regard to this position?

5. Write a response to D'Souza, either refuting his position or several of his arguments, or agreeing with his view but offering different evidence. Alternatively, write an essay analyzing D'Souza's argument. Focus particularly on his appeals to logic. Does he construct a sound argument?

6. Research some of the historical events D'Souza refers to in this essay, either in America's past or in other countries' histories. For example, you could research the role of the British in the history of India, or twentieth century conflicts in Central America.

America's World

THE ECONOMIST

The Economist (founded in 1843) is a weekly news and business publication from Great Britain with a worldwide circulation (80% outside Britain). It covers domestic and international issues, business, finance, current affairs, science, technology, and the arts, and it includes news, opinion, and analysis. Its aim is to maintain an independent and international perspective, and it seeks to hold to its founding principles of free trade, internationalism, and minimum interference by government. The publication works to maintain independence through its structure—there are no majority shareholders, the editor is appointed by trustees without political or commercial influences, and articles and images generally appear without bylines. The cartoon that follows was published in *The Economist* on October 23, 1999.

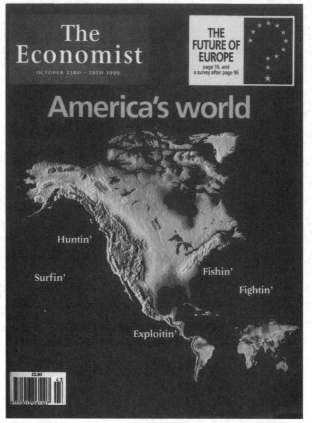

(*THE ECONOMIST* NEWSPAPER)

QUESTIONS FOR DISCUSSION AND WRITING

1. What is your reaction to viewing this image? Does it surprise you that it came from a publication of one of America's strongest allies and supporters?

2. What do you think international readers would think of this map? How do you think other countries would draw themselves?

3. In class, in groups or in pairs, draw a map that reflects what you believe to be a more accurate depiction of America's worldview. Collaboratively, write a brief rationale for your map. Or if you agree with the cartoon's depiction, write a brief response supporting this view.

4. Write an essay challenging *The Economist's* depiction of America's view of the world as oversimplifying and stereotyping the United States. Alternatively, write an essay analyzing the depiction and the argument about America that it makes.

Reflections on America as a World Power: A European View

PASCAL BONIFACE

Pascal Boniface is executive director of the Institute of International and Strategic Relations (IRIS), one of France's leading think tanks. He lectures extensively and is also professor of international relations at the Institut D' acute Etudes Politiques in Lille and Paris and the author of numerous books including, most recently, *Atlas des Guerres,* and, in English, *The Will to Powerlessness* (Toronto: Queens University Press, 1999). Boniface wrote in favor of France using its veto power against the Gulf War, expressing concern that war in the region would result in chaos. He has also criticized double standards in US policy toward Iraq, Israel, and North Korea, and some critics have, in turn, suggested he is anti-Semitic, a charge he roundly denies. The following essay was published in 2000 in the *Journal of Palestine Studies.*

Abstract:

With the collapse of the Soviet Union, restraints on US power have been greatly diminished, allowing free rein for the unilateralism the author sees as rooted in the US perception of its moral authority and the legacy of Manifest Destiny. Using examples from the Middle East, the author highlights differences in approach between the Europeans and the Americans—the European preference for dialogue with adversaries versus the US tendency toward punishment and sanction. More generally, this essay argues, the difference is between Europe's increased multilateralism and acceptance of the constraints of international law, and America's turning away from international institutions and growing disdain for legality. Such a development can only have adverse consequences for long-term security.

The United States has never had to practice a diplomacy between equals. When it was a nation on the rise, its isolation shielded it from the outside world and from the European powers. In the 19th century, it was up against forces in no way able to resist it: Indian tribes, Mexico, the remnants of a declining Spanish empire. When it decided to break definitively with isolationism after World War II, participating for the first time in a military alliance during peacetime, it did so directly as a superpower, taking over the "leadership of the free world."

A Nation without Rivals

The collapse of the Soviet Union did not lead, as some had hoped, to the emergence of a multipolar world. The United States has neither equals nor rivals: it is the first truly global power in history, the only state ever to possess all military means—nuclear arms, projection force, satellites, sophisticated arms, etc. It is the first world economy with seemingly inexhaustible powers of innovation and flexibility; it has a universally attractive culture. Earlier empires—Roman, Chinese, Mongol— were not global empires but, above all, regional powers. The United States enjoys not superiority but supremacy. No other power can aspire to challenge it in the four essential areas (military, economic, technological, and cultural) that constitute a global power.

Not only can no state compete with the United States in these four areas combined; most would have difficulty competing even in one of them. The French minister of foreign affairs, Hubert Vedrine, finding the term "superpower" inadequate to describe the power of the United States, invented a new term: "hyperpower."

Power allows the United States to dispense with reflection   5 and prudence: its "power reserve" is such that the consequences of carelessness or, indeed, errors are never too serious. "Hyperpower" can thus become, with impunity, hyperarrogance. The United States can decide to define singlehandedly the rules of international law, political or economic, applicable to all countries; to determine what is good for all humanity according to its own conscience; to judge that those who oppose it are antidemocratic and antiliberal; to treat the United Nations like an agency of the State Department and totally ignore it if it does not conduct itself as such; to believe that its European and Japanese allies have no right to challenge its preeminence by virtue of the protection it grants them; to allow Israel to interpret international law as it sees fit and to applaud it as a peacemaker when it signs agreements (Wye, Sharm al-Shaykh) that merely confirm (while scaling back) agreements it had signed earlier. None of this has any importance. Never has La Fontaine's adage "Your power or weakness will always decide your lot" been more appropriate.

Manifest Destiny

The U.S. belief in its uniqueness goes beyond the crude assessment of a balance of power. The United States, from the outset, saw itself as exceptional from a moral standpoint. Indeed, messianism is a fundamental component of the dynamic of American history. It is in keeping with its entire project of colonizing the New World, a project involving the will to attain perfection and to assure the triumph of its founding values. It's what Jefferson called "the empire of liberty": the newly conquered lands representing both the promotion of freedom and national grandeur. This quasi-religious collective mythology is at the root of America's relationship to the world. As Thomas Paine wrote in his famous pamphlet "Common Sense," several months before the Americans declared their independence from England: "It is in our power to reconstruct the world."

This messianism was theorized in particular by John Lee O'Sullivan, editor of the *United States Magazine* and *Democratic Review*, through the concept of "Manifest Destiny." Inveighing in the summer of 1845 against those foreign nations that were attempting to prevent the annexation of Texas, he wrote that the United States would beat back all those who would try to stand in the way of its power, limit its grandeur, or prevent "the fulfillment of our Manifest Destiny to overspread the continent allotted by Providence for the free development of our yearly multiplying millions." When the geographical limits of the nation were reached, Manifest Destiny lost its connotation of territorial aggression. Instead, it became a central element in the nationalist discourse attributing to the United States a universal civilizing mission, a future of commercial and cultural expansion and the destiny of great power. One of the first applications of this doctrine—once the territorial expansion phase was over—was to place the Philippines under its trusteeship in 1898, thus anticipating the principle of the "American private preserve" dear to President Theodore Roosevelt.

During and after World War I, President Woodrow Wilson and the United States always put forward moral aspirations for the international order (the people's right to self-determination, democracy, etc.), which they readily contrasted with European cynicism or realpolitik, the reign of brute force, and the will of the powers.

It was the emergence of a superpower at the eastern edge of Europe in 1945, creating by its sole weight a strategic imbalance, apparently able and willing to dominate the entire continent and endowed with a Communist regime to boot, that forced the United States to break forever with isolationism. But there, too, moral objectives (the struggle for the defense of freedom) mingled with geopolitical ones (preventing a power from dominating Europe and/or Eurasia). Dean Acheson declared that since Rome and Carthage there had not been such a polarization in the world: "For the United States, measures to reinforce countries threatened by Soviet aggression or Communist subversion protect the security of the United States, and indeed, freedom itself."

The battle continued at both levels: geopolitical (the Soviet Union had reached strategic parity with the United States by the beginning of the 1970s, albeit by sinking most of its resources into the contest) and politico-moral. As seen by the United States, the Soviet regime was the absolute negation of the American political system: a dictatorial regime versus a liberal regime, the power of the state versus individual freedoms, and so on. The Soviets thus had to be fought not only in the name of interest, but in the name of morality. With the collapse of the Soviet Union in 1991, the battle between East and West was finally won—without a shot being fired—by the United States.

In his State of the Union address of 1992, George Bush declared: "Thank God, America has won the cold war; a world formerly divided in two armed camps today recognizes the superiority of a single power: the United States. This fact no longer inspires fear, for the world has confidence in our nation, and it is right." In an earlier interview, Bush had remarked: "The sole responsibility of the United States is to advance the cause of freedom, for which it has both the moral stature and the necessary means."[1]

The war of Kosovo only reinforced America's moral vision of its foreign policy. Thus, the United States did not intervene to defend its strategic interests, but to uphold its moral duty. As President Bill Clinton declared on 14 April 1999: "It is America in the best it can offer . . . it's America trying to assure that the world lives in a human way, so that we have peace and freedom in Europe and that our people do not have to wage a more extensive war."

The Era of the Rogue States

But the US conception of freedom differs somewhat from that of other peoples. Washington believes that, in the nature of things, it should be the sole and uncontested orchestra leader for the common good. Other countries are more inclined to see a concert of nations where each can make its own music heard, even if all are not audible in the same way.

Moreover, with the collapse of the Soviet Union, the moral argument no longer had the same weight. Without a powerful state seen as bent on world domination in the name of a messianic ideology, what states could be condemned in the name of morality?

What was left after the establishment of the New World   15
Order was states guilty of irregular behaviors out of sync with internationally accepted norms. These would be states with ex-
pansionist policies toward their neighbors, those acting
aggressively toward democracies (through terrorism, drug trafficking, etc.), or those guilty of a flagrant violation of human
rights—provided they are not close allies of the United States.

To describe such states, the Americans devised a new category—"rogue states." This new category of states beyond the
pale of civilized behavior legitimizes a more muscular action
against those thus designated. The problem, of course, is not
only determining which states to include on the list but also, and
especially, determining who is qualified to establish it.

Overcoming these difficulties, the American leaders regularly cite Cuba, Iran, Iraq, Libya, North Korea, Sudan, and Yugoslavia as rogue states. But aside from Yugoslavia, where
international force was employed to force Serbian troops out of
Kosovo, and Iraq, which since December 1998 has been subjected to a regular "self-defense" bombing campaign (albeit without a clear objective) by the United States backed by Britain, the
sanctions established by Washington are limited to economic
sanctions intended to lead these states to adopt behaviors more
in keeping with "universal standards."

The limits of the economic sanctions, however, soon become clear. First of all, the sanctions' effects are limited, either
because of the ease with which the targeted countries can find
alternative outlets for exports and sources of supplies or because
the sanctions' effects fall mainly on the civilian populations
rather than the leaderships of the countries concerned. Considering that rogue states almost by their nature are ruled by dictators, the civilian population cannot be held responsible for the
actions of their leaders. By the same token, the leaders seem to
have little concern for the fate of their populations.

Second, economic sanctions in most cases are unilaterally
decreed by Washington, without consulting with the other major
economic actors, such as the Europeans and the Japanese. This
being the case, these last do not feel constrained to apply the
sanctions, which leads to disputes within the club of industrialized nations.

The classic example in this regard is the August 1996   20
Kennedy-D'Amato bill, better known as the "Iran Libya Sanctions
Act," which "authorizes" the United States to impose sanctions
on third parties investing more than $40 million annually in the
petroleum industries of Iran or Libya. The application of sanctions to the contravening companies was left to the State

Department, while their severity was to be determined by the president from a list of applicable penalties (total ban on access to the American market for products of the implicated firm, ban on American technology transfers, and so on). The first major challenge to the law came in September 1997, when France's TOTAL, heading a consortium including the Russian Gazprom and the firm Petronas, signed a $2 billion gas contract with Tehran. The deal rankled the Americans all the more because the contract had been promised in 1995 to the American firm Conoco, which had been forced by Washington to withdraw from the deal. But in actual fact, faced by a unanimous European outcry, the American attempt to apply the sanctions was rather feeble: after a communiqué from the State Department expressing "hope" that Paris would revoke its decision, and following tense relations for several months, Washington quietly abandoned its efforts to impose sanctions against TOTAL. Since the May 1998 creation of the Transatlantic Economic Partnership, the law, though still on the books, has lain dormant.

The US propensity to sanction and exclude predates the "rogue state era." A case in point is the PLO. Ever since the Venice Declaration of June 1980, Europe recognized the PLO as the sole representative of the Palestinian people and as such considered it entitled to a place at the negotiating table. Washington, on the other hand, running counter to near unanimous world opinion and in support of Israeli inflexibility, continued to sanction the "terrorist" organization with a "diplomatic gag" for another eight years, thus complicating the search for Arab-Israeli peace.

Such differences in approach continue to hold true, with the Europeans favoring dialogue and diplomacy even during periods of extreme tension and sharp disagreement. The most egregious ongoing example is that of Iraq, where the maintenance of the embargo since the end of the Gulf War is without question due to the determination of America, backed by Britain. France, backed by many of the European Union countries, has repeatedly stressed the inadequate nature of the sanctions on the grounds that, far from destablizing the Iraqi regime as Washington claims, they seem only to plunge the civilian population in ever more desperate straits. It is thus that France has long called for the need to "replace the logic of punishment by a logic of solution." France's proposals—involving rigorous surveillance of Iraqi weapons sites with a view toward lifting the oil embargo (even while applying strict controls on the use of export revenues) to ensure Iraqi compliance with its obligations—have been repeatedly and categorically rejected by the United States. The effectiveness of the European approach can perhaps be discerned in recent events in Iran. While the United States has totally boycotted the regime, the Europeans engaged Iran first in "critical dialogue" and then, after the election of President Mohamed Khatami in 1997, in "constructive dialogue." The international support implicit in this dialogue unquestionably helped the reformers' camp.

What is a Rogue State?

Above and beyond the problems of implementing sanctions involving the rogue states, the definition of rogue states leaves a great deal to be desired.

These states, certainly, are hardly models of democracy, but there are a number of states on the planet with even worse records in this domain that continue all the same to maintain good relations with Washington. Respect for human rights can thus not be the true criterion for the definition of rogue state.

Indeed, on closer examination, it does not take long to discern that what these countries have in common despite their diversity is not so much their national or international behavior, however worthy of criticism it may be, but their open defiance of Washington. They have all, either within their own region or on an international level, challenged American supremacy, sometimes violently (e.g., Castro's attempts to export revolution in the 1960s, Libya's attacks against American regional interests, Iraq's defiance of the United States in the Gulf War). Long after such defiance against the American order by force has ceased, Washington's rancor persists. The leaders of these countries are often demonized and presented as the very archetype of the dictator.

Finally, these countries are not really powers, neither on the military nor on the economic plane, and in no way represent a real threat to the United States. It is thus that states that contest American supremacy but which are real powers (China, Russia) are not on the list. The true definition of a rogue state is one that rises against the United States without really having the means to do so. Such states are all the easier to designate as adversaries in that they pose few dangers. This moreover allows the United States to confer legitimacy or moral rectitude on its actions against those it considers troublemakers with respect to the international order. Also excluded from the rogue list are countries that flout human rights but which do not, for all that, contest America's leadership of world affairs.

Looking closely, the United States could itself qualify for the category of states not overly concerned with the rules accepted by most states. Its attitude concerning the death penalty puts it on a par with states like China, which can hardly constitute a reference. Several years ago, two German citizens were executed in the United States despite the German government's repeated pleas for clemency. Question: What would happen if two American citizens were executed in Germany, despite Washington's entreaties?

The pilot of the US military plane that severed the cable of a ski lift in Italy, causing the death of some twenty persons, was acquitted by an American court martial, the flight recordings having been erased "by mistake." Certainly, the American president presented excuses, which has become habitual, and suggested financial compensation. Nonetheless: What would happen if an Italian pilot who had caused through negligence the death of twenty Americans were acquitted by an Italian court martial?

In Khartoum, Sudan, the United States bombed a pharmaceutical plant, totally destroying the plant and killing or injuring around twenty employees, on the basis of information—never proven and moreover questioned by the CIA—that it was involved in the manufacture of chemical agents for chemical weapons. The Sudan vigorously denied the charges, and the Pentagon has produced only sketchy information. The owner of the plant, meanwhile, is suing the US government. Question: What would happen if another country bombed a US factory rumored to be manufacturing components for cluster bombs?

The United States continues to bomb Iraq without any international mandate, without any UN authorization. How would the United States react if Iraq, or any other country, adopted a USA Liberation Act (on the order of the Iraq Liberation Act adopted by Congress) and appointed within its foreign ministry a "chief coordinator for the transition in the United States," as Washington has done with regard to Iraq, earmarking $97 million to help the Iraqi opposition overthrow Saddam Hussein?

The United States has refused to sign the convention signed by most other countries banning the manufacture of antipersonnel land mines, even though it is highly unlikely that this type of weapon is necessary for its security. Washington is likewise remaining aloof from the international penal code being devised to judge war crimes. While the European countries, Japan, and the developing world all fight for the protection of the environment, Washington refuses to accept the constraints required to participate in this common action and has refused to sign the convention on global warming. And while the United States is pressing India and Pakistan to sign the nuclear test ban treaty, the US Congress refuses to ratify it and turns a blind eye to Israel's nuclear capacity. Question: How would the United States react if other states imposed on it economic sanctions as long as it did not sign the antipersonnel mine treaty?

The Kosovo War: Dispensing with The UN

The United Nations, which George Bush made the centerpiece of his New World Order following the Gulf War, is increasingly seen by Washington not merely as serving little purpose but as an outright impediment to its action; indeed, it is no accident that the United States, even after its recent payment of a first installment in arrears, remains the world organization's largest debtor.

It was because of its reservations about the UN that Washington set out to define a new strategic concept for NATO, where it has greater weight, in preparation for the organization's fiftieth anniversary celebrations. Not coincidentally, this was the time when the Kosovo crisis was heating up. Since the Serbian military operations in Kosovo took place on Yugoslav soil—partly in response to the military operations of the Kosovo Liberation Army (KLA)—Article 51 of the UN Charter authorizing the use of force as a legitimate defense against aggression did not apply. While UN Resolution 1199 of 23 September 1998, by presenting the deterioration of the Kosovo situation as a threat to international security, left an opening with regard to Chapter 7 of the UN Charter, the linkage was ambiguous at best. And it was precisely because it was known that the Security Council would refuse to allow the strikes that permission was not even asked.

As French foreign minister Vedrine declared to the Defense Committee of the French National Assembly after the NATO campaign ended, "The Allied intervention against Yugoslavia in Kosovo coincided with the finalization of the new strategic concept of NATO whereby the Americans, through Ms. Albright, attempted to substitute NATO for the United Nations."[2] While the Europeans, who were not prepared to tolerate a repetition of Slobodan Milosevic's ethnic cleansing in Kosovo, were not against military intervention, they wanted the new NATO concept to respect the preeminence of the Security Council. Washington, on the other hand, was determined to preserve the autonomy of NATO—in other words, to give NATO the right to use force without a mandate from the UN. In the end, as a result of France's insistent pressures, the new strategic concept did contain explicit references to the UN Charter and to the Security Council's primordial role, which the United States had previously refused. But, as a member of the French delegation emphasized, "We are not naive. We know very well that in future crises, each time 'special circumstances' will lead to 'practical solutions.' But at least it is written as such, and the exception has not been enshrined as the rule." Or, as Foreign Minister Vedrine told the National Assembly, future implementation of the clause safeguarding the Security Council's role "depends in large measure on the American attitude concerning the UN's role in settling future crises."[3]

Something of Washington's intentions concerning the UN could be gleaned from Secretary of State Madeleine Albright at the height of the NATO campaign. According to *Le Monde,* she informed UN Secretary-General Kofi Annan on 7 May 1999 that "any political and military interference by the UN will be unacceptable. The international military presence in Kosovo will not be a United Nations force, and it will in no case be under the control of the United Nations. The UN, Mr. Kofi Annan was told, should be satisfied with what concerns it, that is to say, humanitarian affairs."[4]

For all its flaws, the United Nations, successor of the League of Nations, was created as the guarantor of world peace, a viable alternative to an international system based on realpolitik and conflicting raison d'état. Yet here, in a simple phrase of Secretary Albright, the UN's role is reduced to that of humanitarian affairs. It is clear that what we are witnessing is a reversal of logic. It stands to reason that the United Nations, a world organization representing all the peoples of the planet, should not be subordinate to a great power, but, on the contrary, that the great power should respect the superiority of the UN. But Washington considers that this multilateral framework cannot be allowed to pose a hindrance to the free exercise of its power.

The Kosovo war, the first to take place under the new strategic concept, was waged illegally from NATO's standpoint as well: because Yugoslavia neither attacked nor threatened any NATO countries, Article 5 of the NATO treaty could not be invoked. In the contradiction between the principle of respecting the territorial integrity of states and the principle of the people's right to protect themselves, the NATO countries opted for the latter at the expense of the former, bypassing legality in the name of morality. They did so with full awareness of what they were doing, for it is false to pretend, as some have tried to do, that the Europeans were made to go along with an operation decided by the Americans (even though Washington does carry more weight within NATO than the other eighteen countries combined). But even though the Europeans went along willingly, it is also true that they are far more preoccupied with the question of whether the way the war was waged was an exception or a precedent. Beyond Kosovo, what is at stake is two approaches to the international order: the Europeans are prepared to accept the constraints of international law, the Americans are less inclined to do so.

The Question of Double Standards

Inevitably, the Kosovo war raises the issue of double standards. Before the NATO intervention, the fighting in Kosovo between the Yugoslav army and the KLA claimed two thousand lives. That is about the same as the number of unarmed Palestinians killed by Israeli troops during the intifada. Why intervene in one place but not in other regions where people's rights are likewise trampled on, sometimes in more egregious fashion? Israel has constantly violated not only the Palestinian right to self-determination, but also international law by illegally occupying territories seized by force and by not respecting the Geneva conventions in those territories. Yet there have been no threats to bomb Tel Aviv to impose Palestinian self-determination.

The double standard issue, of course, goes back a long way. Its most recent international manifestation was at the time of the Gulf War. For if Saddam Hussein fatally miscalculated international reaction to his invasion of Kuwait, he did score a point in his media war by calling attention to this issue that had long rankled in the Middle East. Indeed, the actual prosecution of the Gulf War could not have provided a more telling illustration of the problem: while it took less than twenty-four hours after the expiration of the ultimatum in UN Security Council Resolution 678 for the US led coalition to strike Iraq, Resolution 242 calling for Israel's withdrawal from the territories occupied in June 1967—reinforced and confirmed by more than 100 other resolutions—still awaits full implementation thirty-three years later. With the end of the cold war, during which Moscow to a certain extent acted as counterweight to the US-Israeli duo in the UN, the United States, with its pretensions of establishing a New World Order, almost had to do something to clear up the anomaly. Its role in convening the Madrid Conference and sponsoring the subsequent Israeli-Arab negotiations can be seen as a tour de force, though the double standards problem persists. The United States, with varying degrees of subtlety, continues to support Israeli positions in the negotiations, at least on the essential issues.

Resolution 425 of 19 March 1978 calling on Israel to "with- ⁴⁰ draw forthwith its forces from all Lebanese territory" and re- questing the secretary-general to report to the council within twenty-four hours on the resolution's implementation is even more telling because it is unconditional and unambiguous. Twenty-three years later, Israel contemplates withdrawal from southern Lebanon as a result of relentless and punishing local re- sistance, but its massive destruction of Lebanese civilian infra- structure over the years has never elicited strong U.S. censure. Moreover, following its most recent bombing, in February 2000, destroying Lebanese power plants that plunged over half the country in darkness at a cost of over $50 million, Secretary Al- bright's first reaction was to declare that the bombing was meant to "prevent escalation," echoing the phrase of Israeli Prime Min- ister Ehud Barak.

A New Isolationism?

Writing in *Foreign Affairs,* Samuel Huntington noted that the United States practices a policy of "world unilateralism," that is, the promotion of its own interests without consideration of the interests of other nations.[5] Needless to say, there is little danger of the United States reverting to the isolationism of the past, but it could become an isolated country, and this at a time when, as Madeleine Albright herself has recognized, the United States de- votes fourteen times fewer resources to supporting democracy and growth abroad than it did at the time of Secretary of State George Marshall.[6]

What is good for General Motors may be good for the United States, but what is good for the United States is not necessarily good for the rest of the world. Confident of its Manifest Destiny and of its role as the only "indispensable nation," confident that it embodies universal values, the United States does not under- stand that others might be opposed to its policies. Indeed, op- position to its policies is inevitably seen as opposition to universal values rather than to American high-handedness. Just as the Soviet Union confused the interests of the Soviet state with the higher interests of socialism, so the Americans begin to confuse the interests of the United States with those of the West- ern world.

In four years, the European Union has profoundly trans- formed the concept and practice of the international life of its members: a distinctive diplomatic culture has taken root among them consisting of attachment to international institutions, multilateralism in the sense of compromise, and preference for engagement.

The basic trends in the United States seem to go in exactly the opposite direction. After the phase of "institution building" and promotion of international law in the post-World War II period, there has been, since the end of the Cold War, a turning away from international institutions, an increase in unilateral and coercive practices, a disdain for legality, and, more generally, a growing reluctance to tolerate any international constraints whatsoever on its freedom of decision.

The Europeans have an obvious common interest in promoting their own concept of international order—that is, the development of multilateral constraints that are assumed, codified, and reciprocal. A natural outgrowth of this concept are actions aimed at strengthening multilateral frameworks and international institutions and promoting attitudes of cooperation and negotiation. The Kyoto conference on global warming, the Ottawa conference on land mines, and the Rome conference to establish an international criminal court show the ability of the Europeans not only to reach consensus but to reflect the aspirations more widely shared at the global level for a more egalitarian international society with greater respect for the law. This is an undeniable comparative advantage for the European Union.

45

The United States, on the other hand, lacking an adversary or a partner of comparable power, can give priority to unilaterally defined policy and dispense with the rules of dialogue. The cost, of course, is not only to lessen its power of attraction and moral prestige, but ultimately to undermine its effectiveness as a world power.

Notes

1. *Le Monde* January 31, 1991.
2. French National Assembly, Commission for the Defense and Armed Forces, *Minutes* 38, June 22, 1999.
3. French National Assembly.
4. *Le Monde* May 10, 1999.
5. Huntington, Samuel. "The Lonely Superpower." *Foreign Affairs* 78. 2 (1999): 35–49.
6. Albright, Madeleine. "The Testing of American Foreign Policy." *Foreign Affairs* 77.6 (1998): 62.

QUESTIONS FOR DISCUSSION AND WRITING

1. What are your expectations about the perspective on America that a European might offer? Does the fact that the selection is an academic article affect its appeals to authority? What about its appearing in *Journal of Palestine Studies*? This article is preceded by an abstract or summary of its content, written in the third person. Do you feel your reading of the essay benefits from this summary? Restate the thesis in your own words.

2. Do the section titles help guide you through this relatively long essay? Does the author utilize good lead-in or topic sentences to guide the reader? Give examples of more and less effective topic or lead-in sentences.

3. Examine the sections "A Nation without Rivals" and "Manifest Destiny." Does the author make a case for his assertions in these sections? Is his definition of Manifest Destiny consistent with your understanding of the term? If not, how would you change it? Does the author support his assertions about America's ethics and beliefs about itself?

4. The author argues that the chief criteria America uses to define a rogue state are that it openly defies the United States and it is not a credible threat. Do the examples adequately support this view?

5. According to the author, what type of isolationism does America seem to be moving toward? What do you infer are the disadvantages of such a position? A chief concern of the author is that the United States will not engage in dialogue and will act unilaterally. Do you see why he has come to this opinion? Do you share this opinion? Why or why not?

6. Write a brief reflection on your response to this essay and on hearing an alternative perspective on the US role in world affairs. Alternatively, write an essay analyzing the assumptions, claims, and reasoning process in this essay. Are its logical appeals persuasive?

7. Research the origins of the principle of Manifest Destiny or US isolationism before its entry into World War II.

Chapter Two: Connections

1. How does the Bourke-White photograph compare with other types of images (painting, posters) in this chapter and in this book? Do you find one medium more persuasive than another? What role do audience, point of view, composition, and the like play in persuasive appeal?

2. Contrast D'Souza's essay with Edward Said's in Chapter Four. How might either author refute the other's views? You might focus, for example, on D'Souza's suggestion that America's dropping food while fighting in Afghanistan is evidence of American magnanimity.

3. Compare the themes in "Letter from a Birmingham Jail" with those in one of King's other well known texts, such as the "March on Washington Address." How does the difference in audience and purpose, or written essay versus speech, affect matters of style? You could also consider researching contextualizing information and historical background at the Martin Luther King, Jr. Papers Project Web site (listed with end-of-chapter Web sites)

4. King has made references to Gandhi in a number of his speeches or texts. Read selected texts by Gandhi's essay on the concept related to passive resistance, Satyagraha, at <*http://www.meadev.nic.in/Gandhi/satyagraha.htm*> or in the Appendix. Do you observe influences from Gandhi's writings in this speech? Do you recognize the influence of other source readings from the Appendix?

5. Compare and contrast the views in the cartoon "America's World" with other texts in this chapter. For example, how might Dinesh D'Souza respond to this cartoon? How does this cartoon compare with Benjamin Franklin's cartoon?

6. Construct a dialogue between Anzaldua and D'Souza, or between D'Souza and Boniface, or between another pair of authors in this chapter, or set up a discussion in class with different students taking on the point of view of various authors. Have the rest of the class observe and analyze each author's approach to argumentation.

7. In small class groups, create a dialogue among Anzaldua, Keola and Agard, and Needleman on the ways in which America does, or does not, reflect the Founders' philosophy of democracy.

8. Reflect on the points raised in "The Native Hawaiians Today" in view of the stereotypes discussed in the Takaki essay.

9. Compare the prose discussion of America in the Boniface essay with the cartoon from *The Economist*. What common threads or contrasts do you find?

Chapter Two: End-of-Chapter Assignments

1. Research the discourse preceding and during the American Revolutionary War. Pay particular attention to materials such as broadsides, letters, and newspaper accounts, as well as to traditional accounts in historical and scholarly books, because such personal and primary materials often provide perspectives and immediacy to the event that are less evident in textbooks and historical accounts.

2. Conduct research on the Civil Rights or Free Speech movement. You could start with the Martin Luther King, Jr. Papers Project (see end of chapter for Web site), view a video series such as *Eyes on the Prize,* or start with the King essay in this chapter and then review the "March on Washington Address" or other key text.

3. Research the origins and organization of the Pacific News Service. What is its mission? How does it complement—or duplicate—services from other news agencies? Analyze the articles and stories it presents. Where would you place it on the political spectrum? How authoritative is it as a source? (See the end of chapter for Web site.)

4. Follow a news story on at least two international Web sites as well as on an American Web site. What are the similarities and differences in how the story is presented? Take into account space and emphasis, connotative and denotative language, photographic coverage, and the like.

5. With peers, participate in an international forum or cultural exchange through a Web site listed at the end of this chapter, in another chapter in this textbook, or through some other forum that you or classmates identify. Participants should listen to opinions from other countries and cultures and attempt to participate meaningfully in the discussion. After participating for an agreed-upon period of time, have individuals, pairs, or groups from the class assess their findings and share what they learned about different perspectives with the rest of the class.

6. Through your campus public service center or through your own connections, pursue a placement at a local agency with a focus on American issues or on America's connections with other countries. For example, you could volunteer for the American

Red Cross or Habitat for Humanity, or you could work on behalf of a local organization with global or international ties. As described in the introduction, your community writing could take different forms depending on your interest and the organization's needs; you could write educational brochures, flyers, or promotional materials—for example, on behalf of a blood drive on campus or a tissue- or marrow-matching program. This option may particularly appeal to you if you are interested in pursuing a career in health care or medicine.

7. On the Web or in library books and periodicals, research representations of America or Americans in posters, editorial cartoons, or other visual media. Consider focusing on images from the mid- to late nineteenth century, also known as the golden age of cartooning, and review popular culture of the times, such as *Puck* magazine in the United States and *Punch* in Britain.

Chapter Two: Web Sites for Further Exploration

Public Broadcasting System: Great American Speeches
http://www.pbs.org/greatspeeches/
Pacific News Service
http://news.pacificnews.org/news/
The Making of America site—primary sources on American social history
http://moa.umdl.umich.edu/
The White House
http://www.whitehouse.gov/
US National Archives and Record Administration
http://www.archives.gov/
Martin Luther King, Jr. Papers Project
http://www.stanford.edu/group/King/
Council on Foreign Relations
http://www.cfr.org
Smithsonian National Museum of American History
http://americanhistory.si.edu/
Bishop Museum, Hawaii and the Pacific
http://www.bishopmuseum.org/
"Crossfire" television program
http://www.cnn.com/CNN/Programs/crossfire/

"Hardball" television program
http://www.msnbc.com/news/hardball_front.asp?cp1=1
Asia Pacific Universe
http://asiapacificuniverse.com/
A journal of Asian American Cultural Criticism
http://socrates.berkeley.edu/~critmass/

3

CROSSING CULTURES

INTRODUCTION

Values and beliefs make a society unique, give it strength, and transmit cultural practices from one generation to the next. In the previous chapter, we read about values and beliefs important both to America's founders and to contemporary writers. In the selections that follow we read about values and beliefs in communities beyond the United States; we also examine other societies' concerns about American cultural influence or even domination and the ways in which those cultures handle interactions with the ubiquitous American culture and technology. Although some societies see themselves as open to the cultural practices and diverse beliefs and values immigrants bring with them, others are more alarmed by the prospects of cultural encroachment from countries with divergent values. Still others aim for a cautious acceptance of some Western influences but a rejection of others. Concerns are evident not only in parts of the Islamic Middle East, with pronounced religious and cultural differences from the United States and other Western nations, but also in Western countries such as France, where a government culture ministry fends off English-language intrusions, most recently rejecting use of the term "e-mail" and creating a new French word to take its place.

Our focus in this chapter is on culture as it relates to a society's values and beliefs, including those situations where these values come into conflict with those of other societies. The selections in this chapter range in genre from essays on personal and academic topics, with and without documented research, to photographs, to online question-and-answer format, to newspaper reporting. Each selection demonstrates a way in which values and assumptions underlie cultural practices; each demonstrates an attempt to grapple with a social or cultural tension—between the traditional and the modern, for example, or between the familiar and the esoteric. Each selection also makes a point and then supports it, drawing on evidence such as narrative, example, and logic.

We begin the selections with an exercise in perspective—an analysis of two photographs conveying different perspectives. The pair of photographs in "Two Views: Women and Veils" exemplifies the ways in which the author or artist's point of view can affect the viewer's perception of and attitudes about a subject. We then turn to an essay that describes and explains a society and its cultural practices, beliefs, and values. Human rights activist and Nobel Peace Prize-winner Aung San Suu Kyi, in her essay about Buddhist influence on Burmese society, "My Country and People," suggests that Buddhism continues to influence beliefs, values, and behavior in Burmese people of all ages. Despite some inroads by Western clothing, style, and ideas, T-shirt–wearing youngsters still perform religious rituals and Buddhism has remained a primary influence on the culture. She acknowledges that one's distinctive culture may be better retained in isolation, but that the trade-offs may include being less advanced in science and other areas that benefit from intellectual or cultural exchange. This selection provides an opportunity to learn how a society draws strength from its religious heritage and learns to live with the inconsistencies that an ancient religion and a modern world present. Culture and custom also guide, and reflect, ways in which people handle conflict and differences of opinion. In the next selection, "Listening to Other Cultures," linguist Deborah Tannen provides examples of how different cultures view argument and the ways in which these approaches, which seem natural and logical to the participants, can lead to misperceptions by others as well as to misunderstandings.

One word that may well describe the conflict societies face as they attempt to retain cultural practices in the midst of modernizing is ambivalence. Technological advancement, for example, is not always without cost to the culture it serves. In the next selection, "In Kabary the Point Is to Avoid the Point," reporter Danna Harman writes that an innovation such as a cell phone may affect, even erode, not only a community's traditional style of communication but also the values from which that style is derived.

In the next reading, we learn how leaders in one Islamic society are dealing with unwanted cultural influence by co-opting that influence and turning it to their own purposes. The late journalist Daniel Pearl, tragically killed while pursuing a story in Pakistan post–9/11, had a particular interest in music and researched and wrote about the burgeoning pop rock music scene in Iran. His essay discusses the ways in which rock music has been supported by the Iranian government insofar as it meets their ends and satisfies the public's wishes as well.

Some commentators argue that the encroachment of Western cultures, particularly American culture, is overstated, and that the cultural exchange is a two-way street, with America assimilating customs and practices from all over the world. Student writer Sarala Nagala, for example, researched Hindu influences in American popular culture; she discusses her findings in her essay "Om: Hinduism in American Pop Culture: Global Strategy or Sacrilegious Mistake?" But many non-US commentators would argue that the exchange remains heavily biased toward US cultural domination, and it is such dominance that seems to drive the Fatwas, or religious/legal opinions, included here. These two opinions, "Islamic View of Barbie" and "Boycotting Locally-Owned McDonalds," speak to concerns about preserving an Islamic society and living according to the values and beliefs of Islam. These brief articles provide an opportunity to understand the logical and ethical basis on which the Islamic experts evaluate and resolve, the issues raised, as well as what concerns others have about Western cultural products. Ironically, these online Fatwas demonstrate an innovative use of technology that seems to support rather than undermine the cultural values of Islam.

After reading and analyzing a number of texts and images that provide perspectives on cultures and values within a society's context, we turn to anthropologist Carolyn Fluehr-Lobban's thoughtful discussion "Cultural Relativism and Universal Rights." Fluehr-Lobban explores the balance between respecting individual cultures' autonomy and supporting basic, universal human rights that should be accorded to all human beings regardless of the practices of their cultures. This argument, as in Fluehr-Lobban's essay, often notes pervasive violence against women as evidence of the need to rethink the "hands-off" policy of anthropologists and others concerned with the study of diverse cultures.

Confucian values rather than religious beliefs have been credited with phenomenal economic success in a number of Asian countries and political scientist Lucian Pye, in "Asian Values: From Dynamos to Dominoes?", analyzes the role attributed to these values in Asian economic progress. He suggests that the same values may contribute to economic progress or decline depending on other aspects of the cultural and economic contexts, focusing on the rise and decline of Asian economies at the close of the twentieth century. This selection explicitly addresses assumptions about the role of cultural values in a society's economic success or failure and suggests that the complex interaction between the two is often oversimplified.

Over time, economic needs and evolving policy can drive social change and influence popular culture, a transformation the image of a Vietnamese billboard photograph documents. It captures and graphically illustrates the shift from a Communist billboard focusing on workers to a new image promoting tourism.

As you read and view these selections, consider the ways in which your own culture and cultural apparatus—your perspective and the media filters through which you have developed that perspective—have contributed to the ways in which you absorb and evaluate information. In evaluating information, you can always use a basic framework: What point does the author make? And how does the author support it? For every reading, consider extending your understanding of the topic by doing additional reading, reflection, and research. The materials included here are also often part of the media through which we obtain information. But something as basic as regularly reading or listening to international news sources or discussing issues with people who do not share your background or opinions can help inform your views and can contribute to your thinking critically about the world. And being mindful that your own views are in part developed through the culture around you may help you to assess information from your own society as well as others. At the end of this chapter, questions connecting the various readings, additional research suggestions, and a number of Web sites are included to help you take this discussion beyond the textbook and the classroom.

Two Views: Women and Veils

The following photographs were taken by two different photographers and suggest different impressions of an object that has come to have iconic or symbolic associations: the burka. The first photograph, of the lady getting into a taxi, is credited to Behrouz. The second photograph, of Afghan mothers waiting for their children's vaccinations, is credited to Emmanuel Dundand. (Please see color images on pages C–1 and C–2 of the insert.)

WOMAN GETTING INTO A TAXI

(BEHROUZ MEHRI)

THREE AFGHAN MOTHERS AT A VACCINATION CLINIC

Original Caption: Three Afghan mothers, two of them holding their babies under their burka, or veil, wait for their children to be vaccinated, November 28 2001, as part of a vaccination campaign sponsored by UNICEF. The 6.5-million-dollar vaccination program against the six most common diseases is aimed at curbing child mortality in Afghanistan. One in four Afghan children dies before reaching adulthood. (AFP PHOTO/EMMANUEL DUNAND)

QUESTIONS FOR DISCUSSION AND WRITING

1. Write out your reactions and response to each photograph. Do you have more positive or negative reactions to one or the other? Why do you believe that you respond as you do? What do you think influences your response? What do you infer to be the point of view of each photographer?

2. In what ways could the perspective of a viewer, who might accept and perhaps attribute positive connotations to the burka, be different from someone who might view the garment as unusual or even oppressive?

3. Write an essay analyzing the ways in which the photographer's point of view may affect the viewer's response to the image and to the symbolism of the burka.

My Country and People

AUNG SAN SUU KYI

Aung San Suu Kyi was born in Rangoon, Burma, in 1945, the daughter of national liberation leader General Aung San, who was assassinated two years after her birth, and of Daw Khin Kyi, who became Burma's ambassador to India and Nepal. Aung San Suu Kyi received a degree in philosophy, politics, and economics from Oxford University and served in the UN Secretariat. A follower of the nonviolent resistance of Gandhi, she has led a prodemocracy movement, the National League for Democracy (NLD), since the 1988 uprising against the current regime in Burma, now called Myanmar. Burma became independent in 1948 after being ruled by Britain and occupied by Japan during World War II. The current military junta has essentially ruled Burma for decades. The democratic opposition won elections in 1990, but the ruling junta has refused to give up power; because she would not leave the country, Aung San Suu Kyi was under strict house arrest from 1989 to 1995, and then again in September 2000; she had been released and again arrested as of this writing. She was awarded the Nobel Peace Prize in 1991. Despite her detention, her NLD party won victory in the general elections with eighty-two percent of the seats; the military junta refuses to recognize the results of the election and continues to hold power. Aung San Suu Kyi has given numerous speeches, and her writings include the book *Freedom from Fear,* published in 1991, in which the following selection was published. In this essay she describes the influence of Buddhism on the people of Burma.

The Burmese

The one single factor which has had the most influence on Burmese culture and civilization is Theravada Buddhism. In all parts of the country where the Burmese people live there are pagodas and Buddhist monasteries. The graceful tapering shape of a pagoda, painted white or gilded to a shining gold, is a basic part of any Burmese landscape. Burma is often called the "Land of Pagodas."

Buddhism teaches that suffering is an unavoidable part of existence. At the root of all suffering are such feelings as desire, greed, and attachment. Therefore to be free from suffering it is necessary to be free from those undesirable feelings. This free-dom can be obtained by following the Noble Eightfold Path:

Right Understanding
Right Thought
Right Speech
Right Action
Right Livelihood
Right Effort
Right Mindfulness
Right Concentration

This path is also known as the Middle Way, because it avoids two extremes: one extreme is the search for happiness through the pursuit of pleasure, the other extreme is the search for happiness through inflicting pain on oneself. The final goal of a Buddhist is to be liberated from the cycle of existence and rebirth, called *samsara*. Once this final liberation is achieved, one may be said to have attained *nirvana;* this word means "extinction" and might be explained as Ultimate Reality for all Buddhists.

The teachings of the Buddha are known as the Dharma, and these teachings are generally passed on to ordinary people by the Buddhist monks, collectively known as the Sangha. There-fore, the Buddha, the Dharma, and the Sangha are called the "Triple Gem." Because the Lord Buddha was a great teacher, the Burmese have a great reverence for all teachers. Parents are also regarded with "awe, love, and respect." Consequently, the Triple Gem, teachers, and parents make up the "five that must be revered" by Burmese Buddhists.

All good Buddhists undertake to abide by the Five Precepts: not to take life, not to steal, not to commit adultery, not to tell lies, not to take intoxicating drinks. Although the taking of life is considered such an evil that many Burmese will go out of their way to avoid stepping on an insect, there are few who avoid eat-ing meat. This is considered inconsistent by some people. The Burmese would probably argue that the Lord Buddha himself ate meat. The Burmese people are a practical people. They have also been described as happy-go-lucky.

As might be expected, many Burmese festivals are based on Buddhist events. Festival days are determined by the Burmese calendar, which is calculated according to the phases of the moon. The full moon days of the month of *Kason* (April/May), *Waso* (June/July), and *Thidingyut* (October/November) are special

5

days for the Buddhists. The full moon day of *Kason* celebrates the birth, enlightenment, and death of the Buddha. The Buddha achieved enlightenment—that is, he finally shed all false beliefs and saw through to the ultimate truth—underneath a *bodhi* tree. On the full moon of *Kason,* therefore, people pour offerings of water on *bodhi* trees.

The full moon day of *Waso* also celebrates important events in the life of the Buddha, in particular the first sermon he preached on the truth he had learnt. In addition, this day marks the beginning of the 'Buddhist Lent,' which lasts for three months. During this time the monks are not allowed to travel. Many Buddhists observe what are known as the Eight Precepts on all the holy days during Lent. The Buddhist holy days are the day of the dark moon, the eighth day of the new moon, the day of the full moon, and the eighth day after the full moon. The Eight Precepts are four of the basic Five Precepts (not to kill, steal, lie or take intoxicating drinks) with the addition of four others: not to commit any immoral acts; not to take any food after twelve noon; not to indulge in music, dancing, and the use of perfume; not to sleep in high places. (The last is taken to mean that one should not sleep in a luxurious bed.) Some devout Buddhists keep these eight precepts throughout the three months of Lent. Because it is a time when people should be thinking of their spiritual development, Buddhists should not get married during this period. Marriage brings family life and therefore greater ties and attachments. Thus it is likely to make the achieving of *nirvana* more difficult.

The end of Lent coincides with the end of the monsoon rains in October. It is a time for happiness and rejoicing. Tradition has it that the Lord Buddha spent one Lent in the *Tavatimsa* heaven to preach to his mother. (His mother had died in giving birth to him and had been reborn in *Tavatimsa,* one of the many Buddhist heavens.) At the end of Lent, he came back to earth and the people of the world welcomed him with lights. In celebration of this, during the three days of the *Thidingyut* festival, pagodas, monasteries, and homes are decorated with lights and lanterns. Cities like Rangoon and Mandalay are ablaze with coloured lights, and there are competitions to see which part of the town is the most beautifully decorated. *Thidingyut* is a time for expressing reverence towards older people. Many Burmese visit older friends and relatives to bow down before them and to offer gifts.

There are other Buddhist festivals apart from the ones just described. In addition, many pagodas have their own festival day. One of the most important pagoda festivals is that of the great Shwedagon in Rangoon, which takes place in March. Soaring to a height of almost 100 metres (over 300 feet), covered with layers of solid gold leaf and topped with a hollow gold orb encrusted with many precious gems, the Shwedagon is the most famous landmark in the country. Foreigners come to look at it with curiosity and wonder. For the Burmese it is not just an interesting and beautiful monument, but a very central part of their religious life—and not just on festival days. Every day, an endless stream of people climb up to the Shwedagon from one of its four great stairways (an electric lift has also been installed near one stairway). They buy flowers, incense sticks, gold leaves, and candles to offer at the pagoda from the stalls that line the stairs. (These stalls sell a variety of other things apart from religious objects.)

The atmosphere of the Shwedagon is steeped in the religious faith of the people who have worshipped there for generations. Everywhere are the sounds of prayers and the clear ring of prayer gongs. On the platform which surrounds the pagoda are many smaller pagodas, shrines, and pavilions. Each person goes to his or her favourite place of worship to pray there and to make offerings. Apart from the main prayer pavilions, the eight planetary posts which mark the days of the week are popular places of worship. (Each day of the week, together with Rahu—Wednesday night—has its own planet.) People go to the post marking the day of their birth to pray, light candles and incense sticks, and to make offerings of flowers and water. In a hot country like Burma, the coolness of water is symbolic of peace.

All Burmese know the day of the week on which they were born. The name given on a person's birth horoscope is decided according to the day of birth. For example, those born on a Monday should have names beginning with the letters *ka, hka, ga, nga,* those born on a Tuesday are given names beginning with *sa, hsa, za, nya,* and so on. Not just horoscope names but also those given by parents are usually chosen according to these rules. The horoscope shows the position of the planets at the time of a person's birth. Astrologers use it to make predictions about the future. This practice is not really in line with the teachings of the Buddha, according to which one's future is decided by one's own actions rather than by the stars.

Another side of Burmese life which is not strictly in accordance with Buddhist teachings is spirit-worship. Like the other peoples of Burma, the Burmese were spirit-worshippers before the arrival of Buddhism. The Burmese use the word *nat* to mean supernatural beings, the good ones who dwell in the various heavens as well as the frightening ones who interfere in the affairs of the human world. Little *nat* shrines can often be seen in Burma, especially under big trees which are believed to harbour spirits. The most powerful of all the *nats* are the *Thonzekhuna Min,* or "Thirty-Seven Lords". There are people who take *nat* worship very seriously in spite of their belief in Buddhism. Even those who avoid having anything to do with spirit-worship will not do anything which is known to be offensive to *nats.*

The most important place for *nat* worship in Burma is Mount Popa, an extinct volcano. Mount Popa is considered to be the home of 2 of the thirty-seven powerful *nats.* A great festival takes place there every year which attracts people from all over the country, *nat* worshippers as well as curious observers.

It is often asked why even educated Burmese can sometimes be found taking part in *nat* worship. Perhaps the answer lies in two aspects of Burmese life. One is the strong hold which old beliefs from the days before Buddhism still have on the minds of the people. The other is the extreme self-reliance which Buddhism demands from the individual. In Buddhism there are no gods to whom one can pray for favours or help. One's destiny is decided entirely by one's own actions. While accepting the truth of this, most people find it difficult to resist the need to rely on supernatural powers, especially when times are hard.

The Burmese may put great importance on their religious life, but that does not stop them from being a fun-loving people. This is particularly obvious during the celebrations for the Burmese New Year, which takes place in April. *Thingyan* is also known as the Water Festival because the last three days of the old year are a time for people to throw water at one another all over the country. This is very refreshing at a time of year when the hot weather is at its worst. The water-throwing can sometimes get too rough, but nobody is supposed to get angry.

Thingyan is also a time when many Burmese boys celebrate one of the most important landmarks of their life. This is the *shinbyu,* when a Buddhist boy enters the monastery for a short time as a novice monk. All Burmese parents see it as their duty to make sure that their sons are admitted to the religious life in this way. The *shinbyu* ceremony can be performed once the boy is old enough to say certain Buddhist prayers correctly, manage the robes of a monk, and "drive away crows from his begging bowl." This period of novicehood during which boys live the life of monks (although they do not keep all the rules which adult monks must observe) is a good introduction to the religious life. Burmese men like to enter monastic life at least three times during their lifetime: once as a boy, once as a young man, and once as an adult.

The *shinbyu* ceremony is a joyful occasion. The candidate for novicehood (*shinlaung*) is usually dressed in princely costume. This recalls the fact that the Buddha was a prince before he gave up his royal position to follow the religious life. The *shinlaung* is paraded through the streets with great ceremony before his head is shaved and he is given the robes of a novice. How simple or elaborate a *shinbyu* ceremony is depends on the inclinations and resources of the family. Often a number of boys take part in a single ceremony. Apart from the *Thingyan* period, the Buddhist Lent is a popular time for *shinbyu* ceremonies.

When brothers are having their *shinbyu,* it is usual for the sisters to have their ears pierced. This gives the girls a chance to dress up as princesses and have their share of fuss and attention. Many see this as an expression of the Burmese belief in the equality of men and women. Although, theoretically, men are considered nobler because only a man can become a Buddha, Burmese women have never really had an inferior status. They have always had equal rights of inheritance and led active, independent lives. Secure in the knowledge of her own worth, the Burmese woman does not mind giving men the kind of respectful treatment that makes them so happy!

A big *shinbyu* ceremony may be accompanied by a *pwe.* *Pwe* is a particularly Burmese word which can mean a festival, feast, celebration, ceremony, gathering, or public performance. One common use of the word is to describe a popular entertainment which is a marvellous mixture of dance, drama, music, and clowning.

The origins of Burmese dance are considered to go back at least to the Pagan period, judging from old wall paintings and references in stone inscriptions. However, many of the dances performed today owe a considerable amount to Thai influences introduced in the eighteenth century when a son of Alaungpaya brought back many artists from his invasions of Thailand. The movements of both male and female dancers are very graceful, involving beautiful hand gestures and extremely skilled footwork.

Burmese drama, which is a little like western opera with music, singing, and much dramatic action, also owes a considerable amount to the tradition of court plays brought back from Thailand in the eighteenth century. Popular dramas such as the *Yamazat,* based on the famous *Ramayana* epic of India, are performed again and again. The nineteenth century produced many fine Burmese dramatists whose works also remain popular to this day.

Dance drama is always accompanied by orchestral music. Burmese musical instruments fall into five categories: bronze instruments, stringed instruments, leather instruments, hollow wind instruments and non-metallic percussion instruments used for keeping time. Burmese orchestral music has a great range, from soft, gentle tunes to the loud, stirring clashes which so often announce the presence of a *pwe*. The leading instrument of the orchestra is the *hsaingwaing,* a circle of 21 small leather-faced drums which are played with amazing virtuosity by the performer, who sits in the centre. Another instrument considered particularly Burmese is the gently curving harp, which is held in the lap of the performer as he plays.

There are many different types of classical Burmese song. To mention a few, there are the *kyo* (meaning string), which is always preceded by little phrases of music on the *hsaingwaing;* and the *bawle,* invented by a princess of the last royal dynasty at Mandalay.

Although classical music is always performed at the much loved *pwes,* modern music showing a strong western influence is increasingly gaining popularity, especially among young people. However, Burmese music and dance have not only strong traditions but also the support and encouragement of the government. There is, therefore, little danger that they will fall into decline, in spite of modern developments.

One form of entertainment which has lost some of its popular appeal is the puppet show. This was first introduced in the late eighteenth or early nineteenth century for the amusement of the royal court. A traditional puppet show has twenty-eight characters, including *nats,* a king, queen, courtiers, and various animals and birds. Different kinds of wood must be used to make different characters. There are many other rules, such as the order in which the characters come on stage and the direction from which they emerge. Puppeteering is, therefore, a very specialized art. It is a great pity that the public no longer seem very interested in this fascinating form of entertainment.

Today, the cinema has much appeal for the Burmese. The 25 Burmese film industry began before the Second World War. As in other countries, actors and actresses have many fans. But although successful film stars can make a good living, they do not become as rich as the big stars in the Western countries. Traditionally, actors and dancers were considered an inferior class, but these old prejudices are fast disappearing. Television, which was introduced several years ago, is quickly gaining in popularity.

The Burmese are an agricultural people, depending on the land for their living. Even today, in spite of some industries and the many professions open to people in the towns, agriculture is the backbone of the country. The number of those engaged in such professions as medicine, engineering, and teaching is increasing all the time. The Burmese have always had a high proportion of people who could read and write. This is due to the custom of sending children to the local monastery for their schooling. Traditionally the monasteries limited themselves to religious teachings, but gradually more and more of them added modern subjects to their teaching programme. Nowadays, with the growth of state education, there are few monasteries serving as schools. However, there are still many Burmese who owe their early education to Buddhist monks.

It has already been mentioned that Burmese writing first began to develop in the Pagan period. Much of the traditional literature was concerned with religious themes. But there is also a considerable body of classical works, mainly verse, which deals with nonreligious matters. Before the nineteenth century, the Burmese seem to have preferred poetry to prose. However, since the first novel in Burmese was published at the beginning of the twentieth century, prose writing, especially fiction, has developed greatly. Today, Burmese is a vigorous, continuously developing language.

The Burmese have a great respect for education. There is a popular old saying that riches can vanish as if by magic, but knowledge is a truly precious treasure which nobody can take away. Traditionally, education was seen not just as the acquisition of knowledge but as the development of Buddhist values. The needs of the present age have led to more emphasis on formal qualifications, but parents still place importance on bringing children up as good Buddhists.

The family is very important in Burma. Children are brought up to honour and respect their elders. It is believed that the love and care given by parents are beyond repayment. Burmese are taught that even though the Lord Buddha showed his mother the way to *nirvana,* he did not manage to repay more than a minute portion of what he owed her.

In spite of the strong feelings of family, the Burmese do not   30
have a system of family names. Each individual has his or her own personal name, which is often quite different from those of everybody else in the family. Moreover, women do not change their names on marriage. For example, the father may be called U Thein, the mother Daw Saw Tin, the son Maung Tun Aye, and the daughter Ma Khin Khin. *U, Daw, Maung,* and *Ma* are prefixes like "Mr" or "Mrs." In Burma, age is an important factor in deciding which prefix to use. *U* literally means "uncle" and *Daw* means "aunt," so these cannot be used for young children. *Maung,* meaning "younger brother," is suitable for a boy, but

when he is older the prefix *Ko* ("older brother") will be used. However, *Ma* ("sister") is the only prefix used for girls. Sometimes it is the person's position that decides which prefix should be used. A young man who has achieved a very important position will be addressed as *U*, while an older man, if his status is low, may still be addressed as *Ko* or *Maung.*

A person's position may decide how much respect is shown to him, but Burmese society has no rigid class system. It is not possible to tell from a person's name or accent whether his father is a manual labourer or a wealthy businessman. Even his appearance is not always an indication of his background, as there is not a great deal of difference in the kinds of clothes people wear. Many of those who are in high positions come from humble homes. A person is judged by his own achievements rather than by his family.

An important part of Burmese life is food. Both Burmese men and women take a lively interest in cooking. The basic item of a Burmese meal is usually rice, taken with what Westerners would describe as a "curry." However, Burmese "curries" are not quite the same as the better known Indian ones. The Burmese use less spices but more garlic and ginger. Fish products are an important part of Burmese cooking. Fish sauce and dried shrimps are used for flavouring. *Ngapi,* a paste of preserved fish with a very strong smell, is taken as a relish at almost every meal. Meat is not eaten in large quantities. A great variety of vegetables are available all the year round and Burmese cooking makes full use of them. It has been said that no tender leaf or shoot is safe from the Burmese.

The number of Indians and Chinese in Burma have added further variety to the food of the country. In the towns there are many restaurants and food stalls. It is quite usual for people to stop by the roadside to have a snack or a meal. Two of the most popular dishes are *mohinga* and *khaukswe. Mohinga* is a dish of slightly fermented rice noodles eaten with a thick fish soup. *Khaukswe* simply means noodles, and these can be prepared in many different ways. But the *Khaukswe* dish considered most typically Burmese is the one eaten with a kind of chicken stew cooked in coconut milk.

In general, the Burmese do not eat many sweets. Hot, spicy snacks are more to their taste. Fruits often take the place of puddings. As in many other South Asian countries, the mango is very popular. There are many varieties and the Burmese eat them in a number of ways. Small green mangoes are taken with *ngapi* as part of the main meal, or eaten as a snack dipped in salt and chili powder. Larger, slightly underripe mangoes can be made into a curry. But of course there is nothing to compare with a ripe, sweet mango eaten on its own.

Green tea is one of the most usual drinks in Burma. Tea with milk and sugar is also taken, but this is usually brewed in such a way that foreigners do not always recognize it as tea. As Buddhists, the Burmese frown upon alcoholic drinks, but there are strong country liquors made from the juice of the toddy palm. Bottled beer of the Western variety is also produced nowadays.

Food is a popular subject of conversation. It is quite usual for friends and acquaintances to ask each other on meeting: "And what did you have for lunch today?" This constant interest makes Burmese cooking one of the most imaginative and varied in the world.

Both Burmese men and women wear the *longyi,* a long tube of cloth which they wrap around themselves and tuck in at the waist. Men wear Western-style shirts with their *longyis* and women wear short, fitted tops. Young girls have now taken to wearing Western-style blouses and T-shirts. For formal occasions, men wear collarless shirts with short jackets and a *gaungbaung* (a kind of turban) on their heads. Chains of sweet-smelling white jasmines coiled around a knot of glossy black hair are one of the most attractive sights. Traditionally, both Burmese men and women kept their hair very long. Men started to cut their hair soon after British rule was established in the country. However, men with large top-knots can still be seen in the villages. Women have continued to keep their hair long, but in recent years it has become fashionable for girls to adopt short, Westernized hairstyles.

Burmese women are noted for their fine complexions. It is thought that they owe this in some degree to the use of *thanakha.* This is a paste made by grinding the bark of the *thanakha* tree. It gives the skin protection from the sun and is also thought to have medicinal properties. *Thanakha* is a yellow-beige paste and when applied thickly can make the face look as though it has been smeared with mud. In spite of this, it remains the most important item of a Burmese woman's beauty treatment. Even the arrival of modern cosmetics has not diminished the popularity of *thanakha.*

In Burma, as in many Asian countries, Western goods are much sought after. Western ideas and attitudes have also crept in through books, films, and foreign visitors. Under the policy of the present government, tourists are only allowed into the country for one week at a time. This goes some way towards keeping out foreign influences and, compared with most South-east Asian countries, Burma has done a much better job of preserving its

own culture and traditions. The country is to some extent isolated from the rest of the world through restrictions on Burmese
wishing to travel abroad as well as on foreigners wishing to come
to Burma. This enforced isolation has resulted in giving things
foreign the appeal of "forbidden fruit" for some Burmese. It also
means that in many areas of scientific and technological education, Burma has fallen behind modern developments.

Whatever attraction western goods and culture may hold for   40
some of the Burmese people, Buddhism is still the greatest influence on their daily lives. Young people who dress in T-shirts
and listen eagerly to Western-style pop music still visit the pagodas frequently. The religious life of the Burmese is not separated
from their social life. Most Burmese gatherings are centred
around a religious event. The most common social occasion is
perhaps the *hsoongway,* offering of food to monks. Friends will
come to help, listen to the sermons, and join in the chanting of
prayers. It is usual to repeat the Five Precepts and undertake to
keep them. On holy days people undertake to keep the Eight Precepts. After the monks have left, friends and family will eat together. It will have been an enjoyable as well as a spiritually
rewarding occasion.

By international standards, Burma is not a wealthy country
and life is hard for many of its people. But there is still a quality
of calmness and serenity which is very precious. For this the
Burmese are greatly indebted to their religion.

QUESTIONS FOR DISCUSSION AND WRITING

1. Summarize the core principles of Buddhism as articulated
   by this author and the goal for following them. According to
   the author, in what ways do these principles influence
   Burmese culture? How effective are her examples in supporting her views?

3. If you were raised in a society such as the United States that
   values a degree of separation of church and state, how does
   that affect your assessment of this article and its description
   of a culture deeply influenced by religious principles?

4. In what ways are roles and customs for men, women, and
   children similar to or different from those in Western cultures
   such as in Europe and the United States?

5. Find a Web site on Burma, Burmese culture, or the various types of Buddhism. Write a brief reflection on how it either reinforces or extends what you learned from this essay.

6. With this selection as a starting point and perhaps drawing from your response to question 1, research some element of culture discussed in this essay and present your findings to your class or peer group. Consider working with peers to research diverse areas of culture and put them together on a Web site.

7. Write an essay analyzing the author's style of presentation, particularly use of example and handling of paradoxes or inconsistencies in the culture.

Listening to Other Cultures

DEBORAH TANNEN

Deborah Tannen, linguist and scholar, is University Professor and Professor of Linguistics at Georgetown University in Washington, D.C. Her nineteen books include *You Just Don't Understand* (2001), *That's Not What I Meant!* (1986), *Talking Voices* (1989), and *Talking from 9 to 5: Men and Women at Work* (2001). Recently she has published *I Only Say This Because I Love You: Talking to Your Parents, Partner, Sibs, and Kids When You're All Adults* (2002). The selection that follows is from her book *The Argument Culture: Stopping America's War of Words* (1999). In this selection, Tannen offers examples that illustrate how culture and custom relate to argument and conflict.

How Much Confrontation is Confrontational?

An American woman of European descent (her mother was Italian, her father Jewish Hungarian) who grew up in New York City went to live for a time in the Netherlands. She was dismayed to discover that the Dutch often saw her as far too confrontational. At times she felt they regarded her as something of a monster. But the same style earned her opposite reactions in Israel, where people felt she was too much of a lady. They complained, "We don't know where you stand." Her style hadn't changed; it just looked very different in comparison to the contrasting norms of Dutch and Israeli culture. The level of confrontation considered normal by the Dutch was lower than what she had grown up with; the level considered appropriate by the Israelis was higher.

Jewish tradition requires people to speak up and protest when they disagree, and many individuals of Eastern European background (like those of Mediterranean, Armenian, African, South American, and many other backgrounds as well) enjoy friendly contentiousness, lively argument, and bantering opposition. In India and Sri Lanka, people are often expected to be confrontational; in Bali, they are generally not allowed to be. A linguist who spent many years in Bali commented that emotional arguments are almost unheard of there, so Balinese who come to the United States are frightened when they experience one. Yet Americans, for their part, can be if not frightened, then certainly put off, by the level of confrontation they encounter in some European countries—or in the homes of other Americans.

"If We Can Fight, We're Close"

People in many cultures feel that arguing is a sign of closeness. This can be startling to Americans who go to such countries in Europe as Germany, France, Italy, or Greece. For example, many American students who have spent time in France comment on their French families' and friends' bluntness and taste for dynamic argument. In France, as in many other countries, agreement is deemed boring; to keep things interesting, you have to disagree—preferably with great animation. Students in my classes provided many accounts from their own experience. Joanna Repczynski, for example, recalled her year in France:

> During one dinner my host mother ran through a litany of subjects, changing them every time I agreed or when there was general agreement. She would bring up one controversial topic after another, looking to start a heated intellectual debate over dinner.

Another country in which lively argument is valued is Germany. An American student majoring in political science with a special focus on Central America spent his junior year abroad in Germany. Years later, he still recalled with frustration conversations with German students who, early in their acquaintance, regaled him with their conviction that American foreign policy in Central America was self-serving, destructive, and generally venal, made worse by the hypocritical American claims to high-minded motives. The American student disagreed with his German verbal attackers and knew of numerous specific facts to counter their claims, but he found himself unable to respond—not for lack of language (his German was fluent) but because he was so taken aback by their manner: Their aggressive approach seemed hostile and rude. In order to counter their charges he would have had to respond in kind, something he did not want to do, since he did not want to be like them.

German-born linguist Heidi Byrnes relates this tale in explaining why Americans and Germans have negative stereotypes about each other. Germans tend to assume that intelligence and knowledge should be displayed through aggressive argumentation and forceful disputation of others' arguments. This behavior results in American students' impressions that German students are self-aggrandizing, pigheaded, given to facile right/wrong dichotomies, and generally inclined to put people on the defensive and humiliate them publicly. Conversely, Americans' refusal to engage in arguments in this way leads Germans to conclude that American students are superficial, uncommitted, ignorant, and unwilling (or, more likely, unable) to take a stand.

An Israeli professor visiting the United States had the opposite experience. When she met an American scholar prominent in her field, she almost immediately launched into a rundown of the points on which she disagreed. She hoped thereby to show the American how carefully she had read her work—and begin a fruitful exchange of ideas. But the American professor was offended by the assault: She did not consider it appropriate to begin an acquaintance by criticizing. Not eager to let herself in for more of the same, the American professor assiduously avoided the Israeli visitor for the remainder of her stay, exactly the opposite of what the visitor had hoped to accomplish.

You do not have to go to a foreign country to experience these cultural differences. Americans of different ethnic backgrounds can experience them just by making friends. After my class discussed these issues, Andrea Talarico wrote:

> I find it amusing how the last girl to raise her hand in class today discussed how in the Italian family voices would be raised and objects would be thrown in an intense discussion over which television show to watch, whereas in the British household a serious disagreement could be undertaken without any apparent show of emotion or distress. My Italian-American family is much the same as the Italian family. My friends have often crept up to my room in fear when the screaming begins and don't understand or believe me when I stress that what's going on is no big deal.

Andrea sees advantages to her Italian-American family's style: "We always know how each other feels at all times."

A Japanese woman who is happily married to a Frenchman recalls that she spent much of the first two years of their relationship in tears. He frequently started arguments with her, which she found so upsetting that she did her best to agree and be conciliatory. This only led him to seek another point on which to argue. Finally, she lost her self-control and began to yell back. Rather than being angered, he was overjoyed. Provoking arguments was his way of showing interest in her, letting her know how much he respected her intelligence. To him, being able to engage in spirited disagreement was a sign of a good relationship.

It is not simply the idea of arguing but the form it takes— the level of opposition and the way it is expressed—that accounts for surprise, confusion, or alarm when people of one cultural background encounter those of another expressing disagreement or conflict. I doubt there is any culture in which there isn't some form of opposition that can be a sign of intimacy.

Even in Japan, for example, the ability to argue can be taken as evidence of intimacy. Kimberly Jones observed that the Japanese sometimes refer to conflict as positive, even though references to harmony are more frequent. One example she gives illustrates how conflict can create solidarity among those who take the same side. Two men, Nakamura and Watanabe, were discussing the graduate program each had attended at different times. Nakamura mentioned two students who had quit before finishing. When asked why that happened, he explained that they had never really become part of the group. They had not joined the others in encouraging each other or in bad-mouthing their teachers, so they could not take advantage of the group support as the other students did. In other words, bad-mouthing the teachers was necessary to build solidarity with the other students.

Talking against teachers is very different from arguing with someone who is actually there, but positive conflict was not limited to the kind directed at absent parties. As the conversation continued, Nakamura asked whether things had been any different when Watanabe was in the program. Watanabe replied, No, the students in his time did not form factions but were a cohesive unit. Nakamura then asked, "Did everyone get along?" Humorously, Watanabe replied, "No one got along!" and added, "Everyone arguing and stuff." Here, Jones explains, the ability to argue openly was a sign of intimacy: The students in the program were a cohesive unit *because* they could argue with each other openly.

These examples all show that arguing can be a way of establishing intimacy, though the level, type, and context by which it does so can differ from one culture to another.

QUESTIONS FOR DISCUSSION AND WRITING

1. What attitudes toward argument do you have? What are your family's or culture's customs regarding argument? Do you identify with any of the examples or experiences Tannen cites?

2. This brief excerpt from Tannen's book gives examples to support a larger point or conclusion. What is that point? Where is it placed in the essay? How does its placement affect your engagement with the text?

3. Summarize Tannen's assertion about the perception of argument in the different cultures she highlights. How do different concepts of argument lead to misunderstandings?

4. Write an essay in which you reflect on your own attitudes about argument or ways to discuss differences of opinion, paying particular attention to the role of custom and culture.

5. Observe a discussion board with international participants and examine the ways in which people handle difference and conflict.

6. Read additional material on this topic in Tannen's book or in other scholarly sources and consider developing a research project in this area.

In Kabary, the Point Is to Avoid the Point

DANNA HARMAN

Recently based in Nairobi but currently in transition back to the United States, Danna Harman has covered sub-Saharan Africa for *The Christian Science Monitor,* reporting on political and economic news as well as a broad range of social issues such as the AIDS epidemic and regional famine. Prior to joining the *Monitor* in 2001, Harman was a diplomatic correspondent for *The Jerusalem Post,* where she covered the prime minister's office, the foreign ministry, and the peace process. She also worked as a print and radio reporter for the Associated Press in Jerusalem and as a correspondent for *The Jewish Chronicle.* Harman has also written for *Elle, The New Republic,* and *The Chicago Sun Times.* Harman holds degrees from Harvard and Cambridge universities and did course work at Oxford, the University of California at Berkeley, and the Sorbonne. She spent two years with the Israeli Defense Force and also served as a UN electoral observer in South Africa. She speaks Hebrew, French, English, and Arabic. The article that follows, published in the *Monitor* in May, 2002, discusses the term *kabary,* an expression that conveys highly ritualized oratory with specific context and function. This traditional oratory is highly regarded and is rooted in early political assemblies with individuals speaking in turn. Madagascar, the fourth largest island in the world, which includes several smaller islands, is a nation that lies off the coast of Mozambique, in the Indian Ocean. Madagascar was a French colony from 1896 until independence in 1960; a military government held power beginning in the 1970s; then a series of political and economic crises ensued and the political system became more open in 1990 when opposition parties were legalized. The Malagasy, the majority of people on the island, have ties both to Africa and Asia. The economy is primarily agricultural. Some commentators suggest that Malagasy don't see their struggle as one to "modernize," but rather as a result of past French colonialism. Consider researching both the cultural and the historical roots of kabary as a follow-up to this reading.

The biggest potential threat to Madagascar's culture, sighs local poet Ranoe, is the cellphone. Each minute of talk is so **expensive,** he says, that people have to get to the point quickly— not the Malagasy way.

"We are about circular movement. We are about our ancestors and their words of wisdom. We are about harmony," waxes Hanitravio Rasoanaivo, a singer. "Basically," he concludes, "we are about taking it slow."

Self-made millionaire Marc Ravalomanana, the newly elected president of this island nation in the Indian Ocean, knows this truth well.

The crowds in the capital who came out to celebrate the victory of their "American dream" candidate may have been sporting cowboy hats emblazoned with "OK Ravalomanana!" in English, and they may have been cheering for the "US style" economic reforms they hope he will introduce, but when it came time for their leader to address them, they wanted nothing like a US politician's barrage of sound bites.

They wanted kabary.   5

A form of traditional Malagasy oratory, kabary is based on the unhurried telling of ancestral proverbs, metaphors, and riddles, frequently in a dialogue using call and response.

Originally used in public gatherings and political assemblies of a pre-literate era, the form has since evolved and been popularized, but it has kept its specific rules. Today, despite the rising literacy rate and the familiarity with different manners of speech, kabary is still considered necessary for communication during ritual events, and is also used widely in regular, day-to-day talk.

"I'm a businessman," says the Western-educated Mr. Ravalomanana in an interview. "I am all about setting an agenda. Setting a time frame. Going through that agenda. One. Two. Three." In theory, he muses, the people might respect that directness— but not if it comes at the expense of their traditional ways. "I have been learning," he admits with a smile.

"No, no, no straight talk," says primary school teacher Bonnard Ohiria, putting her hands over her ears as she explains that only twenty percent of any good oratory should be "to the point." The rest—"the very long rest"—she says, should be all about word play.

One of the main rules of kabary is that the subject or point of   10
the conversation can never be broached directly—and in some instances cannot be stated at all. During a funeral or condolence call, for instance, uttering aloud the name of the deceased is taboo. To express that someone is missed, Ranoe offers, one might begin

with a story about the short grass on the highlands plateau that a great grandfather once trod upon. Then, the speaker might embark on a tale about the pearls of the deep sea and how grass and great grandfather and sea have become torn apart.

Kabary is spoken solely in the Malagasy language, which—like the Malagasy themselves—is a synthesis of Indonesian, Polynesian, African, Arab, and European influences.

"The idea is to roll our thoughts and our ancestors' thoughts all around on our tongues in pleasure—but never give voice to the main point," says Tsiky Rakolomavo, a professional mpikabary—a person skilled in kabary—who is often hired to represent brides or grooms in the lengthy, crucial kabary meetings between families before a wedding ceremony.

Such meetings, explains local musician Ndrina, are of major significance.

"If one family does not like the word play or the proverbs the other family is using," he says solemnly, "the whole wedding can be called off."

The concept of including ancestors and their words of wis- 15
dom in daily existence is found throughout Malagasy culture. During the Famadihana ceremony, for example, the dead are exhumed and treated as if they were alive and just returned from an extended absence. The relatives are entertained, danced with, regaled with stories of recent family events, turned to for advice, and then reburied with new shrouds and presents.

Malagasies acknowledge that in striving to modernize their society, in electing a "modern man" as their leader and in giving their children access to modern communications, they risk losing parts of their cultural heritage.

"We want to move forward, but we want our past to move forward with us," says Malala Rafam'Anducenjly, an English professor and mother of four. So she envisions her children moving easily between the e-mail chat forums in their school computer classes and school assemblies where they speak in kabary. In recent years, popular kabary classes and after-school clubs have sprouted up in Antananarivo to help parents educate their increasingly busy children in the ways of the past. Meanwhile, kabary is opening up to new metaphors, and even slang associated with modern life.

"Today we don't need kabary for communication," says Ranoe, "but it is important for our culture. It is essential for our souls."

As the poet talks on, a Christmas jingle sounds. It is his cell-phone. His cousin Sylvain is on the line, and the two break into

a staccato kabary conversation, with Ranoe laughing heartily
and waving his arms in the air. After ten minutes they hang up.

"What did he want?" the poet is asked. "I don't know," he   20
replies. "We didn't get that far."

QUESTIONS FOR DISCUSSION AND WRITING

1. Evaluate the introduction. How does the specific example engage your interest? How does the short sentence of paragraph 5 create an effect? Evaluate the conclusion and the
   ways in which it provides closure, reiterates the point, and invokes the introduction.
2. Do paragraphs 6 and 7 define kabary adequately and give
   you a clear sense of the term? How is kabary a part of and a
   reflection of the culture of Madagascar?
3. How does "one of the main rules of kabary"—being indirect—compare with your understanding of American com-
   muncation styles?
4. Write an essay reflecting on the dilemma that Madagascar and
   other cultures face and discussing whether people can "find a
   way to move forward" but be accompanied by their past.

Rock Rolls Once More in Iran

DANIEL PEARL

Daniel Pearl (1963-2002), born in Los Angeles in 1963, was a prominent journalist who began writing for the *Wall Street Journal* in the late 1980s after graduating from Stanford University in 1985 with a degree in communication. Pearl built a reputation as a sympathetic journalist interested in the lives of ordinary people, covering genocide in the former Yugoslavia, influences of American popular culture on the Islamic Middle East, and more recently the roots of terrorism. While researching convicted shoe bomber Richard Reid's connection to the al Qaeda terrorist organization in Karachi, Pearl was kidnapped by Islamic extremists, who forced him to participate in a propaganda videotaping that ended with his on-camera death. At Stanford University the Daniel Pearl Memorial Journalism Internship has been established to commemorate his work and is awarded annually to an outstanding student journalist who exemplifies Pearl's work with "a commitment to explaining different cultures to each other, an emphasis on the stories of ordinary people rather than those in positions of power, and a focus in his or her writing on the dignity of individuals." Pearl was also a musician, and the essay that follows, written for the *Wall Street Journal* in 2000, reflects his interest in music as well as in Middle Eastern cultural and political issues.

In a basement studio here, Iranian pop singer Alireza Assar and his crew are mixing their latest rock ballad. Mr. Assar's strong solo voice rings out in Farsi, singing, "We should find love in the rain." As the music swells, an electric guitar begins to wail, and women's voices take up the song.

If Iran's political hard-liners ever heard this, there'd be hell to pay, right?

Wrong. In fact, the conservatives sponsor Mr. Assar. They own this digital recording studio, they promote his $5-a-ticket concerts, and they approve each of his songs before its release.

Pop music, prohibited for most of the *Islamic Republic of Iran's* two decades of existence, has made a comeback in the past two years. And its revival owes more to the nation's conservatives than to its reformists. Iranian TV, a hard-liner stronghold, gave most of the new popular-music stars their start. A related record label is the nation's biggest producer of pop. Iran's most original recording, critics say, is Mr. Assar's 1999 debut album, which was conceived by an arts center aligned with the hard-liners.

On the surface, this nation's hard-liners are doing all they   5
can to prevent cultural change, but the reality is more complex. These days, the real political struggles here are over the pace of change—and who gets the spoils. That shows in the hard-liners' strategy of championing the new home-grown pop, which they hope will pre-empt the unruly Western variety.

Pop music is a good window into Iran's all-consuming politics. Most developments in the industry trace back to one faction or the other: a guitar is shown on TV (conservatives), a book of translated Pink Floyd lyrics appears in a city-run bookstore in Tehran (reformists), a young crowd gathers to hear a local rock band play the Dire Straits hit "Sultans of Swing" (conservatives), and Googoosh, a reclusive prerevolution star, hints she will soon return to the stage (reformists).

"Music has always been in the service" of the state, says Fouad Hejazi, Mr. Assar's 29-year-old composer. Mr. Hejazi doesn't mind. He gets what he wants: seven days in the studio to polish each song and free rein in arranging the music.

What the government wants is a bulwark against the "cultural invasion of the West." For their part, the hard-liners used the judiciary recently to shut down fifteen newspapers, some of which they decried as "bases of the enemy." And they tried without success to derail Sunday's installation of a new Parliament that favors greater freedoms for Iran's youth.

Conservatives fret about the Madonna and Michael Jackson songs blaring illegally from car stereos in Tehran, but they worry even more about the Iranian artists in exile who record in Farsi in Los Angeles, evoking prerevolutionary nostalgia and new social freedoms. That music seeps into Iran via smuggled cassettes, hidden satellite dishes, and the Internet. A hard-line judge recently decriminalized the private use of such music, but selling it is still against the law.

"With your sexy moves, you provoke me," goes a typical L.A.   10
song. Young Iranians laugh with embarrassment at the suggestive lyrics but find the fast six-count rhythm perfect for co-ed dancing.

Co-Opting Pop

Iran's Islamic government doesn't condone dancing or dating, however. So, led by the conservatives, it came up with a plan to co-opt the forbidden pop. It put Tehran pop on the airwaves, with singers who could match the voices and melodies of the popular LA acts, but with slower rhythms and ambiguous lyrics. One example: "I wish it were possible, for the spring of my dreams, with you, to come true."

Is this poem about God or a girl? It's hard to tell, and that's why it lends itself so well to the new Iranian pop scene.

Now, the Shandaz Nights restaurant can present live cover bands, under the watchful eye of government inspectors. If diners request a song by Iranian exile Dariush, they often get one from Khashayar Etemadi, who has the same rasp in his voice. Mr. Etemadi's career was launched by the conservatives, but the singer, who typically sports a goatee and suspenders, recently formed his own record company and wrote a song for Iran's reformist president, Mohammed Khatami—"In the age of coin and gunpowder, come and believe in humanity."

In the Permitted Music store in a downtown alley here, shoppers asking for an under-the-counter tape of LA-based singer Ebi may end up with Tehran teen idol Shadmehr Aghili, with his silky voice, slick hair, and showy violin solos. His songs have jazz, funk, and Latin influences. "You know that life is hard without you, but how easily your eyes take death from my heart," Mr. Aghili sings in a track titled "Skylike."

The strategy works, according to those who deal in contraband tunes. One such merchant, who goes by the name Akbar, has operated downtown for the past eight years, approaching passersby with the whispered offer of "new tapes." Akbar says his business is off 50 percent since the Iranian pop cassettes became available.

As the novelty wears off, however, sales of sanctioned pop are slipping, too. "You feel that they want to talk about earthly love, but they have to talk about love for God. They should say whatever they want to say, frankly," says Morteza, 24, as his clandestine date nods. Shabnam Assadi, a 20-year-old management student, says the seven or eight Iranian pop tapes she owns aren't suitable for dancing, but "for listening to them once, they're not bad."

Iran's music industry is trying to break new ground. Mr. Etemadi's coming album features a samba tune called "Wow." People who have heard the bootleg versions of Mr. Aghili's next release say it has words that are clearly about girls. Mr. Assar's next effort features "lambada and rap" rhythms, says his composer. Saxophones, Spanish guitar, techno-electronic beats, and lush string arrangements are all being squeezed behind Iranian pop's typically oriental melodies. Still, most of the music has the same 1970s-film-soundtrack style that Iran's pop musicians used before the 1979 Islamic Revolution.

For centuries here, music was restricted to Islamic mystics who played only for themselves, or motrebi singers, who provided the royal court with cheap entertainment. The once-disdained motrebis moved into downtown cabarets in the 1970s, and some became superstars, with the aid of the shah's government, which subsidized record producers.

The Islamic Revolution initially banned all but traditional and classical music and barred women from singing in public. Most of the top performers fled to the West.

In 1990, Mr. Khatami, then minister of culture, tried to liberalize the arts. Mr. Assar, for example, recalls playing in a three-month blues show called "Victory of Chicago." But the establishment rebelled, and Mr. Khatami lost his job. Mr. Assar resorted to giving piano lessons.   20

Many people cite Mr. Khatami's 1997 election as president as the beginning of Iran's musical reform. Actually, it began a few years earlier with Iran's supreme leader, Ayatollah Ali Khamenei. A champion of the hard-liners, he is also a shrewd politician who knows a bit about music; he plays the dotar, a traditional stringed instrument. His cultural advisers convinced him that if Iran didn't produce its own pop, music from abroad would corrupt Iran's youth and undermine Islamic values.

Ayatollah Khamenei quietly sought the approval of top Islamic scholars. "He told them he would look for classical poems and military themes," says one adviser.

One tool he used was the Islamic Arts Center in Tehran, which was set up at the beginning of the revolution to help spread Islamic culture. The center put aside its traditional-music projects and learned to rock. It installed a modern studio on its tree-lined campus, and in 1997 started a one-year search for musicians.

Television was there to help. Iran's five TV channels are all run by Islamic Republic of Iran Broadcasting, whose politics are clear from the portraits hanging in the studio's lobby: Ayatollah Khamenei's, not President Khatami's. IRIB's music director is a close friend of the ayatollah.

The conservatives introduced pop to Iran in gradual doses, to let religious hard-liners get used to it. IRIB started Radio Payam, which aired instrumentals by such acts as the Gipsy Kings. Some songs featuring drums and guitar were played on TV. Soroush Distribution, an affiliate of IRIB, issued a pop tape two years ago, a compilation of patriotic songs tied to the soccer World Cup. "Iran, Iran, ey-mahd-e daliran. Iran, Iran, eftekhar-e dowran," one singer intones over a disco-like beat. ("Iran, Iran, the land of the brave. Iran, Iran, the honor of the era.") IRIB polled young people about their preferences and auditioned singers.   25

Unlikely Material

Mr. Assar and Mr. Hejazi, his composer, seemed unlikely material. The two musicians had grown up together listening to progressive rock. But Mr. Hejazi had a friend at IRIB and went to Mr. Assar's apartment one day to persuade him to audition. Their recording, with Mr. Assar singing a classical text by the poet Hafez, aired on TV over a nature film.

An Islamic Arts Center producer heard Mr. Assar and signed him up. Arts center officials interpreted classical poems with him. Looking for "thoughtful" music, the center encouraged the singer to emphasize the words through careful articulation, like Canadian superstar Céline Dion.

Mr. Assar says he isn't "into politics" and has warned his backers he would withdraw if they used him to pursue a right-wing agenda. He has, however, developed an interest in Islamic mysticism, and the image that goes with it. The singer grew a beard, started wearing a black robe, and avoided parties where men and women mixed or alcohol was served. The sleeve of Mr. Assar's first album, "Kooch," which means migration, shows his profile in blue light, with liner notes citing his lineage to the prophet Mohammed and asking God's help "not to fall out of the honest path." The album, with its tense, syncopated tunes, sold an estimated 300,000 copies, producing a windfall for the arts center.

Meanwhile, the reformists were establishing their own pop empire, centered on the Ministry of Culture and Islamic Guidance, whose approval is needed to release an album. The ministry is under Mr. Khatami's control, but that doesn't mean it lets artists do what they want.

On a recent day, Farid Salmanian of the ministry's Music Council sits in his office and listens to a demo tape, with a clipboard that holds marked-up lyrics of a soft-rock song about traveling. The ministry's Lyrics Council has changed the words: "It's the start of the hard road of the hot weather of the West" becomes "It's the demands of the long road." Mr. Salmanian says the tape will be rejected anyway because the singer is out of tune.

A Shocking Decision

The Ministry of Culture gives some record labels financial aid and advice on music and packaging, and labels close to the ministry have recruited some of the TV-launched singers. In November, the ministry shocked the music industry when a Khatami appointee overruled the Music Council by approving a Shadmehr Aghili album that included songs with a fast, six-count rhythm. The album has sold more than a million copies.

The musical battles between the two camps have escalated. Iranian TV shows only singers who have stayed on its own record label. Several pop singers appeared at a rally for a pro-reform political party before the February parliamentary elections. Conservatives and reformists have vied for control of civic centers where many concerts are held.

The reformists may hold the ultimate pop weapon: Googoosh, the sensuous empress of 1970s Iranian pop. Iranian expatriates still adore her, and sometimes portray her as a silenced prisoner of the Islamic regime. These days, women are allowed to sing solos only before female audiences, and they can perform for mixed audiences or on recordings only as part of a chorus.

Googoosh was in the first row recently at a women-only pop festival sponsored by the Ministry of Culture. And she may well perform at the next festival, in October, says the head of Revelations of Dawn, a record label with connections to the singer. If Googoosh returned to the stage, the regime would score a propaganda coup and, music-industry insiders say, the reformists would get the credit.

QUESTIONS FOR DISCUSSION AND WRITING

1. Summarize the main point of this essay. Does the title accurately forecast this point? Does Pearl's statement in paragraph 5 capture the complexity of the topic and the paradox of the conservatives' co-opting of rock music? Analyze Pearl's introduction. How effectively does the anecdote provoke interest and lead you into the essay?
2. Pearl argues that pop music is a window into Iran's politics. How does he develop this point? Do you agree, in the case of Iran? Do you agree as a general principle?
3. Does it seem likely that Iran's government will withstand the "invasion of the West" by taking over the pop music industry? Does the author seem to believe so?
4. According to the author, what is the role of music in the state and the culture?

5. Research some aspect of culture—music, film, art, or literature—in a country other than the United States. In addition to writing your findings, give a brief oral presentation to your class. Consider including audio, video, or text files to support your presentation.

Fatwas:
McDonald's and
Barbie Dolls

ISLAM ONLINE

Islam Online is a Web site devoted, as its developers state, to offering a global Internet presence that presents a "unified and lively Islam that keeps up with modern times in all areas." The site is overseen by a committee of Islamic scholars headed by Dr. Yusuf Qardawi to ensure the site does not violate Islamic law and aims to provide services to Muslims and non-Muslims alike in several languages, initially in Arabic and English. One of the services offered on this site is an Online consultation for a *fatwa,* or legal statement in Islam that is issued by a mufti or religious lawyer on a specific issue and is rendered based on precedent. According to some sources, today fatwas have limited importance in most Muslim societies and draw what importance they do have from people's acceptance of their authority. At the same time, requests for fatwas and the responses to them can inform readers about cultural issues. The fatwas that follow, published on *Islam Online,* offer an opportunity to examine issues of cultural conflict from a non-US dominant cultural perspective.

Islamic View of the Barbie Doll

Inquiry

Please, I'd like to know the Islamic ruling concerning baby dolls, especially the one called "Barbie" designed mainly for girls? Secondly, I'd like to know the fatwa concerning the act of making and selling outfits for dolls, especially that I know that taking a doll as a toy is something permissible in Islam. Thirdly, what is the fatwa concerning the act of putting a doll on display rather than taking it as a toy?

Islam Online Fatwa Committee

Dr. Fu'aad Mekheimar, professor of Islamic Studies at Al-A-Azhar University, answers: In the Name of Allah, Most Gracious, Most Merciful. All praise and thanks are due to Allah, and peace and blessings be upon His Messenger. Some Muslim scholars maintain that dolls that are mainly for children's amusement are something permissible in Islam, for they are just toys, specially made for kids. Thus, it is permissible to put them on display and take them as trade objects, for this is how people normally deal with them, they are not considered as sacred objects. As for Barbie, it is purely American. It embodies popular American culture, displaying sexual attractions and being fashion conscious. It promotes an un-Islamic way of dressing, and rather encourages materialism and brushes aside spiritual values. Thus, it negatively affects female Muslim children who are supposed to be brought up wearing hijab and guarding their chastity. Accordingly, Barbie is forbiden in Islam. Every Muslim should fear Allah and bring up his children according to the teachings of Islam. May Allah protect Muslim children from evil and keep them on the straight path of Islam. Almighty Allah knows best.

Boycotting Locally-owned McDonald's

Inquiry

As-Salaam 'Alaykum! Sheikh Qaradawi recently called on all Muslims to boycott Israeli and American goods. The boycott has gained much popularity now, and many people are boycotting American as well as Israeli goods. However, recently, someone informed me that in the Gulf countries (live in the UAE), fast food outlets, such as McDonald's or KFC, are 100% locally owned. These are American products. However, they are owned by locals. Should we boycott such companies, which are in fact locally owned. If we do boycott them, this will harm our fellow Muslims who run such companies. I was also told that the earnings made by Coca Cola or Pepsi in the UAE and other Gulf countries do not go to any American, but to locals. Should we, nevertheless, boycott these goods, which may end up causing harm economically to our fellow Muslims? Wassalamu Alaykum.

Dr. Monzer Kahf

Wa 'alykum As-Salaamu wa Rahmatullahi wa Barakaatuh.

In the Name of Allah, Most Gracious, Most Merciful.

All praise and thanks are due to Allah, and peace and blessings be upon His Messenger.

Dear brother in Islam, we would like to thank you for showing keenness on knowing the teachings of Islam, and we appreciate the great confidence you have in us. We hope our efforts meet your expectations.

With regard to your question, Dr. Monzer Kahf, a prominent Muslim economist and counselor, answers:

"McDonalds, KFC, Pepsi, Coke, and other American brands that operate in the Gulf and most other Arab countries are locally owned and their profits go to local owners, Muslim and non-Muslim alike. However, these companies are granted franchise by the American mother companies, hence they use their products and systems and pay them either an annual lump sum amount or in accordance with their sale or a combination of both.

The problem with these products, brands of donuts, and pizza is that they are not only using American products and paying franchise fees, they also represent the "American culture." I think the businessmen who started them in our Muslim countries have done a grave mistake in importing the "American way of life" in place of our traditional *hommos, fool* (beans), *shawerma, falafel/ta'miyyah* (mashed beans), *lahm mashwi* (fried meat), *aima' 'arab/booza,* and other traditional fast food that you see all over the Muslim land from Morocco to Malaysia and Indonesia.

I believe that the declaration of boycott applies to them for two reasons:

1. They are American products that pay to the American companies franchise fees.

2. They are American cultural symbols that are included in the declaration of boycott more than anything else. In fact, both nutritionwise and beautywise the national fast food in each and all Muslim countries are superior. You can't compare the *irqisus* of Istanbul and Cairo and the *laban 'airan* of Aleppo and *Bursa* with the Pepsi and the cola of Uncle Sam!"

Do keep in touch. If you have any other question, don't hesitate to write to us.

Allah Almighty knows best.

QUESTIONS FOR DISCUSSION AND WRITING

1. How does the expert or Islamic scholar structure a response to each query? What appeals to authority are evoked in each reply?

2. With regard to the Barbie doll, how does the author differentiate between dolls in general and this doll in particular?

3. What are the scholar's specific objections to the Barbie doll? How does the Islamic expert appeal to ethos in his discussion?

4. With regard to the query about boycotting McDonald's, how does the author of the question make a case for not boycotting locally owned McDonald's?

5. How does the Islamic expert respond to the inquirer's case? What is the scholar's chief objection to American brands in the Gulf? What is wrong with these fast food chains in terms of what they represent?

6. What is your response to these fatwas and the arguments they make? Do you see the point of these rulings or do you believe they are unreasonable? Might American feminists, coming from a quite different perspective, come to a similar conclusion about Barbie dolls?

"OM"
Hinduism in American Pop Culture: Global Strategy or Sacrilegious Mistake?

SARALA NAGALA

Sarala V. Nagala was born in 1983 in Oakes, North Dakota. She attended high school in her hometown and became interested in this topic after moving to the more cosmopolitan California for her undergraduate studies. After seeing products representing Hindu images hanging in storefronts, Nagala began investigating these items, examining both the culturally blended artifacts that seemed problematic and those that had the potential to lead to greater multicultural understanding. Nagala is currently studying public policy and plans to attend law school.

As the stage is illuminated, the colorful backdrop decorated with depictions of the Hindu deities Krishna and Shiva appears. Then the focus shifts to the woman dressed in the ephemeral, shimmering black dress. Her forehead is adorned with tilaka markings, which symbolize devotion in the Hindu religion; her hands are bedecked in traditional Indian mehendi hand paint. The song she performs is "Shanti," with lyrics written entirely in Sanskrit. This seemingly religious scene is instantly transformed when, for her next number, American pop singer Madonna changes into a see-through tank top and launches into a provocative dance with guitarist Lenny Kravitz. Though the background images were gone, Madonna remained in the Indian makeup, juxtaposing two cultures in a way that has not become uncommon in America. This performance is only one instance of the burgeoning trend of borrowing Hindu religious and cultural symbols for use in mainstream American pop culture. Several other celebrities have also integrated Hindu symbols into their dress, behavior, and art. Trying to emulate America's entertainment elite, young people are flocking to fashion boutiques to purchase various manifestations of this cultural borrowing. Shirts, shoes, and accessories have been screen-printed with such images as India's elephant god, Ganesha, and the word comparable to Christianity's "amen," Om.

Conflicting opinions about this apparent exploitation have prompted a heated debate. On one side are some Hindus who consider the images, in this context, sacrilegious to what they perceive as an already tolerant religion. On the other are those who believe that utilizing such symbolism allows for freedom of artistic expression and, furthermore, draws attention to an Eastern culture often neglected in a predominantly Eurocentric worldview. Therefore, the question must be posed: Is the emergence of Hindu symbols in Western popular culture inappropriate or simply an innocent side effect of evolving fashion trends? To answer this question effectively, we must elucidate the underpinnings of Hinduism, the manner in which these images are portrayed, the motivations behind those who use and purchase the images, and the broader conceptions of Hinduism in America. Acknowledging that various definitions of Hinduism lead to both positive and negative interpretations of Hindu images, it can be hypothesized that the positive, harmless fashion examples are most pervasive in mainstream society.

Before examining America's escalating use of Hindu symbols, it is important to review some basic aspects of Hinduism. Although the exact numbers are uncertain, Stanford University Professor of Cultural and Social Anthropology Akhil Gupta estimates that over 850 million people in India and significant diasporas in the Caribbean, Africa, South America, the Pacific Islands, and North America identify themselves as members of the Hindu religion (Interview). In the United States alone, there are 1.4 million Hindus in the last census count, a ten-fold increase since 1990 ("New Study"). Due to this immense world-wide following, Hinduism, a pantheistic religion, has evolved quite differently in disparate regions. Anantanand Rambachan, Hindu scholar and author of *The Hindu Vision,* explains: "The term 'Hindu' was used originally to describe a geographical entity rather than uniform religious culture. Today, it refers to a multiplicity of beliefs and practices." (1). Hinduism differs from Western religions in that it lacks a single identifiable founder, specific theological system, or a central religious organization. Over the centuries, various sects of the religion have developed and, due to this variation, beliefs and rituals of worship are not uniform across the whole religion. The diversity that exists within this religion prompts the foregrounding of certain beliefs by a sect that another group may consider inconsequential. Because priorities are skewed among different deities, beliefs, and practices, the reactions of Hindus to the use of their symbols in Western fashion greatly vary.

Various experts have attempted to define Hinduism, and
they have failed to agree on a solid characterization. India's first
prime minister, Jawaharlal Nehru, expressed both his views and
those of Mahatma Gandhi, who led India to independence
through his campaign of non-violence:

> Hinduism, as a faith, is vague, amorphous, many-sided, all
> things to all men . . . In its present form, and even in the
> past, it embraces many beliefs and practices, from the
> highest to the lowest, often opposed to contradicting each
> other. . . . Mahatma Gandhi has attempted to define it: "If
> I were asked to define the Hindu creed, I should simply
> say: A man may not believe in God and still call himself a
> Hindu. Hinduism is a relentless pursuit after truth. . . .
> Hinduism is the religion of truth. Truth is God." (75)

This hazy, indistinct picture given of Hinduism by two of   5
India's premier leaders is testament to the religion's lack of a
clear-cut definition. Stanford's Professor Akhil Gupta goes so far
as to claim that "there is no such thing as 'Hinduism,' per se" and
also notes that Hinduism as a classification emerged only during
the parallel construction of a Muslim community in nineteenth
century colonial India. The ancient roots of Hinduism have
evolved greatly over time. Because of the paucity of dogmatic
principles laying out precisely what "is" and "is not" Hinduism,
the religion has formed a metaphorical umbrella, accepting various—and often contradicting—viewpoints as doctrine. The lack
of an accepted overarching definition of Hinduism accentuates
the role of the individual in determining his or her own personal
depiction of the religion. This room for individual interpretation
is central to the debate over the use of Hindu symbols in American popular culture, as some Hindus consider it innocuous while
others are strongly offended.

This disparity provokes the question: What are these symbols and how are they being used? India has been called the
"land of 33 million gods," and "individual Hindus might worship
any of thousands of different deities" (KRON-TV). Several of
these deities are prevalent in Western fashion designs: Ganesha,
depicted as an elephant, is seen as the remover of obstacles;
Goddess Laksmi, often decked in beautiful clothing and sitting
on a lotus flower, represents prosperity; Shiva, the destroyer of
evil, is also the lord of art and dance; and many other deities represent complex combinations of different traits (see Figure 1).
Moreover, many American women have taken to wearing bindi
and mehendi, markings of cultural importance to Indians. Generally, America's entertainment industry has been the foremost

FIGURE 1   DESIGNS FROM T-SHIRTS DEPICTING HINDU DEITIES.

Clockwise from top left: Ganesha, Laksmi, Krishna, and Shiva. *Siamese Dream: Elegance from Around the World,* March 3, 2002.   (MARK ROMERO/SIAMESE DREAM)

151

propagator of Hindu symbols. Use within the entertainment industry itself can be divided into three categories: Those entertainers who use the symbols with an understanding of their significance to Hindu culture; those people who adopt the symbols simply as a fashion trend; and those artists who, deliberately or inadvertently, use symbols of Hinduism in a derogatory manner.

First we shall address the inquisitive individuals who have learned about the cultural significance of the images they use. One such figure is American pop singer Madonna. Although her performance at the 1998 MTV Music Awards described earlier forced the issue of cultural borrowing to the surface, she has been known to embrace many aspects of Hinduism (see Figure 2).

FIGURE 2   MADONNA AT THE 1998 MTV MUSIC AWARDS.

Madonna Shots. March 3, 2002.   (AP/WIDE WORLD PHOTOS).

Shibani Patnaik, a college student who performed classical Indian dance with Madonna in that controversial performance, extols Madonna's respect for and knowledge of Hinduism. Patnaik states: "Madonna knows everything about the deities—her baby daughter even has a statue of Krishna. She is very aware of Hindu practices and traditions, incorporating some of them into her own wedding. She also practices yoga and studies Sanskrit" (Interview). This demonstrated interest in Hinduism is testament to Madonna's appreciation of multiculturalism. Because of her earnestness, a watchdog group named American Hindus Against Defamation (AHAD) had to concede that her actions at the MTV performance were sincere and therefore warranted forgiveness ("Hindus React"). Other entertainers who have expressed genuine appreciation for Hindu culture are such singers as Sting and the late George Harrison, a member of the Beatles. Sting has incorporated typical Indian melodies into his songs. Harrison's interest began when the Beatles traveled to India. After meeting an Indian swami in London, the Beatles were exposed to Hindu philosophy and music. In fact, "During the 1960s many Hindu ideas and practices came to the West and had a large impact upon the counter-culture then developing. Dominant figures in popular culture—pop stars such as the Beatles—promoted Hindu ideas and gurus" (Flood 271). While these ideas mushroomed in the 1960s and 1970s, their popularity receded until the late 1990s when they began to appear again in the entertainment industry.

Though entertainers such as Madonna and Sting have set trends of embracing Hinduism, there are those who get swept up in the trend and use the images without understanding their cultural importance. In the entertainment industry, this paradigmatic "I do it because it's cool" view is represented by Gwen Stefani, the lead singer of the band No Doubt. She has integrated Indian jewelry and traditional adornment into her wardrobe, and she has been photographed numerous times wearing a bindi, the dot between the eyebrows on the lower part of the forehead (see Figure 3). To Indian women, this mark has a significant meaning. It represents a symbolic third eye that "promotes prosperity and festivity within a person" (Mangla). Stefani's use of the bindi can be deemed superficial because she typically wears it when dressed in Western outfits. Her marginalization of a single Hindu symbol leads to the conclusion that Stefani's interest is spurious. In contrast, Madonna tends to incorporate several Hindu features such as dress, bindi, and mehendi at once, therefore demonstrating multifaceted interest rather than borrowing simply for fashion's sake. However, Stefani has not received univer-

FIGURE 3　GWEN STEFANI, LEAD SINGER OF NO DOUBT, WEARING BINDI.

"Gwen Stefani Pictures," March 3, 2002.　(FRANK TRAPPER; CORBIS/SYGMA)

sal criticism for her utilization of the bindi, as the prevailing sentiment is that her method is relatively harmless and not disparaging to Hinduism.

Nevertheless, her actions, and those of others in Hollywood who use the images purely for their fashion appeal, have had far-reaching effects. Their somewhat flippant attitude has filtered down to mainstream American popular culture and is partially the reason that stores like Dharma, a fashion boutique in San Francisco's trendy Upper Haight district, have noticed a dramatic increase in sales of shirts, bags, and other accessories emblazoned with Hindu insignia. Jackie Wilson, longtime owner of Dharma, states that her most popular items have been apparel with Hindu deities Ganesha, described earlier; Krishna, a blue-bodied deity whom Hindus worship as an incarnation of the universe's creator, Vishnu; Rama and Sita, where Rama is another form of Vishnu and Sita his ideal wife; and images of the Tibetan Buddha. "In the last couple of years we have sold hundreds of these shirts and now we have the wrap skirts with the same deities," says Wilson (Interview). Among those designers who use these deities in their contemporary fashion lines are Donatella Versace, Christian Dior, and Indian designers Ravi Chawla and Rohini Khosla (Verma). Surprisingly, these designers are not being criticized for producing the clothes that instigate controversy. One may infer that where demand exists, products will be supplied. Designers are simply acting as these suppliers. While most of the patterns are for women's clothing, some are emerging for men as well. This trend is quickly engulfing the nation, as apparel and accessories with Hindu symbols are becoming ubiquitous in cosmopolitan America. This evidence prompts curiosity about why this fascination with all things Hindu has blossomed so rapidly in recent years.

It is difficult to pinpoint one main motivation for those who 10 purchase these images; rather, an intricate combination of factors has catalyzed this trend. These reasons are key because they help to explain the trend's popularity. In general, the American public seems to perceive Eastern culture as mystical and mysterious, compared to the mundane, ordinary life of the United States. Linda Hess, a religious scholar, explains: "Hinduism has fantastically rich mythic/religious imagery, and the American market has an insatiable appetite for novel and vivid images to sell" (qtd. in KRON-TV). Americans are attracted to the perceived exoticism of India and its images. They desire an element of exoticism in their own lives and feel that by wearing Ganesha or Om, they can embody the mysticism of both the deity and the religion as a whole. Added to this fascination is the visual appeal of the symbols. Hess also attributes the images' appeal to their colorfulness and beautiful detail, calling them "arresting" (qtd. in KRON-TV). Professor Gupta of Stanford agrees, asserting that while the interest in Hinduism in the 1960s was steeped more in such aspects as Indian philosophy, yoga, and incense, contemporary society has developed into a "visual culture" more concerned with physical images than philosophical roots. This tendency away from deeper understanding toward superficial appropriation is also the reason Gupta considers this fashion trend a fleeting fad that will likely die out when the fashion market evolves to other styles (Interview). However, there is no evidence that this transformation will come any time soon because consumer demand for these products is not ebbing. Due to this enormous fixation, the entertainment industry has tried to sell Hindu culture—sometimes going too far.

While most of Hollywood uses symbols of Hinduism in a respectful manner, there are those instances where the entertainment industry has, in a twisted attempt to quench the public's thirst for Hindu imagery, used the images in a way considered disparaging and disrespectful to the religion. However, negative depictions have been so quickly retaliated against that, other than negative publicity toward the images' producers, they have had no significant effect on mainstream popular culture.

Take, for example, the April 1999 issue of *Vanity Fair* magazine, which featured a two-page spread of Mike Myers, star of the *Wayne's World* and *Austin Powers* films, with a partially shaved hairstyle, saffron-colored silk robes, traditional mehendi body paint, and a jeweled bindi on his forehead. An accompanying photo showed Myers seated in the lotus position with an elongated tongue like the Hindu goddess Kali and surrounded by naked, blue-skinned models and an odd "monkey" god (Johnson 6). Myers also has the phrase "Call my agent" henna-painted on his hand and poses holding a Palm Pilot that reads "Om" on its screen. American Hindus Against Defamation (AHAD) encouraged the deluge of incensed letters *Vanity Fair* received in response to the photographs. Those who protested felt that the depictions violated the religious sanctity of Hindu imagery. "What bothers me is the ease with which religious symbols important to a peripheral group can be appropriated and used in this manner," said one distraught Hindu (qtd. in *Newsweek* March 22, 1999). The photographer, David LaChapelle, later apologized on the South Asian Journalists Association Web site. The important distinction here is the egregious nature of the images: There is little argument that the photos were inappropriate. Whereas

American teenagers might try to dress or act like Madonna because of her positive use of Hindu symbols, Myers' depiction crosses an invisible boundary into a realm that is vulgar, disrespectful, and clearly derogatory.

Several other instances have been judged disparaging as well, and, consequently, shunned by mainstream America. For example, AHAD was initially formed to protest the 1997 release of the Aerosmith album "Nine Lives," of which the cover featured a traditional depiction of Lord Krishna, but with a cat's face and female breasts. After Sony Music was inundated with over 20,000 e-mails, it agreed to redesign the cover ("Hollywood Hinduism"). In another incident, Stanley Kubrick's 1999 film *Eyes Wide Shut,* starring Tom Cruise and Nicole Kidman, was supposed to include chanted verses from the Bhagavad Gita, the holy text of Hinduism, during a sexually explicit scene. AHAD called its inclusion "utterly tasteless and insensitive" (qtd. in KRON-TV) and the scene was eventually deleted. Furthermore, in July 2001, a Los Angeles shoe company was forced to discontinue production of shoes decorated with the Hindu goddess Laksmi. The shoe protest illuminates how an interest in Hindu imagery can backfire. First, Hindus will not stand for anything representative of the religion to be printed on leather, because cows are seen as sacred in the religion and are not killed under any circumstance. Second, Hindus consider the feet unclean and wearing shoes that bear the image of God means tracking that image through dirt, which is considered sacrilegious. Organized resistance stopped these items in the production stage, therefore not allowing them to become part of the fashion trend. For if they did, outrage from Hindus would be swift. This evidence supports the conclusion that, due to appropriate protests and awareness of what is in good taste, most Americans are exposed to the positive Hindu imagery perpetuated by the entertainment industry.

These positive uses have larger implications in society. Viewed from a different perspective, the entertainment industry's usage of Hindu symbols actually encourages multicultural understanding and appreciation. For one, it has drawn attention to a southeastern Asian culture that has remained predominantly unrecognized in America. Amazingly, a 2001 study commissioned by the Hindu Leaders Forum found that 96 percent of Americans do not know what Hinduism is, despite the fact that the 1.4 million American Hindus contribute $20 billion to the United States economy ("New Study"). Professor Gupta reinforces this statistic, saying that "most people don't have a clue about what Hinduism is" (Interview). However, apparel decorated with Hindu images gives both the wearer and the observer a link to Hinduism, if only in recognizing that the images are derived from Hinduism rather than another religion. This realization is only the first step, though. The purchasers and observers will begin to inquire about which deity the shirt depicts and then what that deity represents in Hinduism. This cycle, now initiated by the existence of Hindu symbols in American popular culture, will lift Hinduism from its obscure position into one of more prominence. Thomas Wendell, author of *Hinduism Invades America,* speaks of America's potential: "As oriental countries in the recent past furnished good soil for the sowing of Western culture because of their material helplessness and subjection, so America today offers good soil for the sowing of Eastern culture because of its growing liberalism" (244). This "growing liberalism" also precipitates greater multicultural awareness in the United States. Prior to this recent emergence of Hindu imagery, Indians were represented by such characters as *The Simpsons'* Apu Nahasapeemapetilon, whose Indian movie characters babble nonsensically and whose idol of a six-armed God was displayed at the Kwik-E-Mart where he worked (Mangla). Although this image persists today, the other more positive, or, at the least, harmless fashions perpetuated by Madonna, Sting, and even Gwen Stefani have permeated American culture and have encouraged young men and women to wear Ganesha, Krishna, Om, and bindi. As Americans aim to build a stronger multicultural society, deviation from archetypal American fashion styles to more international designs exposes us to new ideas. This novelty undoubtedly has benefits, one of which is augmented appreciation and understanding of different cultures.

Based on this perspective, it is important to realize that 15 while there are some negative portrayals of Hinduism by the entertainment industry, these are carefully patrolled by watchdog groups such as AHAD and are also spurned by the American public's good judgment. Rather, America accepts the vibrant, colorful depictions perpetuated by sincere stars like Madonna that are ultimately innocuous. This warm reception has effects which leave the individual sphere, having instead the potential to change America's global awareness. And as for those Hindus who still take offense to the images, refer to Gotham Chopra, son of Indian new-age philosopher Deepak Chopra: "The principal problem with any faith is when the followers begin to take themselves too seriously" ("All the Raj"). Although their concerns are well-intentioned, these followers are misplaced in the changing tides of both American fashion and culture.

The true beauty of Hindu imagery is that it stands to shrink the globe and bridge cultural divides. As Gavin Flood, author of *An Introduction to Hinduism,* states, "Global Hinduism has a sense of India as its point of reference, but has transcended national boundaries" (265). It is just this essence of transformation which we have to endorse, encourage, and embrace if we are to see beyond the images to the underlying message of multiculturalism. It is the first step to a coalescence of continents and a smaller, more tightly-knit global community.

Works Cited

"All the Raj." Editor's note. *Vanity Fair* June 1999.

"A Vanity Fair Controversy." March 3, 2002. < *http://www.saja.org/vfdetail.html* > .

Flood, Gavin. *An Introduction to Hinduism.* Cambridge: Cambridge University Press, 1996.

Gupta, Akhil. Personal interview. February 21, 2002.

"Gwen Stefani Pictures," March 3, 2002. < *http://www.musicfanclubs.org/nodoubt/Pictures/Group/Gwen/Normal/Gwen111.jpg* > .

"Hindus React to Madonna's MTV Show." *Hinduism Today* January 1999, 50.

"Hollywood Hinduism: Art Vs. Morality." July 30, 2000. February 3, 2002. < *http://hinduism.about.com/library/weekly/aa073000a.htm* > .

Johnson, Richard, and Jeane MacIntosh. "Star's Photo Stunt Enrages Hindus." *New York Post* March 16, 1999: 6.

KRON-TV. "Krishna Culture" (story synopsis). January 21 2001. *ACF News Source.* < *http://www.acfnewsource.org/general/filesheet_religion.html* > .

"Losing Their Religion." *Newsweek* March 22, 1999.

Madonna Shots: March 3, 2002. < *http://www.madonnashots.com/mtvaw98zj.jpg* > .

Mangla, Marla. "Indianism: The New American Fad." *360 Degrees.* 2000-01. Vol. 3, No. 1. Feburary 27, 2002 < *http://students.syr.edu/360/winter/indianism.html* > .

Mehta, Monica. "Express Yourself." *Little India.* February 20, 2002 < http://206.20.14.67/achal/archive/Oct98/express.htm > .

Nehru, Jawaharlal. *The Discovery of India.* Calcutta: The Signet Press, 1946.

"New Study Reveals Hindu Myths and Misconceptions." *U.S. Newswire* national desk, August 15, 2001.

Patnaik, Shibani. Personal interview. February 5, 2002. (http://206.20.14.67/achal/archive/Oct98/express.htm).

Rambachan, Anantanand. *The Hindu Vision.* Delhi: Motilal Banarsidass Publishers Private Limited, 1992.

Siamese Dream: Elegance from Around the World: March 3, 2002. < *http://www.siamese-dream.com/clothing/shirts_hindu.html* > .

Verma, Neharika. "Ram On Your Bust!" IndiaBytes Bureau, *Sify Entertainment.* February 3, 2002. < *http://www.entertainment.sify.com/content/weekendstory.asp?news_code_num = 236&lang_code = Fashion* > .

Wendell, Thomas. *Hinduism Invades America.* New York City: The Beacon Press, Inc., 1930.

Wilson, Jackie. Telephone interview. February 26, 2002.

QUESTIONS FOR DISCUSSION AND WRITING

1. Does the title of this piece capture the central problem or does it seem to oversimplify the issue? Does the introduction provide sufficient background for the thesis?

2. To what degree is the background information about Hinduism necessary? Is there more information than you need to understand the issue? Does the writer assume you have more knowledge than you do about this topic and then provide less background information than you need?

3. Does the writer provide sufficient examples to warrant the conclusions she draws? If not, where should she provide additional support or clarification?

4. What has been your impression of cultural symbols in popular culture, whether they are symbols from your own religion or ethnic group or another? Have you seen symbols from other religions—Christian, Jewish, or Islamic symbols, for example—used in popular culture in ways that seemed questionable?

5. Research and write about religious symbols or motifs in popular culture in America or in another country.

Cultural Relativism and Universal Rights

CAROLYN FLUEHR-LOBBAN

Carolyn Fluehr-Lobban is a professor of anthropology and director of the Study Abroad/International Studies program at Rhode Island College. With her family, she has lived in and conducted field research in Africa and the Middle East. She is the author of six books, including *Islamic Law and Society in the Sudan* (1987) and *Islamic Society in Practice* (UPF, 1994). In the following essay, published in the *Chronicle of Higher Education* in 1995, she challenges the concept of cultural relativism and articulates the concept of universal human rights, asserting that "when there is a choice between defending human rights and defending cultural relativism, anthropologists should choose to protect and promote human rights. We cannot just be bystanders."

Cultural relativism, long a key concept in anthropology, asserts that since each culture has its own values and practices, anthropologists should not make value judgments about cultural differences. As a result, anthropological pedagogy has stressed that the study of customs and norms should be value-free, and that the appropriate role of the anthropologist is that of observer and recorder.

Today, however, this view is being challenged by critics inside and outside the discipline, especially those who want anthropologists to take a stand on key human-rights issues. I agree that the time has come for anthropologists to become more actively engaged in safeguarding the rights of people whose lives and cultures they study.

Historically, anthropology as a discipline has declined to participate in the dialogue that produced international conventions regarding human rights. For example, in 1947, when the executive board of the American Anthropological Association withdrew from discussions that led to the "Universal Declaration of Human Rights," it did so in the belief that no such declaration would be applicable to all human beings. But the world and anthropology have changed. Because their research involves extended interaction with people at the grassroots, anthropologists are in a unique position to lend knowledge and expertise to the international debate regarding human rights.

Doing so does not represent a complete break with the traditions of our field. After all, in the past, anthropologists did not hesitate to speak out against such reprehensible practices as Nazi genocide and South African apartheid. And they have testified in U.S. courts against government rules that impinge on the religious traditions or sacred lands of Native Americans, decrying government policies that treat groups of people unjustly.

However, other practices that violate individual rights or op-   5
press particular groups have not been denounced. Anthropologists generally have not spoken out, for example, against the practice in many cultures of female circumcision, which critics call a mutilation of women. They have been unwilling to pass judgment on such forms of culturally based homicide as the killings of infants or the aged. Some have withheld judgment on acts of communal violence, such as clashes between Hindus and Muslims in India or Tutsis and Hutus in Rwanda, perhaps because the animosities between those groups are of long standing.

Moreover, as a practical matter, organized anthropology's refusal to participate in drafting the 1947 human-rights declaration has meant that anthropologists have not had much of a role in drafting later human-rights statements, such as the United Nations' "Convention on the Elimination of All Forms of Discrimination Against Women," approved in 1979. In many international forums discussing women's rights, participants have specifically rejected using cultural relativism as a barrier to improving women's lives.

The issue of violence against women throws the perils of cultural relativism into stark relief. Following the lead of human-rights advocates, a growing number of anthropologists and others are coming to recognize that violence against women should be acknowledged as a violation of a basic human right to be free from harm. They believe that such violence cannot be excused or justified on cultural grounds.

Let me refer to my own experience. For nearly 25 years, I have conducted research in the Sudan, one of the African countries where the practice of female circumcision is widespread, affecting the vast majority of females in northern Sudan. Chronic infections are a common result, and sexual intercourse and childbirth are rendered difficult and painful. However, cultural ideology in the Sudan holds that an uncircumcised woman is not respectable, and few families would risk their daughter's chances of marrying by not having her circumcised. British colonial officials outlawed the practice in 1946, but this served only to make it surreptitious and thus more dangerous. Women found it harder to get treatment for mistakes or for side effects of the illegal surgery.

For a long time I felt trapped between, on one side, my anthropologist's understanding of the custom and of the sensitivities about it among the people with whom I was working, and, on the other, the largely feminist campaign in the West to eradicate what critics see as a "barbaric" custom. To ally myself with Western feminists and condemn female circumcision seemed to me to be a betrayal of the value system and culture of the Sudan, which I had come to understand. But as I was asked over the years to comment on female circumcision because of my expertise in the Sudan, I came to realize how deeply I felt that the practice was harmful and wrong.

In 1993, female circumcision was one of the practices deemed harmful by delegates of the international Human Rights Conference in Vienna. During their discussions, they came to view circumcision as a violation of the rights of children as well as of the women who suffer its consequences throughout life. Those discussions made me realize that there was a moral agenda larger than myself, larger than Western culture or the culture of the northern Sudan or my discipline. I decided to join colleagues from other disciplines and cultures in speaking out against the practice.

Some cultures are beginning to change, although cause and effect are difficult to determine. Women's associations in the Ivory Coast are calling for an end to female circumcision. In Egypt, the Cairo Institute of Human Rights has reported the first publicly acknowledged marriage of an uncircumcised woman. In the United States, a Nigerian woman recently was granted asylum on the ground that her returning to her country would result in the forcible circumcision of her daughter, which was deemed a violation of the girl's human rights.

To be sure, it is not easy to achieve consensus concerning the point as to which cultural practices cross the line and become violations of human rights. But it is important that scholars and human-rights activists discuss the issue. Some examples of when the line is crossed may be clearer than others. The action of a Japanese wife who feels honor-bound to commit suicide because of the shame of her husband's infidelity can be explained and perhaps justified by the traditional code of honor in Japanese society. However, when she decides to take the lives of her children as well, she is committing murder, which may be easier to condemn than suicide.

What about "honor" killings of sisters and daughters accused of sexual misconduct in some Middle Eastern societies? Some anthropologists have explained this practice in culturally relativist terms, saying that severe disruptions of the moral order occur when sexual impropriety is alleged or takes place. To restore the social equilibrium and avoid feuds, the local culture required the shedding of blood to wash away the shame of sexual dishonor. The practice of honor killings, which victimizes mainly women, has been defended in some local courts as less serious than premeditated murder, because it stems from long-standing cultural traditions. While some judges have agreed, anthropologists should see a different picture: A pattern of cultural discrimination against women.

As the issue of domestic violence shows, we need to explore the ways that we balance individual and cultural rights. The "right" of a man to discipline, slap, hit, or beat his wife (and often, by extension, his children) is widely recognized across many cultures in which male dominance is an accepted fact of life. Indeed, the issue of domestic violence has only recently been added to the international human-rights agenda, with the addition of women's rights to the list of basic human rights at the Vienna conference.

The fact that domestic violence is being openly discussed and challenged in some societies (the United States is among the leaders) helps to encourage dialogue in societies in which domestic violence has been a taboo subject. This dialogue is relatively new, and no clear principles have emerged. But anthropologists could inform and enrich the discussion, using their knowledge of family and community life in different cultures. 15

Cases of genocide may allow the clearest insight into where the line between local culture and universal morality lies. Many anthropologists have urged the Brazilian and Venezuelan governments to stop gold miners from slaughtering the Yanomami people, who are battling the encroachment of miners on their rain forests. Other practices that harm individuals or categories of people (such as the elderly, women, and enslaved or formerly enslaved people) may not represent genocide *per se,* and thus may present somewhat harder questions about the morality of traditional practices. We need to focus on the harm done, however, and not on the scale of the abuse. We need to be sensitive to cultural differences but not allow them to override widely recognized human rights.

The exchange of ideas across cultures is already fostering a growing acceptance of the universal nature of some human rights, regardless of cultural differences. The right of individuals to be free from harm or the threat of harm, and the right of cultural minorities to exist freely within states, are just two examples of rights that are beginning to be universally recognized—although not universally applied.

Fortunately, organized anthropology is beginning to change its attitude toward cultural relativism and human rights. The theme of the 1994 convention of the American Anthropological Association was human rights. At the sessions organized around the topic, many anthropologists said they no longer were absolutely committed to cultural relativism. The association has responded to the changing attitude among its members by forming a Commission for Human Rights, charged with developing a specifically anthropological perspective on those rights, and with challenging violations and promoting education about them.

Nevertheless, many anthropologists continue to express strong support for cultural relativism. One of the most contentious issues arises from the fundamental question: What authority do we Westerners have to impose our own concept of universal rights on the rest of humanity? It is true that Western ideas of human rights have so far dominated international discourse. On the other hand, the cultural relativists' argument is often used by repressive governments to deflect international criticism of their abuse of their citizens. At the very least, anthropologists need to condemn such misuse of cultural relativism, even if it means that they may be denied permission to do research in the country in question.

Personally, I would go further: I believe that we should not let the concept of relativism stop us from using national and international forums to examine ways to protect the lives and dignity of people in every culture. Because of our involvments in local societies, anthropologists could provide early warnings of abuses—for example, by reporting data to international human-rights organizations, and by joining the dialogue at international conferences. When there is a choice between defending human rights and defending cultural relativism, anthropologists should choose to protect and promote human rights. We cannot just be bystanders. 20

QUESTIONS FOR DISCUSSION AND WRITING:

1. How does the author define cultural relativism? Put her definition into your own words. Does she also define human rights? If not, how would you define the term?

2. Identify the author's thesis and explain how she uses the structure of the introduction to set up her argument. How does the author refute opposing views? Give specific examples and discuss the effectiveness of each. How persuasive is the example of female circumcision as a human rights issue, compared to honor killings and suicide?

3. What is your view of the concept of universal human rights that transcend cultural differences? Should anthropologists take a position rather than attempting to work from a value-free perspective? What are the benefits, and drawbacks, of such a position?

4. Write an essay analyzing this author's argument. You could focus on examples and evidence or perhaps on her strategies of refutation.

5. Research one of the topics generated by this essay, such as female circumcision, honor killings, genocide, or domestic violence. Alternatively, research the profession of anthropology, interviewing faculty on your campus about the issues raised in this essay.

"Asian Values": From Dynamos to Dominoes?

LUCIEN PYE

Lucien Pye was born in 1921 in Shansi Province, China. He received his BA from Carlton College and his MA and Ph.D. from Yale University. He served in the US Marine Corps during World War II and is a professor of political science and senior staff at the Center for International Studies at MIT. He has written extensively, in books and articles, about Asia and Asian politics. A former president of the American Political Science Association, his numerous publications include *Southeast Asia's Political Systems* (1967), *China: An Introduction* (1972), *The Dynamics of Chinese Politics* (1981), and *The Spirit of Chinese Politics* (1992). The essay that follows was published in *Culture Matters: How Values Shape Human Progress* (2000), edited by Lawrence E. Harrison and Samuel P. Huntington.

There is no example in history to match the dramatic reversals in fortune of the Asian economies during the second half of the twentieth century. Widely shared views about the fundamental cultural determinants of the Asian countries have been turned on their heads two times in four decades. First, the long-established assumption that Asian cultures lacked the capacity to generate economic growth was dramatically shattered in the 1970s and 1980s by the emergence of the "miracle" economies and especially the "four little tigers." As the region became the envy of the developing world, there was for a time much talk about an Asian model for economic development. But then, even more suddenly, in the late 1990s there came crises and collapses. First, Japan went into a severe recession, if not depression, that has lasted a full decade, and then the Southeast Asian and South Korean economies went from financial crises to more fundamental setbacks. A decade of hype about superior "Asian values" was tellingly deflated.[1]

After a decade of 10 percent annual growth rates, the Asian economies contracted 15 percent in 1998, their stock markets losing over half their value and their currencies 30 to 70 percent of their value. In 1996, some $96 billion in capital had flowed into the five countries of South Korea, Thailand, Malaysia, Indonesia, and Singapore, but in 1997 there was an outflow of over $150 billion. In one year, Indonesia's per capita GNP fell from $3,038 to about $600. The International Labor Organization estimated that some ten million Asians lost their jobs.[2]

Thus, in a matter of a year, the future of Asian economies became uncertain, and the trumpets heralding the greatness of Asian practices were silenced. Yet the collapse of the "miracles" should not end the discussion about "Asian values" but should ignite a more sober and critical analysis of the importance of values in producing sustainable economic development. Instead of the somewhat obnoxious nationalistic chest beating that went with a great deal of the Singapore and Malaysia version of the "debate" over Asian values, what is now called for is an explanation of how the same set of cultural values could have produced both the dynamos and the dominoes. The fact that Asia could go from the extremes of stagnation to dynamic economic growth and then to collapse raises a serious challenge as to the validity of cultural factors for explaining national development. Clearly, the fundamental cultures did not change.

To examine this significant problem, we need first to expose some of the exaggerated rhetoric about the supposed superiority of Asian values and seek a more realistic understanding of the economic performance of the Asian countries. We also need to clarify some points in the theories about Asian cultures and economic development, including another look at what Max Weber had to say about Confucianism and the development of capitalism.

I will then propose two hypotheses that can help explain how the same cultural values can produce such dramatically different results. The first is that the same values, operating, however, in quite different circumstances, can and usually will produce different effects. That is, the values of the Asian cultures have remained the same but the contexts have changed, and hence what had been positive outcomes became negative ones.

The second hypothesis is that cultural values are always clusters of values that at different times can be combined in different ways and thus produce different effects. This is a tricky argument that must be made with care to avoid the danger of reinforcing the criticism that it is always possible to find some cultural considerations to "explain" whatever has happened. Valid explanations require appropriately solid cultural variables, as well as precise linking of cause and effect.

Just the Facts, Not the Hype about "Miracle Economies"

It is easy to dismiss much of the rhetoric generated in the Asian values debate as just a manifestation of Asian triumphalism in the wake of success, which may have reflected a need to be heard over the din of the West's triumphalism about winning the Cold War. Yet the emergence of the "four little dragons" and the impending emergence of China as a potential new superpower, all in varying degrees emulating the Japanese model of state-guided capitalism, did provide the basis for claims of Asian distinctiveness. The combination of economic successes and authoritarian rule clearly suggested that the Asian countries had hit upon something deserving of attention. The concept of Asian values quickly became a shorthand explanation for economic achievements and a justification for authoritarian governmental practices.

The Asian values debate was further complicated by the fact that, in the 1970s, not just Asians but Westerners got carried away with the vision of "miracle" economies in Asia and of a West in decline. There is thus a need to put into perspective some of the exaggerated claims about how exceptional the Asian achievements actually were.

First, there was a strange tendency in some quarters to think of Japan, the leader of the miracle economies, as a Third World country that almost overnight rose to become the second largest economy in the world. In fact, Japan began to industrialize with the Meiji Restoration in the last third of the nineteenth century. The United States started to industrialize at about the same time. Japan was a significant industrial power by the time of the First World War and was able to take advantage of disruptions in the European economies to capture markets for consumer goods and especially textiles, first in Asia and Africa and then in Europe and America.

By the 1920s, Japan had the world's third largest navy and a merchant marine of equal magnitude. By the late 1930s, its economy was the third or fourth largest in the world, depending on whether its investments in Korea, Taiwan, and Manchuria were included. Its prewar auto industry was the match of most in Europe, and of course it produced a very impressive military airplane, the Zero. Those who see the emergence of a powerful Japan only in the 1960s tend to forget the challenge Japan posed in the Pacific War.

The pre-miracle backwardness of other parts of Asia has also been overstated. It has been much too easy to treat Emperor Qianlong as a buffoon because of his arrogant letter to King George III, declaring that "we have never valued ingenious articles, nor do we have the slightest need of your country's manufactures." Yet at the time of his reign, the Chinese economy was in fact larger than Great Britain's. Indeed, before the Industrial Revolution transformed the world economy, and when agriculture was still king, the huge agricultural populations of Asia produced a disproportionate share of the world's economic output. At the end of the eighteenth century, Asia as a whole registered 37 percent of the world's economic output, and for all the hype about their miracle economies, by the mid-1990s Asia's share had dropped back to 31 percent. The outlook before the disasters struck was that Asia would not regain its earlier share until 2010.

What had impressed people in the last few decades was of course the growth rates of the Asian economies. With Asian economies boasting 10 percent rates and the West 3 percent or less, Asians were held in awe. But attention was all on the percentage figures and not on the net growth in absolute terms. For all the excitement about a "decade of 10 percent growth" in the Chinese economy, the fact remains that not during a single year of that decade did the growth produce an addition to the Chinese economy that matched the net growth of the U.S. economy for that year. Thus in every year in what was called its decade of growth, China was not catching up but was actually falling further behind. The inescapable fact of arithmetic is that 10 percent of a $600 billion economy is less than a third of 2.5 percent of a $7.5 trillion economy—$60 billion compared to $187.5 billion. The moral is that focusing on growth percentage figures without regard to the base numbers can produce seriously false impressions.

I make these points not to belittle the accomplishments of the Asians but rather to counter a tendency to think in magical terms about miracles. It is true that there has been a historic transformation in living conditions as Asian households benefited from the growth rates. For the Chinese, going from less than $100 per capita income in 1985 to $360 in 1998 has meant that now there is more than one color television set per household, whereas then fewer than one in five households owned one; whereas 7 percent had refrigerators then, 73 percent do now.[3] There have indeed been manifest improvements in living conditions, and the Chinese are justified in believing that their children's future will be brighter still.

What Max Weber Really Said

Having clarified the facts to some degree, I now turn to examine the theoretical considerations in the analysis of the relationship of Asian cultural values and economic development. As a preface, however, I will review what Max Weber had to say on that subject. Weber, of course, remains the unsurpassed master of the cultural origins of capitalism. As everyone knows, he found those origins in the Protestant ethic, which, on being popularized, has unfortunately come down to little more than a version of the Boy Scout oath, a banal listing of such virtues as hard work, dedication, honesty, thrift, trustworthiness, willingness to delay gratification, and respect for education. Weber, in fact, saw the cultural origins of capitalism in far more complex terms. In particular, he was intrigued with two paradoxes.

The first was the historical fact that monks, devoted solely to otherworldly considerations and living totally ascetic lives in their monasteries, created extraordinarily efficient organizations for making worldly profits. The second paradox was that the critical actors in creating capitalism were Calvinists, who believed in predestination, and not those Christians who believed that virtuous living and good deeds would be rewarded in the hereafter. Weber recognized that an account book approach to rewards and punishments got people off too easily, whereas with predestination there was a profound sense of psychic insecurity that would drive people to grasp for any possible sign that they might belong among the "elect." The key drive was psychic anxiety.

In his detailed analysis of Chinese culture and in his comparison of Confucianism with Puritanism, Weber emphasized the degree to which the ideal of the Confucian gentleman stressed "adjustment to the outside, to the conditions of the 'world.' "[4] Confucian culture idealized harmony without producing any intense inner tensions or psychic insecurities; none of the problems with "nerves," as Weber puts it, that Europeans have—a reference to the problems that Freud analyzed.

Weber goes into great detail describing Chinese character as being well adjusted, as having "unlimited patience" and "controlled politeness," of being "insensitive to monotony" and having "a capacity for uninterrupted hard work." But these, he insists, were not the qualities that could spontaneously produce capitalism. At the same time, Weber was remarkably prescient in recognizing that they were qualities that could make for great skill in emulating capitalistic practices. He wrote that "the Chinese in all probability would be quite capable, *probably more capable than the Japanese,* of assimilating capitalism which has technically and economically been fully developed in the modern culture area."[5]

Thus the criticism that the recent economic successes of the Confucian countries disprove Weber is an incorrect reading of his theories. Weber foresaw that China might indeed be able to emulate capitalistic practices in time. In fact in many ways Weber shared the Enlightenment's positive views about China. The historic fact remains, however, that the Asian successes came about through access to the world economic system and not as the result of internal, autonomous developments.

The Paradoxical Relationship between Confucian Values and Economic Behavior

Considering the assimilation of capitalism by Confucian cultures, we come upon some paradoxes that are the match of those in Max Weber's theories about the economic behavior of monks and Calvinists. For example, Confucianism formally placed the merchant near the bottom of the social scale, below even the peasant. However, as a consequence of having to live with this stigma, Chinese merchants had no choice but to excel at making money. True, they could educate their sons to pass the imperial examinations and become mandarin officials, but that would mean the successful business would last only one generation. Otherwise, they had no alternative but to specialize in a skill that the Confucian mandarin-scholars despised. As marginalized people in their own society, their situation was somewhat analogous to that of the Jews in feudal Europe.

A second paradox, and one that is troubling to Americans raised on Horatio Alger stories extolling hard work as the sure path from "rags to riches," is that Confucianism scorned hard work and all forms of physical exertion while idealizing leisure and effortlessness. The Confucian gentleman wore long fingernails to prove that he did not have to work with his hands. Taoism, of course, reinforced this view by elevating to the highest philosophical level the principle of *wu-wei,* or non-effort, of accomplishing things with the minimum expenditure of energy. In Chinese military thinking, the ideal was to win battles not by exerting prodigious effort but by compelling the opponent to exhaust himself. As far as I know, no other culture is the match of the Chinese in idealizing effortlessness and decrying the folly of hard physical work. For the Chinese, Sisyphus is not a tragedy but a hilarious joke. Certainly in Chinese culture, hard work is not a prime value in itself but only an imperative dictated by necessity.

Instead of idealizing hard work, the Chinese emphasize the importance of "good luck," the likelihood of which can be increased by proper ritual acts. Again, it is Taoism with its concept of the Tao, the Way, or the forces of nature and history, that gives a philosophical foundation to the basic Chinese view that much of life is determined by forces external to the actors involved. Some people are more skilled than others in flowing with the current and thus being blessed with good luck. Others foolishly buck the tide and are born losers. This stress on good fortune does not, however, produce a fatalistic approach to life—there are always things that can be done to increase the chance of good luck, and if things turn out badly, it was only bad luck, which it is hoped will change in time.

This stress on the role of fortune makes for an outward-looking and highly reality-oriented approach to life, not an introspective one. People need to be ever alert to exploit opportunistically anything that might improve their chances for good fortune. This appreciation of the prime importance of external forces makes for extreme sensitivity to objective circumstances, to the lay of the land, and to the importance of timing in taking action. The focus of decision making is on judging carefully the situation and exploiting any advantages.

Thus, what might seem at first an otherworldly emphasis on luck has the paradoxical effect of instilling a vivid appreciation of objective realities. This orientation has made the Chinese very appreciative of the character and structure of markets. Markets are not a theoretical abstraction for Chinese but are vivid and dynamic realities.

This readiness to think in terms of clearly conceptualized markets explains a critical difference between Chinese and Western capitalism. Western capitalism is technology driven — build a better mousetrap, and people will come to your doorstep. But the driving force in Chinese capitalism has always been to find out who needs what and to satisfy that market need. Western firms seek to improve their products, strengthen their organizational structures, and work hard to get name recognition. Chinese entrepreneurs try to diversify, avoid getting a reputation for producing just a prime product, and always be ready to change production in response to what the market wants. Americans know that they are being flooded by consumer goods from Taiwan and China, but they do not know the names of the companies producing those goods.

Although scorning physical exertion and hard work, Confucianism upheld the importance of self-improvement, and hence the culture respected achievement motivation. The concept of "need for achievement" as formulated by David McClelland describes an important Chinese cultural value. McClelland demonstrated that countries that have had success in development also rated high in "need for achievement," as measured in such ways as the motivations taught in children's books. Every attempt to measure need for achievement among Chinese people confirms what any general, impressionistic understanding of Chinese culture would suggest—that the Chinese rank high in such a drive. Chinese children are taught the importance of striving for success and the shame of not measuring up to parental expectations.

Yet, paradoxically, Chinese culture also stresses the rewards of dependency, a psychological orientation that goes against the grain of the Horatio Alger ideal of the self-reliant individual. The paradoxical combination of achievement and dependency was central to the traditional Chinese socialization practices, which sought to teach the child early that disciplined conformity to the wishes of others was the best way to security and that being "different" was dangerous. The result was a positive acceptance of dependency.

The combination of achievement and dependency dictated an implicit goal of the traditional Chinese socialization process, which was to strive to resolve achievement needs by diligently carrying out the assigned role within the family, and hence by being properly dependent. On this score, Chinese and Japanese family norms significantly differed. In China, achievement was rewarded within the family, and the Confucian duties of the sons to the father, and of the younger and older brothers to each other, were lifetime obligations. The tradition was thus inward looking, and there was a basic instinct to distrust people in the non-family world.[6] In Japan, however, the tests of achievement in both samurai and merchant families were in terms of competition against outside parties and forces. Moreover, a younger brother could strike out on his own; if successful, he become a *gosenzo*—the head of a new family line.[7]

The balancing of the need for achievement and the blessings of dependency is closely related to the operations of trust and the dynamics of personal relationships that provide the linkages that make possible social networks. In the case of Chinese culture, the bonds of family extend outward to the clan and then on to more general ties of *guanxi,* or personal connections based on shared identities. What is most significant about the Chinese practices of *guanxi* for economic development is that parties are expected to share mutual obligations even though they may not personally know each other well. It is enough that they were classmates or schoolmates, came from the same town or even province, belonged to the same military outfit, or otherwise had a common element in their backgrounds. The bases of *guanxi* ties are thus objective considerations that others can recognize as existing, not primarily the subjective sentiments of the parties involved.

The comparable Japanese ties of *kankei* are far more subjective and are based on deep feelings of indebtedness and obligation—the importance of *on* and *giri*. Outsiders can assume that two Chinese with a shared connection will have a *guanxi* relationship, whereas the Japanese ties depend more on personal experiences.

The Cultural Factor in Economic Behavior

As stated earlier, the central hypothesis of this essay is that the same values will produce different consequences in different circumstances. The key values of reliance on social networks *(guanxi)*, of taking the long-run view, of seeking market share rather than profits, of delaying gratification, and of aggressively saving for the future all have different consequences according to the state of the economy and its level of development.

The rules of family trust and of *guanxi* meant that in the earlier and more unstable political environment, Chinese enterprises were largely limited to family operations. Distrusting outsiders, family firms could not expand by having more branches than they had sons to manage them.[8] However, as the political environment in East and Southeast Asia became more stable, networking rapidly expanded along the lines of *guanxi* connections. Banking operations in the region in particular tended to be highly personalized and to follow the chain of personal connections. Unger makes the interesting argument that the overseas Chinese practices of networking gave them a form of "social capital" that was not the basis for democracy as Robert Putnam's social capital is, but rather a form of social capital that can provide the basis for economic development. Focusing on Thailand, Unger shows how the Chinese relied upon their connections to facilitate the flow of capital so as to make Thailand an economic "miracle."[9]

Guanxi is also fundamental in explaining the astonishingly rapid expansion of overseas Chinese investments in coastal China. With Deng Xiaoping's opening to the outside world, people from Hong Kong, Taiwan, and the Chinese communities in Southeast Asia went back to their ancestral hometowns and villages in China, and they were instantly accepted and encouraged to invest in the development of the local economies. Hong Kong people went into Guangdong, Taiwanese into Fujien, and others into Shanghai to set up joint ventures, usually with the local political leadership, for manufacturing export items. The result was the spectacular expansion of village and township enterprises. The deals were made on highly personalized bases, not legalistic ones. The overseas Chinese investors sought all manner of favored arrangements, from multiple years of tax exemptions to fixed low wages.

Thus for a time the tradition of informal networking worked wonders in moving capital rapidly into China for setting up new enterprises far faster than legalistic contractual negotiations could have. Even foreign bankers were caught up in the spirit of what they took to be Asian values and were prepared to make loans based on winks and nods from Chinese officials. Yet in time the lack of transparency or firm legal understandings led inevitably to crony capitalism and widespread corruption. The lack of legal foundations for business transactions, which may have facilitated deals when conditions were good, also meant that there were no clear procedures for handling bankruptcies if things went bad.

The tradition of networking in Japan set the stage for the pattern of close informal ties among businessmen, bureaucrats, and politicians that came to be called "Japan Inc." The patterns of mutual obligation and particularistic ties meant that huge amounts of credit could flow with minimum need for formal accounting or checks on the soundness of the projects. For a time, it was assumed that just as long as the state guidance "got the prices right," there was little need to worry about insider dealings and the possibilities for corruption. But then came the shocks: The Japanese elite were not as upright as they had been made out to be. The practice of close cooperation between government and business meant that when it came time for the state to engage in greater regulating of financial institutions, it seemed powerless in dealing with its former partners.

The practices of networking also encouraged the idea that making short-term checks on the profitability of enterprises was unnecessary. Rather, it was desirable to take a "long view" and seek to capture an ever larger share of the market. The supposed virtue of such long-term perspectives was reinforced by the cultural propensity to see great virtue in delayed gratification and the willingness to suffer in the short run in the expectation that in time there would be greater rewards for steadfastness. For a time, when all the economies were on the rise, there were benefits to be gained from this approach, and the successes of the Japanese made many Westerners believe that the Japanese had hit upon a superior strategy for producing wealth. Consequently, many elsewhere in Asia sought to emulate the Japanese drive to capture market share and to postpone worries about profitability.

In time, however, the approach proved disastrous because in- 35
debtedness piled up, and the compulsive drive to capture a greater share of the market produced gross excesses in capacity.

The lack of transparency and legal norms in bank lending allowed for huge expansions in loans based on unrealistic expectations of what expanding production might bring. It turned out that the approach provided no effective checks on whether capital was being allocated rationally. In industry after industry, surplus capacity became the norm. It was strange that the world did not recognize that a crisis was in the making in 1995 when a leading Korean *chaebol* declared with exuberant hubris that it planned to invest $2.5 billion in a new steel complex, at a time when the world was already awash in more steel than it could use.

The Western accounting practice of quarterly profit-and-loss statements provides managers and investors with critical feedback as to whether capital is being efficiently allocated and thus provides a steering mechanism to guide the invisible hand of the market. The combination of a drive for greater market share above all else, a fixation on only the long run, and the notion that it is heroic to suffer the pains of delayed gratification—all essential Asian values—inspired economically useful behavior during the initial stages of economic development, but the combination led in time to serious problems of overcapacity and numerous bubble economies.

Indeed, nearly all the East Asian countries have had major real estate bubbles. In Japan it was said that real estate prices had reached such ridiculous heights that the Imperial Palace grounds in Tokyo were worth more than all the real estate in California. It was not just uninformed people who believed such talk; many supposedly serious Japanese bankers also believed it. In Shanghai, cranes were everywhere in the Putung district putting up skyscrapers—some Chinese liked to say that the crane had become the Chinese national bird. But the buildings finished in 1997 have only 15 percent occupancy, and those finished in 1998 have even fewer tenants. Buildings were still going up as investors felt that they must take the long view and bravely suffer the pains of delayed gratification.

Another dramatic example of how a cultural value can operate usefully under some conditions but then become a source of disaster is the East Asian propensity to save. The Chinese have one of the world's highest savings rates, some 30 percent in recent years, providing much of the capital for economic growth at the start of the reforms. The state banks welcomed the flow of savings that grew as prosperity spread, for they provided the funds necessary for bank lending to the state-owned enterprises (SOEs). But the SOEs have now become huge white elephants and the state banks have no hope of ever recovering their "loans." What keeps the system going is the citizens' propensity to save. The banks could no more honor the private accounts of the savers than the SOEs could honor their debts. However, as long as the people have nowhere else to put their money, the state banks will get it, and an otherwise failed system will manage to stay afloat.

The same propensity to save initially provided bountiful capital for the postwar Japanese economic recovery, but what was a virtue is now making it hard for Japan to get out of its prolonged recession. Japanese officials find it frustratingly difficult to generate a rise in demand that might pull the economy out of its stagnation because the Japanese people, with something of a peasant mentality, believe that if the times are bad, they should postpone consumption and increase savings. Even if fiscal and monetary policies are able to put more money into people's pockets, they refuse to spend more and may even try to save more in anticipation of further troubles ahead.

Getting the Context Right in Cultural Analysis

Although the story is too complex to tell in this essay, it is clear   40
that the ups and downs of the Asian economies have created serious problems for the advocates of Asian values. But these developments do not challenge a more sophisticated understanding of the relationship of culture to economic growth. Problems arise when an attempt is made to jump all the way from generalized cultural characterizations to economic outcomes without taking into account all the intervening variables and the situational contexts. It is thus unscientific to try to draw up a universal list of positive and negative cultural values for economic development. What may be positive in some circumstances can be quite counterproductive under other conditions.

Moreover, our current state of knowledge leaves us with many mysteries about the dynamics of economic development. Our theories do not provide us with sharp enough cause-and-effect relationships to make it possible to assign definite weights to specific cultural variables. Leaving aside all the general considerations such as geography, climate, resource endowment, capacity of the government, and the wisdom of its public policies, the general category of economic behavior is so broad as to make it impossible to be rigorous in evaluating the significance of any specific cultural value. Some behavior is tied to individual conduct, such as the initiative essential for entrepreneurship, while other behavior is more collective, defining the character and structure of the general society. We need to be somewhat humble in ascribing precise weights to cultural variables. We know that they are important, but exactly how important at any particular time is hard to judge. We are dealing with clouds, not clocks, with general approximations, not precise cause-and-effect relationships.[10]

Thus, as we pull these threads of analysis together, it is clear that the advocates of Asian values have grossly overstated the wonders of the Asian economies and the helplessness of the West. Nevertheless, it is true that Asia will continue to modernize and, in doing so, will produce forms and practices that are distinctive. This should not be surprising, for the West as the leader in modernization has not produced a homogeneous culture—there are dynamic differences among all the leading Western societies. Cultural differences will endure, and in most cases there is little point in trying to say which cultures are superior and which ones inferior. Their strengths and weaknesses will be in different areas and will involve different practices. Economic development is not a single event but an ongoing process of history, so there will be many ups and downs in all countries. Organizational forms that were effective in exploiting one state of technology can turn out to be liabilities with newer technologies.

This having been said, it is true that several of the East Asian economies have recovered more rapidly than many expected, and the recovery doubtlessly reflects in part the same cultural factors that contributed to the rapid growth of recent decades.

Notes

1. Needless to say, many other factors were important in causing the Asian economic crises, including mistakes by the International Monetary Fund (IMF) and the U.S. Treasury, as well as the actions of Western investors. For our purposes, however, we shall address only the cultural factor.

2. The numbers are from Nayan Chanda, "Surges of Depression" *Far Eastern Economic Review*, December 31, 1998, 22.

3. *Economist*, January 2, 1999, 56.

4. Max Weber, Trans., Ed., Hans H. Gerth, *The Religion of China: Confucianism and Taoism*. (Glencoe, IL: Free Press, 1951), 235.

5. Weber, 248. Italics added. Contrary to Weber, Robert Bellah has demonstrated that the Japanese do have some cultural traditions that match the Protestant ethic. See his *Tokugawa Religion: The Values of Pre-Industrial Japan*. Glencoe, IL: Free Press, 1957.

6. Francis Fukuyama suggests that a key to China's slow economic development was precisely this lack of trust for non-family members,

in contrast to the Japanese, who learned that they would have to deal with non-family actors. See Fukuyama, *Trust: The Social Virtues and the Creation of Prosperity.* (New York: Free Press, 1995).

7. For a comparison of the influences of family patterns on East Asian developments, see Lucian W. Pye, *Asian Power and Politics: The Cultural Dimensions of Authority.* (Cambridge: Harvard University Press, 1985), ch. 3.

8. The advantages and limitations of family firms are not limited to Chinese cultural practices, but were also central to the successes of the Rothschild family, with the five brothers operating at the five bases in London, Paris, Frankfurt, Vienna, and Naples. See Niall Ferguson, *The World's Banker.* (London: Weidenfeld & Nicolson, 1998).

9. Danny Unger, *Building Social Capital in Thailand.* (New York: Cambridge University Press, 1998), esp. ch. 1.

10. For a sophisticated examination of culture and economic development, see Peter Berger and Hsian-Huang Michael Hsiao, Eds., *In Search of an East Asian Model.* (New Brunswick, NJ: Transaction, 1998).

QUESTIONS FOR DISCUSSION AND WRITING

1. This essay discusses a number of "Asian values." Summarize these values as outlined by the author.

2. The first paragraph summarizes the "reversal of fortune" in the Asian economies over the recent past. After his synopsis, Pye ends his first paragraph with an inference that the economic reverses contradict notions about "Asian values." Does this assertion seem warranted from the information in the introduction?

3. Pye refers to Max Weber's discussion of Confucian and Puritan values. Do you find his argument that "psychic anxiety" is a force in Puritanism, but not apparently in Confucianism, persuasive? Explain why or why not.

4. What is your assessment of Pye's assertions about values that scorn unnecessary hard work and favor effortlessness and good luck? Assess his subsequent conclusion that these values lead to an opportunistic approach to life as well as a focus on external forces. How does your own ethnicity or value system affect your view of these assertions?

5. Compare and contrast Pye's assertions about Chinese and Japanese values with regard to social networks. According to the author, what are the economic implications of these connections?

6. Pye notes that "cultural values can operate usefully under some conditions but then become a source for disaster." Discuss the examples he uses to support this claim.

7. Write a paragraph summarizing your sense of Confucian values and one summarizing your understanding of Puritan values. Share your summaries with classmates and discuss the ways in which these values are, or are not, a part of your own values or of dominant culture American values.

8. Research the philosophies of Confucianism, Taoism, and Buddhism. Present your findings by writing a comparative analysis of these approaches, developing an informative Web site, or giving a PowerPoint presentation to your class. For the latter two suggestions you could consider working with a peer or in a small group.

Vietnam Tourism

The following photograph was taken at Hai Van pass, Vietnam, in September 2001. Under a communist propaganda billboard a worker is completing installation of a billboard promoting tourism, reflecting a transformation from collective agriculture to private enterprise. The words on the billboard read "Pushing up industrialization and modernization."

Under a communist propaganda billboard, a Vietnamese worker puts the finishing touches on a billboard promoting tourism at Hai Van pass, Vietnam, on September 2, 2001. Today's Vietnam is a far cry from the visions of the three communist theoreticians: Marx, Lenin, and Ho Chi Minh, and far from what it was just fifteen years ago. Collectivized agriculture is gone. Private business, once banned, has become the economy's main motive force, with state planners increasingly sidelined.   (AP/WIDE WORLD PHOTOS)

QUESTIONS FOR DISCUSSION AND WRITING

1. Analyze the composition of this photograph. What point do you think it makes?
2. Discuss the irony conveyed in this juxtaposition of an old communist propaganda billboard with tourism promotion. What does it say in view of the legacy of the Vietnam War, communism, capitalism, and the changing face of Vietnamese society?
3. Research contemporary Vietnamese culture and society with regard to its transformation from an agrarian focus to private business ownership.
4. Research tourism campaigns from other countries. What are the common themes and appeals? In what ways are the tourism campaigns culture-specific, either to the culture being represented or to the cultures being sought as tourists?

Chapter Three: Connections

1. Compare representations of women in burkas with other images or stories about women in this text or images in the news. Do any common themes or issues emerge?
2. What might Lucian Pye say about the role of cultural values in adapting to a changing economic context? Discuss Pye's assertions in view of the information on Puritanism in the Appendix, or research the writings of Confucius to explore Pye's premises in this essay.
3. Is the description of Buddhism as practiced in Myanmar (Burma) consistent with your understanding of Buddhism from the selection in the Appendix?
4. Compare and contrast the values articulated in "My Country and People" with those of other cultural groups as discussed in another selection from the Appendix or from this chapter—such as conventionally "Puritan" values, fundamentalist values from any religion, or what you perceive to be capitalistic or Western values.

5. Compare and contrast the role of religion in Burmese life with the interplay between religion and society in a selection from this chapter discussing the Middle East in Women and Society, Issues in Globalization, or America: Perceptions at Home and Abroad. Consider, for example, religious motifs in popular culture as discussed by Nagala in this chapter.

6. What similarities and contrasts do you find between Fluehr-Lobban's position and that of authors who are concerned about cultural autonomy?

7. Compare and contrast Harman's discussion of technology's influence on society with images in this chapter and others.

8. Compare the ways in which authorities in Iran are dealing with rock music, as discussed in Pearl's essay, and the opinions outlined in *Islam Online* regarding dealing with American cultural products.

Chapter Three: End-of-Chapter Assignments

1. Write a paragraph summarizing your sense of Confucian values and one summarizing your understanding of Puritan values, based on the Pye selection, the Appendix resources, or your own information or research. Share your summaries with classmates and discuss common themes and differences; also consider developing an informational PowerPoint presentation or Web site documenting your findings.

2. Research the philosophies of Confucianism, Taoism, and Buddhism. Present your findings by writing a comparative analysis of these approaches, developing an informative Web site, or giving a PowerPoint presentation to your class. For the latter two suggestions you could consider working with a peer or in a small group.

3. Research the fatwa and its role in religious and cultural instruction or regulation of behavior. Is it comparable to a bishop's pastoral letter or a pope's encyclical? Does it carry the authority of a pope's edict Ex Cathedra, in which the pope is held to be infallible? Are contradictory fatwas ever issued? What topics generally concern them?

4. Research current debate among anthropologists and other academics regarding the tension between cultural relativism and universalism. You could focus the discussion on specific topics, such as ritual female circumcision, honor killings, capital pun-

ishment, or some other cultural practice that has challenged academic policies of noninterference.

5. Research the current state of a certain type of technology (e.g., cellular phones, computers, Internet connections) in a society other than the United States. Alternatively, consider the growth of technology industries in countries such as India and Ireland.

6. Research the current status of tourism in Communist and formerly Communist countries including those in Asia and the former Soviet Union.

7. Research popular culture, particularly music and film, in a country outside of the United States. Consider focusing on a particular industry, such as the film industry in India and the growth of "Bollywood."

Chapter Three: Web Sites for Further Exploration

The Hindu Universe
http://www.hindunet.org/
Arab News: Saudi Arabia English Language Daily
http://www.arabnews.com
IslamOnline
http://www.islamonline.org/English/index.shtml
Buddhist Information and Education
http://www.buddhanet.net/
The Vatican
http://www.vatican.va/phome_en.htm
United Methodist Church
http://www.unitedmethodist.org/
Judaism 101
http://www.jewfaq.org/
Submission (to God), Islamic site
http://www.submission.org/
Burma/Myanmar
http://www.burmaproject.org/
http://www.myanmars.net/
China
http://englishcenter.sina.com/
http://english.people.com.cn/

China News Digest, Global Edition
http://www.cnd.org/Global/
Vietnam
http://www.vnagency.com.vn/Public/newse.asp
Asia Week
http://www.asiaweek.com/

ISSUES
IN GLOBALIZATION

INTRODUCTION

In Chapter Three we examined some perspectives on individual cultures, observing in particular the ways in which assumptions, values,
and beliefs are expressed in cultural practices. We also noted concerns about the encroachment of certain practices on other cultures.
In this chapter we examine selections that focus on cultural, political, and economic issues in a larger global context, with special attention to the integration of economic and political systems across
national boundaries and identities through globalization. This international discussion assesses some of the benefits and perils of increasing economic interdependence.

The readings in this chapter grapple with defining globalization,
generally describing it as the integration and interdependence of
economic systems across borders and cultures; and with assessing
the implications of globally integrated economies, technology, and
cultures. Much of the current debate considers whether globalization
will foster development and higher standards of living, as its proponents suggest, or whether it will increase exploitation of labor, as
others argue, or be moderated by sound policy and democratic principles, as UN Secretary-General Kofi Annan hopes. We then examine
global consequences of this integration and turn to discussions
about the nature of culture clash on a global scale, exploring both
alarmist and more modulated perspectives. Core writers in this area
such as Samuel Huntington and Edward Said outline key concerns in
the current debates.

The texts and images in this chapter include highly argumentative essays, rebuttals, documented research, informative exposition
with implied thesis statements, and Web sites that persuade as well

as inform. These selections are by authors from diverse cultures and belief systems; they range from a basic definition essay to the extensive Huntington essay to an undergraduate research paper to a speech by the Secretary General of the United Nations. They include academic discourse and journalistic accounts as well as an overview of the culture clash hypothesis and a response.

We begin with an image that seems to exemplify the idea of a global village: A Samburu warrior with a mobile telephone. We then turn to an essay defining globalization, in order to understand a core term in the discussion and to contextualize the essays that follow. Epping's brief essay, "What is Globalization?", is from his *Beginner's Guide to the World Economy,* but it conveys a point of view about globalization that is not universally shared. In the next selection, "The Global Village Finally Arrives," Pico Iyer draws together threads of cultural and economic integration, describing a global cultural exchange that he terms "a common multiculturalism—call it Planet Hollywood."

An author expressing reservations about the effects of globalization on developing nations is UN Secretary-General Kofi Annan. Focusing on political issues of globalization, he notes in "The Politics of Globalization" that economic interdependence does not in and of itself prevent conflict; according to Annan, politics are both the root of globalization's problems and also the potential solution, and he argues that "prosperity and peace are political achievements" and not simply the consequences of trade or technology. The next essay, "Blood Diamonds" by Greg Campbell, graphically details the interaction of global trade, local warfare, and international terrorism by discussing the lucrative international trade in diamonds from regions of conflict to the world markets, with profits from war-ravaged Sierra Leone ultimately funding terrorist organizations such as al Qaeda. In the next selection, offering a potentially positive outcome of global market forces, a program of international aid organization Oxfam discusses its development project in Laos, working with women to generate income and preserve their traditional weaving crafts while considering how and whether to enter the global marketplace.

As global media have fostered the global village described in the Iyer essay, so has the Internet fostered the globalization of ideas, some of which are repugnant to those who confront them. In the next essay, "Racism and the Internet: The Need for Global Consensus," German national Philipp Schloter, studying and working in the United States, addresses this concern. Schloter calls for implementation of a global fundamental standard for Internet discourse that depends on international consensus.

We then turn to a core reading in the field, Samuel Huntington's "A Clash of Civilizations?" Although it is one of the longer essays in this chapter, this selection presents a hypothesis that many other scholars and commentators cite in their own discussions. Huntington suggests that "the clash of civilizations will dominate global politics" and that most major conflicts will be cultural. For Huntington, the conflict between cultures is writ large, at the level of whole civilizations rather than the more commonly considered national boundaries and identities. Huntington argues that "civilizations are differentiated from each other by history, language, culture, tradition, and, most important, religion. The people of different civilizations have different views on the relations between God and human, the individual and the group, the citizen and the state, parents and children, husband and wife, as well as different views of the relative importance of rights and responsibilities, liberty and authority, equality and hierarchy." Given a premise of such profound differences, one can understand why Huntington draws the conclusions he does about the nature of future conflict.

The late Palestinian scholar Edward Said (pronounced Sigheed'), however, writing in *The Nation*, takes issue with Huntington's hypothesis and the broad brushstrokes with which he paints his theory. In his essay "A Clash of Ignorance," Said, who had been a frequent commentator on Middle Eastern affairs, responds to Huntington and suggests that putting diverse groups and cultures into large catch-all categories misses complexity in the issues and may even lead to drawing invalid conclusions.

Our last two selections, the Web sites of the World Trade Organization and Global Trade Watch, offer divergent views on globalization and on organizations that either promote global trade or see themselves as observers concerned about global trade and its effects on workers and societies. These and related Web sites offer a starting point to expand your discussion and enlarge your frame of reference for understanding the benefits and costs of global economic, political, and cultural exchange. Whether the discussion is framed in terms of opening up markets, developing multinational corporations, finding large supplies of labor to fill jobs (or to exploit, depending on whom you poll), exporting culture, outsourcing jobs, or increasing communication, it is a discussion focused on enormous economic, political, social, and cultural shifts. As with other topics in this text, take advantage of international Web sites, newspapers, and other media for additional and ongoing research to help address the complexities of global issues. The Web sites included here and in other chapters provide a starting point for this research.

Samburu Warrior

SALLY WIENER GROTTA

The mobile or cellular telephone, a staple of Western urban life, now pervades societies worldwide, as also discussed in Chapter Three ("In Kabary, the Point is to Avoid the Point"). This photograph of a Samburu Warrior was taken in Kenya in 1995.

This photograph of a Samburu warrior was taken in Kenya in 1995. (SALLY WIENER GROTTA; CORBIS/BETTMANN)

QUESTIONS FOR DISCUSSION AND WRITING

1. In view of the previous readings on crossing cultures and those in this chapter on globalization, what is your response to this image? In what ways does it confirm, or contradict, assertions made in the selections you have studied to date?

2. What point do you think this image makes? What makes the image noteworthy enough to photograph?

3. Study the composition of this photograph (e.g., elements included, placement, foreground, background) and discuss what these contribute to the photograph's effect.

4. In what ways does this image capture an overall theme of this text or any of its chapters?

5. Research the current status of technology, whether communication, computer, or media, in Kenya or in another African nation and share your findings with peers, perhaps collaborating on a project that presents findings on a number of nations or societies.

What is Globalization?

RANDY CHARLES EPPING

Randy Charles Epping, an American based in Switzerland and fluent in six languages, has worked in international finance and investment banking; he is currently with a Switzerland-based consulting company. Epping has degrees from the University of Notre Dame and the University of Paris–Sorbonne and a master's degree in international relations from Yale University. The selection that follows is from his book *A Beginner's Guide to the World Economy* (1992; revised and updated 2001), a readable handbook dedicated to economic literacy.

The American actress Joan Crawford once said, "The only thing worse than being talked about is not being talked about." Countries that have seen their borders opened by the forces of global trade and finance could say something similar: the only thing worse than opening your economy to the world is *not* opening it.

Many critics of globalization say that it is a major cause of poverty, that it opens up developing countries to exploitation by big foreign corporations, and that it results in people in wealthy countries losing jobs when cheaper foreign imports put their companies out of business. They also criticize foreigners for "buying up" local companies and creating a homogenized world run by multinational corporations not accountable to any government.

Capitalism, it must be said, is by no means a perfect system. People do lose jobs, and some people do earn a lot more money than others. In centrally planned socialist economies, jobs and income are guaranteed at fixed levels for life; in a capitalist economy nothing is guaranteed, especially not equality of income. But it also must be said that, despite all its faults, capitalism is the best system we have for eliminating poverty and creating wealth. One need only look at the crumbling economies of Eastern Europe to see that socialism, despite its claim to distribute the wealth evenly, ends up essentially with little wealth to distribute to anyone.

Globalization, for all its faults, helps economies grow—which means improving standards of living for billions of people around the world. The UN Human Development Index, an indicator of literacy, longevity, and standard of living in countries around the world, shows that during the last years of the twentieth century, more than a billion people around the world escaped absolute poverty through economic growth. Those countries that embraced globalization, especially those in the Third World, have enjoyed rates of growth that were, on average, 50 percent higher than those with closed borders.

For many people in developing countries, economic growth is the ultimate antipoverty weapon. It means access to clean water, a safe house to live in, and a chance to educate their children to prepare for a better future. Countries with expanding economies also enjoy greater political freedom, more social spending, and higher standards of living, for both rich and poor. 5

Even in the United States, the economic boom of the 1990s was fueled in no small part by globalization. Open borders allowed new ideas and technology to flow in freely from around the globe, fueling an increase in productivity. Living standards went up when consumers and businesses were able to buy from countries that had a *comparative advantage,* producing better-made products at better prices. Free trade has also kept local producers on their toes, making them more efficient and forcing them to keep their own prices in line with those from other countries. In addition, export-oriented jobs generally pay more than those that are dependent on the local economy.

Globalization, it must be noted, does benefit some people more than others. Access to technology and capital has created many new jobs for workers in developing countries, and those countries and companies with technology and capital to sell have also benefited enormously from globalization. For example, millions of information technology jobs have been created in Ireland and India—not just in Silicon Valley.

Those left out, especially the high-salary workers in developed countries with little or no education, have seen millions of jobs taken away by newly productive Third World workers, and until they get the training and education they need to find new jobs, they will justifiably blame the world economy for their loss.

QUESTIONS FOR DISCUSSION AND WRITING

1. After reading this selection, what do you understand to be the meaning of the term "globalization"?
2. Why do you think the author gave an extended explanation of the term rather than a brief definition?

3. The title of this selection suggests that the author is defining a term. To what degree do you think this selection is an argument? What is the author's position on globalization?

4. Write a paragraph summarizing your understanding of the term based on this reading. Alternatively, write a definition of globalization with a stance or point of view that differs from Epping's.

The Global Village Finally Arrives

PICO IYER

Pico Iyer was born in England in 1957 to Indian parents. He grew up in California and was educated at Eton and Oxford in England and then at Harvard University. Iyer is the author of six books: *The Global Soul* (2001), *Tropical Classical* (1998), *Cuba and the Night* (1996), *Falling Off the Map* (1994), *The Lady and the Monk* (1992), and *Video Night in Kathmandu* (1989). A correspondent for *Time* magazine for a number of years, Iyer has also published in *Harpers,* the *New Yorker,* the *New York Review of Books,* and many other publications around the world. He has described himself as a "multinational soul on a multicultural globe." The essay that follows, written for *Time* in 1993, uses the term "global village," popularized by Marshall McLuhan, who referred to the contracting of the world into essentially a large village through communication media.

Dec. 2, 1993

This is the typical day of a relatively typical soul in today's diversified world. I wake up to the sound of my Japanese clock radio, put on a T-shirt sent me by an uncle in Nigeria and walk out into the street, past German cars, to my office. Around me are English-language students from Korea, Switzerland, and Argentina—all on this Spanish-named road in this Mediterranean-style town. On TV, I find, the news is in Mandarin; today's baseball game is being broadcast in Korean. For lunch I can walk to a sushi bar, a tandoori palace, a Thai cafe, or the newest burrito joint (run by an old Japanese lady). Who am I, I sometimes wonder, the son of Indian parents and a British citizen who spends much of his time in Japan (and is therefore—what else?—an American permanent resident)? And where am I?

I am, as it happens, in southern California, in a quiet, relatively uninternational town, but I could just as easily be in Vancouver or Sydney or London or Hong Kong. All the world's a rainbow coalition, more and more; the whole planet, you might say, is going global. When I fly to Toronto, or Paris, or Singapore, I disembark in a world as hyphenated as the one I left. More and more of the globe looks like America, but an America that is itself looking more and more like the rest of the globe. Los

Angeles famously teaches eighty-two different languages in its schools. In this respect, the city seems only to bear out the old adage that what is in California today is in America tomorrow, and next week around the globe.

In ways that were hardly conceivable even a generation ago, the new world order is a version of the New World writ large: a wide-open frontier of polyglot terms and postnational trends. A common multiculturalism links us all—call it Planet Hollywood, Planet Reebok, or the United Colors of Benetton. Taxi and hotel and disco are universal terms now, but so too are karaoke and yoga and pizza. For the gourmet alone, there is tiramisu at the Burger King in Kyoto, angel-hair pasta in Saigon, and enchiladas on every menu in Nepal.

But deeper than mere goods, it is souls that are mingling. In Brussels, a center of the new "unified Europe," one new baby in every four is Arab. Whole parts of the Paraguayan capital of Asuncion are largely Korean. And when the prostitutes of Melbourne distributed some pro-condom pamphlets, one of the languages they used was Macedonian. Even Japan, which prides itself on its centuries-old socially engineered uniculture, swarms with Iranian illegals, Western executives, Pakistani laborers, and Filipina hostesses.

The global village is defined, as we know, by an interna- 5
tional youth culture that takes its cues from American pop culture. Kids in Perth and Prague and New Delhi are all tuning in to "Santa Barbara" on TV, and wriggling into 501 jeans, while singing along to Madonna's latest in English. CNN (which has grown 70-fold in thirteen years) now reaches more than 140 countries; an American football championship pits London against Barcelona. As fast as the world comes to America, America goes round the world—but it is an America that is itself multi-tongued and many-hued, an America of Amy Tan and Janet Jackson and movies with dialogue in Lakota.

For far more than goods and artifacts, the one great influence being broadcast around the world in greater numbers and at greater speed than ever before is people. What were once clear divisions are now tangles of crossed lines: there are 40,000 "Canadians" resident in Hong Kong, many of whose first language is Cantonese. And with people come customs: while new immigrants from Taiwan and Vietnam and India—some of the so-called Asian Calvinists—import all-American values of hard work and family closeness and entrepreneurial energy to America, America is sending its values of upward mobility and individualism and melting-pot hopefulness to Taipei and Saigon and Bombay.

Values, in fact, travel at the speed of fax; by now, almost half the world's Mormons live outside the United States. A diversity of one culture quickly becomes a diversity of many: the "typical American" who goes to Japan today may be a third-generation Japanese American, or the son of a Japanese woman married to a California serviceman, or the offspring of a Salvadoran father and an Italian mother from San Francisco. When he goes out with a Japanese woman, more than two cultures are brought into play.

None of this, of course, is new: Chinese silks were all the rage in Rome centuries ago, and Alexandria before the time of Christ was a paradigm of the modern universal city. Not even American eclecticism is new: many a small town has long known Chinese restaurants, Indian doctors, and Lebanese grocers. But now all these cultures are crossing at the speed of light. And the rising diversity of the planet is something more than mere cosmopolitanism: It is a fundamental recoloring of the very complexion of societies. Cities like Paris, or Hong Kong, have always had a soigne, international air and served as magnets for exiles and emigres, but now smaller places are multinational too. Marseilles speaks French with a distinctly North African twang. Islamic fundamentalism has one of its strongholds in Bradford, England. It is the sleepy coastal towns of Queensland, Australia, that print their menus in Japanese.

The dangers this internationalism presents are evident: not for nothing did the Tower of Babel collapse. As national borders fall, tribal alliances, and new manmade divisions, rise up, and the world learns every day terrible new meanings of the word Balkanization. And while some places are wired for international transmission, others (think of Iran or North Korea or Burma) remain as isolated as ever, widening the gap between the haves and the have-nots, or what Alvin Toffler has called the "fast" and the "slow" worlds. Tokyo has more telephones than the whole continent of Africa.

Nonetheless, whether we like it or not, the "transnational" future is upon us: As Kenichi Ohmae, the international economist, suggests with his talk of a "borderless economy," capitalism's allegiances are to products, not places. "Capital is now global," Robert Reich, the US secretary of labor, has said, pointing out that when an Iowan buys a Pontiac from General Motors, 60% of his money goes to South Korea, Japan, West Germany, Taiwan, Singapore, Britain, and Barbados. Culturally we are being re-formed daily by the cadences of world music and world fiction: where the great Canadian writers of an older generation had names like Frye and Davies and Laurence, now they are called Ondaatje and Mistry and Skvorecky.

As space shrinks, moreover, time accelerates. This hip-hop mishmash is spreading overnight. When my parents were in college, there were all of seven foreigners living in Tibet, a country the size of Western Europe, and in its entire history the country had seen fewer than 2,000 Westerners. Now a Danish student in Lhasa is scarcely more surprising than a Tibetan in Copenhagen. Already a city like Miami is beyond the wildest dreams of 1968; how much more so will its face in 2018 defy our predictions of today?

It would be easy, seeing all this, to say that the world is moving toward the Raza, Cosmica (Cosmic Race), predicted by the Mexican thinker Jose Vasconcelos in the 1920s—a glorious blend of mongrels and mestizos. It may be more relevant to suppose that more and more of the world may come to resemble Hong Kong, a stateless special economic zone full of expats and exiles linked by the lingua franca of English and the global marketplace. Some urbanists already see the world as a grid of thirty or so highly advanced city-regions, or technopoles, all plugged into the same international circuit.

The world will not become America. Anyone who has been to a baseball game in Osaka, or a Pizza Hut in Moscow, knows instantly that she is not in Kansas. But America may still, if only symbolically, be a model for the world. *E Pluribus Unum,* after all, is on the dollar bill. As Federico Mayor Zaragoza, the director-general of UNESCO, has said, "America's main role in the new world order is not as a military superpower, but as a multicultural superpower."

The traditional metaphor for this is that of a mosaic. But Richard Rodriguez, the Mexican-American essayist who is a psalmist for our new hybrid forms, points out that the interaction is more fluid than that, more human, subject to daily revision. "I am Chinese," he says, "because I live in San Francisco, a Chinese city. I became Irish in America. I became Portuguese in America." And even as he announces this new truth, Portuguese women are becoming American, and Irishmen are becoming Portuguese, and Sydney (or is it Toronto?) is thinking to compare itself with the "Chinese city" we know as San Francisco.

QUESTIONS FOR DISCUSSION AND WRITING

1. The author writes, "More and more of the globe looks like America, but an America that is itself looking more and more like the rest of the globe." Does he argue that the process is essentially a two-way exchange, or does the balance seem tipped on one side or the other?

2. According to Iyer, what role do youth and "youth culture" play in the international nature of culture? What other factors are involved?

3. Paragraph 10 notes the economic nature of crossing cultures and nations—with allegiance to "products, not places." Does Iyer support this claim? What evidence does he offer? What evidence to the contrary comes to mind?

4. According to Iyer, what factors promote the global village? What keeps it going?

5. Iyer wrote this essay in 1993. How has increased access to the Internet and cable or satellite television affected the phenomena Iyer describes?

6. Write a description of the global village based on your personal observation and experience or examples from your own community or travels.

The Politics of Globalization

KOFI ANNAN

Kofi Annan, born in 1938 in Ghana, is the secretary-general of the United Nations. Annan joined the United Nations in 1962 as an administrator for the World Health Organization. Annan filled a number of other administrative positions in the UN before assuming high-level leadership in the late 1980s, serving as special representative of the secretary-general to the former Yugoslavia in 1996. After Annan's election in 1997, he began implementing his plan to renew the United Nations and address changing humanitarian concerns in, among others, the poor regions of Africa. In 2001 Annan received the Nobel Peace Prize and was appointed to a second term as secretary-general.

The following selection is an address delivered at Harvard University, sponsored by the Harvard Academy for International and Area Studies, Cambridge, Massachusetts, on September 17, 1998.

I speak to you at a time of global turmoil, of economic crisis, political challenge, and conflict throughout much of the world. To cast a glance on the map of the world is to be not only concerned, but humbled. Concerned, of course, because long-simmering *intra*-state conflicts have in recent months intensified and been joined by *inter*-state tensions from Africa to Asia.

Humbled, because we all perhaps have been surprised by the swiftness with which these crises have accumulated in the space of twelve months. Any belief that either the end of major ideological competition or the revolutionary process of economic globalization would prevent conflict has been revealed as utterly wishful thinking. And yet, since these crises and conflicts are the product of human folly and human evil, I am convinced that they can be solved by human wisdom and human effort. But if we are to solve them, we must rededicate ourselves to addressing the *political* roots as well as the economic roots of the problems now gripping much of the world. That is why I have chosen to speak to you today about the politics of globalization.

To many, it is the phenomenon of globalization that distinguishes our era from any other. Globalization, we are told, is redefining not only the way we engage the world, but how we communicate with each other. We speak and hear often about the economics of globalization—of its promise and its perils.

Rarely, however, are the *political* roots of globalization addressed in a way that would help us understand its *political* consequences—both in times of progress and in times of crisis. Rarely, indeed, are the *political* aspects of globalization recognized by either its friends or its foes.

Today, globalization is rapidly losing its luster in parts of the world. What began as a currency crisis in Thailand fourteen months ago has, so far, resulted in a contagion of economic insolvency and political paralysis. Globalization is seen by a growing number not as a friend of prosperity, but as its enemy; not as a vehicle for development, but as an ever tightening vise increasing the demands on states to provide safety-nets while limiting their ability to do so.

At a time when the very value of globalization is being questioned, it may be prudent to revisit the role of politics and good governance in sustaining a successful process of globalization. Before doing so, however, let me say that great efforts are being made in every part of the world to contain and reverse the negative impact of globalization.

The fundamental recognition that lasting prosperity is based on legitimate politics has been joined by a growing appreciation of the need to maximize the benefits of the market while minimizing its costs in social justice and human poverty. To do so, regulatory systems must be improved in every part of the world; solid and sustainable safety-nets must be crafted to shield the poorest and most vulnerable; and transparency must be advanced on all sides.

Globalization is commonly understood to describe those advances in technology and communications that have made possible an unprecedented degree of financial and economic interdependence and growth. As markets are integrated, investments flow more easily, competition is enhanced, prices are lowered, and living standards everywhere are improved.

For a very long time, this logic was borne out by reality. Indeed, it worked so well that in many cases underlying political schisms were ignored in the belief that the rising tide of material growth would eliminate the importance of political differences.

Today, we look back on the early 1990s as a period of savage wars of genocide in Bosnia and Rwanda that cruelly mocked the political hubris attending the end of Communism. Soon, we may well look back on the late 1990s as a period of economic crisis and political conflict that with equal cruelty mocked the political hubris attending the heyday of Globalization.

In time, these twin awakenings—rude as they have been—may be recalled as a form of blessing in disguise, for they will have reminded us that any peace and every prosperity depend on legitimate, responsive politics.

They will have shown beyond a doubt that the belief in the ability of markets to resolve all divisions neglected the reality of differences of interest and outlook; differences that *can* be resolved peacefully, but *must* be resolved politically.

In a sense, it may be said that politics and political development as a whole suffered a form of benign neglect during globalization's glory years. Extraordinary growth rates seemed to justify political actions which otherwise might have invited dissent. Autocratic rule which denied basic civil and political rights was legitimized by its success in helping people escape centuries of poverty. What was lost in the exuberance of material wealth was the value of politics. And not just any politics: the politics of good governance, liberty, equity, and social justice.

The development of a society based on the rule of law; the establishment of legitimate, responsive, uncorrupt government; respect for human rights and the rights of minorities; freedom of expression; the right to a fair trial—these essential, universal pillars of democratic pluralism were in too many cases ignored. And the day the funds stopped flowing and the banks started crashing, the cost of political neglect came home.

Throughout much of the developing world, the awakening to globalization's down side has been one of resistance and resignation, a feeling that globalization is a false God foisted on weaker states by the capitalist centres of the West. Globalization is seen, not as a term describing objective reality, but as an ideology of predatory capitalism.

Whatever reality there is in this view, the perception of a siege is unmistakable. Millions of people are suffering; savings have been decimated; decades of hard-won progress in the fight against poverty are imperiled. And unless the basic principles of equity and liberty are defended in the political arena and advanced as critical conditions for economic growth, they may suffer rejection. Economic despair will be followed by political turmoil and many of the advances for freedom of the last half-century could be lost.

In this growing backlash against globalization, one can discern three separate categories of reaction. All three threaten to undermine globalization's prospects. All three reflect globaliza-

15

tion's neglect of political values. All three call for a response at the global level to what is, at root, a global challenge.

The first, perhaps most dangerous reaction, has been one of nationalism. From the devastated economies of Asia to the indebted societies of Africa, leaders in search of legitimacy are beginning to view globalization, and its down side, as a process that has weakened them vis-a-vis their rivals and diminished them in the eyes of their allies. Globalization is presented as a foreign invasion that will destroy local cultures, regional tastes, and national traditions.

Even more troubling, political leaders are increasingly seeking to sustain popular support amidst economic difficulties by exploiting historic enmities and fomenting trans-border conflict. That these steps will do nothing to improve their nations' lot— indeed just the opposite—must be evident even to them. But the costs of globalization have given them a rhetorical vehicle with which to distract their peoples' attentions from the penury of tomorrow to the pride of today.

The irony, of course, is that globalization's promise was based on the notion that trading partners become political partners, and that economic interdependence would eliminate the potential for political and military conflict. This notion is not new. In the early years of this century, the rapid expansion in trade and commerce even led some to predict an end to conflict. However, no degree of economic interdependence between Germany and Britain prevented the First World War. But this lesson was soon forgotten.

It was assumed that the political nature of inter-state relations had been transformed by a quantum leap similar if not equal to that which has revolutionized technology in the information age.

The fallacy of this doctrine—that trade precludes conflict— is not simply that nations and peoples often act out of a complex web of interests that may or may not favour economic progress. Power politics, hegemonic interests, suspicion, rivalry, greed, and corruption are no less decisive in the affairs of state than rational economic interests. The doctrine also underestimates the degree to which governments often find that the relentless pace of globalization threatens their ability to protect their citizens. Without addressing this concern, globalization cannot succeed.

The second reaction has been the resort to illiberal solutions—the call for the man on the white horse, the strong leader who in a time of crisis can act resolutely in the nation's interests. The raw, immediate appeal of this idea seems most apparent in newly liberalized nations with weak political systems, incapable of reacting with effectiveness or legitimacy in the face of economic crisis.

As central power disintegrates and breadlines grow, there is a growing temptation to forget that democracy is a condition for development—and not its reward. Again—and again falsely—democracy is seen as a luxury and not a necessity, a blessing to be wished for, not a right to be fought for.

Here, too, there is an irony: the proponents of globalization   25
always argued that greater trade would naturally lead to greater prosperity, which in turn would sustain a broad middle class. As a consequence, democratic rule would take firm and lasting root, securing respect for individual liberties and human rights. This, too, proved to be overly optimistic.

Some of globalization's proponents believed too much in the ability and inclination of trade and economic growth to foster democracy. Others, too little in the importance of democratic values such as freedom of speech and freedom of information in sustaining firm and lasting economic growth. Traders will trade, with or without political rights. Their prosperity alone, however, will not secure democratic rule.

In all the debates of the post-cold war years about whether political liberalization should precede economic liberalization or vice versa, one question was left out. What if, regardless of which comes first, the other does not follow? What if economic liberalization, however profitable in the short term, will never beget a political liberalization that is not already integral to economic progress? What if political liberalization, however desirable on its own, is no guarantee of economic growth, at least in the short term?

These are the questions that globalization's friends must face—and answer—in *political* terms, if they are to win the argument against those who would seek solutions in tyranny. Freedom itself is too valuable, its spirit too important for progress, to be bargained away in the struggle for prosperity.

The third reaction against the forces of globalization has been a politics of populism. Embattled leaders may begin to propose forms of protectionism as a way to offset losses supposedly incurred by too open an embrace of competition, and too free a system of political change. Their solution is for a battered nation to turn away and turn inward, tend to its own at whatever cost, and rejoin the global community only when it can do so from a position of strength.

In this reaction, globalization is made the scapegoat of ills   30
which more often have domestic roots of a political nature.

Globalization, having been employed as political cover by reformers wishing to implement austerity programs, comes to be seen as a force of evil by those who would return to imagined communities of earlier times.

Notwithstanding its flaws and failed assumptions, this reaction is a real challenge with real power. Those who would defend the policies of openness, transparency, and good governance must find ways to answer these critics at two levels: at the level of principle and at the level of practical solutions which can provide some kind of economic insurance against social despair and instability.

The lesson of this reaction is that economic integration in an interdependent world is neither all-powerful nor politically neutral. It is seen in strictly political terms, particularly in times of trouble, and so must be defended in political terms. Otherwise, the populists and the protectionists will win the argument between isolation and openness, between the particular and the universal, between an imaginary past and a prosperous future. And they must not win.

If globalization is to succeed, it must succeed for poor and rich alike. It must deliver rights no less than riches. It must provide social justice and equity no less than economic prosperity and enhanced communication. It must be harnessed to the cause not of capital alone, but of development and prosperity for the poorest of the world. It must address the reactions of nationalism, illiberalism, and populism with political answers expressed in political terms.

Political liberty must be seen, once and for all, as a necessary condition for lasting economic growth, even if not a sufficient one. Democracy must be accepted as the midwife of development, and political and human rights must be recognized as key pillars of any architecture of economic progress.

This is, undoubtedly, a tall order. But it is one that must be met, if globalization is not to be recalled in years hence as simply an illusion of the power of trade over politics, and human riches over human rights. As the sole international organization with universal legitimacy and scope, the UN has an interest—indeed an obligation—to help secure the equitable and lasting success of globalization.

We have no magic bullet with which to secure this aim, no easy answers in our common effort to confront this challenge. But we do know that the limitations on the ability of any state or any organization to affect the processes of globalization call for a global, concerted effort.

If this effort is to make a genuine difference, it is clear that the creation of lasting political institutions must form a first line of response. Such steps must, however, be combined with a clear and balanced acceptance of the roots of the precipitous collapse of so many economies. To some extent, this collapse was rooted in flaws and failures of already existing economies characterized by unsound policies, corruption, and illiberal politics.

However, we must not be blind to the fact that irresponsible lending practices and aggressive investment policies pursued by outsiders played their part, too. Without improvements in these practices, we cannot expect political reform to succeed in creating the basis for lasting economic growth. All sides matter; all sides must play a role.

I have argued today that politics are at the root of globalization's difficulties, and that politics will be at the heart of any solutions. But where will solutions be found? In the heyday of globalization, it was assumed that all nations, once secure in prosperity, would turn to multilateral institutions out of maturity; today, I believe, they may turn to those same institutions out of necessity.

The challenge facing the United Nations is to ensure that the   40
difficulties facing globalization do not become an impediment to global cooperation, but rather give such cooperation new life and new promise.

We will do so in two key ways: by emphasizing in all our development work the importance of civil society and institutional structures of democracy at the national level; and by seeking to strengthen the effectiveness of multilateralism in sustaining free economies while securing genuine protection for the poorest and most vulnerable of our world.

After World War II, there was a recognition that ultimately, economic problems were political and security problems. There was a recognition that prosperity and peace are *political* achievements, not simply natural consequences either of trade or of technological progress.

We owe the wisdom of this view and the consequences of its implementation to one man in particular, Franklin Delano Roosevelt. In his fourth inaugural address, President Roosevelt— a founder of the United Nations and surely the greatest Harvard Man of this century—made a passionate plea for global engagement: "We have learned that we cannot live alone, at peace; that our own well-being is dependent on the well-being of other nations, far away. We have learned that we must live as men, and not as ostriches, nor as dogs in the manger. We have learned to be citizens of the world, members of the human community."

In this era, we have learned our lessons, too: that democracy   45
is the condition for true, lasting, and equitable development; that

the rewards of globalization must be seen not only at the centre, but also, at the margins; and that without free, legitimate, and democratic politics, no degree of prosperity can satisfy humanity's needs nor guarantee lasting peace—*even* in the age of Globalization.

QUESTIONS FOR DISCUSSION AND WRITING

1. Early in the essay Annan defines globalization. Is the definition consistent with your view and that of other writers in this text?
2. How does Annan make his case for the importance of "legitimate, responsive politics" in both peace and prosperity? What role does democracy play?
3. Annan describes a backlash against globalization. What are the three main reactions he describes? Why, according to the author, must economic integration be defended in political terms?
4. According to Annan, what interest does the UN have in globalization and its difficulties? What role might the UN play? Besides citing the UN, what other appeals to authority does the author make that are likely to persuade his immediate audience?
5. Research the founding and history of the UN, or explore one of the other topics raised in this issue—post–World War II era, France and Britain's relations prior to World War I, genocide in Rwanda, effects of globalization on developing nations, or Franklin Delano Roosevelt's presidency or involvement in forming the UN.

Blood Diamonds

GREG CAMPBELL

Greg Campbell is editor of the *Fort Collins Weekly* and the author of the book *Blood Diamonds: Tracing the Deadly Path of the World's Most Precious Stones* (2002). The article that follows appeared in the online publication *Amnesty Now,* from Amnesty International, accessed in 2003. In this article the author notes the connections among the diamond trade, civil war, and terrorism.

In April 2001, when Jusu Lahia was fifteen years old, he was wounded by an exploding rocket-propelled grenade. A lieutenant in Sierra Leone's Revolutionary United Front (RUF), Lahia was picked off during a battle in one of the most remote corners of the planet. He was among thousands of victims of a war fought for control of one of the world's most precious commodities: a fortune in raw diamonds that have made their way from the deadly jungles of Sierra Leone onto the rings and necklaces of happy lovers the world over.

Arms merchants, feeding on the diamond trade, bank-rolled local armies and made fortunes for transnational corporations. The profits also filled the coffers of al Qaeda, and possibly Hezbollah—terrorist organizations notorious for committing human rights violations, including crimes against humanity.

When Lahia sprawled to the earth—shards of hot metal ripped his body from face to groin, destroying his left eye—few who eventually wore the gems he fought over could even locate Sierra Leone. And fewer still could find the Parrot's Beak, a small wedge of land that juts between the borders of neighboring Liberia and Guinea, directly into the line of fire between warring rebel factions in those countries. Rebel forces of all three nations were shooting it out with one another, as well as with the legitimate governments of all three countries and with an unknown number of local indigenous militias that were fighting for reasons of their own. The baffling and intense crossfire made the Parrot's Beak one of the deadliest 50-square-mile plots of land on the planet in 2001, and when Lahia went down in a hail of exploding shrapnel, he likely knew that he was far from the type of medical help that could save his life.

The RUF child soldier did not suffer alone. In the Parrot's Beak in mid-2001, some 50,000 refugees from Sierra Leone, Liberia, and Guinea were steadily dying from starvation, disease, and war wounds. The region was too hot for even the most daredevil humanitarian relief organizations.

Lahia was carried to a bare, fire-blackened hospital room in   5
Kailahun, the RUF's stronghold in the Parrot's Beak, and dumped on a pile of hay that served as a bed. When I first saw him there, surrounded by chaos, heat, and filth, I found it hard to remember that the cause of all this suffering—thousands of doomed refugees, well-armed but illiterate and drugged combatants, fallen wounded like Lahia, and injured civilian children—was brutally simple: The greed for diamonds. Certainly, there was nothing nearly as lustrous or awe-inspiring as a diamond in the bloodstained room where Lahia was dying of a tetanus infection, next to another felled fifteen-year-old. Powerless to treat him, the RUF field medics had simply taped his wounds shut and left him wracked with sweats and shivers.

Amputation is Forever

Sadly, Kailahun wasn't the worst of it. The RUF began its jewelry heist in 1991, using the support of neighboring Liberia to capture Sierra Leone's vast wealth of diamond mines. Since then, the rebels have carried out one of the most brutal military campaigns in recent history, to enrich themselves as well as the genteel captains of the diamond industry living far removed from the killing fields. The RUF's signature tactic was amputation of civilians: Over the course of the decade-long war, the rebels have mutilated some 20,000 people, hacking off their arms, legs, lips, and ears with machetes and axes. This campaign was the RUF's grotesquely ironic response to Sierra Leone President Ahmad Tejan Kabbah's 1996 plea for citizens to "join hands for peace." Another 50,000 to 75,000 have been killed. The RUF's goal was to terrorize the population and enjoy uncontested dominion over the diamond fields.

While the RUF terrorized and looted the countryside, thousands of prisoner–laborers worked to exhaustion, digging up the gems from muddy open-pit mines. Many ended up in shallow graves, executed for suspected theft, for lack of production, or simply for sport.

The international diamond industry's trading centers in Europe funded this horror by buying up to $125 million worth of diamonds a year from the RUF, according to UN estimates. Few cared where the gems originated, or calculated the cost in lives lost rather than carats gained. The RUF used its profits to open foreign bank accounts for rebel leaders and to finance a complicated network of gunrunners who kept the rebels well-equipped with the modern military hardware they used to control Sierra Leone's diamonds. The weapons—and the gems the rebels sold unimpeded to terrorist and corporate trader alike—allowed the RUF to fight off government soldiers, hired mercenaries, peacekeepers from a regional West African reaction force, British paratroopers, and, until recently, the most expansive and expensive peacekeeping mission the UN has ever deployed.

Throughout most of the war from 1991 to January 2002, this drama played itself out in obscurity. During the RUF's worst assaults, international media pulled journalists out of the country in fear for their safety. Local citizens were left to fend for themselves against bloodthirsty and drugged child soldiers. Commanders often cut the children's arms and packed the wounds with cocaine; marijuana was everywhere.

Until the deployment of the UN mission in 1999, the developed countries also washed their hands of the situation, doing little more than imposing sanctions on diamond exports and weapons sales to the small country. These efforts did nothing to end the RUF's diamonds-for-guns trade because most of the RUF'S goods were smuggled out of Sierra Leone and sold into the mainstream from neighboring countries.

10

Home to Roost

In a mistake that was to come home to roost, the West dismissed Sierra Leone's war as little more than a baffling and tragic waste of life that had little impact on their own economic interests—and even less on their national security.

Then on September 11, 2001, the world saw horrifying evidence of the peril of ignoring such conflagrations and their related gross violations of human rights.

For years, terrorists had been exploiting both the world's disdain for intervening in Sierra Leone and the international diamond industry's tacit funding of war. At least three African wars—in Sierra Leone, Angola, and the Democratic Republic of Congo—had been good for business, ensuring high and stable global prices for diamonds.

Beginning as early as 1998, the same year al Qaeda operatives reportedly blew up US embassies in Kenya and Sudan, Osama bin Laden's terrorist network began buying diamonds from the RUF of Sierra Leone, according to FBI sources quoted in the *Washington Post*.

The paper also reported that two of the al Qaeda men im- 15
plicated in those attacks—Ahmed Khalfan Ghailani and Fazul Abdullah Mohammed—were in Sierra Leone in 2001, overseeing RUF diamond production.

As recently as mid-2001, a mere three months before the World Trade Center and Pentagon attacks, al Qaeda had laundered millions of dollars by buying untraceable diamonds from the rebels. In the wake of 9/11, the United States and its allies in the "war on terrorism" froze more than $100 million worth of al Qaeda assets worldwide. But the terrorists likely have an ace in the hole in the form of diamonds from Sierra Leone, wealth that can be easily and quickly sold and is virtually untraceable.

Unspinnable Disaster

Even before 9/11, the diamond merchants were getting nervous. Media and human rights groups began exposing the complicity of the romance industry in fueling wars. They also challenged the notion that Sierra Leone was simply another isolated post-cold war conflict that was troubling in its brutality but irrelevant to the national interests of developed countries.

Campaigns launched by Global Exchange and Amnesty International against conflict diamonds threatened to replace the image of a diamond sparkling on the graceful hand of a lover with that of the truncated stump of a child amputee's arm. One diamond company executive is rumored to have had nightmares in which the tag line at the end of De Beers television commercials read, "Amputation is Forever."

The industry grew increasingly amenable to the idea of curtailing the flow of blood diamonds. In 2000, Global Witness, a San Francisco-based non-governmental organization, joined with diamond industry representatives and officials from diamond exporting and importing countries to form the Kimberley Process. Amnesty International soon joined the negotiating effort, but according to Adotei Akwei, AIUSA's senior advocacy director for Africa, "the NGOs never had much power. We were allowed at the table but were seldom diners."

Despite many meetings, the panel failed to reach a consen- 20
sus on how to end the trade in blood diamonds. The US Congress, too, faced intense lobbying. In 2000, Rep. Tony Hall (D-Ohio) introduced the Clean Diamond Act, a bill that sought to enact into law whatever import and export controls the Kimberley Process would adopt. The bill languished because of serious concerns

over provisions added at the request of the Bush administration that—according to NGOs, the industry, and some senators—fatally compromised the bill.

The 9/11 terrorist attacks, along with a blistering *Washington Post* investigation by Doug Farrah into al Qaeda's large purchases of Sierra Leone diamonds, raised the stakes. While associating with bloodthirsty rebels was a formidable public relations challenge for the diamond industry, funding the terrorists who attacked the United States was simply unspinnable.

Last November, the Kimberley Process agreed to a set of regulations that would require that all cross-border diamond transactions be accompanied by a non-forgeable paper trail, indicating when and where every imported stone was discovered. The Clean Diamond Act followed suit and was passed by the House of Representatives 408–6. It is currently awaiting a vote in the Senate.

Unfortunately, neither action is halting the lucrative trade: "Efforts to end the trade in conflict diamonds ran into a major obstacle in the Bush administration, which has been reluctant to impede business in any way or have its hands tied by any international agreements, even when the US diamond industry has called for it," says Akwei.

Nor is a better paper trail foolproof. Diamonds are sufficiently small and portable to make it unlikely that any regime of certificates or guarantees will ensure that diamonds originate in conflict-free areas. Indeed, it seems that the only sure-fire way to eradicate conflict diamonds is to see an end to the conflicts where diamonds are found. As evidence, we can look again at Sierra Leone, where the war was officially declared over in January. With hostilities ended and the RUF disarmed and disbanded, diamond production is once again in the hands of the government and international exploration companies. The trick now is to see if the government can adeptly handle the complexities of mining and taxing so that the majority of revenue is reinvested, and to ensure that Sierra Leone finally benefits from diamonds rather than being torn apart by them.

The Shame of It All

Throughout the 1990s, children like Jusu Lahia armed themselves with diamond-purchased AK-47s and, under the nose of the United Nations, helped the rebels sell the gems to terrorists. People had their hands chopped off by RUF units and were sent wandering hopelessly to spread the message of terror. West African "peacekeepers" were so inept in their defense of Sierra

Leone's civilian population that charges of human rights violations are leveled at them as frequently as they are at the RUF.
Nigerian soldiers serving a regional West African peacekeeping
force killed civilians suspected of aiding RUF, tortured children
suspected of being RUF, and slaughtered hospital patients in
their efforts to rid Freetown of rebels. It is no stretch to say that
Sierra Leone disintegrated during the 1990s into a murderous
sinkhole of death and torture, all of it fueled by the sale of diamonds to respectable merchants throughout the world.

The shame of it all is that it took a catastrophic attack on
American soil for anyone to notice. Developed nations bought
Sierra Leone's blood-soaked diamonds without question throughout the 1990s, apparently untroubled that the sales affected millions of Africans in a mostly forgotten and impoverished jungle.

Only after the effects of the RUF's diamond war were
slammed home—like a blade through the bones of a forearm—
did anyone sit up and take notice.

If nothing else, the story of Sierra Leone's diamond war has
proved unequivocally that the world ignores Africa and its problems at its peril. Events far from home often have very tangible
impacts, and Sierra Leone has shown the world that there is no
longer any such thing as an "isolated, regional conflict." Perhaps
there never was.

QUESTIONS FOR DISCUSSION AND WRITING

1. How do you find yourself responding to the essay? Starting
   with the introduction to this essay, how does the author engage interest and encourage readers to be concerned about
   events happening at both a geographical and in some ways a
   psychological distance from themselves?

2. What is Campbell's thesis? What evidence does he offer to
   support his view? What appeals to logic, ethics, and emotion
   does he make? Which do you find most persuasive?

3. Discuss the author's use of contrast, as in the contrast of diamonds' image in jewelry and romance with the source of
   diamonds and the product of diamond profits.

4. Research the current status of the political situation in Sierra
   Leone, with particular attention to issues raised in this essay,
   such as child soldiers, conflict diamonds, terrorist funding
   and activities, or human rights or UN efforts in this region.

Women's Weaving Project

March 1995
Vang Vieng District, 150 km north of Vientiane, Lao People's Democratic Republic

Background

Vang Vieng is a place of extraordinary beauty, with sheer limestone mountains rising up from flat valley floors, through which the Nam Mom River and its tributaries flow. Despite its high rainfall and lush vegetation, however, it is not an easy area to farm, as the sandy-loamy soil drains rapidly, and without supplementary irrigation, rice cannot be grown.

War and upheaval in Laos, where arable land is in short supply, have led to the displacement of large numbers of people, and many of Vang Vieng's inhabitants were moved there from more remote mountain provinces fifteen to twenty years ago.

The success of several communities in making this huge transition has been remarkable. With Community Aid Abroad's technical and financial support, communities have built irrigation systems, allowing them to grow paddy rice, rather than depend on slash-and-burn upland agriculture. Farming has been diversified to include fish and vegetables, and villages are producing their own organic pesticides.

Like its Indochina neighbours, Vietnam and Cambodia, Laos has been moving from a centrally controlled economy, which emphasised autonomy, to an open market economy, which has also meant an inflow of foreign investment. Garment factories are springing up around Vientiane, and in Vang Vieng itself, a vast Chinese-built cement factory now sits at the southern end of the valley, while power lines from the new hydro-electric schemes cut across the ridges to feed Thailand's power grids.

Women's Economic Role

Amongst the lowland Lao, women have always had a central role in rice agriculture, being responsible for transplanting, weeding, and much of the harvesting and threshing, while men had charge of ploughing and maintenance of irrigation works. In addition to this, women have been chiefly responsible for vegetable gardening and small livestock raising; their working day is longer than men's, and their role is a very complex one.

    Traditional weaving has been one of women's chief economic strengths. In Vang Vieng district, women often control every stage of fabric production, growing cotton, spinning yarn, preparing dyes, and weaving fabric which is then sold or made into garments. Laotian women are renowned for their skill in this area, and many traditional patterns are intricate and beautiful.

    Weaving is usually a dry-season activity; when the rice harvest is in, and women have "free" time from their other tasks, time is spent on spinning, dye production, and weaving. Sale of the finished products is often one of the family's main sources of cash income.

Shifting Patterns

As imported fabrics and factory-made garments have taken a large share of the Laotian market, traditional weaving has been remarkably resilient. As well as the pride local communities take in their own work, Lao fabrics are attracting increasing interest in urban and overseas markets for their high quality, intricate designs, and natural dyes. Several cooperative ventures based in Vientiane are successfully incorporating traditional, village-woven fabrics into goods for export to the upper end of European and North America markets.

The Project

Since 1989, Community Aid Abroad has been working with women in Vang Vieng district to help them achieve their aims of generating income from their work and preserving their traditional skills. Enhancing these skills helps both to improve the quality of their products and to deal with the modern market-place.

Manivanh Suyavong, Community Aid Abroad's Community   10
Development worker, organises training sessions for the women, assists in the marketing of their cloth, and provides advice on designs and articles suited for the Vientiane and international markets. Emphasis is on skills sharing; within the Vang Vieng district, there are women with a very diverse range of skills, and the project allows them to learn from each other.

Hak Boung is seventy years old, but has a degree of agility and energy beyond that of many younger people. When she and her neighbours of the Tai Dam ethnic group were moved to Vang Vieng district in 1978, she brought with her the skill passed on through the women of her family of preparing indigo dye and weaving the beautiful blue-and-white ikat cloth.

Indigo is a weedy-looking plant that is grown on the fields between rice crops. As it fixes nitrogen, it helps restore the soil without the use of chemical fertiliser. Hak Boung has now conducted several training sessions for women of other villages on how to harvest indigo plants, steep them to prepare dye, and dye locally-grown and -spun cotton to achieve even and consistent quality.

Indigo cloth, traditionally worn by Lao farmers, is now sought after from far beyond Vang Vieng, and cloth dyed and woven by Hak Boung and the women she has trained is gaining them a place in the markets which might otherwise undermine their economic status.

The Future

The Community Aid Abroad team in Laos is continuing to work on long-term community development strategies in Vang Vieng, but is also establishing programs in the remote and dry provinces of Saravane and Sekhong in southern Laos. Many of the target communities are comprised of highland minority groups, quite outside the market economy.

Here also, weaving is a prized traditional skill for women,   15
and beautiful and durable blankets and other fabrics are woven. The idea of marketing their work, however, is quite alien to most women, who weave only for their families' use. Community Aid Abroad is working with women in these areas on preserving and enhancing their skills, and planning on how, if at all,

they will enter the market economy that is increasingly making its presence felt.
http://www.caa.org.au/AWARE/1995/march-1995.html

QUESTIONS FOR DISCUSSION AND WRITING

1. What do you think the purpose of this essay is? How do you respond to it as a reader? How does the essay engage and maintain your interest?

2. Explain the role of weaving in the family, community, and culture as discussed in this article. How do you think entry into a global market, should the weavers pursue it, might impact this craft and the women weavers? Consider both positive and negative effects.

3. Research this program and other craft collectives, weaving projects, or other local programs for artisans with links to global or international organizations.

Racism and the Internet: The Need for Global Consensus

PHILIPP SCHLOTER

Philipp Schloter was born and raised in Germany. He graduated from a German Gymnasium (secondary school) where he learned English as his second language. He received a BA in economics and a BS in computer science at Stanford University in 2003 and is a candidate for a master's degree in electrical engineering. He is currently on leave from his graduate studies to work at Microsoft Corporation in Redmond, Washington, as a product manager. He developed the idea for this essay, written in 2000, from his interests in technology and also from discussions in class about related social and cultural issues. As you read his essay, consider both the argument he makes and the extent to which he offers his views about how such a goal could be accomplished. Also note that he uses a documentation style more prevalent in science disciplines.

The US Defense Advanced Research Projects Agency (originally ARPA until March 23, 1972[1]) began developing the ArpaNet in the late 1960s as a robust network for military use.[2] It is doubtful that anyone at that time expected that the ArpaNet, which evolved into the Internet, would ever carry racist propaganda. With increasing commercialization of the Internet during the 1990s, the Internet community grew to about 200 million users in over 200 countries and territories by December 1999 and is likely to grow even further.[3]

The democratic nature of the Internet allows every one of these 200 million or more users to send and receive information from every other user worldwide. Although the Internet seems to be the embodiment of America's dream of unlimited freedom of speech, problems surface when considering that, unfortunately, agitators and racists are also part of this Internet community. The decentralized architecture of the Net makes information difficult to control, and racist groups can freely broadcast their propaganda to a global audience.

When arguing against other countries' attempts to censor the Internet, Americans often use the First Amendment of the United States Constitution to measure freedom of speech in these countries. One must have a global perspective to understand that free access to racists' Net propaganda has a greater impact on relatively homogenous societies, such as the French or the German, than on America's multicultural society. Because the Internet is global and ubiquitous, local authorities cannot effectively decide whether or not the Internet should be censored. A global Internet policy that considers the cultural differences between countries is required.

One does not have to look far: Cultural differences exist even within the Western world. Although the United States was founded by Europeans, there are fundamental differences between typical European and American concepts of freedom of speech. Because the American society is heterogeneous, it has to tolerate hate speech as a part of its diversity. The US Constitution's First Amendment laid the foundation for this tolerance:

> Congress shall make no law respecting an establishment of religion, or prohibiting the free exercise thereof; or abridging the freedom of speech, or of the press; or the right of the people peaccably to assemble, and to petition the government for a redress of grievances.[4]

People may articulate their thoughts freely, even if they are offensive to some parties. Offensive actions, although, are illegal in the United States. American citizens have diverse ethnic backgrounds. People of Hispanic origin account for 11.9 percent of the US population, 12.2 percent are black, 4.1 percent are Asian and Pacific Islander, and 71.4 percent are white (non-Hispanic). Only 0.9 percent are American Indian, Eskimo, or Aleut (i.e., Native American[5]). In total, over 99 percent of the US population is of non-native descent. In other words, they are either immigrants or descendants of immigrants who came to the United States from all over the world with the desire for freedom and independence. Thus, the people living in the United States have built a heterogeneous society. Often the American society is depicted as a "melting pot." Nonetheless, the metaphor of a "fruit salad bowl" seems more appropriate, as different beliefs, political views, and aspirations can still be seen separately in the United States and are not "melted" into one uniform belief, view, or aspiration. In order to function well, it is necessary for Americans to tolerate each other's views.

Given this premise, even if an ultimate truth did exist, no one would have either the right or the ability to decide which viewpoint is the best. Thus, the founding fathers considered it reasonable to allow everyone to express their opinions, regardless of how radical and how hateful they are. Most Americans do not see a danger in racist groups because they think that they are minorities and are unable to gain political power. This assumption is based on the concept of a self-regulating "marketplace of ideas," in which "bad" ideas will lose in popularity and "good" ideas will gain in popularity. According to this view, popular ideas will prosper, whereas unpopular ideas will wither.

In contrast to the United States, in many European countries where hate speech is generally not tolerated, people tend to share a common view or background. For example, in France, 90 percent of the population is Roman Catholic,[6] and in Germany the population consists primarily of Germans. A Danish minority lives in the north and a Serbian minority lives in the east, but overall fewer than 1 percent are non-citizens.[7] Because many share the same religion or ethnic background, most Europeans feel that they are part of homogenous societies. People are allowed to express themselves freely as long as their opinions are based on the institutional rights[8,9] i.e., are not offending other members of their society. Most perceive it as a "human right" not to be exposed to offensive speech. They see a fundamental threat in "hate speech" as it could potentially lead to actions because European history has taught them how compelling "hate speech" and propaganda can be in a homogenous society. The horrors of World War II created a desire for security that led many people to believe that agitators and racists should not have the right to express their opinion.

The lack of a global consensus on Internet censoring policy has caused a number of obscure lawsuits in Europe. As the origin of information is often impossible to determine and as differences in countries' laws make criminal prosecution of authors of offensive information difficult, plaintiffs generally tend to sue local access providers who allow people to view the offensive information, rather than the actual content provider or author. For example, in May 1998, Somm, the German CEO of CompuServe, was sentenced to two years in prison and issued a DM100,000 fine for complicity in distributing unlawful material. However, this judgment was declared invalid in November 1999;[10] it is unreasonable to convict a respectable entrepreneur just because his company is providing access to the Internet. But because no effort has been made to find a global solution to this problem, racist groups are continuing to hide behind the First Amendment of the United States Constitution and the anonymity which the

Net provides. As a result, the suing and blaming of local Internet providers continues in Europe. The most recent case is the suing of Yahoo! by the International League against Racism and Anti-Semitism (LICRA) and the Union of French Jewish Students (UEJF).[11] On November 20, 2000, Yahoo! was ordered to restrict access of French Net surfers to Web pages which contain content that is unlawful under French law. If Yahoo! is not able to install such a system within three months, the company will be fined FF100,000 per day.[12,13] A team of experts is now trying to develop and implement an IP address-based system for local Internet censorship for Yahoo!.

The experts agree, however, that such a system will be limited and cannot guarantee a full exclusion of French surfers from racist Web pages accessible through Yahoo!. The global and decentralized nature of the Internet makes it uncontrollable.[14] There will always be ways to circumvent net censorship barriers. Technologies such as satellite Internet access, data encryption,[15] software cracks,[16] remailers, and IP anonymizers[17] allow people to bypass censorship easily. Furthermore, these existing technologies are complemented by new innovations to undermine censorship every day—dozens of programmers are just waiting for the challenge of hacking the latest Web filter. One has to understand that bits and bytes underlie different laws than the laws of the physical world.[18] As long as one country exists where "racist bytes" are legal, everyone in the world has the possibility to access them, regardless of the physical location of the bytes. It follows that only a global Internet policy or guideline can be successful.

The question now is what should such a guideline look like? Should it resemble the American First Amendment or the French or German constitution? Which understanding of freedom of speech is the right one? There are good arguments for both the European and the American sides. First of all, censorship and filters may confine academic research and education.[19] Would a letter from Martin Luther King, Jr. also fall under censorship and, thus, would educational projects such as the Martin Luther King, Jr. project at Stanford University have to be stopped?[20] Secondly, censorship could drive racist groups underground, which would make it even harder to keep them under surveillance. Thirdly, in some instances, exposure to racist materials may enhance critical thinking, heighten people's understanding of history, and, hence, allow them to learn from past mistakes.[21] Last but not least, there is one fundamental question with no satisfactory answer: Who ultimately determines what racism is? To define one group as racist and another group as non-racist might in some cases be racist itself.

Despite these arguments against Internet censorship, even the United States does not completely renounce it. In the case of pornography the US government implements its own guidelines[22] and contradicts typical American opposition to censorship. Further, racist organizations seem to prosper[23,24] on the Net rather than wither as the "marketplace of ideas" theory would predict. The increasing potential Net audience[25] and the increasing richness of information[26] through larger network bandwidths seem to attract more and more racist organizations who distribute their propaganda through the Internet. While the full effects of spreading hate speech over the Internet have yet to be determined, it is clear that one has to draw attention to the need of a global consensus on this issue.

If local censorship on the Internet clearly cannot work, global censorship cannot work either. Every day the Web grows by thousands of Web pages and becomes even more uncontrollable. As one page is censored or rated, three others surface in its place. Their authors can hardly be tracked down or stopped in anonymous cyberspace, and protection mechanisms such as filters do not present a remedy either because they can easily be circumvented or disabled. Given the failure of these traditional techniques, the chances of eradicating racist material on the Net seem to be remote, inevitably leading to a need for developing alternative measures. The development of a global definition of free speech is one such alternative. Although it will not eliminate racist or incendiary material, it will at least enable those most affected to pursue their course in court. Consistent laws and policies could finally put an end to racists hiding behind another country's laws.

The first step in implementing this plan is the creation of a multinational or, even better, an international consortium to develop a new definition of free speech. A global fundamental standard, based on mutual understanding and human rights, could build a basis for such a unified definition of free speech. If every country in the world would accept this speech code, America's desire for liberty and Europe's desire for protection could both be satisfied while working toward one joint future. One also has to consider that even though the cultural gap between the United States and Europe is wide, the cultural gap between Western countries and countries such as China[27] is even wider. Thus, the path toward reaching an agreement on such a standard is long, but there is no other choice. Although heterogeneous societies and homogenous societies may have difficulties understanding each others' concerns about racism on the Internet, the problem of Net racism must be solved together.

Notes

1. Defense Advanced Research Projects Agency. ARPA-DARPA: The History of the Name. Available: < *http://www.darpa.mil/body/ arpa_darpa.html* > .

2. Leiner, Cerf, Clark, Kahn, Kleinrock, Lynch, Postel, Roberts, and Wolff. A Brief History of the Internet, version 3.31. Revised August 04, 2000. Available: < *http://www.isoc.org/Internet-history/brief.html* > .

3. Kahn and Cerf. What is The Internet (And What Makes It Work). December 1999. Available: < *http://www.worldcom.com/about_the_ company/cerfs_up/Internet_history/whatIs.phtml* > .

4. United States of America. Bill of Rights, Amendment I [Religion, Speech, Press, Assembly, Petition]. 1791.

5. US Census Bureau. Resident Population Estimates of the United States by Sex, Race, and Hispanic Origin: April 1, 1990 to July 1, 1999, with Short-Term Projection to October 1, 2000. November 29, 2000.

6. US Department of State, Bureau of European Affairs. Background Notes: France. October 1999.

7. US Department of State, Bureau of European Affairs. Background Notes: Germany. May 2000.

8. Federal Republic of Germany. Grundgesetz Artikel 5, Absatz 2. Available: < *http://www.bundestag.de/gesetze/gg/gg_5.htm* > .

9. Assemblée nationale. La Constitution de la République francaise. Déclaration des Droits de L'Homme et du Citoyen de 1789, Article XI. October 4, 1958.

10. ARD Aktuell, Tagesschau. Ex-CompuServe-Chef freigesprochen. November 11, 1999. Available: < *http://www.tagesschau.de/archiv/1999/11/ 17/sendung/ts2000/meldung/compuserve?layout = print* > .

11. Michel Alberganti. Des barbelés dans le cyberespace?. Le Monde. August 9, 2000.

12. Thierry Lévêque. Condamnation confirmée de Yahoo. Le Figaro. November 21, 2000.

13. Acacio Pereira. Yahoo condamné à empêcher l'accès des internautes français aux sites illégaux. *Le Monde,* November 22, 2000.

14. Acacio Pereira. Devant la justice française, Yahoo affirme l'impossibilité d'interdire l'accès à des sites illégaux. *Le Monde,* July 26, 2000.

15. Bruce Schneier. Applied Cryptography. (John Wiley & Sons: 1994.)

16. Patricia Jacobus. Judge sides with Net filtering firm in copyright case. CNET News.com. March 28, 2000. Available: < *http://news .cnet.com/news/0-1005-200-1596115.html* >.

17. Ian Goldberg, David Wagner, and Eric Brewer. Privacy-enhancing technologies for the Internet. University of California, Berkeley. 1997. Available: < *http://www.cs.berkeley.edu/~daw/papers/privacy-compcon97-www/privacy-html.html* >.

18. Nicholas Negroponte. MIT Media Lab. Being Digital. Vintage Books: 1996.

19. Jamie McCarthy. Mandated Mediocrity: Blocking Software Gets a Failing Grade. Peacefire and Epic. October 2000. Available: < *http://www.epic.org/censorware/mandated_mediocrity.html* >.

20. Stanford University, MLK Research. Martin Luther King, Jr. Papers Project. < *http://www.stanford.edu/group/King/* >.

21. Lorenz Lorenz-Meyer. Nizkor - We shall remember!. Spiegel Publishing Company: 1996. Available: < *http://www.nizkor.org/hweb/orgs/german/der-spiegel-online/article-961018.html* >.

22. Istook, Dickey, Franks, Myrick, Souder, Tancredo, and Terry. Internet Minors Protection and Cyberspace. House of Representatives. May 25, 2000. Available: < *http://thomas.loc.gov/cgi-bin/query/D?c106:6:./temp/-c106ZmAwIE::* >.

23. Lisa Guernsey. Mainstream Sites Serve as Portals to Hate. *New York Times,* November 30, 2000.

24. Bundesamt für Verfassungsschutz. Rechtsextremismus in Deutschland—Ein Lagebild zu Beobachtungsschwerpunkten des Verfassungsschutzes. November 2000.

25. Cerf. Internet in the next five to ten years. 1999. Available: < *http://www.worldcom.com/about_the_company/cerfs_up/issues/Internet_in5to10.phtml* >.

26. Larry Downes, Chunka Mui, and Nicholas Negroponte. Unleashing the Killer App. Harvard Business School Press: 2000.

27. David Raths. Great Wall. Interactive Week. November 27, 2000. Available: < *http://www.zdnet.com/intweek/stories/news/0,4164,2659146,00.html* >.

QUESTIONS FOR DISCUSSION AND WRITING

1. The author gives three paragraphs of background before asserting his thesis. Do you think it is necessary to do so to convince his readers of the merit of his claim? If not, where would you place the thesis?

2. Evaluate the thesis statement, topic points, and paragraph structure. How well is the essay organized? How well-developed are the tone, stance, and integration of evidence? How argumentative is this essay in terms of the continuum discussed in Chapter One? Does the author anticipate opposing views and respond to them? Has he made a convincing case for his proposal?

3. Schloter argues that the diversity in the United States makes racist material on the Internet less problematic than it is in smaller, more homogenous societies such as France and Germany. Does this view seem logical to you? Why or why not? Were you aware of how extensive the cultural differences are among Western countries with regard to attitudes toward free speech?

4. With a peer or in small groups, draft a "global fundamental standard" for regulating hate speech on the Internet. Alternatively, write a response to Schloter either agreeing with him or arguing that the Internet should remain unregulated with regard to racist speech.

The Clash of Civilizations?

SAMUEL HUNTINGTON

Samuel Huntington (1927-) is a political scientist who often analyzes the conflict between military and civilian governments. He is University Professor at Harvard University and director of the John M. Olin Institute for Strategic Studies. He was director of security planning for the National Security Council during the Carter administration, the founder and co-editor of *Foreign Policy,* and president of the American Political Science Association. In "The Clash of Civilizations?", Huntington claims that the primary conflicts of the twenty-first century will be between civilizations rather than nations. Huntington asserts that the world is divided into roughly eight different civilizations: Western, Confucian, Japanese, Islamic, Hindu, Slavic-Orthodox, Latin American, and African. Huntington believes these civilizations will conflict with each other because basic differences in history, language, and especially religion produce major differences in, for example, legal systems, the citizen's relationship to the state, social norms, and economic practices. The essay that follows was published in *Foreign Affairs* in 1993. He has also authored a book, *The Clash of Civilizations and the Remaking of World Order* (1996) and co-edited *Culture Matters* (2000).

The Next Pattern of Conflict

World politics is entering a new phase, and intellectuals have not hesitated to proliferate visions of what it will be—the end of history, the return of traditional rivalries between nation states, and the decline of the nation state from the conflicting pulls of tribalism and globalization, among others. Each of these visions catches aspects of the emerging reality. Yet they all miss a crucial, indeed a central, aspect of what global politics is likely to be in the coming years.

It is my hypothesis that the fundamental source of conflict in this new world will not be primarily ideological or primarily economic. The great divisions among humankind and the dominating source of conflict will be cultural. Nation states will remain the most powerful actors in world affairs, but the principal conflicts of global politics will occur between nations and groups of different civilizations. The clash of civilizations will dominate global politics. The fault lines between civilizations will be the battle lines of the future.

Conflict between civilizations will be the latest phase in the evolution of conflict in the modern world. For a century and a half after the emergence of the modern international system with the Peace of Westphalia, the conflicts of the Western world were largely among princes—emperors, absolute monarchs, and constitutional monarchs attempting to expand their bureaucracies, their armies, their mercantilist economic strength and, most important, the territory they ruled. In the process they created nation states, and beginning with the French Revolution the principal lines of conflict were between nations rather than princes. In 1793, as R.R. Palmer put it, "The wars of kings were over; the wars of peoples had begun." This nineteenth-century pattern lasted until the end of World War I. Then, as a result of the Russian Revolution and the reaction against it, the conflict of nations yielded to the conflict of ideologies, first among communism, fascism-Nazism, and liberal democracy, and then between communism and liberal democracy. During the Cold War, this latter conflict became embodied in the struggle between the two superpowers, neither of which was a nation state in the classical European sense and each of which defined its identity in terms of its ideology.

These conflicts between princes, nation states, and ideologies were primarily conflicts within Western civilization, "Western civil wars," as William Lind has labeled them. This was as true of the Cold War as it was of the world wars and the earlier wars of the seventeenth, eighteenth, and nineteenth centuries. With the end of the Cold War, international politics moves out of its Western phase, and its centerpiece becomes the interaction between the West and non-Western civilizations and among non-Western civilizations. In the politics of civilizations, the peoples and governments of non-Western civilizations no longer remain the objects of history as targets of Western colonialism but join the West as movers and shapers of history.

The Nature of Civilizations

During the Cold War the world was divided into the First, Second, and Third Worlds. Those divisions are no longer relevant. It is far more meaningful now to group countries not in terms of their political or economic systems or in terms of their level of economic development but rather in terms of their culture and civilization.

What do we mean when we talk of a civilization? A civilization is a cultural entity. Villages, regions, ethnic groups, nationalities, religious groups, all have distinct cultures at different levels of cultural heterogeneity. The culture of a village in southern Italy may be different from that of a village in northern Italy, but both will share in a common Italian culture that distinguishes them from German villages. European communities, in turn, will share cultural features that distinguish them from Arab or Chinese communities. Arabs, Chinese, and Westerners, however, are not part of any broader cultural entity. They constitute civilizations. A civilization is thus the highest cultural grouping of people and the broadest level of cultural identity people have short of that which distinguishes humans from other species. It is defined both by common objective elements, such as language, history, religion, customs, institutions, and by the subjective self-identification of people. People have levels of identity: a resident of Rome may define himself with varying degrees of intensity as a Roman, an Italian, a Catholic, a Christian, a European, a Westerner. The civilization to which he belongs is the broadest level of identification with which he intensely identifies. People can and do redefine their identities and, as a result, the composition and boundaries of civilizations change.

Civilizations may involve a large number of people, as with China ("a civilization pretending to be a state," as Lucian Pye put it), or a very small number of people, such as the Anglophone Caribbean. A civilization may include several nation states, as is the case with Western, Latin American, and Arab civilizations, or only one, as is the case with Japanese civilization. Civilizations obviously blend and overlap, and may include subcivilizations. Western civilization has two major variants, European and North American, and Islam has its Arab, Turkic, and Malay subdivisions. Civilizations are nonetheless meaningful entities, and while the lines between them are seldom sharp, they are real. Civilizations are dynamic; they rise and fall; they divide and merge. And, as any student of history knows, civilizations disappear and are buried in the sands of time.

Westerners tend to think of nation states as the principal actors in global affairs. They have been that, however, for only a few centuries. The broader reaches of human history have been the history of civilizations. In *A Study of History,* Arnold Toynbee identified twenty-one major civilizations; only six of them exist in the contemporary world.

Why Civilizations Will Clash

Civilization identity will be increasingly important in the future, and the world will be shaped in large measure by the interactions among seven or eight major civilizations. These include

Western, Confucian, Japanese, Islamic, Hindu, Slavic-Orthodox, Latin American, and possibly African civilization. The most important conflicts of the future will occur along the cultural fault lines separating these civilizations from one another.

Why will this be the case?

First, differences among civilizations are not only real; they are basic. Civilizations are differentiated from each other by history, language, culture, tradition, and, most important, religion. The people of different civilizations have different views on the relations between God and man, the individual and the group, the citizen and the state, parents and children, husband and wife, as well as differing views of the relative importance of rights and responsibilities, liberty and authority, equality and hierarchy. These differences are the product of centuries. They will not soon disappear. They are far more fundamental than differences among political ideologies and political regimes. Differences do not necessarily mean conflict, and conflict does not necessarily mean violence. Over the centuries, however, differences among civilizations have generated the most prolonged and the most violent conflicts.

Second, the world is becoming a smaller place. The interactions between peoples of different civilizations are increasing; these increasing interactions intensify civilization-consciousness and awareness of differences between civilizations and commonalities within civilizations. North African immigration to France generated hostility among Frenchmen and at the same time increased receptivity to immigration by "good" European Catholic Poles. Americans react far more negatively to Japanese investment than to larger investments from Canada and European countries. Similarly, as Donald Horowitz has pointed out, "An Ibo may be . . . an Owerri Ibo or an Onitsha Ibo in what was the Eastern region of Nigeria. In Lagos, he is simply an Ibo. In London, he is a Nigerian. In New York, he is an African." The interactions among peoples of different civilizations enhance the civilization-consciousness of people that, in turn, invigorates differences and animosities stretching or thought to stretch back deep into history.

Third, the processes of economic modernization and social change throughout the world are separating people from longstanding local identities. They also weaken the nation state as a source of identity. In much of the world, religion has moved in to fill this gap, often in the form of movements that are labeled "fundamentalist." Such movements are found in Western Christianity, Judaism, Buddhism, and Hinduism, as well as in Islam. In most countries and most religions the people active in

10

fundamentalist movements are young, college-educated, middle-class technicians, professionals, and business persons. The "un-secularization of the world." George Weigel has remarked, "is one of the dominant social facts of life in the late twentieth century." The revival of religion, "la revanche de Dieu," as Gilles Kepel labeled it, provides a basis for identify and commitment that transcends national boundaries and unites civilizations.

Fourth, the growth of civilization-consciousness is enhanced by the dual role of the West. On the one hand, the West is at a peak of power. At the same time, however, and perhaps as a result, a return to the roots phenomenon is occurring among non-Western civilizations. Increasingly one hears references to trends toward a turning inward and "Asianization" in Japan, the end of the Nehru legacy and the "Hinduization" of India, the failure of Western ideas of socialism and nationalism and hence "re-Islamization" of the Middle East, and now a debate over West-ernization versus Russianization in Boris Yeltsin's country. A West at the peak of its power confronts non-Wests that increasingly have the desire, the will and the resources to shape the world in non-Western ways.

In the past, the elites of non-Western societies were usually   15
the people who were most involved with the West; had been educated at Oxford, the Sorbonne, or Sandhurst; and had absorbed Western attitudes and values. At the same time, the populace in non-Western countries often remained deeply imbued with the indigenous culture. Now, however, these relationships are being reversed. A de-Westernization and indigenization of elites is occurring in many non-Western countries at the same time that Western, usually American, cultures, styles, and habits become more popular among the mass of the people.

Fifth, cultural characteristics and differences are less mutable and hence less easily compromised and resolved than political and economic ones. In the former Soviet Union, communists can become democrats, the rich can become poor and the poor rich, but Russians cannot become Estonians and Azeris cannot become Armenians. In class and ideological conflicts, the key question was "Which side are you on?" and people could and did choose sides and change sides. In conflicts between civilizations, the question is "What are you?" That is a given that cannot be changed. And as we know, from Bosnia to the Caucasus to the Sudan, the wrong answer to that question can mean a bullet in the head. Even more than ethnicity, religion discriminates sharply and exclusively among people. A person can be half-French and half-Arab and simultaneously even a citizen of two countries. It is more difficult to be half-Catholic and half-Muslim.

Finally, economic regionalism is increasing. The proportions of total trade that were intraregional rose between 1980 and 1989 from 51 percent to 59 percent in Europe, 33 percent to 37 percent in East Asia, and 32 percent to 36 percent in North America. The importance of regional economic blocs is likely to continue to increase in the future. On the one hand, successful economic regionalism will reinforce civilization-consciousness. On the other hand, economic regionalism may succeed only when it is rooted in a common civilization. The European Community rests on the shared foundation of European culture and Western Christianity. The success of the North American Free Trade Area depends on the convergence now underway of Mexican, Canadian, and American cultures. Japan, in contrast, faces difficulties in creating a comparable economic entity in East Asia because Japan is a society and civilization unique to itself. However strong the trade and investment links Japan may develop with other East Asian countries, its cultural differences with those countries inhibit and perhaps preclude its promoting regional economic integration like that in Europe and North America.

Common culture, in contrast, is clearly facilitating the rapid expansion of the economic relations between the People's Republic of China and Hong Kong, Taiwan, Singapore, and the overseas Chinese communities in other Asian countries. With the Cold War over, cultural commonalities increasingly overcome ideological differences, and mainland China and Taiwan move closer together. If cultural commonality is a prerequisite for economic integration, the principal East Asian economic bloc of the future is likely to be centered on China. This bloc is, in fact, already coming into existence. As Murray Weidenbaum has observed,

> Despite the current Japanese dominance of the region, the Chinese-based economy of Asia is rapidly emerging as a new epicenter for industry, commerce, and finance. This strategic area contains substantial amounts of technology and manufacturing capability (Taiwan); outstanding entrepreneurial, marketing, and services acumen (Hong Kong); a fine communications network (Singapore); a tremendous pool of financial capital (all three); and very large endowments of land, resources, and labor (mainland China). . . . From Guangzhou to Singapore, from Kuala Lumpur to Manila, this influential network—often based on extensions of the traditional clans—has been described as the backbone of the East Asian economy.[1]

Culture and religion also form the basis of the Economic Cooperation Organization, which brings together ten non-Arab Muslim countries: Iran, Pakistan, Turkey, Azerbaijan, Kazakhstan,

Kyrgyzstan, Turkmenistan, Tadjikistan, Uzbekistan, and Afghanistan. One impetus to the revival and expansion of this organization, founded originally in the 1960s by Turkey, Pakistan, and Iran, is the realization by the leaders of several of these countries that they had no chance of admission to the European Community. Similarly, Caricom, the Central American Common Market, and Mercosur rest on common cultural foundations. Efforts to build a broader Caribbean-Central American economic entity bridging the Anglo-Latin divide, however, have to date failed.

As people define their identity in ethnic and religious terms, they are likely to see an "us" versus "them" relation existing between themselves and people of different ethnicity or religion. The end of ideologically defined states in Eastern Europe and the former Soviet Union permits traditional ethnic identities and animosities to come to the fore. Differences in culture and religion create differences over policy issues, ranging from human rights to immigration to trade and commerce to the environment. Geographical propinquity gives rise to conflicting territorial claims from Bosnia to Mindanao. Most important, the efforts of the West to promote its values of democracy and liberalism as universal values, to maintain its military predominance, and to advance its economic interests engender countering responses from other civilizations. Decreasingly able to mobilize support and form coalitions on the basis of ideology, governments and groups will increasingly attempt to mobilize support by appealing to common religion and civilization identity. 20

The clash of civilizations thus occurs at two levels. At the micro-level, adjacent groups along the fault lines between civilizations struggle, often violently, over the control of territory and each other. At the macro-level, states from different civilizations compete for relative military and economic power, struggle over the control of international institutions and third parties, and competitively promote their particular political and religious values.

The Fault Lines between Civilizations

The fault lines between civilizations are replacing the political and ideological boundaries of the Cold War as the flash points for crisis and bloodshed. The Cold War began when the Iron Curtain divided Europe politically and ideologically. The Cold War ended with the end of the Iron Curtain. As the ideological division of Europe has disappeared, the cultural division of Europe between

Western Christianity, on the one hand, and Orthodox Christianity and Islam, on the other, has reemerged. The most significant dividing line in Europe, as William Wallace has suggested, may well be the eastern boundary of Western Christianity in the year 1500. This line runs along what are now the boundaries between Finland and Russia and between the Baltic states and Russia, cuts through Belarus and Ukraine separating the more Catholic western Ukraine from Orthodox eastern Ukraine, swings westward separating Transylvania from the rest of Romania, and then goes through Yugoslavia almost exactly along the line now separating Croatia and Slovenia from the rest of Yugoslavia. In the Balkans this line, of course, coincides with the historic boundary between the Hapsburg and Ottoman empires. The peoples to the north and west of this line are Protestant or Catholic; they shared the common experiences of European history—feudalism, the Renaissance, the Reformation, the Enlightenment, the French Revolution, the Industrial Revolution; they are generally economically better off than the peoples to the east; and they may now look forward to increasing involvement in a common European economy and to the consolidation of democratic political systems. The peoples to the east and south of this line are Orthodox or Muslim; they historically belonged to the Ottoman or Tsarist empires and were only lightly touched by the shaping events in the rest of Europe; they are generally less advanced economically; they seem much less likely to develop stable democratic political systems. The Velvet Curtain of culture has replaced the Iron Curtain of ideology as the most significant dividing line in Europe.

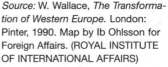

Source: W. Wallace, *The Transformation of Western Europe*. London: Pinter, 1990. Map by Ib Ohlsson for Foreign Affairs. (ROYAL INSTITUTE OF INTERNATIONAL AFFAIRS)

As the events in Yugoslavia show, it is not only a line of difference; it is also at times a line of bloody conflict.

Conflict along the fault line between Western and Islamic civilizations has been going on for 1,300 years. After the founding of Islam, the Arab and Moorish surge west and north only ended at Tours in 732. From the eleventh to the thirteenth century the Crusaders attempted with temporary success to bring Christianity and Christian rule to the Holy Land. From the fourteenth to the seventeenth century, the Ottoman Turks reversed the balance, extended their sway over the Middle East and the Balkans, captured Constantinople, and twice laid siege to Vienna. In the nineteenth and early twentieth centuries as Ottoman power declined Britain, France, and Italy established Western control over most of North Africa and the Middle East.

After World War II, the West, in turn, began to retreat; the colonial empires disappeared; first Arab nationalism and then Islamic fundamentalism manifested themselves; the West became heavily dependent on the Persian Gulf countries for its energy; the oil-rich Muslim countries became money-rich and, when they wished to, weapons-rich. Several wars occurred between Arabs and Israel (created by the West). France fought a bloody and ruthless war in Algeria for most of the 1950s; British and French forces invaded Egypt in 1956; American forces went into Lebanon in 1958; subsequently American forces returned to Lebanon, attacked Libya, and engaged in various military encounters with Iran; Arab and Islamic terrorists, supported by at least three Middle Eastern governments, employed the weapon of the weak and bombed Western planes and installations and seized Western hostages. This warfare between Arabs and the West culminated in 1990, when the United States sent a massive army to the Persian Gulf to defend some Arab countries against aggression by another. In its aftermath NATO planning is increasingly directed to potential threats and instability along its "southern tier."

This centuries-old military interaction between the West and Islam is unlikely to decline. It could become more virulent. The Gulf War left some Arabs feeling proud that Saddam Hussein had attacked Israel and stood up to the West. It also left many feeling humiliated and resentful of the West's military presence in the Persian Gulf, the West's overwhelming military dominance, and their apparent inability to shape their own destiny. Many Arab countries, in addition to the oil exporters, are reaching levels of economic and social development where autocratic forms of government become inappropriate and efforts to introduce democracy become stronger. Some openings in Arab political systems have already occurred. The principal beneficiaries of these openings have been Islamist movements. In the Arab

25

world, in short, Western democracy strengthens anti-Western political forces. This may be a passing phenomenon, but it surely complicates relations between Islamic countries and the West.

Those relations are also complicated by demography. The spectacular population growth in Arab countries, particularly in North Africa, has led to increased migration to Western Europe. The movement within Western Europe toward minimizing internal boundaries has sharpened political sensitivies with respect to this development. In Italy, France, and Germany, racism is increasingly open, and political reactions and violence against Arab and Turkish migrants have become more intense and more widespread since 1990.

On both sides the interaction between Islam and the West is seen as a clash of civilizations. The West's "next confrontation," observes M. J. Akbar, an Indian Muslim author, "is definitely going to come from the Muslim world. It is in the sweep of the Islamic nations from the Maghreb to Pakistan that the struggle for a new world order will begin." Bernard Lewis comes to a similar conclusion:

> We are facing a mood and a movement far transcending the level of issues and policies and the governments that pursue them This is no less than a clash of civilizations— the perhaps irrational but surely historic reaction of an ancient rival against our Judeo-Christian heritage, our secular present, and the worldwide expansion of both.[2]

Historically, the other great antagonistic interaction of Arab Islamic civilization has been with the pagan, animist, and now increasingly Christian black peoples to the south. In the past, this antagonism was epitomized in the image of Arab slave dealers and black slaves. It has been reflected in the ongoing civil war in the Sudan between Arabs and blacks; the fighting in Chad between Libyan-supported insurgents and the government; the tensions between Orthodox Christians and Muslims in the Horn of Africa; and the political conflicts, recurring riots, and communal violence between Muslims and Christians in Nigeria. The modernization of Africa and the spread of Christianity are likely to enhance the probability of violence along this fault line. Symptomatic of the intensification of this conflict was Pope John Paul II's speech in Khartoum in February 1993 attacking the actions of the Sudan's Islamist government against the Christian minority there.

On the northern border of Islam, conflict has increasingly erupted between Orthodox and Muslim peoples, including the carnage of Bosnia and Sarajevo, the simmering violence between Serb and Albanian, the tenuous relations between Bulgarians and their Turkish minority, the violence between Ossetians and Ingush, the unremitting slaughter of each other by Armenians and Azeris, the tense relations between Russians and Muslims in Central Asia, and the deployment of Russian troops to protect Russian interests in the Caucasus and Central Asia. Religion reinforces the revival of ethnic identities and restimulates Russian fears about the security of their southern borders. This concern is well captured by Archie Roosevelt:

> Much of Russian history concerns the struggle between the Slavs and the Turkic peoples on their borders, which dates back to the foundation of the Russian state more than a thousand years ago. In the Slavs' millennium-long confrontation with their eastern neighbors lies the key to an understanding not only of Russian history, but Russian character. To understand Russian realities today one has to have a concept of the great Turkic ethnic group that has preoccupied Russians through the centuries.[3]

The conflict of civilizations is deeply rooted elsewhere in Asia. The historic clash between Muslim and Hindu in the subcontinent manifests itself now not only in the rivalry between Pakistan and India but also in intensifying religious strife within India between increasingly militant Hindu groups and India's substantial Muslim minority. The destruction of the Ayodhya mosque in December 1992 brought to the fore the issue of whether India will remain a secular democratic state or become a Hindu one. In East Asia, China has outstanding territorial disputes with most of its neighbors. It has pursued a ruthless policy toward the Buddhist people of Tibet, and it is pursuing an increasingly ruthless policy toward its Turkic-Muslim minority. With the Cold War over, the underlying differences between China and the United States have reasserted themselves in areas such as human rights, trade, and weapons proliferation. These differences are unlikely to moderate. A "new cold war," Deng Xiaoping reportedly asserted in 1991, is under way between China and America.

The same phrase has been applied to the increasingly difficult relations between Japan and the United States. Here cultural difference exacerbates economic conflict. People on each side allege racism on the other, but at least on the American side the antipathies are not racial but cultural. The basic values, attitudes, and behavioral patterns of the two societies could hardly be more different. The economic issues between the United States and Europe are no less serious than those between the United States and Japan, but they do not have the same political salience and emotional intensity because the differences between American culture and European culture are so much less than those between American civilization and Japanese civilization.

The interactions between civilizations vary greatly in the extent to which they are likely to be characterized by violence. Economic competition clearly predominates between the American and European subcivilizations of the West and between both of them and Japan. On the Eurasian continent, however, the proliferation of ethnic conflict, epitomized at the extreme in "ethnic cleansing," has not been totally random. It has been most frequent and most violent between groups belonging to different civilizations. In Eurasia the great historic fault lines between civilizations are once more aflame. This is particularly true along the boundaries of the crescent-shaped Islamic bloc of nations from the bulge of Africa to central Asia. Violence also occurs between Muslims, on the one hand, and Orthodox Serbs in the Balkans, Jews in Israel, Hindus in India, Buddhists in Burma, and Catholics in the Philippines. Islam has bloody borders.

Civilization Rallying: The Kin-Country Syndrome

Groups or states belonging to one civilization that become involved in war with people from a different civilization naturally try to rally support from other members of their own civilization. As the post-Cold War world evolves, civilization commonality, what H. D. S. Greenway has termed the "kin-country" syndrome, is replacing political ideology and traditional balance of power considerations as the principal basis for cooperation and coalitions. It can be seen gradually emerging in the post-Cold War conflicts in the Persian Gulf, the Caucasus, and Bosnia. None of these was a full-scale war between civilizations, but each involved some elements of civilizational rallying, which seemed to become more important as the conflict continued and which may provide a foretaste of the future.

First, in the Gulf War one Arab state invaded another and then fought a coalition of Arab, Western, and other states. While only a few Muslim governments overtly supported Saddam Hussein, many Arab elites privately cheered him on, and he was highly popular among large sections of the Arab publics. Islamic fundamentalist movements universally supported Iraq rather than the Western-backed governments of Kuwait and Saudi Arabia. Forswearing Arab nationalism, Saddam Hussein explicitly invoked an Islamic appeal. He and his supporters attempted to define the war as a war between civilizations. "It is not the world against Iraq," as Safar al-Hawali, dean of Islamic Studies at the Umm al-Qura University in Mecca, put it in a widely circulated tape. "It is the West against Islam." Ignoring the rivalry between Iran and Iraq, the chief Iranian religious leader, Ayatollah Ali Khamenei, called for a holy war against the West: "The struggle against American aggression, greed, plans, and policies will be counted as a jihad, and anybody who is killed on that path is a martyr." "This is a war," King Hussein of Jordan argued, "against all Arabs and all Muslims and not against Iraq alone."

The rallying of substantial sections of Arab elites and publics   35 behind Saddam Hussein caused those Arab governments in the anti-Iraq coalition to moderate their activities and temper their public statements. Arab governments opposed or distanced themselves from subsequent Western efforts to apply pressure on Iraq, including enforcement of a no-fly zone in the summer of 1992 and the bombing of Iraq in January 1993. The Western-Soviet-Turkish-Arab anti-Iraq coalition of 1990 had by 1993 become a coalition of almost only the West and Kuwait against Iraq.

Muslims contrasted Western actions against Iraq with the West's failure to protect. Bosnians against Serbs and to impose sanctions on Israel for violating UN resolutions. The West, they alleged, was using a double standard. A world of clashing civilizations, however, is inevitably a world of double standards: people apply one standard to their kin-countries and a different standard to others.

Second, the kin-country syndrome also appeared in conflicts in the former Soviet Union. Armenian military successes in 1992 and 1993 stimulated Turkey to become increasingly supportive of its religious, ethnic, and linguistic brethren in Azerbaijan. "We have a Turkish nation feeling the same sentiments as the Azerbaijanis," said one Turkish official in 1992. "We are under pressure. Our newspapers are full of the photos of atrocities and are asking us if we are still serious about pursuing our neutral policy. Maybe we should show Armenia that there's a big Turkey in the region." President Turgut Özal agreed, remarking that Turkey should at least "scare the Armenians a little bit." Turkey, Özal threatened again in 1993, would "show its fangs." Turkish Air Force jets flew reconnaissance flights along the Armenian border; Turkey suspended food shipments and air flights to Armenia; and Turkey and Iran announced they would not accept dismemberment of Azerbaijan. In the last years of its existence, the Soviet government supported Azerbaijan because its government was dominated by former communists. With the end of the Soviet Union, however, political considerations gave way to religious ones. Russian troops fought on the side of the Armenians, and Azerbaijan accused the "Russian government of turning 180 degrees" toward support for Christian Armenia.

Third, with respect to the fighting in the former Yugoslavia, Western publics manifested sympathy and support for the Bosnian Muslims and the horrors they suffered at the hands of the Serbs. Relatively little concern was expressed, however, over Croatian attacks on Muslims and participation in the dismemberment of Bosnia-Herzegovina. In the early stages of the Yugoslav breakup, Germany, in an unusual display of diplomatic initiative and muscle, induced the other eleven members of the European Community to follow its lead in recognizing Slovenia and Croatia. As a result of the pope's determination to provide strong backing to the two Catholic countries, the Vatican extended recognition even before the Community did. The United States followed the European lead. Thus the leading actors in Western civilization rallied behind their coreligionists. Subsequently Croatia was reported to be receiving substantial quantities of arms from Central European and other Western countries. Boris Yeltsin's government, on the other hand, attempted to pursue a middle course that would be sympathetic to the Orthodox Serbs but not alienate Russia from the West. Russian conservative and nationalist groups, however, including many legislators, attacked the government for not being more forthcoming in its support for the Serbs. By early 1993 several hundred Russians apparently were serving with the Serbian forces, and reports circulated of Russian arms being supplied to Serbia.

Islamic governments and groups, on the other hand, castigated the West for not coming to the defense of the Bosnians. Iranian leaders urged Muslims from all countries to provide help to Bosnia; in violation of the UN arms embargo, Iran supplied weapons and men for the Bosnians; Iranian-supported Lebanese groups sent guerrillas to train and organize the Bosnian forces. In 1993 up to 4,000 Muslims from over two dozen Islamic countries were reported to be fighting in Bosnia. The governments of Saudi Arabia and other countries felt under increasing pressure from fundamentalist groups in their own societies to provide more vigorous support for the Bosnians. By the end of 1992, Saudi Arabia had reportedly supplied substantial funding for weapons and supplies for the Bosnians, which significantly increased their military capabilities vis-à-vis the Serbs.

In the 1930s the Spanish Civil War provoked intervention from countries that politically were fascist, communist, and democratic. In the 1990s the Yugoslav conflict is provoking intervention from countries that are Muslim, Orthodox, and West-

40

ern Christian. The parallel has not gone unnoticed. "The war in Bosnia-Herzegovina has become the emotional equivalent of the fight against fascism in the Spanish Civil War," one Saudi editor observed. "Those who died there are regarded as martyrs who tried to save their fellow Muslims."

Conflicts and violence will also occur between states and groups within the same civilization. Such conflicts, however, are likely to be less intense and less likely to expand than conflicts between civilizations. Common membership in a civilization reduces the probability of violence in situations where it might otherwise occur. In 1991 and 1992 many people were alarmed by the possibility of violent conflict between Russia and Ukraine over territory, particularly Crimea, the Black Sea fleet, nuclear weapons, and economic issues. If civilization is what counts, however, the likelihood of violence between Ukrainians and Russians should be low. They are two Slavic, primarily Orthodox peoples who have had close relationships with each other for centuries. As of early 1993, despite all the reasons for conflict, the leaders of the two countries were effectively negotiating and defusing the issues between the two countries. While there has been serious fighting between Muslims and Christians elsewhere in the former Soviet Union and much tension and some fighting between Western and Orthodox Christians in the Baltic states, there has been virtually no violence between Russians and Ukrainians.

Civilization rallying to date has been limited, but it has been growing, and it clearly has the potential to spread much further. As the conflicts in the Persian Gulf, the Caucasus, and Bosnia continued, the positions of nations and the cleavages between them increasingly were along civilizational lines. Populist politicians, religious leaders, and the media have found it a potent means of arousing mass support and of pressuring hesitant governments. In the coming years, the local conflicts most likely to escalate into major wars will be those, as in Bosnia and the Caucasus, along the fault lines between civilizations. The next world war, if there is one, will be a war between civilizations.

The West versus the Rest

The West is now at an extraordinary peak of power in relation to other civilizations. Its superpower opponent has disappeared from the map. Military conflict among Western states is unthinkable, and Western military power is unrivaled. Apart from Japan, the West faces no economic challenge. It dominates international political and security institutions and, with Japan, international economic institutions. Global political and security issues are effectively settled by a directorate of the United States, Britain, and France, world economic issues by a directorate of the United States, Germany, and Japan, all of which maintain extraordinarily close relations with each other to the exclusion of lesser and largely non-Western countries. Decisions made at the UN Security Council or in the International Monetary Fund (IMF) that reflect the interests of the West are presented to the world as reflecting the desires of the world community. The very phrase "the world community" has become the euphemistic collective noun (replacing "the Free World") to give global legitimacy to actions reflecting the interests of the United States and other Western powers.[4] Through the IMF and other international economic institutions, the West promotes its economic interests and imposes on other nations the economic policies it thinks appropriate. In any poll of non-Western peoples, the IMF undoubtedly would win the support of finance ministers and a few others, but get an overwhelmingly unfavorable rating from just about everyone else, who would agree with Georgy Arbatov's characterization of IMF officials as "neo-Bolsheviks who love expropriating other people's money, imposing undemocratic and alien rules of economic and political conduct and stifling economic freedom."

Western domination of the UN Security Council and its decisions, tempered only by occasional abstention by China, produced UN legitimation of the West's use of force to drive Iraq out of Kuwait and its elimination of Iraq's sophisticated weapons and capacity to produce such weapons. It also produced the quite unprecedented action by the United States, Britain, and France in getting the Security Council to demand that Libya hand over the Pan Am 103 bombing suspects and then to impose sanctions when Libya refused. After defeating the largest Arab army, the West did not hesitate to throw its weight around in the Arab world. The West in effect is using international institutions, military power, and economic resources to run the world in ways that will maintain Western predominance, protect Western interests, and promote Western political and economic values.

That at least is the way in which non-Westerners see the new world, and there is a significant element of truth in their view. Differences in power and struggles for military, economic, and institutional power are thus one source of conflict between the West and other civilizations. Differences in culture, that is, basic values and beliefs, are a second source of conflict. V.S. Naipaul has argued that Western civilization is the "universal civilization" that "fits all men." At a superficial level much of Western culture has indeed permeated the rest of the world. At a more basic level, however, Western concepts differ fundamentally from those prevalent in other civilizations. Western ideas of individualism, liberalism, constitutionalism, human rights, equality, liberty, the rule of law, democracy, free markets, the separation of church and state, often have little resonance in Islamic, Confucian, Japanese, Hindu, Buddhist, or Orthodox cultures. Western efforts to propagate such ideas produce instead a reaction against "human rights imperialism" and a reaffirmation of indigenous values, as can be seen in the support for religious fundamentalism by the younger generation in non-Western cultures. The very notion that there could be a "universal civilization" is a Western idea, directly at odds with the particularism of most Asian societies and their emphasis on what distinguishes one people from another. Indeed, the author of a review of a hundred comparative studies of values in different societies concluded that "the values that are most important in the West are least important worldwide."[5] In the political realm, of course, these differences are most manifest in the efforts of the United States and other Western powers to induce other peoples to adopt Western ideas concerning democracy and human rights. Modern democratic government originated in the West. When it has developed in non-Western societies it has usually been the product of Western colonialism or imposition.

The central axis of world politics in the future is likely to be, in Kishore Mahbubani's phrase, the conflict between "the West and the Rest" and the responses of non-Western civilizations to Western power and values.[6] Those responses generally take one or a combination of three forms. At one extreme, non-Western states can, like Burma and North Korea, attempt to pursue a course of isolation, to insulate their societies from penetration or "corruption" by the West, and, in effect, to opt out of participation in the Western-dominated global community. The costs of this course, however, are high, and few states have pursued it exclusively. A second alternative, the equivalent of "bandwagoning" in international relations theory, is to attempt to join the West and accept its values and institutions. The third alternative is to attempt to "balance" the West by developing economic and military power and cooperating with other non-Western societies against the West, while preserving indigenous values and institutions; in short, to modernize but not to Westernize.

The Torn Countries

In the future, as people differentiate themselves by civilization, countries with large numbers of peoples of different civilizations, such as the former Soviet Union and Yugoslavia, are candidates for dismemberment. Some other countries have a fair degree of cultural homogeneity but are divided over whether their society belongs to one civilization or another. These are torn countries. Their leaders typically wish to pursue a bandwagoning strategy and to make their countries members of the West, but the history, culture, and traditions of their countries are non-Western. The most obvious and prototypical torn country is Turkey. The late twentieth-century leaders of Turkey have followed in the Attatürk tradition and defined Turkey as a modern, secular, Western nation state. They allied Turkey with the West in NATO and in the Gulf War; they applied for membership in the European Community. At the same time, however, elements in Turkish society have supported an Islamic revival and have argued that Turkey is basically a Middle Eastern Muslim society. In addition, while the elite of Turkey has defined Turkey as a Western society, the elite of the West refuses to accept Turkey as such. Turkey will not become a member of the European Community, and the real reason, as President Özal said, "is that we are Muslim and they are Christian and they don't say that." Having rejected Mecca, and then being rejected by Brussels, where does Turkey look? Tashkent may be the answer. The end of the Soviet Union gives Turkey the opportunity to become the leader of a revived Turkic civilization involving seven countries from the borders of Greece to those of China. Encouraged by the West, Turkey is making strenuous efforts to carve out this new identity for itself.

During the past decade Mexico has assumed a position somewhat similar to that of Turkey. Just as Turkey abandoned its historic opposition to Europe and attempted to join Europe, Mexico has stopped defining itself by its opposition to the United States and is instead attempting to imitate the United States and to join it in the North American Free Trade area. Mexican leaders are engaged in the great task of redefining Mexican identity and have introduced fundamental economic reforms that eventually will lead to fundamental political change. In 1991 a top adviser to President Carlos Salinas de Gortari described at length to me all the changes the Salinas government was making. When he finished, I remarked: "That's most impressive. It seems to me that basically you want to change Mexico from a Latin American country into a North American country." He looked at me with surprise and exclaimed: "Exactly! That's precisely what we are trying to do, but of course we could never say so publicly." As his remark indicates, in Mexico as in Turkey, significant elements in society resist the redefinition of their country's identity. In Turkey, European-oriented leaders have to make gestures to Islam (Özal's pilgrimage to Mecca); so also Mexico's North American-oriented leaders have to make gestures to those who hold Mexico to be a Latin American country (Salinas' Ibero-American Guadalajara summit).

Historically Turkey has been the most profoundly torn country. For the United States, Mexico is the most immediate torn country. Globally the most important torn country is Russia. The question of whether Russia is part of the West or the leader of a distinct Slavic-Orthodox civilization has been a recurring one in Russian history. That issue was obscured by the communist victory in Russia, which imported a Western ideology, adapted it to Russian conditions, and then challenged the West in the name of that ideology. The dominance of communism shut off the historic debate over Westernization versus Russification. With communism discredited Russians once again face that question.

President Yeltsin is adopting Western principles and goals   50
and seeking to make Russia a "normal" country and a part of the West. Yet both the Russian elite and the Russian public are divided on this issue. Among the more moderate dissenters, Sergei Stankevich argues that Russia should reject the "Atlanticist" course, which would lead it "to become European, to become a part of the world economy in rapid and organized fashion, to become the eighth member of the Seven, and to put particular emphasis on Germany and the United States as the two dominant members of the Atlantic alliance." While also rejecting an exclusively Eurasian policy, Stankevich nonetheless argues that Russia should give priority to the protection of Russians in other countries, emphasize its Turkic and Muslim connections, and promote "an appreciable redistribution of our resources, our options, our ties, and our interests in favor of Asia, of the eastern direction." People of this persuasion criticize Yeltsin for subordinating Russia's interests to those of the West, for reducing Russian military strength, for failing to support traditional friends such as Serbia, and for pushing economic and political reform in ways injurious to the Russian people. Indicative of this trend is the new popularity of the ideas of Petr Savitsky, who in the 1920s argued that Russia was a unique Eurasian civilization.[7] More extreme dissidents voice much more blatantly nationalist, anti-Western, and anti-Semitic views, and urge Russia to redevelop its military strength and to establish closer ties with China

and Muslim countries. The people of Russia are as divided as the elite. An opinion survey in European Russia in the spring of 1992 revealed that 40 percent of the public had positive attitudes toward the West and 36 percent had negative attitudes. As it has been for much of its history, Russia in the early 1990s is truly a torn country.

To redefine its civilization identity, a torn country must meet three requirements. First, its political and economic elite has to be generally supportive of and enthusiastic about this move. Second, its public has to be willing to acquiesce in the redefinition. Third, the dominant groups in the recipient civilization have to be willing to embrace the convert. All three requirements in large part exist with respect to Mexico. The first two in large part exist with respect to Turkey. It is not clear that any of them exist with respect to Russia's joining the West. The conflict between liberal democracy and Marxism-Leninism was between ideologies which, despite their major differences, ostensibly shared ultimate goals of freedom, equality, and prosperity. A traditional, authoritarian, nationalist Russia could have quite different goals. A Western democrat could carry on an intellectual debate with a Soviet Marxist. It would be virtually impossible for him to do that with a Russian traditionalist. If, as the Russians stop behaving like Marxists, they reject liberal democracy and begin behaving like Russians but not like Westerners, the relations between Russia and the West could again become distant and conflictual.[8]

The Confucian-Islamic Connection

The obstacles to non-Western countries joining the West vary considerably. They are least for Latin American and East European countries. They are greater for the Orthodox countries of the former Soviet Union. They are still greater for Muslim, Confucian, Hindu, and Buddhist societies. Japan has established a unique position for itself as an associate member of the West: it is in the West in some respects but clearly not of the West in important dimensions. Those countries that for reason of culture and power do not wish to, or cannot, join the West compete with the West by developing their own economic, military, and political power. They do this by promoting their internal development and by cooperating with other non-Western countries. The most prominent from of this cooperation is the Confucian-Islamic connection that has emerged to challenge Western interests, values, and power.

Almost without exception, Western countries are reducing their military power; under Yeltsin's leadership so also is Russia.

China, North Korea, and several Middle Eastern states, however, are significantly expanding their military capabilities. They are doing this by the import of arms from Western and non-Western sources and by the development of indigenous arms industries. One result is the emergence of what Charles Krauthammer has called "Weapon States," and the Weapon States are not Western states. Another result is the redefinition of arms control, which is a Western concept and a Western goal. During the cold war the primary purpose of arms control was to establish a stable military balance between the United States and its allies and the Soviet Union and its allies. In the post-cold war world the primary objective of arms control is to prevent the development by non-Western societies of military capabilities that could threaten Western interests. The West attempts to do this through international agreements, economic pressure, and controls on the transfer of arms and weapons technologies.

The conflict between the West and the Confucian-Islamic states focuses largely, although not exclusively, on nuclear, chemical, and biological weapons; ballistic missiles and other sophisticated means for delivering them; and the guidance, intelligence, and other electronic capabilities for achieving that goal. The West promotes nonproliferation as a universal norm and nonproliferation treaties and inspections as a means of realizing that norm. It also threatens a variety of sanctions against those who promote the spread of sophisticated weapons and proposes some benefits for those who do not. The attention of the West focuses, naturally, on nations that are actually or potentially hostile to the West.

The non-Western nations, on the other hand, assert their right   55
to acquire and to deploy whatever weapons they think necessary for their security. They also have absorbed, to the full, the truth of the response of the Indian defense minister when asked what lesson he learned from the Gulf War: "Don't fight the United States unless you have nuclear weapons." Nuclear weapons, chemical weapons, and missiles are viewed, probably erroneously, as the potential equalizer of superior Western conventional power. China, of course, already has nuclear weapons; Pakistan and India have the capability to deploy them. North Korea, Iran, Iraq, Libya, and Algeria appear to be attempting to acquire them. A top Iranian official has declared that all Muslim states should acquire nuclear weapons, and in 1988 the president of Iran reportedly issued a directive calling for development of "offensive and defensive chemical, biological, and radiological weapons."

Centrally important to the development of counter-West military capabilities is the sustained expansion of China's military power and its means to create military power. Buoyed by spectacular economic development, China is rapidly increasing its military spending and vigorously moving forward with the modernization of its armed forces. It is purchasing weapons from the former Soviet states; it is developing long-range missiles; in 1992 it tested a one-megaton nuclear device. It is developing power-projection capabilities, acquiring aerial refueling technology, and trying to purchase an aircraft carrier. Its military buildup and assertion of sovereignty over the South China Sea are provoking a multilateral regional arms race in East Asia. China is also a major exporter of arms and weapons technology. It has exported materials to Libya and Iraq that could be used to manufacture nuclear weapons and nerve gas. It has helped Algeria build a reactor suitable for nuclear weapons research and production. China has sold to Iran nuclear technology that American officials believe could only be used to create weapons and apparently has shipped components of 300-mile-range missiles to Pakistan. North Korea has had a nuclear weapons program under way for some while and has sold advanced missiles and missile technology to Syria and Iran. The flow of weapons and weapons technology is generally from East Asia to the Middle East. There is, however, some movement in the reverse direction; China has received Stinger missiles from Pakistan.

A Confucian-Islamic military connection has thus come into being, designed to promote acquisition by its members of the weapons and weapons technologies needed to counter the military power of the West. It may or may not last. At present, however, it is, as Dave McCurdy has said, "a renegades' mutual support pact, run by the proliferators and their backers." A new form of arms competition is thus occurring between Islamic-Confucian states and the West. In an old-fashioned arms race, each side developed its own arms to balance or to achieve superiority against the other side. In this new form of arms competition, one side is developing its arms and the other side is attempting not to balance but to limit and prevent that arms build-up while at the same time reducing its own military capabilities.

Implications for the West

This writing does not argue that civilization identities will replace all other identities, that nation states will disappear, that each civilization will become a single coherent political entity, that groups within a civilization will not conflict with and even fight each other. This paper does set forth the hypotheses that differences between civilizations are real and important; civilization-consciousness is increasing; conflict between civilizations will supplant ideological and other forms of conflict as the dominant global form of conflict; international relations, historically a game played out within Western civilization, will increasingly be de-Westernized and become a game in which non-Western civilizations are actors and not simply objects; successful political, security, and economic international institutions are more likely to develop within civilizations than across civilizations; conflicts between groups in different civilizations will be more frequent, more sustained, and more violent than conflicts between groups in the same civilization; violent conflicts between groups in different civilizations are the most likely and most dangerous source of escalation that could lead to global wars; the paramount axis of world politics will be the relations between "the West and the Rest"; the elites in some torn non-Western countries will try to make their countries part of the West, but in most cases face major obstacles to accomplishing this; a central focus of conflict for the immediate future will be between the West and several Islamic-Confucian states.

This is not to advocate the desirability of conflicts between civilizations. It is to set forth descriptive hypotheses as to what the future may be like. If these are plausible hypotheses, however, it is necessary to consider their implications for Western policy. These implications should be divided between short-term advantage and long-term accommodation. In the short term it is clearly in the interest of the West to promote greater cooperation and unity within its own civilization, particularly between its European and North American components; to incorporate into the West societies in Eastern Europe and Latin America whose cultures are close to those of the West; to promote and maintain cooperative relations with Russia and Japan; to prevent escalation of local inter-civilization conflicts into major inter-civilization wars; to limit the expansion of the military strength of Confucian and Islamic states; to moderate the reduction of Western military capabilities and maintain military superiority in East and Southwest Asia; to exploit differences and conflicts among Confucian and Islamic states; to support in other civilizations groups sympathetic to Western values and interests; to strengthen international institutions that reflect and legitimate Western interests and values and to promote the involvement of non-Western states in those institutions.

In the longer term other measures would be called for. Western civilization is both Western and modern. Non-Western 60 civilizations have attempted to become modern without becoming Western. To date only Japan has fully succeeded in this quest. Non-Western civilizations will continue to attempt to acquire the wealth, technology, skills, machines, and weapons that are part of being modern. They will also attempt to reconcile this modernity with their traditional culture and values. Their economic and military strength relative to the West will increase. Hence the West will increasingly have to accommodate these non-Western modern civilizations whose power approaches that of the West but whose values and interests differ significantly from those of the West. This will require the West to maintain the economic and military power necessary to protect its interests in relation to these civilizations. It will also, however, require the West to develop a more profound understanding of the basic religious and philosophical assumptions underlying other civilizations and the ways in which people in those civilizations see their interests. It will require an effort to identify elements of commonality between Western and other civilizations. For the relevant future, there will be no universal civilization, but instead a world of different civilizations, each of which will have to learn to coexist with the others.

Notes

1. Murray Weidenbaum, *Greater China: The Next Economic Superpower?*, St. Louis: Washington University Center for the Study of American Business, Contemporary Issues 57, February 1993, 2–3.

2. Bernard Lewis, "The Roots of Muslim Rage," *The Atlantic Monthly* 266, September 1990, 60; *Time,* June 15, 1992, 24–28.

3. Archie Roosevelt, *For Lust of Knowing* (Boston: Little, Brown, 1988) 332–333.

4. Almost invariably Western leaders claim they are acting on behalf of "the world community." One minor lapse occurred during the run-up to the Gulf War. In an interview on "Good Morning America," Dec. 21, 1990, British Prime Minister John Major referred to the actions "the West" was taking against Saddam Hussein. He quickly corrected himself and subsequently referred to "the world community." He was, however, right when he erred.

5. Harry C. Triandis, *The New York Times* December 25, 1990, 41, and "Cross-Cultural Studies of Individualism and Collectivism," Nebraska Symposium on Motivation 37, 1989, 41–133.

6. Kishore Mahbubani, "The West and the Rest," *The National Interest* Summer 1992, 3–13.

7. Sergei Stankevich, "Russia in Search of Itself," *The National Interest* Summer 1992, 47–51; Daniel Schneider, "A Russian Movement Rejects Western Tilt," *Christian Science Monitor* February 5, 1993, 5–7.

8. Owen Harries has pointed out that Australia is trying (unwisely in his view) to become a torn country in reverse. Although it has been a full member not only of the West but also of the America, Britain, Canada, Australia (ABCA) military and intelligence core of the West, its current leaders are in effect proposing that it defect from the West, redefine itself as an Asian country, and cultivate close ties with its neighbors. Australia's future, they argue, is with the dynamic economies of East Asia. But, as I have suggested, close economic cooperation normally requires a common cultural base. In addition, none of the three conditions necessary for a torn country to join another civilization is likely to exist in Australia's case.

QUESTIONS FOR DISCUSSION AND WRITING

1. Huntington states his thesis clearly in paragraph 2 and enumerates a number of points. Does this strategy appear to be an appeal to logos? Does it help you to follow his argument? Do you accept Huntington's assertion in paragraph 4 that most of the conflicts of the past 150 years have been "Western civil wars"? What does this assertion indicate about his perspective?

2. Huntington defines civilization in paragraph 7. Summarize the definition in your own words. Do you find it an acceptable working definition? If not, how would you modify it? In paragraph 12, the author asserts that civilizations will clash because the "world is becoming a smaller place"; do you agree that interaction is likely to lead to culture clash? Could interaction also have positive consequences?

3. Discuss Huntington's point in paragraph 13 that religion provides a means of identity that "transcends national boundaries and unites civilizations."

4. In the section "Fault Line Between Civilizations," Huntington makes numerous assertions without evidence or examples. Do you accept his authority as an author and thus accept these assertions? Does he make his argument through logic? Does the example of the Gulf War in the following section increase your acceptance of his argument?

5. Huntington notes that clashing cultures naturally involve a double standard. Do you agree? Does the kin-country idea adequately explain this viewpoint? In "The West and the Rest," the author notes that non-Westerners see the West as exerting money and influence to "run the world" to its advantage. Do you agree that this view is likely an accurate assessment of the West by the rest of the world? Do you agree with his assessment of why this is the case?

6. Huntington refers to a Confucian-Islamic connection. Does he define this expression? What do you infer that it means? What are the goals of this alliance?

7. Write an essay in which you explain your own sense of the term "civilization" or "culture." Alternatively, research one of the conflicts Huntington discusses. Is his hypothesis supported by in-depth research?

The Clash of Ignorance

EDWARD SAID

Edward Said (1935–2003) was a Christian Palestinian born in Jerusalem shortly before Israel achieved nationhood. He attended school in Jerusalem and in Cairo; he received a BA from Princeton University, an MA and Ph.D. from Harvard University, and was University Professor at Columbia University. Said is known for articulating a school of thought that he terms Orientalism, which criticizes traditional Western attitudes toward the Middle East. He wrote his first political essay, "The Arab Portrayed," after Israeli Prime Minister Golda Meir asserted, "There are no Palestinians," and continued to write of Palestinian dispossession and loss. His works have been translated into twenty-four languages and widely published. His books include *Reflections on Exile and Other Essays* (2000), *Peace and Its Discontents* (1996), *The Politics of Dispossession* (1995), *The Politics of Dispossession* (1994), *Culture and Imperialism* (1993), *Covering Islam* (1981), and *The Question of Palestine* (1979). Said has published numerous articles in various periodicals; the essay that follows appeared in *The Nation* on October 12, 2001.

Samuel Huntington's article "The Clash of Civilizations?" appeared in the Summer 1993 issue of *Foreign Affairs,* where it immediately attracted a surprising amount of attention and reaction. Because the article was intended to supply Americans with an original thesis about "a new phase" in world politics after the end of the cold war, Huntington's terms of argument seemed compellingly large, bold, even visionary. He very clearly had his eye on rivals in the policy-making ranks, theorists such as Francis Fukuyama and his "end of history" ideas, as well as the legions who had celebrated the onset of globalization, tribalism, and the dissipation of the state. But they, he allowed, had understood only some aspects of this new period. He was about to announce the "crucial, indeed a central, aspect" of what "global politics is likely to be in the coming years." Unhesitatingly he pressed on:

"It is my hypothesis that the fundamental source of conflict in this new world will not be primarily ideological or primarily economic. The great divisions among humankind and the dominating source of conflict will be cultural. Nation states will remain the most powerful actors in world affairs, but the

252

principal conflicts of global politics will occur between nations and groups of different civilizations. The clash of civilizations will dominate global politics. The fault lines between civilizations will be the battle lines of the future."

Most of the argument in the pages that followed relied on a vague notion of something Huntington called "civilization identity" and "the interactions among seven or eight [sic] major civilizations," of which the conflict between two of them, Islam and the West, gets the lion's share of his attention. In this belligerent kind of thought, he relies heavily on a 1990 article by the veteran Orientalist Bernard Lewis, whose ideological colors are manifest in its title, "The Roots of Muslim Rage." In both articles, the personification of enormous entities called "the West" and "Islam" is recklessly affirmed, as if hugely complicated matters like identity and culture existed in a cartoonlike world where Popeye and Bluto bash each other mercilessly, with one always more virtuous pugilist getting the upper hand over his adversary. Certainly neither Huntington nor Lewis has much time to spare for the internal dynamics and plurality of every civilization, or for the fact that the major contest in most modern cultures concerns the definition or interpretation of each culture, or for the unattractive possibility that a great deal of demagogy and downright ignorance is involved in presuming to speak for a whole religion or civilization. No, the West is the West, and Islam is Islam.

The challenge for Western policy makers, says Huntington, is to make sure that the West gets stronger and fends off all the others, Islam in particular. More troubling is Huntington's assumption that his perspective, which is to survey the entire world from a perch outside all ordinary attachments and hidden loyalties, is the correct one, as if everyone else were scurrying around looking for the answers that he has already found. In fact, Huntington is an ideologist, someone who wants to make "civilizations" and "identities" into what they are not: shut-down, sealed-off entities that have been purged of the myriad currents and countercurrents that animate human history, and that over centuries have made it possible for that history not only to contain wars of religion and imperial conquest but also to be one of exchange, cross-fertilization, and sharing. This far less visible history is ignored in the rush to highlight the ludicrously compressed and constricted warfare that "The Clash of Civilizations?" argues is the reality. When he published his book by the same title in 1996, Huntington tried to give his argument a little more subtlety and many, many more footnotes; all he did, however, was confuse himself and demonstrate what a clumsy writer and inelegant thinker he was.

The basic paradigm of West versus the rest (the cold war op-   5
position reformulated) remained untouched, and this is what has
persisted, often insidiously and implicitly, in discussion since the
terrible events of September 11. The carefully planned and hor-
rendous, pathologically motivated suicide attack and mass
slaughter by a small group of deranged militants has been turned
into proof of Huntington's thesis. Instead of seeing it for what it
is—the capture of big ideas (I use the word loosely) by a tiny
band of crazed fanatics for criminal purposes—international lu-
minaries from former Pakistani Prime Minister Benazir Bhutto to
Italian Prime Minister Silvio Berlusconi have pontificated about
Islam's troubles, and in the latter's case has used Huntington's
ideas to rant on about the West's superiority, how "we" have
Mozart and Michelangelo and they don't. (Berlusconi has since
made a halfhearted apology for his insult to "Islam.")

But why not instead see parallels, admittedly less spectacular in their destructiveness, for Osama Bin Laden and his followers in cults like the Branch Davidians or the disciples of the
Rev. Jim Jones at Guyana or the Japanese Aum Shinrikyo? Even
the normally sober British weekly *The Economist,* in its issue of
September 22–28, can't resist reaching for the vast generalization, praising Huntington extravagantly for his "cruel and sweeping, but nonetheless acute" observations about Islam. "Today,"
the journal says with unseemly solemnity, Huntington writes
that "the world's billion or so Muslims are 'convinced of the superiority of their culture, and obsessed with the inferiority of
their power.'" Did he canvas 100 Indonesians, 200 Moroccans,
500 Egyptians, and 50 Bosnians? Even if he did, what sort of
sample is that?

Uncountable are the editorials in every American and European newspaper and magazine of note adding to this vocabulary of gigantism and apocalypse, each use of which is plainly
designed not to edify but to inflame the reader's indignant passion as a member of the "West," and what we need to do.
Churchillian rhetoric is used inappropriately by self-appointed
combatants in the West's, and especially America's, war against
its haters, despoilers, destroyers, with scant attention to complex histories that defy such reductiveness and have seeped
from one territory into another, in the process overriding the
boundaries that are supposed to separate us all into divided
armed camps.

This is the problem with unedifying labels like Islam and the
West: They mislead and confuse the mind, which is trying to
make sense of a disorderly reality that won't be pigeonholed or
strapped down as easily as all that. I remember interrupting a

man who, after a lecture I had given at a West Bank university in 1994, rose from the audience and started to attack my ideas as "Western," as opposed to the strict Islamic ones he espoused. "Why are you wearing a suit and tie?" was the first retort that came to mind. "They're Western too." He sat down with an embarrassed smile on his face, but I recalled the incident when information on the September 11 terrorists started to come in: How they had mastered all the technical details required to inflict their homicidal evil on the World Trade Center, the Pentagon and the aircraft they had commandeered. Where does one draw the line between "Western" technology and, as Berlusconi declared, "Islam's" inability to be a part of "modernity"?

One cannot easily do so, of course. How finally inadequate are the labels, generalizations, and cultural assertions. At some level, for instance, primitive passions and sophisticated know-how converge in ways that give the lie to a fortified boundary not only between "West" and "Islam" but also between past and present, us and them, to say nothing of the very concepts of identity and nationality about which there is unending disagreement and debate. A unilateral decision made to draw lines in the sand, to undertake crusades, to oppose their evil with our good, to extirpate terrorism and, in Paul Wolfowitz's nihilistic vocabulary, to end nations entirely, doesn't make the supposed entities any easier to see; rather, it speaks to how much simpler it is to make bellicose statements for the purpose of mobilizing collective passions than to reflect, examine, sort out what it is we are dealing with in reality, the interconnectedness of innumerable lives, "ours" as well as "theirs."

In a remarkable series of three articles published between January and March 1999 in *Dawn,* Pakistan's most respected weekly, the late Eqbal Ahmad, writing for a Muslim audience, analyzed what he called the roots of the religious right, coming down very harshly on the mutilations of Islam by absolutists and fanatical tyrants whose obsession with regulating personal behavior promotes "an Islamic order reduced to a penal code, stripped of its humanism, aesthetics, intellectual quests, and spiritual devotion." And this "entails an absolute assertion of one, generally de-contextualized, aspect of religion and a total disregard of another. The phenomenon distorts religion, debases tradition, and twists the political process wherever it unfolds." As a timely instance of this debasement, Ahmad proceeds first to present the rich, complex, pluralist meaning of the word jihad and then goes on to show that in the word's current confinement to indiscriminate war against presumed enemies, it is impossible "to recognize the Islamic—religion, society, culture, history or

10

politics—as lived and experienced by Muslims through the ages." The modern Islamists, Ahmad concludes, are "concerned with power, not with the soul; with the mobilization of people for political purposes rather than with sharing and alleviating their sufferings and aspirations. Theirs is a very limited and time-bound political agenda." What has made matters worse is that similar distortions and zealotry occur in the "Jewish" and "Christian" universes of discourse.

It was Conrad, more powerfully than any of his readers at the end of the nineteenth century could have imagined, who understood that the distinctions between civilized London and "the heart of darkness" quickly collapsed in extreme situations, and that the heights of European civilization could instantaneously fall into the most barbarous practices without preparation or transition. And it was Conrad also, in *The Secret Agent* (1907), who described terrorism's affinity for abstractions like "pure science" (and by extension for "Islam" or "the West"), as well as the terrorist's ultimate moral degradation.

For there are closer ties between apparently warring civilizations than most of us would like to believe; both Freud and Nietzsche showed how the traffic across carefully maintained, even policed boundaries moves with often terrifying ease. But then such fluid ideas, full of ambiguity and skepticism about notions that we hold on to, scarcely furnish us with suitable, practical guidelines for situations such as the one we face now. Hence the altogether more reassuring battle orders (a crusade, good versus evil, freedom against fear, etc.) drawn out of Huntington's alleged opposition between Islam and the West, from which official discourse drew its vocabulary in the first days after the September 11 attacks. There's since been a noticeable de-escalation in that discourse, but to judge from the steady amount of hate speech and actions, plus reports of law enforcement efforts directed against Arabs, Muslims, and Indians all over the country, the paradigm stays on.

One further reason for its persistence is the increased presence of Muslims all over Europe and the United States. Think of the populations today of France, Italy, Germany, Spain, Britain, America, even Sweden, and you must concede that Islam is no longer on the fringes of the West but at its center. But what is so threatening about that presence? Buried in the collective culture are memories of the first great Arab-Islamic conquests, which began in the seventh century and which, as the celebrated Belgian historian Henri Pirenne wrote in his landmark book *Mohammed and Charlemagne* (1939), shattered once and for all the ancient unity of the Mediterranean, destroyed the Christian-

Roman synthesis, and gave rise to a new civilization dominated by northern powers (Germany and Carolingian France) whose mission, he seemed to be saying, is to resume defense of the "West" against its historical-cultural enemies. What Pirenne left out, alas, is that in the creation of this new line of defense the West drew on the humanism, science, philosophy, sociology, and historiography of Islam, which had already interposed itself between Charlemagne's world and classical antiquity. Islam is inside from the start, as even Dante, great enemy of Mohammed, had to concede when he placed the Prophet at the very heart of his Inferno.

Then there is the persisting legacy of monotheism itself, the Abrahamic religions, as Louis Massignon aptly called them. Beginning with Judaism and Christianity, each is a successor haunted by what came before; for Muslims, Islam fulfills and ends the line of prophecy. There is still no decent history or demystification of the many-sided contest among these three followers—not one of them by any means a monolithic, unified camp—of the most jealous of all gods, even though the bloody modern convergence on Palestine furnishes a rich secular instance of what has been so tragically irreconcilable about them. Not surprisingly, then, Muslims and Christians speak readily of crusades and jihads, both of them eliding the Judaic presence with often sublime insouciance. Such an agenda, said Eqbal Ahmad, is "very reassuring to the men and women who are stranded in the middle of the ford, between the deep waters of tradition and modernity."

But we are all swimming in those waters, Westerners and Muslims and others alike. And since the waters are part of the ocean of history, trying to plow or divide them with barriers is futile. These are tense times, but it is better to think in terms of powerful and powerless communities, the secular politics of reason and ignorance, and universal principles of justice and injustice than to wander off in search of vast abstractions that may give momentary satisfaction but little self-knowledge or informed analysis. "The Clash of Civilizations?" thesis is a gimmick like "The War of the Worlds," better for reinforcing defensive self-pride than for critical understanding of the bewildering interdependence of our time.

QUESTIONS FOR DISCUSSION AND WRITING

1. What tone and stance does Said establish in the title and the first three paragraphs of his essay? How do you take his stance into account as you evaluate the merit and strength of his argument?

2. In paragraph 3, Said criticizes the notion that "Islam" and "the West" can be personified, with the complexities and differences being ignored or misrepresented. Do you agree that discussing Islam and the West in such broad terms is problematic? If so, what would you do instead? If you disagree with Said's point, how would you respond to his criticisms?

3. In paragraph 4, Said summarizes Huntington's argument. Do you agree with his summary and consider it a fair statement of Huntington's view? If not, how would you summarize it?

4. Said recasts the events of September 11 by asserting that they are not proof of Huntington's thesis but rather more comparable to groups such as the Branch Davidians or the Rev. Jim Jones' group that committed mass suicide in Guyana. Examine Said's claims and evidence in this section. Does he make a persuasive case?

5. Assume the perspective of Huntington and write a response to Said, either conceding or refuting Said's points about Huntington's hypothesis.

Web Sites: World Trade Organization and Global Trade Watch

Many organizations provide Web sites to offer information about themselves and their goals and constituencies, often in the "About Us" section. In addition, such sites strive to present the organization credibly. As you consider the Web sites that follow, assess the appeals each makes to support its agenda, arguments, and opinions, including the ways in which it presents information or news.

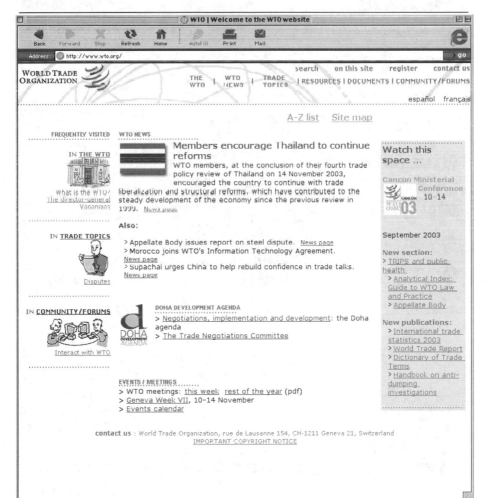

(WORLD TRADE ORGANIZATION)

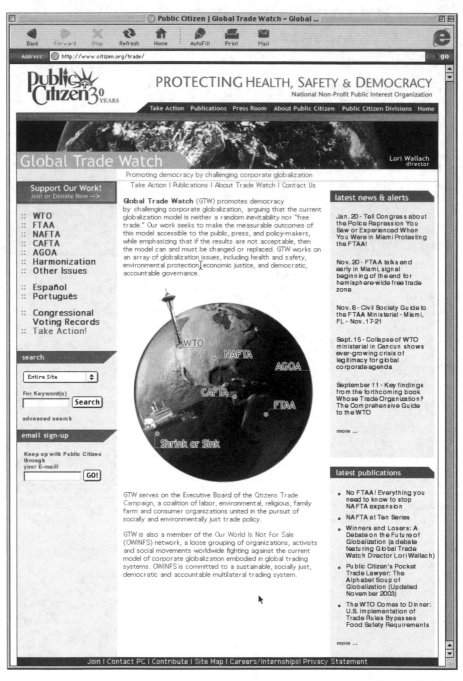

QUESTIONS FOR DISCUSSION AND WRITING

1. Examine each site for appeals to authority. How does each present itself as authoritative? How does each strive to connect with the reader? What kinds of stories, captions, and news briefs are included? Consider Web address, declared purpose of the organization, artwork or photography, placement of text and images, and the like in your assessment.

2. If possible, examine these Web sites online. What additional information do you find? Does your impression of the site or the organization change when you see it online rather than in print?

3. With classmates, perhaps working in groups, analyze the visual and textual rhetoric of the sites and their relative persuasiveness. Then, consider examining related sites in or out of class, depending on your computer access, and summarize your findings for peers.

4. Research in more depth one of the topics raised on either site and develop a researched essay with both online and traditional print sources. Consider presenting your final findings in the form of a Web page, whether an individual page or one that combines findings from others in your class.

Chapter Four: Connections

1. Said's essay responds to Huntington's essay and basic argument and argues for an understanding of the complexities of culture and pluralities within culture. Compare and contrast the essays' different structures for asserting a hypothesis and contradicting a hypothesis.

2. Schloter invokes the First Amendment in articulating the American perspective with regard to censorship. Does he represent alternative American views as well? Discuss this issue in view of the "clash of civilizations" described in the Huntington essay in this chapter.

3. Identify the different approaches toward effects of globalization as expressed or implied in the Campbell, Oxfam, and Epping selections.

4. Huntington argues that "Civilizations are differentiated from each other by history, language, culture, tradition, and, most importantly, religion. The people of different civilizations have different views on the relations between God and man, the individual and the group, the citizen and the state, parents and children, husband and wife, as well as different views of the relative importance of rights and responsibilities, liberty and authority, equality and hierarchy." Based on your examination of different texts in these chapters and on your study of news and popular culture from other sources, do you believe Huntington's point of view is supported? Why or why not? To what degree are human needs and values culturally driven rather than universal and pervasive?

5. Said notes the dualism of good versus evil underlying Huntington's argument and similar views. Discuss this assertion in view of Sam Keen's essay (see Chapter Seven).

6. Divide the class into three groups. Have the first two groups take the position of two authors in this chapter and a third group (a) assess their arguments and (b) point out alternatives to both positions or identify common ground between the two of them. Then, assess what effect class members' cultural identities may have had on their response to each writer.

7. Compare and contrast the Kenyan warrior photograph with other examples of divergent cultures interacting, for example, with those in Chapter Three of this book.

8. What might Lucian Pye (see Chapter Three) say about the role of cultural values in adapting to a changing economic context?

Chapter Four: End-of-Chapter Assignments

1. Research the current state of regulation of hate speech or offensive products on the Internet. What restrictions currently exist and in which countries? How are such regulations enforced?

2. Investigate American-theme businesses in other countries, such as EuroDisney, fast food restaurants, American clothing stores, and the like. How were they introduced? How well received are they?

3. Research intercultural communication in business, perhaps focusing on an area of interest to you, such as international sales or communication via technology.

4. Research Canada and Mexico's current cultural and social climate as well as their relations with the United States. Has NAFTA prompted a change in relations among the three countries?

5. In groups or pairs, select a Web site from a non-US culture and research the site. Consider the information it offers, links to other relevant or useful Web sites, discussion options, or ways to interact with other users. Summarize your findings and present them to the class with recommendations about the usefulness of the site.

6. With a small group from class, a partner, or on your own, identify a local nonprofit organization in the area or accessible by the Internet that provides opportunities for cross-cultural or international interactions. Some examples of groups that could foster such interactions include Cross Cultural Solutions, Los Medicos Voladores (a Central American version of Doctors Without Borders), American Society of International Law, and the Peace Corps. As with other service learning assignments, your work might entail providing written materials for the agency or providing volunteer service and then writing about your experiences in a reflective journal or analytical essays. Consider doing research for the agency and writing up your research findings in a method appropriate for the agency.

7. Review the Web site of the World Trade Organization (WTO) and analyze its arguments on behalf of its mission. Then select a Web site from an organization that opposes the WTO. Write an essay that integrates your research and discusses the question of whether, on balance, the WTO is a positive, benign, or malignant force in contemporary world affairs. You'll need to focus your essay on a specific area such as sustainable growth, trade of cultural products, or some other area where you can develop your paper in some depth.

8. Write an essay exploring the question of marketing cultural artifacts or marketing culture in the travel industry. Who stands to gain or lose? What is the impact on the affected cultures?

Chapter Four: Web Sites for Further Exploration

United Nations
http://www.un.org/
World Trade Organization
http://www.wto.com
Public Citizen Global Trade Watch
http://www.citizen.org/trade/

Europa: The European Union Online
http://europa.eu.int/index_en.htm
International Monetary Fund
http://www.imf.org/
NAFTA (English version)
http://www.customs.gov/nafta/nafta_new.htm
Amnesty International
http://www.amnesty.org/
Woodrow Wilson International Center for Scholars
http://csihp.si.edu/default.htm
Craft cooperative links
http://www.geocities.com/prae_pan/link.html
Business Line Internet Edition, Financial Daily
http://www.blonnet.com/2002/02/22/index.htm
Africa
http://allafrica.com/
Britain
http://www.bbc.com
Oxfam International
http://www.oxfam.org/eng/
Global Exchange
http://www.globalexchange.org/
Marshall McLuhan
http://www.marshallmcluhan.com/
Adforum, a portal for global marketing and advertising
http://ww0.adforum.com/index.asp

5

WOMEN AND SOCIETY

INTRODUCTION

The theme of women and society has pervaded international media in recent years, with headlines reporting stories of women who are killed for transgressions of their kinsmen in so-called honor killings, incidents of women and girls who are victimized by domestic violence, and the persistence of legally and culturally approved genital mutilation of girls. In American media Middle Eastern women often appear behind the veil, although in numerous Islamic societies the veil is the exception and not the rule. Women have also emerged as leaders: The president of Finland, the former prime minister of Pakistan, an exiled dissident leader of Burma, a past and a current president of the Philippines, the socially involved queen of Jordan, the current president and a past president of Ireland, a Palestinian spokeswoman representing Palestinian affairs to the international media, a US House minority leader, and several US senators. Yet these positions of leadership coincide with enormously difficult social, political, and economic status for a majority of women world-wide.

Although gender encompasses certain assumptions, expectations, and values for both men and women, men have historically maintained dominance in human societies. Ancient proverbs and contemporary cultural practices demonstrate the extent and pervasiveness of discrimination against women, from a proverb in which a man thanks God for not making him a woman to a society that maintains a social hierarchy where at the height of an AIDS pandemic a woman fears insisting that her nonmonogamous partner wear a condom to a busload of baby girls discovered packaged and transported to the city to be sold.

Writers in the U.S. and elsewhere argue that subordination of women has biological, social, religious, and economic roots. Women's role in childbearing, men's control of what historian Estelle Freedman calls "reproductive labor," the absence of women's identity as active subject versus passive object, and some cultural traditions and customs have all made respective contributions. For example, traditionally men and women have been segregated in Judaism as well as Islam; in the Catholic Church the priesthood remains restricted to men. Socially and culturally, we find deadly gender bias in some societies that results in selective abortion of female infants; some nations have had to institute legislation against prenatal testing in an effort to stop destruction of female fetuses and the damage to society it ultimately can bring. Economically, we find a complex relationship between women's ability to generate income or contribute to nation building and their limited control over childbearing and childrearing. And much of the current attention on human rights focuses on women and children, particularly the highly charged issue of female genital mutilation, the sex trades, and child labor. At the same time, gender is only one of several variables determining a woman's position and power in society. Race and class are additional, critical factors. Women of higher class or caste generally have more power, power that may rest on the labor of lower-class women and men. Those members of a society who do not belong to the dominant race or ethnicity are often characterized as outsiders regardless of gender.

Contemporary thinkers, writers, and commentators have called for a more vocal and active role for women. As Salman Rushdie notes (see Chapter Eight), "Oh, for the voices of Muslim women to be heard!" Nobel Prize-winning economist Amartya Sen also notes the positive role of women's voices and contributions in nation building. Too often women have had the burden of dealing with the policies and decisions of mostly male leadership—caring for families with AIDS while ill themselves; unable to pursue income-producing activities due to incessant pregnancy and childbirth; and, in some societies, being deliberately denied education and even basic literacy. At times women have unwittingly become agents of their own oppression, in supporting ostensibly liberating regimes that became worse than their historical oppressors—a blatant recent example being the Taliban, who rose to power as a positive alternative to loosely organized, corrupt, and largely self-serving structures but then instituted extraordinarily oppressive rules for women's behavior and punishments for disobedience.

These selections by authors from around the world include diverse genres and perspectives. The chapter includes artistic renderings, theoretical and philosophical perspectives, academic research on historical and political issues of gender, newspaper commentary, and personal essay. The authors support their views with personal narrative and observation, authoritative research, and logic and examples.

We begin this chapter with a British image, an etching that sets forth appropriate behavior for a woman by defining her circumscribed role. The image further demonstrates the consequences of stepping out of the role assigned by the invisible force wielding the compass, presumably male. In the next two selections, also images, we find that the woman herself wields the artistic medium. Artist Frida Kahlo not only paints her self-portraits, but in one image, "Self Portrait with Cropped Hair," she holds the scissors and wears the masculine suit, challenging the image and power differential of gender. In her 1944 painting, "The Broken Column," themes of anguish and suffering emerge.

We then turn to the medium of the essay in a selection from French existentialist and feminist writer Simone de Beauvoir's book *The Second Sex*. This selection, entitled "Woman as Other," outlines the role of man as the norm, the default, and woman as the other, "an 'imperfect man,' an 'incidental being' . . . the 'relative being.'" She argues that women's subordination and dependency is not the result of a specific occurrence or historical event, but in part results because women do not feel a collective consciousness, a sense of women as "we," a history, or in fact even a subjective attitude.

Writing some fifty years later, historian Estelle Freedman acknowledges the power of historical patriarchy, or male domination of social systems, but challenges the notion that women "have no usable history"; she suggests that changes in economics, religion, and families have promoted change in patriarchal systems. She further explores the connections between women's roles and economic class, noting the significance of women's reproductive labor in enabling men to maintain dominance and, among other effects, deny access to education for women. Freedman also notes that other variables, such as class or caste, family, and age, can reduce awareness of gender and to some degree mediate the effects of gender.

In 2003, Japanese politicians made international news when they were repudiated for making sexist and demeaning remarks about women in the workplace. Professional work and status for women are the topic for Japanese writer Yuko Ogasawara; she explores a situation in which the strict segregation of male and female office work paradoxically may empower the structurally subordinate women to evade or at least resist male dominance. In her article "Office Ladies and the Freedom of the Discriminated," Ogasawara suggests that Japan's "office ladies," as one of these workers puts it, turn "weakness into a strength." Although acknowledging their ability to turn the tables on their male superiors by overt and covert behaviors in a "blatantly discriminatory" system, the author suggests that women and society ultimately pay a steep price by reinforcing oppressive stereotypes.

Taking a global view of women's labor, Arlie Russell Hochschild and Barbara Ehrenreich, writing in "Global Woman," the introduction to their book of the same name, explore the "feminization of migration" and the movement of "care workers" from Third World countries to provide care in First World households.

In the next selection, "Outside History," from her book *Object Lessons,* Eavan Boland reflects on images, and to some degree stereotypes, of women in Ireland and in Irish poetry. Boland, an Irish woman and a poet, explores the transformation of women from objects, symbols, and myths in Irish poetry to creators of poems themselves, poems that keep the realities of women's lives, and women's histories, not in the margins but at the center of poems.

We conclude with an essay on the crucial role of women as nation builders. Nobel Prize-winner Amartya Sen outlines connections between population control and women's opportunities in his essay "Population and Gender Equity." He notes the devastating effects on a global level when women are "shackled by persistent bearing and raising of children" and concludes that "advancing gender equality" can benefit not only women and their communities but also more global issues.

These selections are necessarily limited in topic and scope; they have been selected to introduce authors, ideas, and opportunities to help you to take your reading, research, and reflection in interesting, challenging, and perhaps at times perplexing directions. As you read selections in this chapter, consider drawing connections between the other themes in this book, examining the intersections of gender and perceptions, cultures, values, and social and economic systems in a multi-dimensional global exchange.

Keep Within Compass

This British etching, circa 1790, draws upon a centuries-old tradition of emblems that incorporate visual elements and a written moral lesson. Combining several pictures with a moral command, the etching depicts four unpleasant scenes with which the "virtuous" woman is threatened if she does not remain within her own circumscribed world: Raising a child in poverty and misery, working as a domestic or tavern worker, selling in the street, and prostituting herself to soldiers. Such scenes contrast with the prosperous gentlewoman depicted next to flowers and a large home. A metaphor that surfaces decade after decade in conveying social worlds is that of the circle, or in some cases, the three-dimensional sphere. Sometimes referring to social class, other times to occupations, the image has been used to describe the designated and circumscribed roles for men and women: Men's world of greater economic, industrial, and political society, and women's world of the home.

"Keep Within Compass" (England, 1785–1805). Graphic on laid paper, H. 9.310 cm.   (THE HENRY FRANCIS DU PONT WINTERTHUR MUSEUM, INC.)

QUESTIONS FOR DISCUSSION AND WRITING

1. What is your dominant impression of this image? Analyze the argument it makes, including both its core point and supporting reasons and examples. What code of behavior for women does it suggest?

2. Who do you think is the likely audience for this image? What gender would the artist/author likely have been? Discuss the basis for your inferences.

3. In small groups or pairs, develop a contemporary version of this image—targeting either men or women—with advice for gender-appropriate behavior. Discuss in the larger group why you designed the image as you did and what inferences you can draw about assumptions regarding gender.

4. Write an essay analyzing the appeals to logic, emotion, or authority evident in this image.

Self-Portrait with Cropped Hair and The Broken Column

FRIDA KAHLO

Frida Kahlo (1907-1954) was an artist born in Mexico, the daughter of a father who was a Hungarian Jew from Germany and a mother of Native and Spanish descent from Mexico. She was one of the first girls allowed into the National Preparatory Academy of Mexico City. Injury and illness caused profound suffering in her life; at age six she was stricken with polio and at age eighteen she sustained nearly fatal injuries, including fractures to her spine and pelvis, in a devastating bus accident. In her convalescence she focused on her painting, later becoming the third wife of renowned artist Diego Rivera in a somewhat stormy relationship. Many of Kahlo's paintings portray the unseen lives of women in startling and nontraditional ways—frequently juxtaposing pain and suffering with overtly sexual symbolism. Her style has been described as being rooted in surrealism, in magic realism, and in her own world and her life, with its ambiguities and anguish. In part because of her frank exposure of facets of female gender identity previously considered taboo, Kahlo has become a strong icon of *feminism*. The paintings included here, both self-portraits, reflect the dualities that pervaded many of her works, including both gender and cultural themes. (Please see color images on pages C–3 and C–4 of the insert.)

"Self Portrait with Cropped Hair, 1940," Frida Kahlo   (ART RESOURCE/THE MUSEUM OF MODERN ART)

"The Broken Column, 1944" Frida Kahlo. (INSTITUTO NACIONAL DE BELLAS ARTES—MEXICO)

QUESTIONS FOR DISCUSSION AND WRITING

1. How would you describe your initial response to these images? In what ways might your response be tied to your own gender and ethnicity? Compare and contrast your response to others in your class or discussion group and see what common threads or differences you find.

2. What is the point or theme of each image? What in each image supports or develops this point? What do the images suggest about gender or identity? About suffering?

3. Drawing from your responses to question 1 or 2, write an essay analyzing these images and the appeals they make to support their point.

4. Research the life and art of Frida Kahlo, selecting some aspect or theme on which to focus your research. How might her cultural background have affected acceptance of her work or evaluation of her artistic merit?

5. View the film *Frida* (2002); write a review of the film and then look up reviews critics have published. In what ways did your analysis of the film differ? What similarities did you find? Did your analysis of these images affect your view of the film?

Woman as Other

SIMONE DE BEAUVOIR

Simone (Lucie Ernestine Marie Bertrand) de Beauvoir (1908–1986), was a French author and an existentialist, or philosopher, concerned with the individual and his or her relationship to the universe and to God. She was closely associated with existentialist Jean-Paul Sartre, and her works spanned the pre-World War I era to the 1980s. Educated at the Sorbonne in Paris, Beauvoir taught philosophy at several colleges until 1943, after which she devoted herself to writing. Her novels include *All Men Are Mortal* (1946, tr. 1955), *The Blood of Others* (1946, tr. 1948), and *The Mandarins* (1955, tr. 1956). Among her most celebrated works is her analysis of the status of women, *The Second Sex* (1949–1950, tr. 1953), in which the following selection was published. Her monumental work *The Coming of Age* (1970, tr. 1972) considers the social treatment of the aged in many cultures. Beauvoir's autobiographical writings include *Memoirs of a Dutiful Daughter* (1958, tr. 1959), *The Prime of Life* (tr. 1962), *Force of Circumstance* (1963, tr. 1964), *A Very Easy Death* (1964, tr. 1966), and *All Said and Done* (tr. 1974). She also edited Jean Paul Sartre's letters to her (tr. 1994).

What is a woman?

To state the question is, to me, to suggest, at once, a preliminary answer. The fact that I ask it is in itself significant. A man would never get the notion of writing a book on the peculiar situation of the human male. But if I wish to define myself, I must first of all say: "I am a woman"; on this truth must be based all further discussion. A man never begins by presenting himself as an individual of a certain sex; it goes without saying that he is a man. The terms *masculine* and *feminine* are used symmetrically only as a matter of form, as on legal papers. In actuality the relation of the two sexes is not quite like that of two electrical poles, for man represents both the positive and the neutral, as is indicated by the common use of *man* to designate human beings in general; whereas woman represents only the negative, defined by limiting criteria, without reciprocity. In the midst of an abstract discussion it is vexing to hear a man say: "You think thus and so because you are a woman"; but I know that my only defense is to reply: "I think thus and so because it is true," thereby removing my subjective self from the argument. It would be out of the question to reply: "And you think the contrary because you are a man," for it is understood that the fact of being a man is no peculiarity. A man is in the right in being a man; it is the woman who is in the wrong. It amounts to this: Just as for the ancients there was an absolute vertical with reference to which the oblique was defined, so there is an absolute human type, the masculine. Woman has ovaries, a uterus; these peculiarities imprison her in her subjectivity, circumscribe her within the limits of her own nature. It is often said that she thinks with her glands. Man superbly ignores the fact that his anatomy also includes glands, such as the testicles, and that they secrete hormones. He thinks of his body as a direct and normal connection with the world, which he believes he apprehends objectively, whereas he regards the body of woman as a hindrance, a prison, weighed down by everything peculiar to it. "The female is a female by virtue of a certain *lack* of qualities," said Aristotle; "we should regard the female nature as afflicted with a natural defectiveness." And St. Thomas for his part pronounced woman to be an "imperfect man," an "incidental" being. This is symbolized in Genesis where Eve is depicted as made from what Bossuet called "a supernumerary bone" of Adam.

Thus humanity is male and man defines woman not in herself but as relative to him; she is not regarded as an autonomous being. Michelet writes: "Woman, the relative being. . . ." And Benda is most positive in his *Rapport d'Uriel:* "The body of man makes sense in itself quite apart from that of woman, whereas the latter seems wanting in significance by itself. . . . Man can think of himself without woman. She cannot think of herself without man." And she is simply what man decrees; thus she is called "the sex," by which is meant that she appears essentially to the male as a sexual being. For him she is sex—absolute sex, no less. She is defined and differentiated with reference to man and not he with reference to her; she is the incidental, the inessential as opposed to the essential. He is the Subject, he is the Absolute—she is the Other.

The category of the *Other* is as primordial as consciousness itself. In the most primitive societies, in the most ancient mythologies, one finds the expression of a duality—that of the Self and the Other. This duality was not originally attached to the division of the sexes; it was not dependent upon any empirical facts. It is revealed in such works as that of Granet on Chinese thought and those of Dumézil on the East Indies and Rome. The feminine element was at first no more involved in such pairs as

Varuna-Mitra, Uranus-Zeus, Sun-Moon, and Day-Night than it was in the contrasts between Good and Evil, lucky and unlucky auspices, right and left, God and Lucifer. Otherness is a fundamental category of human thought.

Thus it is that no group ever sets itself up as the One without at once setting up the Other over against itself. If three travelers chance to occupy the same compartment, that is enough to make vaguely hostile "others" out of all the rest of the passengers on the train. In small-town eyes all persons not belonging to the village are "strangers" and suspect; to the native of a country all who inhabit other countries are "foreigners"; Jews are "different" for the anti-Semite, Negroes are "inferior" for American racists, aborigines are "natives" for colonists, proletarians are the "lower class" for the privileged.

Lévi-Strauss, at the end of a profound work on the various forms of primitive societies, reaches the following conclusion: "Passage from the state of Nature to the state of Culture is marked by man's ability to view biological relations as a series of contrasts; duality, alternation, opposition, and symmetry, whether under definite or vague forms, constitute not so much phenomena to be explained as fundamental and immediately given data of social reality." These phenomena would be incomprehensible if in fact human society were simply a *Mitsein* or fellowship based on solidarity and friendliness. Things become clear, on the contrary, if, following Hegel, we find in consciousness itself a fundamental hostility toward every other consciousness; the subject can be posed only in being opposed—he sets himself up as the essential, as opposed to the other, the inessential, the object.

But the other consciousness, the other ego, sets up a reciprocal claim. The native traveling abroad is shocked to find himself in turn regarded as a "stranger" by the natives of neighboring countries. As a matter of fact, wars, festivals, trading, treaties, and contests among tribes, nations, and classes tend to deprive the concept *Other* of its absolute sense and to make manifest its relativity; willy-nilly, individuals and groups are forced to realize the reciprocity of their relations. How is it, then, that this reciprocity has not been recognized between the sexes, that one of the contrasting terms is set up as the sole essential, denying any relativity in regard to its correlative and defining the latter as pure otherness? Why is it that women do not dispute male sovereignty? No subject will readily volunteer to become the object, the inessential; it is not the Other who, in defining himself as the Other, establishes the One. The Other is posed as such by the One in defining himself as the One. But if the Other

5

is not to regain the status of being the One, he must be submissive enough to accept this alien point of view. Whence comes this submission in the case of woman?

There are, to be sure, other cases in which a certain category has been able to dominate another completely for a time. Very often this privilege depends upon inequality of numbers—the majority imposes its rule upon the minority or persecutes it. But women are not a minority, like the American Negroes or the Jews; there are as many women as men on earth. Again, the two groups concerned have often been originally independent; they may have been formerly unaware of each other's existence, or perhaps they recognized each other's autonomy. But a historical event has resulted in the subjugation of the weaker by the stronger. The scattering of the Jews, the introduction of slavery into America, the conquests of imperialism are examples in point. In these cases the oppressed retained at least the memory of former days; they possessed in common a past, a tradition, sometimes a religion or a culture.

The parallel drawn by Bebel between women and the proletariat is valid in that neither ever formed a minority or a separate collective unit of mankind. And instead of a single historical event it is in both cases a historical development that explains their status as a class and accounts for the membership of *particular individuals* in that class. But proletarians have not always existed, whereas there have always been women. They are women in virtue of their anatomy and physiology. Throughout history they have always been subordinated to men, and hence their dependency is not the result of a historical event or a social change—it was not something that *occurred*. The reason why otherness in this case seems to be an absolute is in part that it lacks the contingent or incidental nature of historical facts. A condition brought about at a certain time can be abolished at some other time, as the Negroes of Haiti and others have proved; but it might seem that a natural condition is beyond the possibility of change. In truth, however, the nature of things is no more immutably given, once for all, than is historical reality. If woman seems to be the inessential which never becomes the essential, it is because she herself fails to bring about this change. Proletarians say "We"; Negroes also. Regarding themselves as subjects, they transform the bourgeois, the whites, into "others." But women do not say "We," except at some congress of feminists or similar formal demonstration; men say "women," and women use the same word in referring to themselves. They do not authentically assume a subjective attitude. The proletarians have accomplished the revolution in Russia, the Negroes in Haiti, the Indochinese are battling for it in Indochina; but the women's effort has never been anything more than a symbolic agitation. They have gained only what men have been willing to grant; they have taken nothing, they have only received.

The reason for this is that women lack concrete means for organizing themselves into a unit which can stand face to face with the correlative unit. They have no past, no history, no religion of their own; and they have no such solidarity of work and interest as that of the proletariat. They are not even promiscuously herded together in the way that creates community feeling among the American Negroes, the ghetto Jews, the workers of Saint-Denis, or the factory hands of Renault. They live dispersed among the males, attached through residence, housework, economic condition, and social standing to certain men—fathers or husbands—more firmly than they are to other women. If they belong to the bourgeoisie, they feel solidarity with men of that class, not with proletarian women; if they are white, their allegiance is to white men, not to Negro women. The proletariat can propose to massacre the ruling class, and a sufficiently fanatical Jew or Negro might dream of getting sole possession of the atomic bomb and making humanity wholly Jewish or black; but woman cannot even dream of exterminating the males. The bond that unites her to her oppressors is not comparable to any other. The division of the sexes is a biological fact, not an event in human history. Male and female stand opposed within a primordial *Mitsein,* and woman has not broken it. The couple is a fundamental unity with its two halves riveted together, and the cleavage of society along the line of sex is impossible. Here is to be found the basic trait of woman: She is the Other in a totality of which the two components are necessary to one another.

One could suppose that this reciprocity might have facilitated the liberation of woman. When Hercules sat at the feet of Omphale and helped with her spinning, his desire for her held him captive; but why did she fail to gain a lasting power? To revenge herself on Jason, Medea killed their children; and this grim legend would seem to suggest that she might have obtained a formidable influence over him through his love for his offspring. In *Lysistrata* Aristophanes gaily depicts a band of women who joined forces to gain social ends through the sexual needs of their men; but this is only a play. In the legend of the Sabine women, the latter soon abandoned their plan of remaining sterile to punish their ravishers. In truth woman has not been socially emancipated through man's need—sexual desire and the desire for offspring—which makes the male dependent for satisfaction upon the female.

Master and slave, also, are united by a reciprocal need, in this case economic, which does not liberate the slave. In the relation of master to slave the master does not make a point of the need that he has for the other; he has in his grasp the power of satisfying this need through his own action; whereas the slave, in his dependent condition, his hope and fear, is quite conscious of the need he has for his master. Even if the need is at bottom equally urgent for both, it always works in favor of the oppressor and against the oppressed. That is why the liberation of the working class, for example, has been slow.

Now, woman has always been man's dependent, if not his slave; the two sexes have never shared the world in equality. And even today woman is heavily handicapped, though her situation is beginning to change. Almost nowhere is her legal status the same as man's, and frequently it is much to her disadvantage. Even when her rights are legally recognized in the abstract, long-standing custom prevents their full expression in the mores. In the economic sphere men and women can almost be said to make up two castes; other things being equal, the former hold the better jobs, get higher wages, and have more opportunity for success than their new competitors. In industry and politics men have a great many more positions and they monopolize the most important posts. In addition to all this, they enjoy a traditional prestige that the education of children tends in every way to support, for the present enshrines the past—and in the past all history has been made by men. At the present time, when women are beginning to take part in the affairs of the world, it is still a world that belongs to men—they have no doubt of it at all and women have scarcely any. To decline to be the Other, to refuse to be a party to the deal—this would be for women to renounce all the advantages conferred upon them by their alliance with the superior caste. Man-the-sovereign will provide woman-the-liege with material protection and will undertake the moral justification of her existence; thus she can evade at once both economic risk and the metaphysical risk of a liberty in which ends and aims must be contrived without assistance. Indeed, along with the ethical urge of each individual to affirm his subjective existence, there is also the temptation to forgo liberty and become a thing. This is an inauspicious road, for he who takes it—passive, lost, ruined—becomes henceforth the creature of another's will, frustrated in his transcendence and deprived of every value. But it is an easy road; on it one avoids the strain involved in undertaking an authentic existence. When man makes of woman the *Other,* he may, then, expect her to manifest deep-seated tendencies toward complicity. Thus, woman may fail to lay claim to the status of subject because she lacks definite resources, because she feels the necessary bond that ties her to man regardless of reciprocity, and because she is often very well pleased with her role as the *Other.*

QUESTIONS FOR DISCUSSION AND WRITING

1. Analyze the opening two paragraphs of this essay. Put Beauvoir's point in your own words. How does she support this point? Do you find her point well taken? If so, which reason or example is most persuasive? if not, what objections do you have?

2. By the time you reach the end of paragraph 3, are you willing to accept her premise that man is subject and woman is the other? In paragraph 4, given her examples across cultures, do you accept her conclusion that "otherness is a fundamental category of human thought"? Do her examples in paragraph 5 provide convincing evidence? Why or why not?

3. At the end of paragraph 7 and in paragraph 8, the author asks why women have not disputed male/female status as one and other, especially given that men are not a numerical majority. Analyze her response to this question in paragraph 10 and her subsequent analogy to master and slave.

4. Write an essay analyzing and critiquing Beauvoir's reasoning and conclusions.

5. Write an essay reflecting on the extent to which Beauvoir's argument is or is not relevant to contemporary US or non-US cultures.

Gender and Power

ESTELLE B. FREEDMAN

Estelle B. Freedman is a U.S. historian specializing in women's history and feminist studies. She has taught at Stanford University since 1976, where she is a professor of history; she also cofounded the Program in Feminist Studies at Stanford and has received numerous teaching awards. Freedman graduated from Barnard College and holds a Ph.D. from Columbia University. She has written extensively about the history of women in the United States. She authored two award-winning studies: *Their Sisters' Keepers: Women's Prison Reform in America, 1830–1930* (1981) and *Maternal Justice: Miriam Van Waters and the Female Reform Tradition* (1996). She also co-authored *Intimate Matters: A History of Sexuality in America* (1997). The following selection is from her book, *No Turning Back: The History of Feminism and the Future of Women* (2002).

> *The history of mankind is a history of repeated injuries and usurpations on the part of man toward woman, having in direct object the establishment of an absolute tyranny over her.*
>
> —ELIZABETH CADY STANTON, UNITED STATES, 1848

> *Patriarchy as a system is historical: it has a beginning in history . . . it can be ended by historical process.*
>
> —GERDA LERNER, UNITED STATES, 1986

At the first U.S. women's rights convention, held in 1848 in the town of Seneca Falls, New York, three hundred women and men launched a major social movement. As convention organizer Elizabeth Cady Stanton read the Declaration of Sentiments, these early feminists heard a litany of complaints about the unjust laws and practices that denied women education, property rights, and self-esteem. Echoing the revolutionary generation that had overthrown British colonial rulers, the declaration boldly called for women to overthrow the male rulers who denied them liberty. Stanton introduced women's grievances with a rhetorical flourish worthy of her rebellious predecessors. She pronounced a sweeping historical generalization: "The history of mankind is a history of repeated injuries and usurpations on the part of man toward woman, having in direct object the establishment of an absolute tyranny over her." Only a movement to empower women legally and politically could correct this injustice.

If the Declaration of Sentiments was right, and men had been tyrants throughout world history, why did it take so long for women to rebel? What could have enforced such total, unrelenting patriarchal power throughout past millennia? Had patriarchy robbed women of their very ability to question male authority? Elizabeth Cady Stanton would have answered yes, women had been deprived of liberty throughout history. They did not rebel because the denial of education and self-respect had contributed to their becoming "willing to lead a dependent and abject life."[1]

Such downtrodden creatures seemed unlikely to foment a revolution. Surely Stanton knew that history was full of resilient women who defied tyranny, whether queens such as Nefertiti, warriors such as Joan of Arc, or simply clever wives and mothers who bowed to no man's will. What distinguished these earlier, strong women from Stanton and later feminists was a new political view of the world. The future society envisioned at Seneca Falls in 1848 incorporated the concept of equality, a relatively recent political ideal that had already helped motivate the American and French revolutions. For most of world history, however, few people questioned the inequality of social hierarchies, including the rule of men over women, or patriarchy. Because they accepted supernatural (theological) and natural (biological) explanations of male dominance, women and men rarely questioned their inherited gender systems—until feminism, that is.

Inspired by democratic ideals of equal rights, when Stanton and her colleagues turned a feminist eye to women's history, they vastly oversimplified the patriarchal past. True, most human societies value men more highly than women. Fortunately for the future of feminism, however, women have not been so tyrannized that they have no usable history. Even a brief review of the past refines the Declaration of Sentiments to show how patriarchy itself has changed over time in response to changing economic systems, family structures, and religious beliefs. In historian Gerda Lerner's words, "Patriarchy as a system is historical: it has a beginning in history . . . it can be ended by historical process."[2] Understanding that history and women's resistance to it is critical to the feminist political project.

The Evidence for Patriarchy

The world before feminism offers ample evidence that men had more power than women. If we simply listen to folk wisdom or read sacred texts, we learn about the virtues of sons and the

5

lesser value of daughters. A girl is "merely a weed," in a Zulu say-ing. According to the Old Testament, "The Lord said to Moses, 'Set the value of a male between ages of twenty and sixty at fifty shekels . . . and if it is a female, set the value at thirty shekels.'" A Dutch proverb declares that "a house full of daughters is like a cellar full of sour beer," while Koreans learn that "a girl lets you down twice, once at birth and the second time when she mar-ries." Even contemporary parents usually prefer male children; a 1983 survey of forty countries found only two with daughter preference and only thirteen with equal preference for boys or girls. Where strong son preferences persist, parents may selec-tively abort female fetuses and neglect girls, leading to higher mortality rates for female infants in parts of the world, such as India and China.[3]

So widespread is the greater privilege, opportunity, and value attached to boys and men that anthropologist Michelle Zimbalist Rosaldo once referred to its occurrence as "universal sexual asymmetry." Almost all societies, Rosaldo wrote in 1974, not only differentiate by gender but, more important, they value the male more highly than the female. She provided a vivid il-lustration of this phenomenon in the case of a New Guinea cul-ture that cultivated both yams and sweet potatoes. Although they were quite similar foods, the yams, raised by men, were reserved for festival consumption, while the sweet potatoes, raised by women, provided daily sustenance. In this case, as in so many features of social life, seemingly neutral traits or activities take on greater symbolic value simply by their association with the male gender.

Stories of human origins help support these beliefs in male superiority. Most of the supernatural theories of how humans came to be assert that a higher power—a God, gods, or other spiritual force beyond human reason—ordained that men should rule over women. When anthropologist Peggy Reeves Sanday surveyed stories of human origins she found that most cultures imagine a male divine force as the origin of life. Fewer than one fifth of all creation stories include a female deity (usually in less patriarchal societies). The major Western monotheistic religions, which originated around five thousand years ago in the ancient Middle East, provide a good example of the use of supernatural theories to support patriarchy. In this settled agricultural region, fathers exercised extensive authority over wives and children, who had few if any rights. The Judeo-Christian Bible reflected this patriarchal gender system, as did later commentaries on the Islamic Qu'ran. Each cited the story of Adam and Eve to justify the rule of men: God created Adam to rule over the earth and the animal kingdom, <u>while Eve, a physical outgrowth from Adam's rib, brought sin into the world.</u>

Aside from origin stories, religious institutions have often enforced patriarchy. In Judaism and Christianity, a male symbol for God the Father set the standard for earthly rule. The elevation of male prophets and male priests showed that only men were worthy of hearing or speaking the word of God. Both traditions denigrated women as mere flesh, closer to nature and less capable of spiritual growth than men. Like traditional Judaism, Islam segregated women during worship. An exclusively male priesthood in Catholicism reproduced patriarchy by treating women like subordinate members of the spiritual family. Even Buddhism, which began with a gender-neutral ideal of enlightenment, came to emphasize male qualities of the Buddha and mandated female obedience to men. As one Japanese Buddhist sect explains, "The husband is the lord and the wife is the servant."[4]

The evidence for patriarchy is not universal, however. Prehistoric artifacts suggest that men and women have at times shared spiritual prestige. Ancient female deities, such as the Middle Eastern fertility goddess Astarte and the Greek earth goddess Gaia, attest to women's powerful role in pantheistic religions. Historically, we know that women have sometimes held other powerful social positions. Women ruled as queens in ancient Egypt and among Bedouins in pre-Islamic Arabia. In ancient Japan, female emperors ruled as often as men. Jewish women, such as the biblical Deborah, played important public roles as judges in the era after the Exodus from Egypt.

Short of formal power, some women have enjoyed rights similar to men, as they did in pastoral, nomadic cultures in Asia and the Middle East, such as the Mongols. In ancient Sumer and Egypt, adult women could own property, serve as clergy, and play active roles in public marketplaces. Women in ancient Japan could also own property. In precolonial Latin America, some native cultures practiced what anthropologists term "gender parallelism," valuing highly the distinct and overlapping tasks performed by men and women. Women traders sold goods in the marketplace, but even their household labors ranked as highly as men's military exploits. In the Andes, girls learned to use brooms and looms—the latter called "weaving swords"—as if they were weapons of war; giving birth was equivalent to taking a prisoner of war, and death in childbirth was as honorable as death in battle.

The Seneca of North America provide another example of the influence women wielded in communal, agricultural societies. Well into the 1800s, Seneca women cultivated the land and shared child rearing with men. Because women controlled the food supply, Seneca men could not hunt or wage war unless elder women agreed to allocate food for these purposes. These elders knew they held political authority. During the American Revolutionary War, they explained to American army officers that "you ought to hear and listen to what we, women shall speak, as well as to the sachems [chiefs]; for *we are the owners of this land—and it is ours.*"[5]

Exceptions to patriarchal rule persist in more recent history. In the 1930s, Margaret Mead shook up our notions of "natural" male dominance when she described three New Guinea cultures, one in which men and women were equally parental, one in which men and women were equally aggressive, and one in which women were businesslike and men were decorative. Male tyranny was far from universal, even in this one region. Sanday too noted that on the pacific island of Bali, male and female social roles are highly interchangeable. Another contemporary case is Vanatinai (the name means "motherland") Island, also in the South Pacific. Both women and men share in child care and decision making and use gender-neutral language. Significantly, both sexes can officiate during the public yam-planting ritual.

What Happened to Women's Power?

At the time Elizabeth Cady Stanton called for a female independence movement, she seemed unaware of the Seneca women who lived just a few dozen miles from her Seneca Falls home. In 1848, the year of the women's rights convention, the Seneca formed a constitution that granted both men and women voting rights. Had Stanton taken notice, the early feminists might have couched their demands for equality in less universal terms; perhaps they would have called for a *return* of women's power. Unlike the subsistence farming villages of the Seneca, however, in the middle-class, commercial, and increasingly urban world that Stanton inhabited, women no longer shared formal authority, nor did they control economic life, although they certainly contributed to it. The democratic governments of the United States denied women voting rights and legitimated a husband's control of his wife's property. For her own culture, Stanton correctly observed that legal inequalities denied women the rights enjoyed by men. Unaware of the alternative histories around her, she failed to ask how a patriarchal world had emerged, given the more egalitarian potential of human cultures.

That question is worth contemplating, even if we can never answer it definitively. The short answer is that as human societies became more complex, they became less egalitarian.

Among the early hunter-gatherers, men and women had distinct but complementary tasks and shared important economic and religious duties. Though women never ruled over men, as the term *matriarchy* implies, they once enjoyed more equal footing. When these egalitarian societies shifted to settled agriculture (around 3100 to 600 BCE), they developed complicated class and gender relations. More-specialized farming, the barter of surplus goods, and an emerging class hierarchy contributed to patriarchal families in which only male children inherited property and wives became subjects in their husbands' homes. Around the same time, female deities seemed to disappear, replaced by a single male god. In Western cultures, by the time of the Hebrew Bible and Greek and Roman civilizations, only men exercised political power. Women retained some authority in the home but little in the public realm. Gone, for example, were the temple priestesses of earlier civilizations. By the time of Christianity the Virgin Mary had become an intermediary to God rather than a goddess in her own right.

Two influential theories of the emergence of patriarchy help 15
explain this process. The first appeared in an 1884 essay, "On the Origin of the Family, Private Property, and the State," by Friedrich Engels (the coauthor, with Karl Marx, of *The Communist Manifesto*). Engels argued that the subjugation of women began only when economic surpluses accumulated; thus private property, which leads to class hierarchy and the formation of states, is the source of women's oppression. When individual families replaced larger clan and communal living groups, women lost their reciprocal roles. In short, Engels argued, private property was the source of "the *world historical defeat of the female sex*."[6] In the second, more recent account, *The Creation of Patriarchy* (1986), feminist historian Gerda Lerner revised Engels's theory. She agreed that male control over women gradually formed during the long transition to settled agriculture. A new farming system in the Middle East, based on private land ownership and domesticated farm animals, coincided with the emergence of a hierarchial state led by military elites and based on the rule of fathers in the family. Male gods and ultimately monotheism replaced earlier female deities. To this story Lerner added a critical point: Reproductive labor was key to men's subordination of women.

In Lerner's view, children helped a family produce more crops, allowing the accumulation of surpluses that created family wealth. Since women's reproductive labor provided these workers, reproduction itself became a commodity, something purchased from a father when a young man's family paid a bride-price to a young woman's family. In order to ensure the husband's paternity, and with it his ownership of the wealth produced by children, women had to be chaste before marriage and faithful within it. Another source of reproductive labor was the theft of women during war raids. By acquiring captive female slaves as additional wives, men could increase the number of children they fathered, adding to the family's workforce and its ability to accumulate surpluses. According to Lerner, women were the first slaves, and all other forms of enslavement built upon female reproductive slavery. "Economic oppression and exploitation," Lerner wrote, "are based as much on the commodification of female sexuality and the appropriation by men of women's labor power and her reproductive power as on the direct economic acquisition of resources and persons."[7] In this way she turned Engels upside down by arguing that the appropriation of women's labor led to the possibility of accumulating surplus private property, rather than private property giving rise to women's subjugation.

Historical theories that emphasize the economic and reproductive origins of patriarchy do not dismiss the role of culture. For Lerner, denying access to education played a key role in the patriarchal control of women, whether as slaves or as wives. Myth, folktales, and religious precepts helped deepen the hold of patriarchy; thus knowledge could enable women to question their status.

Limits of Patriarchy

Whatever its precise origins, the history of patriarchy cannot be understood in isolation from a larger matrix of social relations. Aside from the power of mythology and religion to enforce male dominance, women did not rebel in the past because gender was only one of many power relations affecting their lives. In short, not all men exercised control over all women. The privileges of age or family status could mediate patriarchal power. In simple societies, for example, older women command service from younger men, who are obligated to provide food for both male and female elders. In many patriarchal cultures, the wives of elite men enjoy privileges, and women often exercise authority as mothers. Indeed, as long as they do not challenge the legitimacy of the patriarchal ideal, women could find ways to advance their own interests and those of their children. Allowing some female authority also helped prevent disloyalty to patriarchy.

Given the interconnection of gender and other social hierarchies, the simple fact of being born female was not necessarily the most important one in a woman's life. Consciousness of gender identity, a precondition for feminism, surfaced only rarely when caste, class, and family defined one's social position. Take, for example, the Hindu caste system, which mandates what tasks each group may perform; women and men of a common caste share more than women of different castes. Or consider those African women who as slave owners once benefited from the labor of captive women. In either case, thinking about oneself primarily as a "woman" did not always make sense. The Chinese language illustrates how distinct, age-related kinship identities could be more important than a broader gender identity. The terms for daughter, wife, mother, or mother-in-law once sufficed to name most women. Only after 1900 did terms such as *funü* and *nuxing* define "women as a political category," apart from their family relations.[8]

A final problem with Stanton's assertion of absolute male tyranny is that it presents a static picture. As economic practices, family relations, and religious beliefs change over time, they shift the balance of gender and power. Although the pace of change is uneven across cultures, in each phase of economic development—from settled agriculture to urban trade to early world capitalism—we find evidence of a female resilience that strongly contradicts Stanton's claim of unrelenting sexual oppression.

20

Notes

1. Alice Rossi, Ed. "Declaration of Sentiments," *The History of Woman Suffrage,* in *The Feminist Papers* (New York: Bantam, 1973), 415–418.

2. Gerda Lerner, *The Creation of Patriarchy* (New York: Oxford University Press, 1986), 6.

3. For proverbs and son preference, see Neera Kuckreja Sohoni, *The Burden of Girlhood: A Global Inquiry Into the Status of Girls* (Oakland, CA: Third Party Publishing, 1995), and Leviticus 27:1–4; and Joni Seager, *The State of Women in the World Atlas* (London: Penguin, 1997), 34–35. Parents in Venezuela and Jamaica had daughter preferences.

4. Quoted in Haruko Okano, "Women's Image and Place in Japanese Buddhism," in *Japanese Women: New Feminist Perpectives on the Past, Present, and Future,* eds. Kumiko Fujimura-Fanselow and Atsuko Kameda (New York Feminist Press, 1995), 16.

5. Quoted in Joan Jensen, "Native American Women and Agriculture: A Seneca Case Study," in *Unequal Sisters: A Multi-Cultural Reader in U.S. Women's History,* eds. Ellen Carol DuBois and Vicki L. Ruiz (New York: Routledge, 1990), 57, 73.

6. Friedrich Engels, *The Origin of the Family, Private Property, and the State* (New York: International Publishers, 1942), 50.

7. Lerner, *Creation of Patriarchy,* 216.

8. Tani Barlow, "Theorizing Woman: Funii, Guojia, Jiating (Chinese Women, Chinese State, Chinese Family)," in *Scattered Hegemonies: Postmodernity and Transnational Feminist Practices,* eds. Inderpal Grewal and Caren Kaplan (Minneapolis: University of Minnesota Press, 1994), 173–196.

QUESTIONS FOR DISCUSSION AND WRITING

1. After reading the whole selection, examine paragraph 4 and put Freedman's argument into your own words. Does the rest of the selection support this view convincingly? If so, what evidence is most persuasive? If not, what would persuade you of her view?

2. How does Freedman define patriarchy? What examples does she use? In the section "Limits of Patriarchy," Freedman notes that other variables (e.g., social class) could be more relevant than gender in determining position in society. Does her argument lend credence to the problem with Stanton's assumption of a static, unchanging societal structure, rather than a dynamic view that takes into account economic changes and belief systems?

3. In what ways did Stanton's Declaration evolve from the ethos of equality? What were the limits of the prevailing belief in equality in America at the time? Discuss also the irony Freedman notes of a Seneca Falls Declaration that does not take into account the structure of the nearby Seneca tribe.

4. Review the Seneca Falls Declaration (see the Appendix) and, using Freedman's essay as a secondary source to inform your analysis, write an essay analyzing the Declaration. Consider incorporating the American Declaration of Independence as well.

5. Using question 1 as a starting point, write an essay analyzing Freedman's argument and use of examples and reasoning.

Office Ladies and the Freedom of the Discriminated

YUKO OGASAWARA

Yuko Ogasawara is Assistant Professor of Sociology at Edogawa University. Her recent publications include *Office Ladies and Salaried Men: Power, Gender, and Work in Japanese Companies* (Berkeley: University of California Press, 1998). In a review of this book, anthropology professor Louisa Schein suggests that Ogasawara challenges notions of "victimized, passive Asian women" and the Western views and interpretations of gender relations and power. In the essay that follows, which was published on the *Japan Editorial* Web site, a forum designed to promote Japanese and American dialog, (accessed November 2002), Ogasawara acknowledges the prevailing view of women's office work and lack of advancement while pointing out the ways in which these women in fact have power to resist and subvert, a power which, however, comes at a cost.

Ofisu redi (office lady), or OL for short, is a term coined in the early 1960s for female office workers who do word processing, perform elementary accounting, and operate copiers and facsimile machines. They are sometimes also called to do various chores, such as serving tea to their male colleagues or to company visitors, wiping the surface of desks with wet towels, and taking telephone calls. Not exactly the kind of job that most American women seek. However, approximately one third of working women in Japan hold this position.

Although the Equal Employment Opportunity Law has been in effect for more than a decade, opportunities for OLs to be promoted into management remain limited. In 1996, in companies with 100 or more employees, only 1.4 percent of *bucho* (general managers), 3.1 percent of *kacho* (section managers), and 7.3 percent of *kakaricho* (chiefs) were women.[1] *Kakaricho* is typically the lowest rank of managers to have supervisory responsibility in a white-collar organization. That so few women exist even at this level of organizational hierarchy attests to the ubiquitous pattern of "male managers and female subordinates" in Japan.

The position of OL seems to lead nowhere but to a case study of oppression. However, I have found in my survey, based on participant observation in a Japanese bank and through interviews with thirty OLs and ex-OLs and with thirty businessmen, that this smothering lack of opportunity can in some ways be liberating. While many men work hard to make their way up the corporate ladder, most OLs expect and are expected to quit after several years of service. OLs are usually exempt from strict performance reviews. Because they are excluded from the race for promotion, they have almost nothing to lose. They resist male dominance. Furthermore, they have the potential to spoil, if not ruin, the reputations of their male co-workers.

Because OLs do the majority of menial work for male employees, the men are highly dependent on them. If the menial work is not done, the "man's work" is not done. One source of women's leverage, therefore, is the strict sexual division of labor in most Japanese offices that leaves men dependent on female employees for such details as where files are stored or how to fix a jammed copying machine.

In addition, there is the potency of women's gossip about   5
male co-workers and the fabrication of male reputations by comparing men with one another. The female gaze is a matter of men's concern, since a man's promotion is based in part on how well he manages his subordinates, including his team of OLs. For example, a man whose assistant "boycotted" him after a quarrel and refused to send a telex complained to his (male) boss that he could not get his assistant's cooperation. Instead of reproaching the uncooperative OL, the boss criticized the man for not knowing how to manage women. In the end, the man had to learn to type and send his telex himself.

The result is an office where men take pains not to offend women, study women's moods, and even curry women's favor. Contrary to intuitive thought, men in positions of authority care more about the feelings of subordinate women than subordinate women do about the feelings of men in authority. I therefore argue that macro-level power relations are not necessarily reproduced in micro-level interactions, and may even be reversed.

Some men attempt to maintain good relationships with OLs via small and large gifts, meals at restaurants, and flattery. In one telling incident, a vice-general manager of a bank had to take a call at an OL's desk. When the conversation ended, he took out his handkerchief to wipe off the receiver.

Men who fail to maintain good relationships with OLs must prepare to face their defiance. OLs can annoy and trouble men in various forms. First, they can resist by not taking the initiative.

For example, when typing a document, an OL can make life easier for a man she likes by voluntarily double-checking unclear points, but she may refuse to do the same for a man she dislikes. For the latter man, she may just keep typing as she sees fit, leaving it up to the man to come back to her if he found anything wrong. Many OLs I interviewed admitted that the way they worked varied according to their feelings about a man. As one OL said, "If I were asked to do an ordinary, routine job, I would do work even for a man I didn't like. But let's say you see an extremely busy person. If it's someone I like or someone I respect, I offer to help. If it's someone I don't like, I pretend not to notice. I guess it's in the area of providing additional services that I discriminate in terms of how I work for a man."

Second, OLs can decline men's requests to do extra work. Even if it were a general manager asking for her favor, an OL may refuse politely, saying, "I'm terribly sorry, but I'm very busy right now. Would you please do it yourself?" An OL explained why she could take such a strong attitude even toward a man of high rank and office in the following way: "It's OK to refuse. I won't be put in a difficult position because of it. In a way, I'm turning my weakness into strength. After all, if it makes no difference to your promotion whether or not you say something, isn't it to your advantage to say whatever you want to say?" The OL's words suggest that when a woman does not have a career in the company that can be jeopardized, even a senior manager has limited power to extract favors from her.

Third, OLs can refuse not only to do favors but also to work. 10
If an OL is asked to perform a task by a man she does not like, she may agree and then neglect the task. When the man asks for the completed assignment, she can insist that she is really sorry but that she just hasn't had the time to get around to it. Both men and women I interviewed mentioned that giving certain assignments priority while deliberately moving others to the bottom regardless of the urgency was a frequent tactic used by OLs to put off doing the work of a disliked man. The following statement of a businessman illustrates the situation: "A man is in trouble if he can't get women to cooperate. I mean, it seems like a very common thing for a girl [sic] to do the word-processing or typing for a man she likes first. In our company, the ratio of men to women is about six to two, and so we must scramble for women's help . . . Let's say a girl [sic] was asked to do a word-processing job by Mr. A, B, and C. Because she likes Mr. A, she works hard on his job, and it's finished by the time men come back from sales calls late in the afternoon. Mr. B's work is half done, and she hasn't even started on Mr. C's.

The girl [sic] leaves the office, and Mr. C must type by himself at night." In this act of defiance, an OL is not neglecting work but simply reorganizing the order of assignments. She therefore may feel relatively uninhibited in resorting to this measure. However, as discussed earlier, it is rare but possible for an OL to step up the degree of resistance and refuse to work completely. In either case, an OL's refusal to cooperate with a man is commonly regarded as in part his fault, because a truly capable manager is one who is able to raise the working morale of his subordinates.

Lastly, one of the harshest and most humiliating treatments is called *sosukan* (total neglect). In this, not only the man's assistant but many other OLs plot together to ignore him. They ostensibly behave as though the victim did not exist. They minimize the amount of words they exchange with him, and when they have to speak to him at all, they do so bluntly or without looking in his direction. Even a high-ranking manager with power over personnel management can be defenseless against *sosukan;* it is a movement supported by many OLs. To penalize an OL for acting improperly is one thing, but it is quite another to assert that many OLs had done so. A man who makes such an assertion is likely to embarrass himself by disclosing his inability to supervise OLs.

The dynamics of these gendered relations in the Japanese workplace come into focus in two annual rituals: Valentine's Day, when OLs present male co-workers with gifts of chocolates, and "White Day" in March, when men give return gifts to OLs. On Valentine's Day, OLs give candy primarily to men they like. Therefore, both men and women gauge a man's popularity among women by the number of gifts he receives. A man with few gifts is humiliated in the presence of his colleagues: the desk of a disliked man may be left conspicuously empty, while his colleague's desk groans under mountains of chocolates. Moreover, some women use Valentine's Day to convey subtle criticisms. They devise various tactics of revenge, such as giving fewer boxes, delaying the time to give, or presenting broken chocolate to a man they dislike. In contrast, on White Day many men feel compelled to give reciprocal gifts to OLs, because they know that they risk their reputation among OLs if they fail to do so. Those who do not reciprocate must often be prepared to receive women's criticisms of stinginess.

In sum, the relationship between men and women in the workplace and the question of domination and subordination in large-scale organizations are far more complex than they appear to be. Most OLs are not entrusted with work that fully exercises their abilities, but are instead assigned to dead-end and often demeaning jobs. They have little prospect of promotion, and their individuality is seldom respected.

The employment system that is so blatantly discriminatory to women, however, has, not without irony, empowered them. With considerably less benefits to protect than their male co-workers, women have little to fear. Many OLs are indifferent to threats, such as a boss's scornful look or a suggestion about de-motion, that are sufficient to keep men under control.

OLs' acts of resistance are not without a price, however. For what enables OLs to take subversive actions is their accommo-dation to company policies that set the separate career paths of the two sexes. Only OLs who do not hope to be promoted and who do not care about their performance can annoy men by act-ing irresponsibly. Furthermore, the more OLs resist, the more they promote the stereotype: That women get carried away by emotion; that they are unable to make rational decisions; and that they are not seriously committed to business. The sad irony is that by making demands on men, OLs unwittingly reinforce the very excuse for discriminating against them. My study shows, however, that the stereotype is suspect. Men usually make seri-ous efforts to perform well in their jobs. They put business re-quirements ahead of personal preferences, and will not let the impulse of the moment destroy their career in the company. OLs, in contrast, readily complain and otherwise show discomfort, be-cause they know there is little to be gained by forbearance. If such is the case, we may conclude that it is the wider social and cultural systems that are responsible for the contrasting attitudes men and women assume in the Japanese workplace.

15

Note

1. Ministry of Labor, 1997, Heisei 8-nen chingin kozo kikon tokei chosa (Basic Survey on Wage Structure, 1996).

QUESTIONS FOR DISCUSSION AND WRITING

1. Ogasawara explains that Japanese office ladies may find that "lack of opportunity can in some ways be liberating." Do you agree, given her essay, or do you suspect that the costs may be greater than evident at first?

2. Ogasawara summarizes her essay by noting, "In sum, the relationship between men and women in the workplace and the question of domination and subordination in large-scale organizations are far more complex than they appear." Do you agree that the office ladies' apparent submissiveness gives them power over the dominant male superiors? In what ways does the apparent submission reinforce the dominant order and stereotypes about women?

3. Ogasawara conducted a participant-observation and interviews, tools of ethnographic study. Research this topic in books and periodicals and in online sources to determine if the author's findings have been supported by other research in the field.

4. Write an essay critiquing Ogasawara's essay, paying attention to the inferences she draws from her observations. Do her conclusions seem logical? Can other conclusions be drawn from her evidence?

Global Woman

ARLIE RUSSELL HOCHSCHILD

Arlie Russell Hochschild is Professor of Sociology at the University of California at Berkeley and has received awards from the Fulbright, Guggenheim, and Alfred P. Sloan foundations and from the National Institute of Public Health. She is the author of *The Second Shift* (1989) and *The Managed Heart* (1983). She also directs the Center for Working Families at the University of California at Berkeley. Her articles have appeared in scholarly journals as well as *Harper's, Mother Jones, The New York Times Magazine,* and others. The selection that follows is the introduction to her recent book, *Global Woman* (2003), co-authored with Barbara Ehrenreich.

BARBARA EHRENREICH

Barbara Ehrenreich is the author of numerous books, including *The Hearts of Men: American Dreams and the Flight from Commitment* (1983). Social critic, essayist, and journalist, Ehrenreich has written for many major magazines and newspapers in the United States. Originally a biologist who earned her Ph.D. from Rockefeller University, Ehrenreich became involved in politics during the Vietnam War and has written professionally ever since. Among her books are *The American Health Empire: Power, Profits, and Politics* (1970), *For Her Own Good: One Hundred Fifty Years of the Experts' Advice to Women* (1978), and *Nickeled and Dimed: On (Not) Getting By in America* (2001).

"Whose baby are you?" Josephine Perera, a nanny from Sri Lanka, asks Isadora, her pudgy two-year-old charge in Athens, Greece.

Thoughtful for a moment, the child glances toward the closed door of the next room, in which her mother is working, as if to say, "That's my mother in there."

"No, you're *my* baby," Josephine teases, tickling Isadora lightly. Then, to settle the issue, Isadora answers, "Together!" She has two mommies—her mother and Josephine. And surely a child loved by many adults is richly blessed.

In some ways, Josephine's story—which unfolds in an extraordinary documentary film, *When Mother Comes Home for*

Christmas, directed by Nilita Vachani—describes an unparalleled success. Josephine has ventured around the world, achieving a degree of independence her mother could not have imagined and amply supporting her three children with no help from her ex-husband, their father. Each month she mails a remittance check from Athens to Hatton, Sri Lanka, to pay the children's living expenses and school fees. On her Christmas visit home, she bears gifts of pots, pans, and dishes. While she makes payments on a new bus that Suresh, her oldest son, now drives for a living, she is also saving for a modest dowry for her daughter, Norma. She dreams of buying a new house in which the whole family can live. In the meantime, her work as a nanny enables Isadora's parents to devote themselves to their careers and avocations.

But Josephine's story is also one of wrenching global inequality. While Isadora enjoys the attention of three adults, Josephine's three children in Sri Lanka have been far less lucky. According to Vachani, Josephine's youngest child, Suminda, was two—Isadora's age—when his mother first left home to work in Saudi Arabia. Her middle child, Norma, was nine; her oldest son, Suresh, thirteen. From Saudi Arabia, Josephine found her way first to Kuwait, then to Greece. Except for one two-month trip home, she has lived apart from her children for ten years. She writes them weekly letters, seeking news of relatives, asking about school, and complaining that Norma doesn't write back.

Although Josephine left the children under her sister's supervision, the two youngest have shown signs of real distress. Norma has attempted suicide three times. Suminda, who was twelve when the film was made, boards in a grim, Dickensian orphanage that forbids talk during meals and showers. He visits his aunt on holidays. Although the oldest, Suresh, seems to be on good terms with his mother, Norma is tearful and sullen, and Suminda does poorly in school, picks quarrels, and otherwise seems withdrawn from the world. Still, at the end of the film, we see Josephine once again leave her three children in Sri Lanka to return to Isadora in Athens. For Josephine can either live with her children in desperate poverty or make money by living apart from them. Unlike her affluent First World employers, she cannot both live with her family and support it.

Thanks to the process we loosely call "globalization," women are on the move as never before in history. In images familiar to the West from television commercials for credit cards, cell phones, and airlines, female executives jet about the world, phoning home from luxury hotels and reuniting with eager children in airports. But we hear much less about a far more prodigious flow of female labor and energy: the increasing migration of millions of women from poor countries to rich ones, where they serve as nannies, maids, and sometimes sex workers. In the absence of help from male partners, many women have succeeded in tough "male world" careers only by turning over the care of their children, elderly parents, and homes to women from the Third World. This is the female underside of globalization, whereby millions of Josephines from poor countries in the south migrate to do the "women's work" of the north—work that affluent women are no longer able or willing to do. These migrant workers often leave their own children in the care of grandmothers, sisters, and sisters-in-law. Sometimes a young daughter is drawn out of school to care for her younger siblings.

This pattern of female migration reflects what could be called a worldwide gender revolution. In both rich and poor countries, fewer families can rely solely on a male breadwinner. In the United States, the earning power of most men has declined since 1970, and many women have gone out to "make up the difference." By one recent estimate, women were the sole, primary, or coequal earners in more than half of American families.[1] So the question arises: Who will take care of the children, the sick, the elderly? Who will make dinner and clean house?

While the European or American woman commutes to work an average twenty-eight minutes a day, many nannies from the Philippines, Sri Lanka, and India cross the globe to get to their jobs. Some female migrants from the Third World do find something like "liberation," or at least the chance to become independent breadwinners and to improve their children's material lives. Other, less fortunate migrant women end up in the control of criminal employers—their passports stolen, their mobility blocked, forced to work without pay in brothels or to provide sex along with cleaning and child-care services in affluent homes. But even in more typical cases, where benign employers pay wages on time, Third World migrant women achieve their success only by assuming the cast-off domestic roles of middle- and high-income women in the First World—roles that have been previously rejected, of course, by men. And their "commute" entails a cost we have yet to fully comprehend.

The migration of women from the Third World to do "women's work" in affluent countries has so far received little scholarly or media attention—for reasons that are easy enough to guess. First, many, though by no means all, of the new female migrant workers are women of color, and therefore subject to the racial "discounting" routinely experienced by, say, Algerians in France, Mexicans in the United States, and Asians in the United Kingdom. Add to racism the private "indoor" nature of so much   10 of the new migrants' work. Unlike factory workers, who congregate in large numbers, or taxi drivers, who are visible on the street, nannies and maids are often hidden away, one or two at a time, behind closed doors in private homes. Because of the illegal nature of their work, most sex workers are even further concealed from public view.

At least in the case of nannies and maids, another factor contributes to the invisibility of migrant women and their work—one that, for their affluent employers, touches closer to home. The Western culture of individualism, which finds extreme expression in the United States, militates against acknowledging help or human interdependency of nearly any kind. Thus, in the time-pressed upper middle class, servants are no longer displayed as status symbols, decked out in white caps and aprons, but often remain in the background, or disappear when company comes. Furthermore, affluent careerwomen increasingly earn their status not through leisure, as they might have a century ago, but by apparently "doing it all"—producing a full-time career, thriving children, a contented spouse, and a well-managed home. In order to preserve this illusion, domestic workers and nannies make the house hotel-room perfect, feed and bathe the children, cook and clean up—and then magically fade from sight.

The lifestyles of the First World are made possible by a global transfer of the services associated with a wife's traditional role—child care, home-making, and sex—from poor countries to rich ones. To generalize and perhaps oversimplify: In an earlier phase of imperialism, northern countries extracted natural resources and agricultural products—rubber, metals, and sugar, for example—from lands they conquered and colonized. Today, while still relying on Third World countries for agricultural and industrial labor, the wealthy countries also seek to extract something harder to measure and quantify, something that can look very much like love. Nannies like Josephine bring the distant families that employ them real maternal affection, no doubt enhanced by the heartbreaking absence of their own children in the poor countries they leave behind. Similarly, women who migrate from country to country to work as maids bring not only their muscle power but an attentiveness to detail and to the human relationships in the household that might otherwise have been invested in their own families. Sex workers offer the simulation of sexual and romantic love, or at least transient sexual companionship. It is as if the wealthy parts of the world are running short on precious emotional and sexual resources and have had to turn to poorer regions for fresh supplies.

There are plenty of historical precedents for this globalization of traditional female services. In the ancient Middle East, the women of populations defeated in war were routinely enslaved and hauled off to serve as household workers and concubines for the victors. Among the Africans brought to North America as slaves in the sixteenth through nineteenth centuries, about a third were women and children, and many of those women were pressed to be concubines, domestic servants, or both. Nineteenth century Irishwomen—along with many rural English-women—migrated to English towns and cities to work as domestics in the homes of the growing upper middle class. Services thought to be innately feminine—child care, housework, and sex—often win little recognition or pay. But they have always been sufficiently in demand to transport over long distances if necessary. What is new today is the sheer number of female migrants and the very long distances they travel. Immigration statistics show huge numbers of women in motion, typically from poor countries to rich. Although the gross statistics give little clue as to the jobs women eventually take, there are reasons to infer that much of their work is "caring work," performed either in private homes or in institutional settings such as hospitals, hospices, child-care centers, and nursing homes.

The statistics are, in many ways, frustrating. We have information on legal migrants but not on illegal migrants, who, experts tell us, travel in equal if not greater numbers. Furthermore, many Third World countries lack data for past years, which makes it hard to trace trends over time; or they use varying methods of gathering information, which makes it hard to compare one country with another. Nevertheless, the trend is clear enough for some scholars, including Stephen Castles, Mark Miller, and Janet Momsen, to speak of a "feminization of migration."[2] From 1950 to 1970, for example, men predominated in labor migration to northern Europe from Turkey, Greece, and North Africa. Since then, women have been replacing men. In 1946, women were fewer than 3 percent of the Algerians and Moroccans living in France; by 1990, they were more than 40 percent.[3] Overall, half of the world's 120 million legal and illegal migrants are now believed to be women.

Patterns of international migration vary from region to region, but women migrants from a surprising number of sending countries actually outnumber men, sometimes by a wide margin. For example, in the 1990s, women made up over half of Filipino migrants to all countries and 84 percent of Sri Lankan migrants to the Middle East.[4] Indeed, by 1993 statistics, Sri Lankan women such

15

as Josephine vastly outnumbered Sri Lankan men as migrant workers who'd left for Saudi Arabia, Kuwait, Lebanon, Oman, Bahrain, Jordan, and Qatar, as well as to all countries of the Far East, Africa, and Asia.[5] About half of the migrants leaving Mexico, India, Korea, Malaysia, Cyprus, and Swaziland to work elsewhere are also women. Throughout the 1990s women outnumbered men among migrants to the United States, Canada, Sweden, the United Kingdom, Argentina, and Israel.[6]

Most women, like men, migrate from the south to the north and from poor countries to rich ones. Typically, migrants go to the nearest comparatively rich country, preferably one whose language they speak or whose religion and culture they share. There are also local migratory flows: from northern to southern Thailand, for instance or from the former East Germany to the West. But of the regional or cross-regional flows, four stand out. One goes from Southeast Asia to the oil-rich Middle and Far East—from Bangladesh, Indonesia, the Philippines, and Sri Lanka to Bahrain, Oman, Kuwait, Saudi Arabia, Hong Kong, Malaysia, and Singapore. Another stream of migration goes from the former Soviet bloc to Western Europe—from Russia, Romania, Bulgaria, and Albania to Scandinavia, Germany, France, Spain, Portugal, and England. A third goes from south to north in the Americas, including the stream from Mexico to the United States, which scholars say is the longest-running labor migration in the world. A fourth stream moves from Africa to various parts of Europe. France receives many female migrants from Morocco, Tunisia, and Algeria. Italy receives female workers from Ethiopia, Eritrea, and Cape Verde.

Female migrants overwhelmingly take up work as maids or domestics. As women have become an ever greater proportion of migrant workers, receiving countries reflect a dramatic influx of foreign-born domestics. In the United States, African-American women, who accounted for 60 percent of domestics in the 1940s, have been largely replaced by Latinas, many of them recent migrants from Mexico and Central America. In England, Asian migrant women have displaced the Irish and Portuguese domestics of the past. In French cities, North African women have replaced rural French girls. In western Germany, Turks and women from the former East Germany have replaced rural native-born women. Foreign females from countries outside the European Union made up only 6 percent of all domestic workers in 1984. By 1987, the percentage had jumped to 52, with most coming from the Philippines, Sri Lanka, Thailand, Argentina, Colombia, Brazil, El Salvador, and Peru.[7]

The governments of some sending countries actively encourage women to migrate in search of domestic jobs, reasoning that migrant women are more likely than their male counterparts to send their hard-earned wages to their families rather than spending the money on themselves. In general, women send home anywhere from half to nearly all of what they earn. These remittances have a significant impact on the lives of children, parents, siblings, and wider networks of kin—as well as on cash-strapped Third World governments. Thus, before Josephine left for Athens, a program sponsored by the Sri Lankan government taught her how to use a microwave oven, a vacuum cleaner, and an electric mixer. As she awaited her flight, a song piped into the airport departure lounge extolled the opportunity to earn money abroad. The songwriter was in the pay of the Sri Lanka Bureau of Foreign Employment, an office devised to encourage women to migrate. The lyrics say:

After much hardship, such difficult times
How lucky I am to work in a foreign land.
As the gold gathers so do many greedy flies.
But our good government protects us from them.
After much hardship, such difficult times,
How lucky I am to work in a foreign land.
I promise to return home with treasures for everyone.

Why this transfer of women's traditional services from poor to rich parts of the world? The reasons are, in a crude way, easy to guess. Women in Western countries have increasingly taken on paid work, and hence need others—paid domestics and caretakers for children and elderly people—to replace them.[8] For their part, women in poor countries have an obvious incentive to migrate: relative and absolute poverty. The "care deficit" that has emerged in the wealthier countries as women enter the workforce *pulls* migrants from the Third World and postcommunist nations; poverty *pushes* them.

In broad outline, this explanation holds true. Throughout Western Europe, Taiwan, and Japan, but above all in the United States, England, and Sweden, women's employment has increased dramatically since the 1970s. In the United States, for example, the proportion of women in paid work rose from 15 percent of mothers of children six and under in 1950 to 65 percent today. Women now make up 46 percent of the US labor force. Three-quarters of mothers of children eighteen and under and nearly two-thirds of mothers of children age one and younger now work for pay. Furthermore, according to a recent

International Labor Organization study, working Americans averaged longer hours at work in the late 1990s than they did in the 1970s. By some measures, the number of hours spent at work have increased more for women than for men, and especially for women in managerial and professional jobs.

Meanwhile, over the last thirty years, as the rich countries have grown much richer, the poor countries have become—in both absolute and relative terms—poorer. Global inequalities in wages are particularly striking. In Hong Kong, for instance, the wages of a Filipina domestic are about fifteen times the amount she could make as a schoolteacher back in the Philippines. In addition, poor countries turning to the IMF or World Bank for loans are often forced to undertake measures of so-called structural adjustment, with disastrous results for the poor and especially for poor women and children. To qualify for loans, governments are usually required to devalue their currencies, which turns the hard currencies of rich countries into gold and the soft currencies of poor countries into straw. Structural adjustment programs also call for cuts in support for "noncompetitive industries," and for the reduction of public services such as health care and food subsidies for the poor. Citizens of poor countries, women as well as men, thus have a strong incentive to seek work in more fortunate parts of the world.

But it would be a mistake to attribute the globalization of women's work to a simple synergy of needs among women—one group, in the affluent countries, needing help and the other, in poor countries, needing jobs. For one thing, this formulation fails to account for the marked failure of First World governments to meet the needs created by its women's entry into the work force. The downsized American—and to a lesser degree, Western European—welfare state has become a "deadbeat dad." Unlike the rest of the industrialized world, the United States does not offer public child care for working mothers, nor does it ensure paid family and medical leave. Moreover, a series of state tax revolts in the 1980s reduced the number of hours public libraries were open and slashed school-enrichment and after-school programs. Europe did not experience anything comparable. Still, tens of millions of western European women are in the workforce who were not before—and there has been no proportionate expansion in public services.

Secondly, any view of the globalization of domestic work as simply an arrangement among women completely omits the role of men. Numerous studies, including some of our own, have shown that as American women took on paid employment, the men in their families did little to increase their contribution to the work of the home. For example, only one out of every five men among the working couples whom Hochschild interviewed for *The Second Shift* in the 1980s shared the work at home, and later studies suggest that while working mothers are doing somewhat less housework than their counterparts twenty years ago, most men are doing only a little more.[9] With divorce, men frequently abdicate their child-care responsibilities to their ex-wives. In most cultures of the First World outside the United States, powerful traditions even more firmly discourage husbands from doing "women's work." So, strictly speaking, the presence of immigrant nannies does not enable affluent women to enter the workforce; it enables affluent *men* to continue avoiding the second shift.

The men in wealthier countries are also, of course, directly responsible for the demand for immigrant sex workers—as well as for the sexual abuse of many migrant women who work as domestics. Why, we wondered, is there a particular demand for "imported" sexual partners? Part of the answer may lie in the fact that new immigrants often take up the least desirable work, and, thanks to the AIDS epidemic, prostitution has become a job that ever fewer women deliberately choose. But perhaps some of this demand, as we see in Denise Brennan's chapter* on sex tourism, grows out of the erotic lure of the "exotic." Immigrant women may seem desirable sexual partners for the same reason that First World employers believe them to be especially gifted as caregivers: they are thought to embody the traditional feminine qualities of nurturance, docility, and eagerness to please. Some men feel nostalgic for these qualities, which they associate with a bygone way of life. Even as many wage-earning Western women assimilate to the competitive culture of "male" work and ask respect for making it in a man's world, some men seek in the "exotic Orient" or "hot-blooded tropics" a woman from the imagined past.

Of course, not all sex workers migrate voluntarily. An alarming number of women and girls are trafficked by smugglers and sold into bondage. Because trafficking is illegal and secret, the numbers are hard to know with any certainty. Kevin Bales estimates that in Thailand alone, a country of 60 million, half a million to a million women are prostitutes, and one out of every twenty of these is enslaved.[10] As Bales's chapter in *Global Woman* shows, many of these women are daughters whom northern hill-tribe families have sold to brothels in the cities of the south. Believing the promises of jobs and money, some

25

---

*Another chapter in Hochschild and Ehrenreich's book, *Global Woman*—editor's note begin the voyage willingly, only to discover days later that the "arrangers" are traffickers who steal their passports, define them as debtors, and enslave them as prostitutes. Other women and girls are kidnapped, or sold by their impoverished families, and then trafficked to brothels. Even worse fates befall women from neighboring Laos and Burma, who flee crushing poverty and repression at home only to fall into the hands of Thai slave traders.

If the factors that pull migrant women workers to affluent countries are not as simple as they at first appear, neither are the factors that push them. Certainly relative poverty plays a major role, but, interestingly, migrant women often do not come from the poorest classes of their societies.[11] In fact, they are typically more affluent and better educated than male migrants. Many female migrants from the Philippines and Mexico, for example, have high school or college diplomas and have held middle-class—albeit low-paid—jobs back home. One study of Mexican migrants suggests that the trend is toward increasingly better-educated female migrants. Thirty years ago, most Mexican-born maids in the United States had been poorly educated maids in Mexico. Now a majority have high school degrees and have held clerical, retail, or professional jobs before leaving for the United States.[12] Such women are likely to be enterprising and adventurous enough to resist the social pressures to stay home and accept their lot in life.

Noneconomic factors—or at least factors that are not immediately and directly economic—also influence a woman's decision to emigrate. By migrating, a woman may escape the expectation that she care for elderly family members, relinquish her paycheck to a husband or father, or defer to an abusive husband. Migration may also be a practical response to a failed marriage and the need to provide for children without male help. In the Philippines, contributor Rhacel Salazar Parreñas tells us, migration is sometimes called a "Philippine divorce." And there are forces at work that may be making the men of poor countries less desirable as husbands. Male unemployment runs high in the countries that supply female domestics to the First World. Unable to make a living, these men often grow demoralized and cease contributing to their families in other ways. Many female migrants, including those in Michele Gamburd's chapter in this volume, tell of unemployed husbands who drink or gamble their remittances away. Notes one study of Sri Lankan women working as maids in the Persian Gulf: "It is not unusual . . . for the women to find upon their return that their Gulf wages by and large have been squandered on alcohol, gambling, and other dubious undertakings while they were away."[13]

To an extent then, the globalization of child care and housework brings the ambitious and independent women of the world together: the career-oriented upper-middle-class woman of an affluent nation and the striving woman from a crumbling Third World or postcommunist economy. Only it does not bring them together in the way that second-wave feminists in affluent countries once liked to imagine—as sisters and allies struggling to achieve common goals. Instead, they come together as mistress and maid, employer and employee, across a great divide of privilege and opportunity.

This trend toward global redivision of women's traditional work throws new light on the entire process of globalization. Conventionally, it is the poorer countries that are thought to be dependent on the richer ones—a dependency symbolized by the huge debt they owe to global financial institutions. What we explore in *Global Woman*, however, is a dependency that works in the other direction, and it is a dependency of a particularly intimate kind. Increasingly often, as affluent and middle-class families in the First World come to depend on migrants from poorer regions to provide child care, homemaking, and sexual services, a global relationship arises that in some ways mirrors the traditional relationship between the sexes. The First World takes on a role like that of the old-fashioned male in the family—pampered, entitled, unable to cook, clean, or find his socks. Poor countries take on a role like that of the traditional woman within the family—patient, nurturing, and self-denying. A division of labor feminists critiqued when it was "local" has now, metaphorically speaking, gone global.

To press this metaphor a bit further, the resulting relationship is by no means a "marriage," in the sense of being openly acknowledged. In fact, it is striking how invisible the globalization of women's work remains, how little it is noted or discussed in the First World. Trend spotters have had almost nothing to say about the fact that increasing numbers of affluent First World children and elderly persons are tended by immigrant care workers or live in homes cleaned by immigrant maids. Even the political groups we might expect to be concerned about this trend—antiglobalization and feminist activists—often seem to have noticed only the most extravagant abuses, such as trafficking and female enslavement. So if a metaphorically gendered relationship has developed between rich and poor countries, it is less like a marriage and more like a secret affair.

But it is a "secret affair" conducted in plain view of the children. Little Isadora and the other children of the First World raised by "two mommies" may be learning more than their ABC's from a loving surrogate parent. In their own living rooms, they are learning a vast and tragic global politics.[14] Children see. But they also learn how to disregard what they see. They learn how adults make the visible invisible. That is their "early childhood education."

Notes

1. See Ellen Galinsky and Dana Friedman, *Women: The New Providers,* Whirlpool Foundation Study, Part 1 (New York: Families and Work Institute, 1995), 37.

2. Special thanks to Roberta Espinoza, who gathered and designed the flow maps shown in Appendix I. In addition to material directly cited, this introduction draws from the following works: Kathleen M. Adams and Sara Dickey, eds., *Home and Hegemony: Domestic Service and Identity Politics in South and Southeast Asia* (Ann Arbor: University of Michigan Press, 2000); Floya Anthias and Gabriella Lazaridis, eds., *Gender and Migration in Southern Europe: Women on the Move* (Oxford and New York: Berg, 2000); Stephen Castles and Mark J. Miller, *The Age of Migration: International Population Movements in the Modern World* (New York and London: The Guilford Press, 1998); Noeleen Heyzer, Geertje Lycklama à Nijehold, and Nedra Weerakoon, eds., *The Trade in Domestic Workers: Causes, Mechanisms, and Consequences of International Migration* (London: Zed Books, 1994); Eleanore Kofman, Annie Phizacklea, Parvati Raghuram, and Rosemary Sales, *Gender and International Migration in Europe: Employment, Welfare, and Politics* (New York and London: Routledge, 2000); Douglas S. Massey, Joaquin Arango, Graeme Hugo, Ali Kouaouci, Adela Pellegrino, and J. Edward Taylor, *Worlds in Motion: Understanding International Migration at the End of the Millennium* (Oxford: Clarendon Press, 1999); Janet Henshall Momsen, ed., *Gender, Migration, and Domestic Service* (London: Routledge, 1999); Katie Willis and Brenda Yeoh, eds., *Gender and Immigration* (London: Edward Elgar Publishers, 2000).

3. Illegal migrants are said to make up anywhere from 60 percent (as in Sri Lanka) to 87 percent (as in Indonesia) of all migrants. In Singapore in 1994, 95 percent of Filipino overseas contract workers lacked work permits from the Philippine government. The official figures based on legal migration therefore severely underestimate the number of migrants. See Momsen, 1999, 7.

4. Momsen, 1999, 9.

5. Sri Lanka Bureau of Foreign Employment, 1994, as cited in G. Gunatilleke, *The Economic, Demographic, Sociocultural and Political*

Setting for Emigration from Sri Lanka International Migration 23 (3/4), 1995, 667–98.

6. Anthias and Lazaridis, 2000; Heyzer, Nijehold, and Weerakoon, 1994, 4–27; Momsen, 1999, 21; "Wistat: Women's Indicators and Statistics Database," version 3, CD-ROM (United Nations, Department for Economic and Social Information and Policy Analysis, Statistical Division, 1994).

7. Geovanna Campani, "Labor Markets and Family Networks: Filipino Women in Italy," in Hedwig Rudolph and Mirjana Morokvasic, eds., *Bridging States and Markets: International Migration in the Early 1990s* (Berlin: Edition Sigma, 1993), 206.

8. This "new" source of the Western demand for nannies, maids, child-care, and elder-care workers does not, of course, account for the more status-oriented demand in the Persian Gulf states, where most affluent women don't work outside the home.

9. For information on male work at home during the 1990s, see Arlie Russell Hochschild and Anne Machung, *The Second Shift: Working Parents and the Revolution at Home* (New York: Avon, 1997), 277.

10. Kevin Bales, *Disposable People: New Slavery in the Global Economy* (Berkeley: University of California Press, 1999), 43.

11. Andrea Tyree and Katharine M. Donato, "A Demographic Overview of the International Migration of Women," in *International Migration: The Female Experience,* eds. Rita Simon and Caroline Bretell (Totowa, N.J: Rowman & Allanheld, 1986), 29. Indeed, many immigrant maids and nannies are more educated than the people they work for. See Pei-Chia Lan's paper in *Global Woman*.

12. Momsen, 1999, 10, 73.

13. Grete Brochmann, *Middle East Avenue: Female Migration from Sri Lanka to the Gulf* (Boulder, CO: Westview Press, 1993), 179, 215.

14. On this point, thanks to Raka Ray, Sociology Department at the University of California at Berkeley.

QUESTIONS FOR DISCUSSION AND WRITING

1. How do the authors define globalization of labor? What do the authors see as the primary effects of globalization on women and families?

2. According to the authors, what contributes to the invisibility of migrant women workers?

3. In what ways do men and governments factor into the process of the global transfer of women's labor?

4. What is the new light that "global redivision of women's traditional work" casts on globalization?

5. Research a topic raised in this article (e.g., Hochschild's book, *The Second Shift*) to examine gender and housekeeping roles, or patterns of immigration by country and gender.

Outside History

EAVAN BOLAND

Eavan Boland was born in Dublin, Ireland, in 1944 and was educated in London, New York, and Dublin. She has taught at Trinity College, University College, and Bowdoin College, and was a member of the International Writing Program at the University of Iowa. She has published several poetry collections, including *The War Horse* (1975), *In Her Own Image* (1980), *Night Feed* (1982), *The Journey* (1987), *Selected Poems* (1989), *Outside History* (1990), *An Origin Like Water—Collected Poems* (1967–1987), *Lost Land* (1998), and *Code* (2001). In addition to her poetry, Boland has published a collection of prose writings, *Object Lessons: The Life of the Woman and the Poet in Our Time* (1995), in which the following selection was published. She co-edited *The Making of a Poem* (2000) with Mark Strand. Her awards include the Lannan Foundation Award in Poetry and the American Ireland Fund Literary Award. Boland is also a regular reviewer for the *Irish Times*. She maintains homes in Ireland and in California, where she is currently a professor of English at Stanford University. In a recent interview, Boland discussed being a woman in the context of Irish literature: "When I was young in Ireland, I felt there was almost a magnetic distance between the word 'woman' and the word 'poet.' I don't feel that now. But there was a certain amount of oppression in that in feeling the difficulty of being a woman poet there, and of feeling that there was a heroic tradition on which it was difficult to write your name." In the following selection Boland reflects on this complexity.

I.

Years ago I went to Achill for Easter. I was a student at Trinity then, and I had the loan of a friend's cottage. It was a one-story stone building with two rooms and a view of sloping fields.

April was cold that year. The cottage was in sight of the Atlantic, and at night a bitter, humid wind blew across the shore. By day there was heckling sunshine, but after dark a fire was necessary. The loneliness of the place suited me. My purposes in being there were purgatorial, and I had no intention of going out and about. I had done erratically, to say the least, in my first-year exams. In token of the need to do better, I had brought with me a small, accusing volume of the court poets of the silver age. In other words, those sixteenth-century English songwriters, like Wyatt and Raleigh, whose lines appear so elegant, so offhand yet whose poems smell of the gallows.

I was there less than a week. The cottage had no water, and every evening the caretaker, an old woman who shared a cottage with her brother at the bottom of the field, would carry water up to me. I can see her still. She has a tea towel round her waist—perhaps this is one image that has become all the images I have of her—she wears an old cardigan and her hands are blushing with cold as she puts down the bucket. Sometimes we talk inside the door of the cottage. Once, I remember, we stood there as the dark grew all around us and I could see stars beginning to curve in the stream behind us.

She was the first person to talk to me about the famine. The first person, in fact, to speak to me with any force about the terrible parish of survival and death which the event had been in those regions. She kept repeating to me that they were great people, the people in the famine. *Great people.* I had never heard that before. She pointed out the beauties of the place. But they themselves, I see now, were a subtext. On the eastern side of Keel, the cliffs of Menawn rose sheer out of the water. And here was Keel itself, with its blond strand and broken stone, where the villagers in the famine, she told me, had moved closer to the shore, the better to eat the seaweed.

Memory is treacherous. It confers meanings which are not apparent at the time. I want to say that I understood this woman as emblem and instance of everything I am about to propose. Of course I did not. Yet even then I sensed a power in the encounter. I knew, without having words for it, that she came from a past which affected me. When she pointed out Keel to me that evening when the wind was brisk and cold and the light was going, when she gestured toward that shore which had stones as outlines and monuments of a desperate people, what was she pointing at? A history? A nation? Her memories or mine?   5

Those questions, once I began to write my own poetry, came back to haunt me. "I have been amazed, more than once," writes Hélène Cixous, "by a description a woman gave me of a world all her own, which she had been secretly haunting since early childhood." As the years passed, my amazement grew. I would see again the spring evening, the woman talking to me. Above all, I would remember how, when I finished speaking to her I went in, lit a fire, took out my book of English court poetry and memorized all over again—with no sense of irony or omission—the cadences of power and despair.

II.

I have written this to probe the virulence and necessity of the idea of a nation. Not on its own and not in a vacuum, but as it intersects with a specific poetic inheritance and as that inheritance, in turn, cut across me as woman and poet. Some of these intersections are personal. Some of them may be painful to remember. Nearly all of them are elusive and difficult to describe with any degree of precision. Nevertheless, I believe these intersections, if I can observe them at all properly here, reveal something about poetry, about nationalism, about the difficulties for a woman poet within a constraining national tradition. Perhaps the argument itself is nothing more than a way of revisiting the cold lights of that western evening and the force of that woman's conversation. In any case, the questions inherent in that encounter remain with me. It could well be that they might appear, even to a sympathetic reader, too complex to admit of an answer. In other words, that an argument like mine must contain too many imponderables to admit of any practical focus.

Yet I have no difficulty in stating the central premise of my argument. It is that over a relatively short time—certainly no more than a generation or so—women have moved from being the objects of Irish poems to being the authors of them. It is a momentous transit. It is also a disruptive one. It raises questions of identity, issues of poetic motive and ethical direction which can seem almost impossibly complex. What is more, such a transit—like the slow course of a star or the shifts in a constellation—is almost invisible to the naked eye. Critics may well miss it or map it inaccurately. Yet such a transit inevitably changes our idea of measurement, of distance, of the past as well as the future. And as it does so, it changes our idea of the Irish poem, of its composition and authority, of its right to appropriate certain themes and make certain fiats. And since poetry is never local for long, that in turn widens out into further implications.

Everything I am about to argue here could be taken as local and personal, rooted in one country and one poetic inheritance, and both of them mine. Yet if the names were changed, if situations and places were transposed, the issues might well be revealed as less parochial. This is not, after all, an essay on the craft of the art. I am writing not about aesthetics but about the ethics which are altogether less visible in a poetic tradition. Who

the poet is, what he or she nominates as a proper theme for poetry, what selves poets discover and confirm through this subject
matter—all of this involves an ethical choice. The more volatile
the material—and a wounded history, public or private, is always
volatile—the more intensely ethical the choice. Poetic ethics are
evident and urgent in any culture where tensions between a poet
and his or her birthplace are inherited and established. Poets
from such cultures might well recognize some of the issues
raised here. After all, this is not the only country or the only
politic where the previously passive objects of a work of art have,
in a relatively short time, become the authors of it.

So it was with me. For this very reason, early on as a poet,   10
certainly in my twenties. I realized that the Irish nation as an existing construct in Irish poetry was not available to me. I would not
have been able to articulate it at that point, but at some preliminary level I already knew that the anguish and power of that
woman's gesture on Achill, with its suggestive hinterland of pain,
were not something I could predict or rely on in Irish poetry. There
were glimpses here and there; sometimes more than that. But all
too often, when I was searching for such an inclusion, what I
found was a rhetoric of imagery which alienated me: a fusion of
the national and the feminine which seemed to simplify both.

It was not a comfortable realization. There was nothing
clear-cut about my feelings. I had tribal ambivalences and
doubts, and even then I had an uneasy sense of the conflict
which awaited me. On the one hand, I knew that as a poet I could
not easily do without the idea of a nation. Poetry in every time
draws on that reserve. On the other, I could not as a woman accept the nation formulated for me by Irish poetry and its traditions. At one point it even looked to me as if the whole thing
might be made up of irreconcilable differences. At the very least
it seemed to me that I was likely to remain an outsider in my own
national literature, cut off from its archive, at a distance from its
energy. Unless, that is, I could repossess it. This proposal is about
that conflict and that repossession and about the fact that repossession itself is not a static or single act. Indeed, the argument
which describes it may itself be no more than a part of it.

III.

A nation. It is, in some ways, the most fragile and improbable of
concepts. Yet the idea of an Ireland, resolved and healed of its
wounds, is an irreducible presence in the Irish past and its literature. In one sense, of course, both the concept and its realiza-

tion resist definition. It is certainly nothing conceived in what Edmund Burke calls "the spirit of rational liberty." When a people have been so dispossessed by event as the Irish in the eighteenth and nineteenth centuries, an extra burden falls on the very idea of a nation. What should be a political aspiration becomes a collective fantasy. The dream itself becomes freighted with invention. The Irish nation, materializing in the songs and ballads of these centuries, is a sequence of improvised images. These songs, these images, wonderful and terrible and memorable as they are, propose for a nation an impossible task: To be at once an archive of defeat and a diagram of victory.

As a child I loved these songs. As a teenager I had sought them out for some meaning, some definition. Even now, in some moods and at certain times, I can find it difficult to resist their makeshift angers. And no wonder. The best of them are written—like the lyrics of Wyatt and Raleigh—within sight of the gibbet. They breathe just free of the noose.

In one sense I was a captive audience. My childhood was spent in London. My image makers as a child, therefore, were refractions of my exile: conversations overheard, memories and visitors. I listened and absorbed. For me, as for many another exile, Ireland was my nation long before it was once again my country. That nation, then and later, was a session of images: of defeats and sacrifices, of individual defiances happening offstage. The songs enhanced the images; the images reinforced the songs. To me they were the soundings of the place I had lost: drowned treasure.

It took me years to shake off those presences. In the end, though, I did escape. My escape was assisted by the realization that these songs were effect, not cause. They were only the curators of the dream, not the inventors. In retrospect I could accuse both them and the dream of certain crucial simplifications. I made then, as I make now, a moral division between what those songs sought to accomplish and what Irish poetry must seek to achieve. The songs, with their postures and their angers, glamorized resistance, action. But the Irish experience, certainly for the purposes of poetry, was only incidentally about action and resistance. At a far deeper level—and here the Achill woman return—it was about defeat. The coffin ships, the soup queues, those desperate villagers at the shoreline—these things had actually happened. The songs, persuasive, hypnotic, could wish them away. Poetry could not. Of course, the relation between a poem and a past is never that simple. When I met the Achill woman, I was already a poet, I thought of myself as a poet. Yet nothing that I understood about poetry enabled me to under-

15

stand her better. Quite the reverse. I turned my back on her in that cold twilight and went to commit to memory the songs and artifices of the very power systems which had made her own memory such an archive of loss.

If I understand her better now, and my relation to her, it is not just because my sense of irony or history has developed over the years, although I hope it has. It is more likely because of my own experience as a poet. Inevitably any account of this carries the risk of subjective codes and impressions. Yet in poetry in particular and women's writing in general, the private witness is often all there is to go on. Since my personal experience as a poet is part of my source material, it is to that I now turn.

IV.

I entered Trinity to study English and Latin. Those were the early 1960s, and Dublin was another world—a place for which I can still feel Henry James's "tiger-pounce of homesickness." In a very real sense it was a city of images and anachronisms. There were still brewery horses on Grafton Street, their rumps draped and smoking under sackcloth. In the coffee bars eggs were poached in a rolling boil and spooned onto thick, crustless toast. The lights went on at twilight; by midnight the city was full of echoes.

After the day's lectures I took a bus home from college. It was a short journey. Home was an attic flat on the near edge of a town that was just beginning to sprawl. There in the kitchen, on an oilskin tablecloth, I wrote my first real poems: derivative, formalist, gesturing poems. I was a very long way from Adrienne Rich's realization that "instead of poems about experience, I am getting poems that are experiences." If anything, my poems were other people's experiences. This, after all, was the heyday of the movement in Britain, and the neat stanza, the well-broken line were the very stuff of poetic identity.

Now I wonder how many young women poets taught themselves—in rooms like that, with a blank discipline—to write the poem that was in the air, rather than the one within their experience? How many faltered, as I did, not for lack of answers but for lack of questions. "It will be a long time still, I think," wrote Virginia Woolf, "before a woman can sit down to write a book without finding a phantom to be slain, a rock to be dashed against."

But for now let me invent a shift of time. I am turning down   20
those streets which echo after midnight. I am climbing the stairs of a coffee bar which stays open late. I know what I will find. Here is the salt-glazed mug on a tabletop which is as scarred as

a desk in a country school. Here is the window with its view of an empty street, of lamplight and iron. And there, in the corner, is my younger self.

I draw up a chair, I sit down opposite her. I begin to talk— no, to harangue her. Why, I say, do you do it? Why do you go back to that attic flat, night after night, to write in forms explored and sealed by Englishmen hundreds of years ago? You are Irish. You are a woman. Why do you keep these things at the periphery of the poem? Why do you not move them to the center, where they belong?

But the woman who looks back at me is uncomprehending. If she answers at all, it will be with the rhetoric of a callow apprenticeship: that the poem is pure process, that the technical encounter is the one which guarantees all others. She will speak about the dissonance of the line and the necessity for the stanza. And so on. And so on.

"For what is the poet responsible?" asks Allen Tate. "He is responsible for the virtue proper to him as a poet, for his special *arete:* For the mastery of a disciplined language which will not shun the full report of the reality conveyed to him by his awareness."

She is a long way, that young woman—with the gleaming cup and her movement jargo—from the full report of anything. In her lack of any sense of implication or complication, she might as well be a scientist in the 1930s, bombarding uranium with neutrons.

If I try now to analyze why such a dialogue would be a waste of time, I come up with several reasons. One of them is that it would take years for me to see, let alone comprehend, certain realities. Not until the oilskin tablecloth was well folded and the sprawling town had become a rapacious city, and the attic flat was a house in the suburbs, could I accept the fact that I was a woman and a poet in a culture which had the greatest difficulty associating the two ideas. "A woman must often take a critical stance towards her social, historical, and cultural position in order to experience her own quest," writes the American poet and feminist Rachel Blau de Plessis. "Poems of the self's growth, or of self-knowledge may often include or be preceded by a questioning of major social prescriptions about the shape women's experience should take." In years to come I would never be sure whether my poems had generated the questions or the questions had facilitated the poems. All that lay ahead. "No poet," says Eliot, "no artist of any kind, has his complete meaning alone." In the meantime, I existed whether I liked it or not in a mesh, a web, a labyrinth of associations. Of poems past and present. Contemporary poems. Irish poems.

V.

Irish poetry was predominantly male. Here or there you found a small eloquence, like "After Aughrim" by Emily Lawless. Now and again, in discussion, you heard a woman's name. But the lived vocation, the craft witnessed by a human life—that was missing. And I missed it. Not in the beginning, perhaps. But later, when perceptions of womanhood began to redirect my own work, what I regretted was the absence of an expressed poetic life which would have dignified and revealed mine. The influence of absences should not be underestimated. Isolation itself can have a powerful effect in the life of a young writer. "I'm talking about real influence now," says Raymond Carver. "I'm talking about the moon and the tide."

I turned to the work of Irish male poets. After all, I thought of myself as an Irish poet. I wanted to locate myself within the Irish poetic tradition. The dangers and stresses in my own themes gave me an added incentive to discover a context for them. But what I found dismayed me.

The majority of Irish male poets depended on women as motifs in their poetry. They moved easily, deftly, as if by right among images of women in which I did not believe and of which I could not approve. The women in their poems were often passive, decorative, raised to emblematic status. This was especially true where the woman and the idea of the nation were mixed: where the nation became a woman and the woman took on a national posture.

The trouble was these images did good service as ornaments. In fact, they had a wide acceptance as ornaments by readers of Irish poetry. Women in such poems were frequently referred to approvingly as mythic, emblematic. But to me these passive and simplified women seemed a corruption. Moreover, the transaction they urged on the reader, to accept them as mere decoration, seemed to compound the corruption. For they were not decorations, they were not ornaments. However distorted these images, they had their roots in a suffered truth.

What had happened? How had the women of our past—the women of a long struggle and a terrible survival—undergone such a transformation? How had they suffered Irish history and rooted themselves in the speech and memory of the Achill woman, only to reemerge in Irish poetry as fictive queens and national sibyls?

The more I thought about it, the more uneasy I became. The wrath and grief of Irish history seemed to me, as it did to many, one of our true possessions. Women were part of that wrath, had endured that grief. It seemed to me a species of human insult that at the end of all, in certain Irish poems, they should become elements of style rather than aspects of truth.

The association of the feminine and the national—and the consequent simplification of both—are not, of course, a monopoly of Irish poetry. "All my life," writes Charles de Gaulle. "I have thought about France in a certain way. The emotional side of me tends to imagine France like the princess in the fairy tale, or the Madonna of the Frescoes." De Gaulle's words point up the power of nationhood to edit the reality of womanhood. Once the idea of a nation influences the perception of a woman, then that woman is suddenly and inevitably simplified. She can no longer have complex feelings and aspirations. She becomes the passive projection of a national idea.

Irish poems simplified women most at the point of intersection between womanhood and Irishness. The further the Irish poem drew away from the idea of Ireland, the more real and persuasive became the images of women. Once the pendulum swung back, the simplifications started again. The idea of the defeated nation's being reborn as a triumphant woman was central to a certain kind of Irish poem. Dark Rosaleen. Cathleen ni Houlihan. The nation as woman; the woman as national muse.

The more I looked at it, the more it seemed to me that in relation to the idea of a nation many, if not most, Irish male poets had taken the soft option. The irony was that few Irish poets were nationalists. By and large, they had eschewed the fervor and crudity of that ideal. But long after they had rejected the politics of Irish nationalism, they continued to deploy the emblems and enchantments of its culture. It was the culture, not the politics, which informed Irish poetry: not the harsh awakenings but the old dreams.

In all of this I did not blame nationalism. Nationalism   35
seemed to me inevitable in the Irish context, a necessary hallucination within Joyce's nightmare of history. I did blame Irish poets. Long after it was necessary, Irish poetry had continued to trade in the exhausted fictions of the nation, had allowed those fictions to edit ideas of womanhood and modes of remembrance. Some of the poetry produced by such simplifications was, of course, difficult to argue with. It was difficult to deny that something was gained by poems which used the imagery and emblem of the national muse. Something was gained, certainly,

but only at an aesthetic level. While what was lost occurred at the deepest, most ethical level, and what was lost was what I valued. Not just the details of a past. Not just the hungers, the angers. These, however terrible, remain local. But the truth these details witness—human truths of survival and humiliation—these also were suppressed along with the details. Gone was the suggestion of any complicated human suffering. Instead you had the hollow victories, the passive images, the rhyming queens.

I knew that the women of the Irish past were defeated. I knew it instinctively long before the Achill woman pointed down the hill to the Keel shoreline. What I objected to was that Irish poetry should defeat them twice.

"I have not written day after day," says Camus, "because I desire the world to be covered with Greek statues and masterpieces. The man who has such a desire does exist in me. But I have written so much because I cannot keep from being drawn toward everyday life, toward those, whoever they may be, who are humiliated. They need to hope and, if all keep silent, they will be forever deprived of hope and we with them."

This argument originates in some part from my own need to locate myself in a powerful literary tradition in which until then, or so it seemed to me, I had been an element of design rather than an agent of change. But even as a young poet, and certainly by the time my work confronted me with some of these questions, I had already had a vivid, human witness of the stresses which a national literature can impose on a poet. I had already seen the damage it could do.

QUESTIONS FOR DISCUSSION AND WRITING

1. Respond to the personal voice and prose style of this writer. Do you find the first-person narrative brings you closer to the topic and the writer's thoughts? How might your response have been different were this selection written as a poem or in third-person narrative prose?

2. Why do you think Boland entitled this selection "Outside History"? Who, or what, is outside history, and in what ways can one be outside? In what ways are "the wrath and grief of Irish history" excluded or transformed in the songs and poetry by Irish writers? In what ways did the Achill woman encourage her to consider this perspective?

3. Discuss the author's concept of the identification of Ireland with a woman and the ways in which both are, subsequently, oversimplified. What concerns Boland about women being emblematic or decorative in poetry?

4. In an imaginary conversation with her younger self, Boland writes, "You are Irish. You are a woman. Why do you keep these things at the periphery of the poem? Why do you not move them to the center, where they belong?" Why do you think she wrote that? And in what ways has her perspective changed?

5. Boland explicitly states her argument and then develops her support of this premise. How does this approach strengthen, or detract from, the persuasiveness of this selection? Alternatively, discuss the ways in which marginality, as she describes it, can have advantages.

6. Research and write a documented essay about an area of interest stimulated by this reading, such as the Great Famine, the coffin ships, women in Irish history, historical or contemporary or events such as the 1916 Easter Rebellion and The Troubles.

Population and Gender Equity

AMARTYA SEN

Amartya Sen, the 1998 Nobel Prize-winner in Economics, was born in 1933 in Santiniketan, India. He was educated at Presidency College in Calcutta, India, where he received a BA, and at Trinity College, Cambridge, England, where he received a BA, MA, and Ph.D. His publications include *Collective Choices and Social Welfare* (1970), *Levels of Poverty: Policy and Change: A Background Study for World Development Report* (1980), *Poverty and Famine: An Essay on Entitlement and Deprivation* (1981), *Choice, Welfare, and Measurement* (1982), *On Ethics and Economics* (1987), *Hunger and Entitlements: Research for Action* (1987), *Inequality Reexamined* (1992), *Development as Freedom* (1999), and *Reason Before Identity* (1999). Sen's works have been said to reintroduce ethics into the field of economics, and his areas of study have included world poverty, relative wealth of nations, causes of famine, economic impact of literacy and public health programs, and ways in which governments can improve the lives of the poor. Sen has been described as "a genuine world citizen." These descriptions of Sen and his work are echoed in the following essay, in which he argues that progress for developing countries is ultimately tied to progress and a degree of self-determination for the women of these societies.

The magnitude of the population problem is frequently exaggerated. Anxious commentators have been terrifying others about imagined disasters for a very long time. That roaring tradition goes back at least two hundred years, when Thomas Robert Malthus declared that the world was heavily overpopulated already and that the growth of food supply was losing the race with the growth of population. However, as in Malthus's time, food production now continues to grow significantly faster than world population, with the fastest expansion of food output per head occurring in relatively poor countries, such as China and India. What is particularly remarkable is that the rapid expansion of world food output has continued despite the reduced economic incentive to produce food, as a result of a sharp fall in food prices relative to other prices. Indeed, although international prices of wheat, rice, and other staple foods, in constant US dollars, have fallen by more than 60 percent between 1950–1952 and 1995–1997, more and more of these crops are being produced, staying well ahead of population growth.

But there is a danger of complacency here. The fact that population growth is much slower than the growth of world output (of food as well as of industrial and other commodities) often generates undue placidity, reinforced by the further recognition (correct; as it happens) that fertility rates and population growth are coming down fast for the world as a whole and also for most regions of the world. This reassuring overall picture hides the fact that population growth rates are falling very fast in some regions and very slowly—sometimes not at all—in others.

It is, in fact, extremely important to avoid complacency in dealing with the population problem and to understand that it raises serious issues that are not particularly well captured by the old Malthusian perspective. One such issue is the environment—global as well as local. It is true that environmental adversities such as global warming are influenced by total consumption rather than the total size of the population (poor people consume much less and pollute far less). But one hopes that in the future the poorer nations of today will be rich as well, and the compound effect of a larger population and increased consumption could be devastating for the global environment. There is also the important challenge of overcrowding in a limited habitat. Children, too, have to be raised, not just food crops.

But perhaps the most immediate adversity caused by a high rate of population growth lies in the loss of freedom that women suffer when they are shackled by persistent bearing and rearing of children. Global warming is a distant effect compared with what population explosion does to the lives and well-being of mothers. Indeed, the most important—and perhaps the most neglected—aspect of the population debate is the adverse impact of high fertility imposed on women in societies where their voices don't count for much. Given the connection between overfrequent childbirth and the predicament of women, there are reasons to expect that an increase of gender equity, particularly in the decisional power of young women, would tend to lower fertility rates. Since women's interests are very badly served by high fertility rates imposed on them, they can be expected to correct this adversity if they have more power.

Why, then, do women have little decisional power in some societies, and how can that be remedied? There are various distinct influences to be considered here. (I discuss this question more fully in my book *Development as Freedom*.) First, social and economic handicaps (such as female illiteracy, lack of female employment opportunity, and economic independence) contribute greatly to muffling women's voices in society and within the family. Second, the absence of knowledge or facilities of family planning can also be an important source of helplessness. Third, there are cultural, even religious, factors that place young women in a subservient position, making them accept the burden of constantly bearing and rearing children (as desired by the husband or the parents-in-law). These inequities may not even have to be physically enforced, since women's subservient role as well as frequent childbearing may appear "natural" when these practices have been sanctified by a long history that generates uncritical acceptance.

The promotion of female literacy, female employment opportunities, and family planning facilities, as well as open and informed public discussion of women's place in society, can enhance the voice and decisional role of women in family affairs and also bring about radical changes in the understanding of justice and injustice. Indeed, there is much evidence now, based on intercountry comparisons as well as interregional contrasts within a large country (such as recent empirical comparisons of the more than three hundred districts that make up India), that women's empowerment (through employment, education, property rights, etc.) can have a very strong effect in reducing the fertility rate.

India is a statistician's paradise because of the tremendous variations among its distinct regions. While the total fertility rate for India as a whole is still substantially higher than the replacement level of two per couple, many districts in India not only have below-replacement fertility rates but also substantially lower fertility rates than, for example, the United States, Britain, and China. The fertility rates have been falling more or less everywhere in India (the country average has fallen from six per couple some decades ago to about three per couple now), but the rate of decline has been extremely uneven. Speedy fertility declines in the states of Kerala, Tamil Nadu, or Himachal Pradesh can be closely linked to the rapid enhancement of female education and other sources of empowerment of young women. Indeed, as a number of studies (by Mamta Murthi and Jean Dreze, among others) demonstrate, the two principal variables that explain the bulk of the interdistrict variations in fertility rates in India are female literacy and female employment opportunity. These achievements not only enhance women's voice in family decisions (thereby contributing directly to lowering fertility), they also have other favorable social effects. For example, female literacy has a strong impact in reducing child mortality rates, which also contributes, indirectly, to reducing fertility (since the desire to have a large family is often related to insuring support in one's old age from surviving progeny). The states in India with high fertility (for example, Uttar Pradesh, Bihar, Rajasthan) are precisely those that give few economic and educational opportunities to young women.

It is also interesting in this context to note that while China's sharp fertility decline is often attributed to coercive policies (like the "one-child family"), one could have expected a roughly similar decline because of China's excellent achievements in raising female education and employment. The contrast between China and India is a useful one to examine, in this context, since both countries—like many others in Asia—have had much gender-based inequality and persistent male preference in the treatment of children. As a whole, China has done far more than India to give women educational and economic opportunities. However, there are parts of India (which is much more diverse than China) that have done more than China in this respect. Kerala, for example—a sizable Indian state with about thirty million people—has a higher rate of female literacy than every province of China.

Kerala's rate of expansion of female literacy has also been faster than China's. Correspondingly, Kerala has experienced a substantially faster decline in fertility rates. While the Chinese fertility rate fell from 2.8 to 2.0 between 1979 (when the one-child policy was introduced) and 1991, it fell from 3 to 1.8 in the same period in Kerala. Kerala has kept its lead over China both in female education and in fertility decline (currently, Kerala's fertility rate is around 1.7; China's, about 1.9). Also, thanks to the process of fertility decline being freely chosen without any coercion, the infant mortality rate has continued to fall fast in Kerala while it has not in China, even though they were roughly even in this respect in 1979. The female infant mortality rate now in China is, in fact, more than twice that in Kerala.

Variations within India also bring out the important fact that even cultural and religious influences on fertility can themselves be swayed. For example, it has been argued that Muslim populations tend to have a higher fertility rate. Insofar as there is any truth to this, the linkage seems to operate mainly in an indirect way, through various correlates of gender inequality (including female illiteracy and lower employment opportunity). Significance is sometimes attached to the fact that Pakistan has a much higher fertility rate than India (around five, in contrast to three), but that divergence corresponds closely to the difference between the two countries in terms of female education,

10

women's employment, and other influences on women's empowerment.

Also, the Muslim population in India is itself very large at around 120 million the third largest among all countries in the world (despite the insistence of Hindu political activists as well as the Western press on describing multireligious and constitutionally secular India as a "mainly Hindu country"). As it happens, the most successful state in India in reducing fertility, Kerala, also has the highest percentage of Muslims among all the states, with the exception of Kashmir. In general, the fertility rates of Indian Muslims are much closer to those of other communities in the same region in India, including the Hindus, than to Muslims in Pakistan. Insofar as there are intercommunity contrasts in fertility within India, they too relate to such social and economic variables as education, employment, and property rights, and altogether they are relatively minor within each state, in comparison with the large differences between the different Indian states—matching the contrasts in related social and economic variables.

It is also significant that Bangladesh, with a predominantly Muslim population, has had a sharp reduction in fertility rates, which can be associated with the gains that Bangladeshi women have recently made through the expansion of family-planning opportunities, greater involvement of women in economic activities (for example, through microcredit programs), and much public discussion and political activism on the need to change the prevailing pattern of gender disparity. In a mere decade and a half (between 1980 and 1996), Bangladesh's fertility rate has come down from 6.1 (close to Pakistan's today) to 3.4 (close to India's), and it is continuing to fall sharply. The bottom line, then, is this: While cultural and religious influences on fertility rates cannot be ignored, they are neither immutable nor independent of the social and economic factors through which the cultural connections work.

There are, of course, many different influences that operate on fertility rates, and it would be a mistake to look for one "magic variable" that would work uniformly well in reducing high fertility rates. What is needed instead is a unified approach that places different variables within a general framework of family decisions on fertility. The advantage of bringing gender equity and women's empowerment to the center of the stage is that they provide a broad perspective that can accommodate many of the major influences on fertility decisions. This includes acknowledging the role of educational development (including the schooling of girls), economic arrangements (including female job opportunities), social concerns (including the status of women), and cultural factors (including the value of equity in family decisions), as well as the more traditional variables that can assist family planning (such as the availability of family planning facilities and access to medical attention). The expansion of family planning may appear to be just a demographic intervention, but the real opportunity to practice family planning can also be seen in the broader light of enhancing the decisional freedom of families in general and of vulnerable women in particular.

It is important to bring together, under a unified framework of understanding, the diverse influences on fertility reduction that have been identified in the empirical and statistical research. A variety of institutions have constructive roles in this crucial social transformation, including family planning centers, elementary schools, land reform facilities, microcredit organizations and free newspapers, and other media for unrestrained public discussion. These distinct institutions have their respective roles, but there is a need to integrate the processes of social change that they separately but interactively induce. For example, the debates—often bitter—between advocates of family planning facilities and female education must give way to a more integrated approach.

The crucial issue is the need to recognize that a responsible 15 policy of fertility decline demands gender equity, which is, of course, crucially important for other reasons as well. The way forward is through more freedom and justice, not through more coercion and intimidation. The population problem is integrally linked with justice for women in particular. On this reasoning, it is also right to expect that advancing gender equity, through reversing the various social and economic handicaps that make women voiceless and powerless, may also be one of the best ways of saving the environment—working against global warming and countering the dangers of overcrowding and other adversities associated with population pressure. The voice of women is critically important for the world's future—not just for women's future.

QUESTIONS FOR DISCUSSION AND WRITING

1. The author of this essay has been awarded the Nobel Prize for economics and holds an academic appointment. How does this information develop his authority to discuss gender equity?

2. How do the first three paragraphs establish the context for the points Sen makes? On your own or in groups, map out the logic of Sen's argument in paragraphs 4 through 11. What are the assertions and connections he makes? How does he help the reader follow the steps in his logic?

3. In paragraph 11, Sen notes that "women's empowerment (through employment, education, property rights, etc.) can have a very strong effect on reducing the fertility rate." How does his comparison of states within India, and India with China, offer evidence to support this view?

4. Research one of the issues raised regarding women's education in India, family planning, women's craft cooperatives or weaving enterprises, or nonprofits that support women's business in developing nations.

5. Write an essay analyzing Sen's argument. Do you find it persuasive? If so, what appeals made it most effective? If not, explain your assessment.

Chapter Five: Connections

1. Drawing from the Beauvoir selection, in what ways do other selections in this chapter incorporate the concept of woman as "other"?

2. Discuss Boland's and Friedman's concepts regarding women and history—for example, Friedman's view of women having their own usable history and Boland's observation that Irish poetry has included mythologized and oversimplified motifs of women at the expense of including a more authentic women's history.

3. Friedman notes that conditions other than gender, such as class, caste, and family, influence women's social position. Explore this premise in view of the Beauvoir and Osagawara selections. Also consider this view with regard to the image "Keep Within Compass." For example, to what degree does the central figure in this image maintain her position because of class or race?

4. Analyze the image "Keep Within Compass," in view of Friedman's discussion of patriarchy and control of women.

5. Compare "Keep within Compass" and the Kahlo self-portraits and discuss in view of the selections by Beauvoir, Freedman, and Hochschild and Ehrenreich.

6. Discuss Osagawara's premise that office ladies maintain power in their subservient position in view of Friedman's discussion of patriarchy.

7. In what ways do other selections in this chapter illustrate, or contradict, Ehrenreich and Hochschild's assertions in "Global Woman"?

8. Discuss assumptions about women's identity in "Woman as Other" and "Keep Within Compass." In what ways are these roles informed by Friedman's research on patriarchal and matriarchal societies?

Chapter Five: End-of-Chapter Assignments

1. Research cultural rituals related to gender—not only those in traditional societies, but also those in contemporary American cultures. Consider, for example, teenage rites of passage or dating rituals.

2. Research social and economic roles of women and men in Colonial America, early Islam, or one of the other societies described by Freedman in "Gender and Power."

3. In view of Fluehr-Lobban's discussion of cultural relativism and human rights (Chapter Three), research one of the topics she raises: Female circumcision, honor killings, or ritual suicides.

4. Research the work of Frida Kahlo and Diego Rivera. Consider focusing on the mural as a means of political statement, particularly for issues of gender and culture.

5. Research the role of the prophet Muhammad's wife in the founding of Islam or the role of Mary, mother of Jesus, in early Christianity.

6. Compare beliefs and attitudes pertaining to women in Christianity and Islam, or Hinduism and Islam. Web sites such as those included in this chapter can provide an overview for your research. You could focus on specific topics, such as morals and customs or role in worship.

7. Research representations of women in popular media in the United States or other countries, reviewing magazines, newspapers, Web sites, and other cultural products. What themes emerge? Are views expressed in this text supported by your research?

8. Research roles of women in African cultures, not only in traditional or tribal societies, but in urban areas as well.

9. Research selective abortion practices in societies where it has been an issue in public policy, such as India and China. You could

consider exploring contemporary social problems resulting from this practice, such as the imbalance in the male-to-female ratio for those now reaching traditional age of marriage.

Chapter Five: Web Sites for Further Exploration

Women in Asia: Tradition, Modernity, and Globalization
http://www.mcauley.acu.edu.au/womenasia/Resources.htm
Global Woman
http://www.globalwoman.org
The National Women's Health Information Center
http://www.4woman.gov/
Global Fund for Women
http://www.globalfundforwomen.org/
National Organization for Women
http://www.now.org/
Revolutionary Association of the Women of Afghanistan
http://rawa.fancymarketing.net/index.html
Japan
http://www.newsonjapan.com/
Women in Judaism (Journal)
http://www.utoronto.ca/wjudaism/
Prae Pan and Women's Crafts Collectives
http://www.geocities.com/prae_pan/index.html
Dimitrra, Project with Rural Women, Gender and Development Service (SDWW), Food and Agriculture Organization of the UN.
http://www.fao.org/dimitra/query/start1.idc
A Weekly Newsletter from Isis International Manila
http://www.isiswomen.org/pub/we/thisweek.html
Women's E-news
http://www.womensenews.org

6

ONE WORLD: HEALTH AND THE ENVIRONMENT

INTRODUCTION

Previous chapters have explored questions of globally integrated economics, cultural interactions and clashes, gender across cultures, and perceptions of oneself and others in an international context. However, few issues depend on a global view and on international cooperation more than public health and environmental issues. Poor health, a lack of potable water and clean air, lack of sanitation, and malnutrition should be addressed not only for humanistic and moral reasons, but also as a matter of self-preservation for currently unaffected communities.

This chapter explores two areas that have potentially worldwide implications and ultimately require global cooperation to resolve. Global climate, atmosphere, and air and water quality cross borders and will be damaged, or repaired and maintained, by cooperative international efforts. And as we have seen with the SARS epidemic, and with daily global travel and human encroachment into new territory, exotic and communicable diseases are potentially devastating to world health; the concerns multiply with the prospect of intentional infection through biological warfare or terrorism.

The selections in this chapter include landmark scientific writing on environmental issues, student research in documented essays, a personal essay, professional exposition and argumentation, and satellite photographs. Writers range from Rachel Carson, a marine biologist who predicted environmental catastrophe four decades ago, to the director of Amnesty International, and to students researching water contamination and deforestation. We also present government documentation of environmental damage in the Amazon.

We first turn to global health issues. The first selection is a document summarizing the World Health Organization's response to the SARS epidemic, reinforcing the need for swift and effective global cooperation in combating serious and contagious diseases. The next selection focuses on a disease ravaging Africa and threatening world health: HIV-AIDS. Hope Chigudu, who co-founded the Zimbabwe Women's Resource Center and Network, describes the coping mechanisms of African women in the face of pervasive tragedy. Chigudu notes that women bear the burden of care in the AIDS crisis; she asserts that the disease "will force gender-based social change onto the agenda of every government, nongovernmental organization, and agency working to fight HIV/AIDS in Africa."

We then consider the implications both for human rights and for self-interest in combating disease worldwide in a selection by Amnesty International's director, William F. Schulz. The title, "Only a Plane Ride Away," captures the appeal of self-interest in health and human rights issues by its premise that in our era of global trade and travel, we are all at risk of diseases prevalent elsewhere and transported here. Americans further invite disaster with their patronage of abusive practices such as those that occur in the Asian sex trades; for example, in Thailand, Schulz notes, an estimated 50 percent of "the 200,000 'sex workers'" are infected with HIV/AIDS, "anywhere from 25 percent to 40 percent of whom are under eighteen." In this article Schulz argues that human rights "play a far greater role than our policy makers have generally allowed. . . . To dismiss the interdependence of health and human rights. . . . is very simply to invite disaster." One of Schulz's chief concerns is that in societies without civil and political rights "there can be no effective internal checks" on governments that might use chemical or biological weapons. This premise supports Schulz's more general argument that defending human rights globally potentially benefits everyone.

Tejaswini More's essay, "Drinking Poison: The Lesson of Bhopal," provides an intersection of health and environmental issues. With the best intentions, UNICEF sponsored the digging of numerous wells to provide drinkable water in regions with heavily polluted water. Unforeseen by the authorities, the wells ended up providing water that was contaminated with arsenic and resulted in widespread poisoning. More notes important lessons learned from this disastrous effort.

In our environmental readings we turn to one of the most well-known authorities in environmentalism, Rachel Carson. Among her widely read books is *Silent Spring*, which in 1962 raised the alarm on the degree to which pesticides were irrevocably poisoning our world. Carson's warnings, and her prescient views of agriculture and what is now called integrated pest management, fostered the development of environmentalism. Carson called for full public awareness—not "false assurances" but "the public's right to know."

In the essay that follows, "The Ugly Guzzlers," writer Derrick Jackson describes a new version of the 1950s "ugly American" stereotype: the SUV-driving American oblivious to or uncaring about the environmental effects of driving a huge, fuel-inefficient "tank" in urban and suburban environments. In addition to producing 25 percent of the world's greenhouse gases with only 6 percent of the world's population, rejecting the Kyoto accords without offering an alternative, and declining to insist on higher fuel efficiency standards, the US has provoked Europeans normally friendly to the United States to charge Americans with "ignorance, denial, or selfishness" when it comes to dealing with pressing environmental problems.

On the subject of air pollutants and environmental policy, Warwick McKibbin and Peter Wilcoxen support the US rejection of Kyoto, but they fault the Bush administration for not offering an alternative plan. In their essay "The Next Step for US Climate Change Policy," the authors propose that the United States put forward "a more realistic policy" so that "global reaction can be shifted from outrage to reasoned debate." They argue for a global warming policy that is flexible but that includes provisions to slow carbon emissions when financially feasible, compensate those who will suffer economically, and include international cooperation. The authors argue for a movement away from ideological clashes and toward practical and concrete steps to take immediately to help reduce damaging air emissions.

While global warming and climate change remains one of the most pressing and highly publicized environmental issues, deforestation, or the removal of forest timber by human means, has also commanded intense concern and is addressed in this chapter in both text and image. Pam Mayfield, a student intern in Ohio State University's office of communication, reports on research by an Ohio State professor and colleagues that evokes concern about the worldwide issue of deforestation. The researchers' model, outlined in "US Forest Conservation May Increase Deforestation Elsewhere," suggests that conservation in the United States may, paradoxically, result in loss of tropical rain forests in other regions due to the economics of timber harvesting.

The satellite images that follow, provided by NASA, document the progress of deforestation in the Amazon. The companion photos provide a useful example of visual rhetoric when we compare the vivid red image with the more placid green views and consider the effects on the reader of each view.

This chapter's theme lends itself well not only to research in topics of interest, but also to collaboration and to projects in service learning and community involvement. If you find these topics personally engaging or are concerned about the issues raised here, consider increasing your level of involvement. Through participating in Earth Day, developing materials to educate peers or youth in your community, or volunteering for local public health projects and agencies or environmental nonprofit organizations, you can take your interest and concern about health and the environment beyond the classroom to the community greater. Consider reviewing the service learning section in Chapter One and contacting the office on your campus that supports community learning or community writing options.

SARS: A Global Threat, a Global Response

WORLD HEALTH ORGANIZATION

The World Health Organization (WHO), the United Nations specialized agency for health, was established in 1948 with the goal of attaining "by all peoples of the highest possible level of health. Health is defined in WHO's Constitution as a state of complete physical, mental, and social well-being and not merely the absence of disease or infirmity." WHO is governed by 192 member states who approve its program and the budget for the following biennium and work to formulate policy. In March 2003 WHO issued an extremely rare health warning regarding Severe Acute Respiratory Syndrome (SARS). The disease was first reported among people in Guangdong province in China; in Hanoi, Vietnam; and in Hong Kong. It has since spread to other countries; Toronto, Canada, was designated as an area with a significant SARS outbreak. SARS first appeared in Guangdong province of southern China in November 2002 and has spread to 32 other countries. By June 11, mainland China reported 5,326 probable cases and more than 346 deaths. As of summer 2003, the number of reported cases was decreasing dramatically and the WHO said that China's health system, response, and preparedness was good. Fears of underreporting appear now to be unfounded. In the memo that follows from the WHO's European Union's Council of Health Ministers, the unnamed author, speaking for the Council, describes the SARS response as "Global public health at its very best." As you read the memo, consider its appeal to authority and its rhetorical purpose in justifying WHO's approach to handling the SARS crisis.

Severe Acute Respiratory Syndrome (SARS) has only been with us for a few months but, in that time, it has evolved from an unknown problem in one city in southern China to an infamous global health threat. It is the first new public health epidemic of the twenty-first century and our first opportunity to mount a coordinated early public health response.

From the moment we sent out the global health alert, on March 12 of this year, the response has been rapid and effective.

From a scientific point of view, we have learned about SARS in record time. Collaborating centres, including sites in Paris, Hamburg, Rotterdam, and London as well as in North America and Asia, have been instrumental in helping us learn more about this disease. By working together, sharing information, and communicating the latest findings, we have made unprecedented progress in learning about this virus.

We know it is caused by a new type of coronavirus—a virus family usually associated with the common cold. We know SARS generally spreads through droplets, during close contact with an affected person. And we also know now that it can live on surfaces and in stool. This makes fighting it more challenging, but this expanding knowledge gives us more tools to mount a strong public health response.

We know also that, so far, SARS has been spread to just a limited number of areas and countries. We have seen the epidemic contained and stopped in Vietnam. And we have likely seen it peak in Singapore, Hong Kong, and Toronto, but not before appearing in some twenty-seven countries, including many here in this region. And, of course, we know that SARS is still spreading through China. Cases are increasing in Taiwan. The global fight against SARS is far from over, but our early action has made a difference.

Rapid action in this region has definitely made a difference.   5
Soon after our global alert was issued, Germany saw the very first case in Europe, when a doctor infected with SARS landed in Frankfurt and was quickly put into isolation. Rapid response there ensured no further spread. The same can be said of many European countries, where individual travellers with SARS have been quickly identified and isolated. The result—no community transmission in this region. Continued sensitive surveillance is necessary to ensure rapid case detection and infection control. In future, a European Centre for Disease Prevention and Control could help further coordinate a rapid response to these types of emerging threats. However, the fight against SARS is far from over. We don't yet have a treatment, we don't yet have a vaccine. But we do have a window of opportunity now to contain it—to avoid it becoming endemic in any country. To do this, we will be stretched. We will be tested. But we must try. By doing that, we are giving new meaning to the protection of global public health.

We have already seen the immediate health and economic consequences of SARS. We have seen how this virus can paralyse the health care system—with doctors and nurses themselves sick—unable to care for those with SARS or with other ailments. We cannot afford to have these consequences affect even more countries of the world, particularly in countries with weaker health infrastructures already stretched by a disproportionate burden of disease. These countries could soon face crippled hospitals, the loss of valuable professional staff and the fear and panic which come from a new disease. SARS will not be the last new disease we see in our lifetimes. But our response now is a test for the future. We see the importance of full transparency, as we are reminded again that one country's disease is potentially the world's problem. Openness now will save lives, and will maintain faith in economies in the long term. And while the system now is good, we know that to mount the most effective offence to new diseases, we need to expand the capacity for global surveillance and response. This is an issue that we will report on and that will certainly be the focus of delegations as we meet at the WHO some two weeks from now.

I know you will continue your good work on SARS. Your work to protect your own populations from SARS will also protect others. This is global public health at its very best.

QUESTIONS FOR DISCUSSION AND WRITING

1. Assess the audience for this memo, which was published on the WHO Web site. In addition to those addressed in the council's internal audience—the health ministers from member countries—who else does the report intend to inform and persuade?
2. What appeals to authority does this memo make? How does it establish credibility for the organization? How does it support a view that WHO acted swiftly and responsibly to contain the SARS outbreak?
3. What might this memo suggest to countries who may wish to keep news of disease outbreaks quiet? How does it make a case for global cooperation with regard to communicable diseases or other health issues?
4. Review the WHO Web site and assess the visual and textual rhetoric of the site, paying particular attention to the ways in which it appeals to authority and informs or persuades its audience.

How African Women Are Coping with the HIV/AIDS Crisis

HOPE CHIGUDU

Hope Chigudu is former chair of the board of the Global Fund for Women and is the cofounder and chair of the Zimbabwe Women's Resource Centre and Network (ZWRCN). In 1997 she published a paper entitled "The Zimbabwe Women's Resource Centre and Network" in which she discusses some of the goals of ZWRCN and some of the ways in which it accomplishes those goals (e.g., providing a documentation center, thematic debates, talks on gender and development, advocacy, and book fairs). Chigudu has also co-authored a book, *Reviving Democracy: Citizens at the Heart of Governance* (2002). The essay that follows was published in *Raising our Voices,* the Global Fund for Women newsletter, in August 2001.

I was having lunch with a visiting American friend recently, and she said that she had never seen as much death as she has seen in Zimbabwe. She marveled at the African woman's tenacious spirit, which continues to throb with a rhythmic passion, undulating with the landscape as if she is not surrounded by death. My friend confessed that the spirit she has witnessed here is completely incomprehensible to the outsider. She is right; African women dance and laugh in the midst of poverty, death, civil strife, harsh climatic conditions, and the AIDS pandemic. She dances when she knows she is HIV positive, when the sickly child she is carrying on her back is HIV positive, and when her husband is lying on a mat unable to move without her help. It is a coping mechanism.

Not long ago, I was driving to my office at 6 a.m. and saw a woman carrying a "child" on her back. I was puzzled because the child looked old and shriveled. My conscience would not let me continue. I stopped and was told that the "child" was not really a child, but a husband. She was taking him to the nearest clinic—six kilometers away. They had no money for a wheelbarrow, the cheapest form of transport these days. Interestingly, even as he was being carried on his wife's back, he was giving her orders. She informed me that two of her infants were also infected. I wondered how this woman was surviving. Looking after her husband and children meant that she couldn't engage in income-generating activity. This is not an isolated case; there are many women like her. Although mothers suffer the most, the entire family suffers.

I remember waiting for nights to turn into days and days to turn into nights as my younger brother, an undergraduate student, lay dying. At the tender age of twenty, his body was deteriorating—every day parts of him were dying and we were dying with him. Since then, I have died again and again, with cousins, aunties, and uncles.

Recent UN reports emphasize the extent to which HIV/AIDS is eroding economic, health, and educational development in Africa by wiping out its human resource base. AIDS has shocked Africa's population, as did slavery. The extent of the fear, which the HIV/AIDS pandemic has struck in the hearts of most Africans, can be seen in the countless euphemisms by which the disease is known in different countries—"the slow leak," "slimming disease," "slow puncture," "the modern disease," "the silent killer"— as if mentioning the name would aggravate its incidence!

African countries have allowed the dreadful HIV strains to   5
permeate their societies. When HIV/AIDS was discovered in the early 1980s in Africa, it was met with outright denial in African society. As the decade progressed, Africans half-heartedly acknowledged the disease and began the hypocritical enforcement of "non-disclosure policies." Waking up from this self-delusional stupor in the 1990s, many African countries found their societies decimated by HIV/AIDS. The consequent loss of their youngest and most productive populations and the huge increase in the number of AIDS orphans forced skyrocketing social welfare needs upon already burdened governments.

Since then, the governments of some countries have taken steps toward curbing the incidence of HIV/AIDS by adopting bold policies and mounting aggressive and open campaigns against its spread. Their efforts, assisted by foreign aid, churches, and civil society organizations, have gone a long way toward educating the public and beginning to treat the millions that are infected. The most praised methodology thus far is home-based care.

Home-Based Care

As AIDS-related health concerns escalate, it has become increasingly important for families and communities to be able to take care of infected family members at home. Hospitals are refusing to keep patients for treatment, and many families cannot afford the medical expense associated with keeping relatives in the hospital for long periods of time. There are some advantages to home-based care—reducing the cost of care within the health system and helping patients die at home with their family in dignity. However, long-term sickness impoverishes families due to the time devoted to caring for the patient, as well as the high costs of medicine and food, and the inability of family caregivers to engage in their usual income-generating work.

It is amidst the poverty of the majority of African women that government and civil society organizations are promoting and singing the praises of home-based care. The burden of home-based care falls on women, who are often sick themselves. The programs are based on women's sweat. They take advantage of the fact that African women exude a passion for living no matter how dire the situation, a passion for love and family, for traditions that confirm a heritage, a passion for people and the land, in fact, a passion for everything that epitomizes life!

It is difficult to tackle the problem of HIV/AIDS without tackling the problem of poverty and women's subordinate position. Fortunately, women are increasingly challenging their subservient sexual, social, and economic relation to men because now the cost of submissiveness is potentially death—their own and that of family members. The disease is destroying the social fabric of African communities, to the extent that it has left even the hardest of patriarchs with no doubt as to the strength of female-headed households and the need to provide economic independence for such families. The disease will force gender-based social change onto the agenda of every government, non-governmental organization, and agency working to fight HIV/AIDS in Africa.

QUESTIONS FOR DISCUSSION AND WRITING

1. The author writes of the ways in which the AIDS epidemic is promoting gender-based social change. Outline the changes she describes and the factors leading to them.

2. According to the author, how are African women coping with AIDS? What is their role in the community with regard to AIDS care?

3. Compare the effectiveness of different types of evidence included in this essay—personal narratives, references to authority such as UN reports, and logical arguments (i.e., addressing social conditions while addressing AIDS). Do you find one type of evidence more persuasive than another? Would additional examples of one type be more helpful in supporting the author's view?

4. What is the author's point of view regarding how the AIDS crisis got to be as extensive as it is? For example, why do you infer it took so long for the crisis to be addressed?

5. Research current efforts to address the AIDS epidemic worldwide; in Africa, China, or India; or in the United States. Alternatively, research current drug treatments or clinical trials designed to address the epidemic.

Only a Plane Ride Away: Public Health and Human Rights

WILLIAM F. SCHULZ

William F. Schulz is executive director of Amnesty International USA and former president of the Unitarian Universalist Association of Congregations. A recipient of numerous awards, Schulz is a Phi Beta Kappa graduate of Oberlin College, and holds a master's degree in philosophy from the University of Chicago and the Doctor of Ministry degree from Meadville/Lombard Theological School at the University of Chicago. Schulz was part of a delegation instrumental in improving the rights of religious and ethnic minorities in Romania after the fall of Nicolae Ceausescu, and he has led fact-finding missions to the Middle East and Northern Ireland. In 1997 he led an Amnesty mission to Liberia to investigate atrocities committed during the civil war there and returned to Northern Ireland with the human rights organization in 1999 to insist that human rights protections be incorporated into the peace process. Schulz has lectured and written extensively, including articles in the *New York Times,* the *Los Angeles Times,* the *Christian Science Monitor, The Nation,* and *Atlantic Monthly.* The essay that follows appeared in his book *In Our Own Best Interest: How Defending Human Rights Benefits Us All* (2001).

> *The microbe that felled one child in a distant continent yesterday can reach yours today and seed a global pandemic tomorrow.*
>
> —Joshua Lederberg,
> Nobel Laureate, Rockefeller University

In one respect environmental activists Alexander Nikitin and Grigory Pasko were lucky. As former naval officers whose cases attracted international attention, they were not "average" Russian prisoners. How they were treated is important to Americans because of who they are and what they tried to warn the world about, but surely this cannot be said of the many "common criminals"—more than one million of them—who occupy

Russian penal facilities. What could their fates possibly have to do with Americans?

"When the door to a [Russian] prison cell is opened," remarked Sir Nigel Rodley, the UN special rapporteur on torture in 1995, "one is hit by a blast of hot, dark, stinking (sweat, urine, feces) gas that passes for air." Rodley went on to describe rooms so crowded that their occupants had to take turns lying down; so unsanitary that water had to be boiled by the prisoners themselves with makeshift heating wires; so lacking in light and air that it was almost impossible to breathe; so cold in the winter that prisoners had to huddle together for warmth; and so hot in the summer that even stripped to their underwear, prisoners sweated profusely. "The Special Rapporteur would need the poetic skills of a Dante," he concluded, "adequately to describe the infernal conditions he found in these cells."[1] Since 1995, human rights violations of this order in Russian prisons have only gotten worse.

But it was another remark Rodley made that has proven especially prophetic. "These cells," he reported, "are disease incubators." Indeed, that is exactly what they have turned out to be. Four years after the publication of Rodley's report, the Public Health Research Institute issued this warning:

> The tuberculosis epidemic in Russia, particularly in Russian prisons, has reached alarming proportions. The prison system acts as an epidemiological pump, releasing into society tens of thousands of active TB cases and hundreds of thousands of infected individuals every year. The high rate of multidrug resistant tuberculosis among them is especially threatening.[2]

The incidence of tuberculosis (TB) in Russian prisons is 40 percent to 50 percent higher than in the civilian population; approximately one in ten prisoners is infected, and the bacilli that transmits that infection cannot be contained within a prison wall. After all, TB is a highly infectious airborne disease spread by coughing. Lack of ventilation, over-crowding, and perpetual darkness allow the disease to thrive, and HIV, which runs rampant in prisons, accelerates the disease. Guards, prison visitors, and lawyers go in and out of prisons every day; prisoners make appearances in court, and thousands with TB are released every year back into their communities.[3] It is little wonder that Russia is facing a health crisis.

But how could such a distant crisis possibly have an impact on the United States? Very simply. We live in an era of increased travel and trade. The medical relief organization Doctors Without

Borders has predicted that the threat from uncontrolled TB in Russia "will become the principal epidemic of the next century."[4] Twenty-seven million Americans visit developing countries every year, to say nothing of more common tourist and business destinations.[5] They bring back photographs, tchotchkes, and memories. They also bring back diseases. Every year 190,000 flights from developing countries land in the United States. Passengers bring with them hope and new energy. They also bring myriad microbes. Furthermore, the World Health Organization reported in 2000 that drug-resistant cases of TB had increased by 50 percent in Denmark and Germany.[6] If previous studies of TB's origin in Germany are correct, as many as two-thirds of those cases originated in the former Soviet Union,[7] and close to two million Americans visit Germany every year.[8]

But Americans do not need to go abroad to be susceptible to TB. Almost twenty thousand cases were reported in the United States in 1997, including those of thirteen passengers on a Paris to New York flight who contracted the disease from an infected Ukrainian passenger.[9] The United States is a favorite destination for Russian émigrés. Says health researcher Barry Kreisworth, "On the basis of molecular typing of TB among Russian cases in both the civilian and prison populations, we have identified a highly prevalent multidrug resistant clone that has now been observed in cases of tuberculosis among Russian immigrants in New York City. This resistant strain, and others like it, could easily spread in secondary settings."[10] In fact, New York City already saw a serious TB outbreak, which originated in its own prisons, in 1989. And even when the health of Americans is not put in jeopardy by imported diseases, our pocketbooks certainly are. The treatment of drug-resistant TB costs $250,000 per patient, compared with $25,000 to treat a victim of conventional TB.[11]

TB is resurgent once again for many reasons: poverty and inadequate medical regimens are but two of them. But providing the perfect environment in which TB can thrive dramatically facilitates its spread. The notion therefore that Americans have no self-interest at stake when it comes to how Russian prisoners are treated—that we need not care, beyond a certain vague moral queasiness perhaps, that tens of thousands of young Russians are held for years in pretrial detention centers (where disease is most rampant) without even having been convicted of any crime—is pure folly. For as the chief of Russian prison hospitals put it, "If Westerners don't . . . help treat TB in Russia [now], in two or three years the problem will be theirs and then it will cost them billions."[12] One of the most effective ways to treat the disease would be to insist on respect for human rights.

5

Given the dangers of the transport of disease around the globe, some might speculate that the solution to the problem is simply to shut our borders more firmly. But quite apart from the fact that an even tougher immigration policy than recently adopted in the United States would contribute to even more human rights violations, there are practical reasons why such a "solution" is infeasible. Because the time between infection and appearance of disease is quite lengthy for many illnesses—the incubation period for some diseases may exceed twenty-one days and, in the case of HIV, many years—it is impossible with any degree of certainty to screen travelers who may be carrying dangerous infections.[13] "[Even] having one inspector for every person coming in would not prevent disease from coming in," says New York City's assistant commissioner for communicable diseases.[14] Short of shutting down the worldwide tourist industry, cutting off international business travel, and closing down US borders completely, letting no living soul in or out of the country, we must face the fact that human-borne disease is capable of spreading around the world with remarkable rapidity, carried by anyone, be it the rich or the refugee. In 1991 an Aerolineas Argentinas flight made a scheduled stop in Lima, Peru, picked up a load of passengers, and efficiently delivered cholera to Los Angeles. It doesn't take a planeload of people to transmit disease, however. The Spanish conqueror Hernán Cortés managed to decimate the Aztec population in 1520 when one slave from Spanish Cuba arrived in Mexico infected with smallpox.[15]

Nor are human carriers the only transporters of illness. The growth in global trade with its exchange of goods, including plants, animals, and foodstuffs, is a major vehicle by which vectors—those organisms that transmit pathogenic fungi, viruses, and bacteria—make their way around the globe. A 1985 outbreak of dengue fever in Texas, for example, has been attributed to the arrival of a particularly aggressive mosquito species in a shipment of waterlogged used tires sent to Houston, Texas, from Japan for retreading.[16]

Climate change too—particularly the kind of global warming caused in part by deforestation—is responsible for some of the United States' increased susceptibility to disease. Higher temperatures raise the reproductive rates of vectors like mosquitoes and entice them farther north, bringing with them malaria, encephalitis, leishmaniasis (a facial-disfiguring disease for which there is no vaccine), Chagas' disease (which debilitates muscles), and elephantiasis (which currently afflicts some four hundred million people worldwide).[17] Malarial infections are already on the rise in the United States, some cases having been identified as far north as Michigan. Anyone who lived in metropolitan New York City in the fall of 1999 when a breed of encephalitis previously unknown in the area was linked to a number of deaths knows how unnerving the appearance of a new threat can be to a population, to say nothing of the CIA, which examined the possibility that the outbreak was attributable to bioterrorism on the part of Saddam Hussein.[18]

Regardless of how they get here, however, more than thirty new pathogenic microbes have been identified in the United States since 1973.[19] Other maladies thought to be under control, such as cholera and diphtheria, have reemerged elsewhere in the world.[20] The globalization of disease and the possibility of worldwide pandemics is no longer a fantasy in the mind of a science fiction writer. As international commerce and travel increase, the dangers will become still more real. By the year 2020, for example, China, where many strains of influenza have first appeared, will be the world's number-one tourist destination, hosting some 130 million visitors each year and supplying 100 million tourists to other parts of the globe.[21] All this has led the Centers for Disease Control (CDC) to conclude that "the health of the American people is inextricably linked to the health of people in other nations; infectious diseases can and do spread rapidly around the globe" and to warn that "once considered 'exotic,' tropical infectious diseases are having an increasing effect on the American public."[22]

No longer will the relative isolation of the United States' geography, poised as it is between two great oceans, protect us, for pestilents know no national boundaries. If nothing else can convince us that our interests are tied to those of the rest of the world, perhaps a few errant microbes will.

No matter how or where a disease originates, it is unlikely to spread widely in the absence of one or more "amplifiers," that is, one or more factors that exacerbate and multiply the impact of the initial pathogen. Sometimes these amplifiers are impossible to control, such as cyclical changes in weather, flight patterns of disease-carrying birds, or the evolution of new strains of microbes. But often the amplifiers that spread disease are related to human behavior, and frequently that behavior is related to the issue of respect for human rights.

Wars, for example, have long been known to contribute mightily to the dissemination of disease;[23] in the thirteenth through sixteenth centuries the Mongol conquerors brought with them bubonic plague. Slavery facilitated the spread of malaria and yellow fever throughout the Americas, and British colonizers in India and Africa denied medical treatment to indigenous people on the racist assumption that they were genetically inferior.[24] If the denial of what we now call "human rights" has historically been so closely linked to the amplification of illness, why would we think it any different today? The Nicaraguan dictator Anastasio Somoza invested in the collection of plasma from the poorest and most pathetic of his citizens for sale on the international market out of a facility that Nicaraguans dubbed "the house of the vampires." Somoza's undertaking may well have contributed to the worldwide spread of hepatitis, but what is certain is that when Pedro Joaquin Chamorro, the publisher of the opposition newspaper, *La Prensa,* tried to expose the operation, he paid for it with his life.[25] When countries such as the Congo and Ethiopia, among the world's poorest nations, succumb to war, their governments have even fewer resources than other countries to devote to sanitation and health care. The International Red Cross has estimated that of the 17 million excess deaths in the Congo that have occurred since the recent fighting there, all but 200,000 are a function of disease, malnutrition, and the breakdown of the public health system.[26]

When it comes to social and economic rights, the connection between health and human rights is self-evident and not simply because the UN International Covenant on Economic, Social, and Cultural Rights guarantees "the prevention, treatment, and control of epidemic, endemic, occupational, and other diseases."[27] The relationship between poverty and disease is so well established that were the world to take seriously the covenant's commitment to "the right of everyone to an adequate standard of living,"[28] we would have an abundance of microbes on the run in a jiffy. Such a crusade would also pay economic dividends to investor countries, because healthier populations make for more productive workers and a more vibrant market for goods and services. But it is the relationship between health and the more traditional civil and political rights that is of interest to us here. For although many amplifiers may not have a direct connection to these types of human rights violations, others—and assuredly far more than foreign policy "realists" ever allow—most certainly do.

Dengue fever, particularly in its more acute form, is not a pleasant disease to contract. Viral in nature, transmitted by mosquitoes, it is characterized by high fever, severe headache, disabling muscle pain, and vomiting, but it may also produce hemorrhaging from the nose, mouth, and gums. Not pleasant, potentially fatal, and there is no vaccine.

In May 1991 dengue fever raged through Havana, Cuba, affecting at least 344,000 people. It took six months to get the ailment under control, by which point the Cuban government had spent more than $100 million.[29] By 1994 the CDC could report that Cuba was "the only country in the region that has eliminated dengue as a health problem."[30]

The only problem was that the CDC was wrong. Cuban medical doctor Desi Mendoza Rivero, president of the Colegio Medico Independiente de Santiago de Cuba, knew by 1997 that it was wrong. Dr. Mendoza, then forty-three, had been raised in a family of "believers"—believers in Castro's revolution. His parents had been Young Pioneers in the Cuban Communist movement, and Mendoza was raised to honor Communist ideals. But gradually he began to notice the inequities in this presumably egalitarian society, the fact that those like his parents who were close to the government enjoyed more access to goods and services than did the average Cuban. When Mendoza was fifteen, he dared to criticize the way his school was run and was expelled for his outspokenness. "Soon I was warned," he said later, "that the little people can't win against the big people—even in Cuba."

For a good many years Mendoza kept his opinions to himself because he wanted to study medicine and emulate a family doctor he had known since his youth who often treated his poorer patients for free. Finally, in 1986 Mendoza received his degree in medicine, eventually taking a position at a teaching hospital where his wife, also a physician, held a position as well. But his unhappiness with the Cuban system had not abated, and in 1994 Mendoza fled Cuba on a raft. Rescued at sea, he was interned in a refugee camp at the Guantanamo military base for eight months. When it became obvious that he would not be admitted to the United States, however, he returned to Cuba. By now Mendoza's reputation had been permanently soiled in the eyes of Cuban authorities, and he was refused permission to work in the teaching hospital. This led to the establishment of the private Colegio, where he saw patients informally at his home in Cuba's second largest city, Santiago. While he was treating these patients, he first recognized the symptoms of dengue and the possibility of another epidemic.

But how could he sound the warning? He was, after all, no longer a state-recognized physician. "Many people here were sick with dengue and were being told only that they had come down with a virus," his wife, Dr. Pinon Rodriguez, explained later.[31] Some of them were even dying, but for some reason the government was covering up the disease. Although Mendoza's former colleagues in the public health system confirmed to him that lab results revealed the presence of dengue, the death certificates listed the causes of death as unknown. Fearing that a widespread outbreak might be on the horizon, Mendoza concluded that the only way to get the word out was to contact journalists in Mexico and Spain who would in turn broadcast the news back to Cuba—a communications practice popularly known as "the boomerang."

On June 18, 1997, Mendoza contacted the foreign journalists. Three days later the local Santiago paper printed the news, and four days after that, Mendoza was arrested. It seems that from the Cuban government's standpoint, his warning could not have come at a worse time. Santiago was scheduled to host several large international events, including a cultural festival and trade fair, which thousands of foreign visitors were expected to attend. Rumors of an outbreak of dengue fever could ruin the entire enterprise. Mendoza was charged with spreading "enemy propaganda" with the intention, said the indictment, of creating "uncertainty, confusion, and panic in the Cuban population."

For five months the doctor was held pending trial. Finally, on November 18, he appeared in court, where the authorities even acknowledged that bad publicity resulting from his outspokenness could have adversely affected tourism. Nonetheless, Mendoza was convicted and sentenced to eight years in prison.[32] About a year later, after an appeal by the king and queen of Spain, he was released on the condition that he take up exile in Madrid. Finally, in February 2000, Mendoza, his wife, and three children made it to Miami, where they live today. The doctor's experience serves as a powerful symbol to other Cuban health workers of the perils of telling the truth about disease. Mendoza is trying to renew his medical credentials in the United States, but for the time being he is working as a security guard. "I don't really mind," says this proud, determined man. "After all, I have to start somewhere."[33]

Dengue fever is already well established in the United States (86 cases reported to the CDC in 1995; 179 in 1996[34]), much of it contracted from travel to the Caribbean. Given the growing number of US visitors to Cuba, to say nothing of travel exchanges between Cuba and its Caribbean neighbors, economic sanctions cannot prevent the dissemination of this disease.

The first line of defense against epidemics is transparency—a willingness on the part of governments to compile accurate information about infectious diseases, to distribute that information to its citizens, and to share the facts quickly and honestly with medical and research professionals around the world. Many observers, including a White House working group on global threats from pathogenic microbes, have advocated the establishment of a global system of surveillance by which such data might be readily obtained and communicated. But as the working group noted, "Individual governments may . . . be reluctant to share [such] information, fearing losses in trade, tourism, and national prestige."[35] How much more likely is that reluctance to prevail in countries that lack traditions of transparency, a free press, independent monitoring organizations, and health professionals who have confidence that they will be hailed, not punished, for telling the truth? As Laurie Garrett, Pulitzer Prize-winning author of *The Coming Plague,* has written:

> It is often exceedingly difficult to obtain accurate information about outbreaks of disease. . . . Egypt denies the existence of cholera bacteria in the Nile's waters; Saudi Arabia has asked WHO [World Health Organization] not to warn that travelers to Mecca may be bitten by mosquitoes carrying viruses that cause the new, superlethal dengue hemorrhagic fever; . . . and central authorities in Serbia . . .rescinded an international epidemic alert when they learned that all the scientists WHO planned to send to the tense Kosovo region to halt a large outbreak of Crimean-Congo hemorrhagic fever were from the United States.[36]

What Egypt, Saudi Arabia, and Serbia all had in common, albeit to different degrees, were governments that could hardly be said to have prized the free exchange of critical ideas.

Just as diseases cross borders unimpeded, so the fight to detect and prevent the spread of illnesses around the globe cannot succeed without international cooperation. Had such cooperation been in place when slim disease first appeared in Uganda as early as 1962, it might not have prevented the spread of HIV/AIDS, depending on your theory of its origins. But it certainly could not have hurt to have begun monitoring the virus some two decades before it was first formally diagnosed.[37] That was not the only problem in Uganda that may have amplified the outbreak of HIV/AIDS, however. There was also the little matter of a very big man named Idi Amin.

Whether HIV/AIDS emerged first in Africa or elsewhere, and whether it was transported there through the early testing of a polio vaccine, as one recent controversial book alleges,[38] it is widely agreed, based on seroepidemiological tests, that at some point the African strain of the disease radiated outward from the Lake Victoria region on the Uganda–Tanzania border and spread extensively after 1980 through much of central and southern Africa. The highest infection rates in this period were among prostitutes originally from the Lake Victoria area. Beginning in 1975, the number of cases of aggressive Kaposi's sarcoma (skin lesions associated with AIDS) diagnosed in Kinshasa, Zaire, doubled every year, leading one Zairian health official to observe that "something dramatic happened in 1975."[39]

Idi Amin was president of Uganda from 1971 to 1979. At three hundred pounds he was widely considered one of the continent's most intimidating and ruthless dictators, rumored to practice cannibalism and known to be bloodthirsty in his treatment of his enemies. After overthrowing the government of Milton Obote in 1971, Amin expelled between fifty thousand and eighty thousand Asian Ugandans, many of them Indians, who had, much to the resentment of indigenous Ugandans, constituted the heart of Uganda's commercial sector, having been placed in charge of cotton-ginning and wholesale trade during British colonial rule. Not surprisingly, this mass expulsion of legitimate citizens, itself a human rights violation, led to the quick collapse of the formal Ugandan economy and its replacement by an underground black market largely dependent on smuggling. The young men who plied the smuggling trade led a high-risk life of debauchery and promiscuity.[40] Laurie Garrett picks up the story from there:

> Tiny Lake Victoria fishing villages were transformed overnight into busy smuggling ports. As a business, prostitution was second only to the black market. For most women there were only two choices in life: have babies and grow food without assistance from men, livestock or machinery, or exchange sex for money at black-market rates. . . . The area became a vast lattice of mud roads, brothels, and smuggling centers through which flowed a steady stream of truckers carrying cargoes bound for Kenya, Tanzania, Rwanda, Burundi, and Zaire.[41]

And with those truckers went HIV.

Over the course of his reign, Amin terrorized the professional population, thereby diminishing the number of health workers; looted Makere University, the primary medical training center for East Africa's doctors, "right down to its electrical sockets and bathroom tiles";[42] created a refugee flow of some 300,000 Ugandans fleeing for their lives and carrying their microbes with them to neighboring countries; and during the war with Tanzania in 1977 through 1979, fostered a military in which rape was used as a form of ethnic cleansing. Even his eventual overthrow in 1979 did not stem Uganda's misfortunes as, thanks partly to his policies, famine gripped the country, further decimating the population's resistance to disease. Little wonder, then, that writer Jeffrey Goldberg, in arguing that the United States should take Africa as a continent more seriously than it does, has said that "HIV is a clever microbe—a slow, steady incubator—and it might have spread efficiently even without political chaos. . . . [But] the volatile mix of refugees, soldiers, prostitutes, and the attendant lack of disease surveillance [in Uganda under Idi Amin] may have given HIV the jump-start it needed to travel the world."[43]

It is hazardous enough to deny the facts about a public health crisis. Even as late as a 1985 conference on AIDS in Africa, health professionals on the continent had formally confirmed only a few cases of AIDS, and many rejected the notion that they had an epidemic on their hands.[44] Today Africa accounts for 70 percent of those living with AIDS, 83 percent of AIDS deaths, and 95 percent of its orphans.[45] But couple denial with human rights crimes—expulsion of citizens, intimidation of medical officers, rape, child prostitution, forced migration, and so on—and you create a health situation nothing short of lethal. One of the reasons that orphaned infants in Romania under the dictator Ceausescu were given wholly unnecessary blood transfusions later found to be tainted by HIV is because health professionals feared they would be punished by the government if any of the children died. So they agreed to whole blood transfusions in the mistaken belief that it would offer important nutrients to sick children.[46] Furthermore, when people with HIV/AIDS face discrimination, coercion, and punishment on account of their illness, they are less likely to seek testing and treatment, and the disease is even more likely to spread.

When Idi Amin was in power, the world bemoaned his barbarism but treated it largely as a problem for Ugandans or, at most, for Africans. But the human rights violations contributing to the diffusion of HIV/AIDS today—the subjugation of women, for example, or the creation of refugee camps, or the scourge of war that decimates public health care systems—are finally being recognized as everybody's problem. The question is whether that recognition has come too late.

Regardless of how HIV/AIDS initially arose in the United States,   30
it is now so serious a global problem that in April 2000 the US National Security Council declared the disease a threat to national security. More than forty million people are currently living with HIV/AIDS, and a quarter of the population of southern Africa is likely to die of it.[47] Based on current trends, South Asia and the former Soviet Union could duplicate or even exceed that

rate at some point in the future.[48] Such massive mortality rates would threaten international stability; disrupt potential American markets (nonproductive populations spending what discretionary income they have on treatments are hardly a reliable consumer base for US products); endanger American workers overseas; make it impossible for countries to bolster their share of peacekeeping missions; and, given how readily HIV/AIDS patients succumb to other diseases like tuberculosis, amplify the spread of infectious diseases around the globe.

Other than Africa, the region of the world in which AIDS is now spreading the most quickly is Asia. Incubated along China's border with Burma (Myanmar) beginning in 1990, thanks to the sharing of needles by heroin users, it is now rampaging through China's Xinjiang province and elsewhere.[49] Estimates have it that 2 percent of Cambodian adults suffer from the disease and at least half a million in Thailand.[50] Here too human rights violations have contributed to the menace.

Burma (Myanmar) suffers today under one of the world's most repressive regimes. Once one of Asia's most medically advanced countries, it has witnessed an explosion of heroin use over the years; the erosion of its health care system under brutal military rule; arrest, execution, or emigration of its medical and nursing professionals, a paucity of information about AIDS prevention, thanks to a junta-controlled media; and the absence of nongovernmental health organizations capable of educating the people about their health care needs. All but the first of these facts entail human rights abuses, and all contribute to the explosion of sexually transmitted diseases.

One of the most direct causes of the crisis is the government's persecution of the ethnic Karen and Shan people, many of whom are forced into hard labor on roads, quarries, and railways. Faced with the loss of their men as well as the common incidence of rape by government troops, Shan women and girls are emigrating in high numbers to Thailand to take up the sex trade. Twenty thousand to thirty thousand Burmese women have become prostitutes in Thailand, and it is estimated that they suffer a prevalence of HIV at the level of 40 percent to 60 percent.[51]

Similarly, in Cambodia there has been little replenishment of the enormous numbers of health care professionals executed by the Khmer Rouge (at one point only twenty-five doctors remained in the Ministry of Health[52]). Hundreds of land mine injuries each month require transfusions with blood that is sometimes tainted. And trafficking of Khmer women and girls into the sex trade is increasing[53]—conditions again involving human rights violations.

The results of all of this are staggering for Asia, but it is not 35 only Asia that has cause to worry. There is evidence that American soldiers and officials assigned to the UN Transitional Authority in Cambodia in the mid-1990s, mostly young men, dramatically increased the demand for sex services and brought HIV infections back to the United States.[54] (Indeed, in a larger sense, it has been estimated that since 1980 more UN peace-keeping troops have died of AIDS than in combat.[55]) Moreover, given the growing attractiveness of tourist and business travel to China, Thailand, Cambodia, and even Burma (Myanmar), the likelihood of more Americans contracting sexually transmitted diseases in these countries and transporting them to the United States in their bloodstreams, to pass on to others, increases with each airline ticket.

There could be no more direct link in this chain, of course, than the thousands of Americans who indulge each year in the Asian sex trade, including sex with minors. American travel com-panies such as Big Apple Oriental Tours of Bellerose, New York ("Real sex with real girls, all for real cheap"), and twenty-five oth-ers are known to arrange pre-planned tours.[56] In Thailand, for ex-ample, 200,000 "sex workers" (a conservative estimate), 50 percent of whom are infected with HIV/AIDS and anywhere from 25 percent to 40 percent of whom are under eighteen, service some 500,000 foreign tourists annually, of which some reason-able percentage are bound to be drawn from the 50,000 to 100,000 Americans who visit the country annually. Nor do Americans need to go to South-east Asia to have contact with women who have been forced into prostitution. As many as fifty thousand women and girls may be trafficked into the United States itself for that purpose each year and held for bondage to pay off their $40,000 debts for passage.[57]

Whether it be a sexually transmitted disease, or any another kind, maladies are frequently amplified by human rights viola-tions. Americans, because of a mosquito's breeding habits or their own, can less and less readily escape the consequences. The connection between ill health and human rights is particu-larly obvious when it comes to migration, the majority of which is prompted by war, economic deprivation, ecological disaster (sometimes caused by the greenhouse effect), or ethnic cleans-ing. In 2000 the world contained at least sixteen million refugees, many of them living in camps and settlements that are breeding grounds for pathogens. As one physician has put it, "Should a new disease, such as Ebola, emerge in the setting of a refugee camp, the conditions would be perfectly in place for a global plague"[58]—an observation that sheds more doubt on the notion of US policy makers that the 1994 Rwandan genocide had no relationship to US national interest.

Finally, there is the issue of chemical and biological weapons (which have been called "the poor man's atom bomb"), capable in short order of wiping out entire populations. Such weapons are hardly a new phenomenon. Plague-ridden bodies of Tartar soldiers were catapulted over the walls of the city of Kaffa (now Feodosiya, Ukraine) as early as 1346. Sir Jeffrey Amherst unashamedly provided Native Americans with smallpox-infested blankets during the French and Indian War.[59] Today at least twenty-five countries are thought to possess some level of capability to produce toxic chemical weapons and twelve to manufacture biological weapons that employ disease-causing microorganisms.[60] It goes without saying that many of these countries, Syria and Iraq, for example, have atrocious human rights records.

What particularly worries experts, however—and here I return to the issue of transparency—is that without an organized civil society capable of monitoring compliance with treaties, without independent academics and journalists offering alternative views to the people, without a vibrant political opposition to critique an incumbent government's policies—in short, without a healthy respect for civil and political rights—there can be no effective internal checks on *any* government's predilections to use chemical and biological weapons to terrorize the globe. As what Brad Roberts of the Center for Strategic and International Studies calls a "new tier" of states (from Germany to Egypt, Kazakhstan to India) capable of producing weapons of mass destruction—be they nuclear, chemical, or biological—emerges out of the demise of the Cold War, so the need to ensure structures of accountability for the use of such weapons only grows that much more urgent.[61]

Many factors beyond issues of human rights play a part in the proliferation of weapons or the spread of disease. To ignore the role of power politics or religious fervor in the growth of terrorism or to forget how large a part economic ills, foolish risk-taking, and simple ignorance play in the march of microbes is to see the world through far too narrow a lens. My case is not that human rights violations are the only contributors to global health threats or even the primary ones. My case is that they play a far greater role than our policy makers have generally allowed. To dismiss the interdependence of health and human rights is not only to live in a dream world. To dismiss it is very simply to invite disaster.

Notes

1. UN Economic and Social Council, *Report of the Special Rapporteur on His Visit to the Russian Federation,* 1995.
2. A. Goldfarb and M. E. Kimerlin, *Russian TB Program: An Initiative of the International Center for Public Health* (New York: Public Health Research Institute, 1999).
3. Vivian Stern, *Sentenced to Die? The Problem of TB in Prisons in Eastern Europe and Central Asia* (London: International Centre for Prison Studies, 1999).
4. "Russia's TB Epidemic Creates a Global Threat," *USA Today* March 25, 1999.
5. NBC Nightly News, October 4, 1999.
6. "Resisting Drugs, TB Spreads Fast in the West," *New York Times* March 24, 2000.
7. Harvard Medical School/Open Society Institute, *The Global Impact of Drug-Resistant Tuberculosis* (New York: Open Society Institute, 1999).
8. ITA Tourism Industries Market Analysis, "Departures and Payments for US Travelers Abroad (Outbound), 1997," December 1998.
9. "Russia's TB Epidemic."
10. Barry Kreisworth, interview, June 5, 2000; and see Harvard Medical School/ Open Society Institute, *Global Impact,* 63.
11. Institute of Medicine, *America's Vital Interest in Global Health* (Washington, DC National Academy Press, 1997).
12. Harvard Medical School/Open Society Institute, *Global Impact,* 61.
13. Laurie Garrett, "The Return of Infectious Disease," *Foreign Affairs* January/February 1996: 66–79.
14. "Mosquito Virus Exposes a Hole in the Safety Net," *New York Times* October 4, 1999.
15. Jared Diamond, *Guns, Germs, and Steel: The Fates of Human Societies* (New York: W.W. Norton, 1997), 206, 210.
16. Laurie Garrett, *The Coming Plague: Newly Emerging Diseases in a World out of Balance* (New York: Penguin, 1994), 257. The long-horned beetle, a threat to hardwood forests, probably arrived in the United States from Asia in the 1980s in wooden shipping pallets, and Zebra mussels brought from Eastern Europe in ships have caused $5 billion damage in the Great Lakes; see "Mosquito Virus."
17. Marshall Fisher and David E. Fisher, "Coming Soon: The Attack of the Killer Mosquitoes," *Los Angeles Times* September 15, 1991.
18. See Richard Preston, "West Nile Mystery," *The New Yorker* October 18 and 25, 1999.

19. "Global Microbial Threats in the 1990s," *Report of the Committee on International Science, Engineering, and Technology Policy of the President's National Science and Technology Council,* 1995.

20. World Health Organization, "Emerging and Re-emerging Infectious Diseases," Fact Sheet 97, August 1998.

21. "No. 1 Destination in 2020? Try China, Then France," *New York Times* October 3, 1999.

22. Centers for Disease Control, "Addressing Emerging Infectious Disease Threats," September 6, 1995.

23. William H. McNeill, *Plagues and People* (New York: Doubleday, 1977).

24. Sheldon Watts, *Epidemics and History: Disease, Power, and Imperialism* (New Haven, CT: Yale University Press, 1998).

25. Douglas Starr, *Blood* (New York: Alfred A. Knopf, 1999), 231–49.

26. Cited in Jordan Kassalow, Council on Foreign Relations, Schulz email correspondence, June 22, 2000.

27. UN International Covenant on Economic, Social, and Cultural Rights, Article 12.2.c.

28. UN International Covenant, Article 11.1.

29. Garrett, *Coming Plague,* 256.

30. Centers for Disease Control, "Dengue Surveillance—United States, 1986–1992," July 1994.

31. "Jailed Cuban's Wife Pins Hope on Pope's Words," *New York Times* January 30, 1998.

32. Amnesty International, "Cuba: New Cases of Prisoners of Conscience and Possible Prisoners of Conscience," January 1998.

33. Desi Mendoza Rivero, interview with William F. Schulz, May 25, 2000.

34. Centers for Disease Control, "Imported Dengue—United States, 1996," July 10, 1998.

35. "Global Microbial Threats."

36. Garrett, "Return of Infectious Disease," 74.

37. A point made by the White House working group in "Global Microbial Threats."

38. Edward Hooper, *The River* (Boston: Little, Brown, 1999).

39. Garrett, *Coming Plague,* 366–67.

40. Tony Barnett and Piers Blaikie, *AIDS in Africa* (New York: Guilford Press, 1992), 69–70.

41. Garrett, *Coming Plague,* 368.

42. Garrett, *Coming Plague,* 211.

43. Jeffrey Goldberg, "Our Africa," *New York Times Magazine* March 2, 1997.

44. Mirko Grmek, *History of AIDS* (Princeton, NJ: Princeton University Press, 1990).

45. World Health Organization (WHO), "African Countries Urged to Declare HIV/AIDS a National Emergency," press release, WHO Regional Office for Africa, June 24, 1999.

46. Bradley Hersh, "Acquired Immunodeficiency Syndrome in Romania," *Lancet* September 14, 1991.

47. A figure cited from the UN AIDS Programme in Geneva in Laurie Garrett, "Runaway Diseases and the Human Hand Behind Them," *Foreign Affairs* (January/February 1998):141.

48. "AIDS Is Declared Threat to U.S. National Security," *Washington Post* April 30, 2000; and National Intelligence Estimate, *The Global Infectious Disease Threat and Its Implications for the United States,* January 2000.

49. "Ancient Trade Route Brings Modern Virus to Remote China, Linxia," *AIDS Weekly Plus* August 18, 1997.

50. See Chris Beyrer, "Burma and Cambodia: Human Rights, Social Disruption, and the Spread of HIV/AIDS," *Health and Human Rights 2* (1998): 4; and "Continent Braces Itself for Upsurge in HIV Cases," *AIDS Weekly* February 7, 1994.

51. Beyrer, "Burma and Cambodia," 87–90; and Tezza O. Paret, Aurora Javate-de Dios, Cecelia Hofmann, and Charrie Calalang, "Coalition against Trafficking in Women and Prostitution in the Asia Pacific." < *www.uri.edu/artsci/wms/hughes/catw* > .

52. Mam Bun Heng and P.J. Key, "Cambodian Health in Transition," *British Medical Journal* August 12, 1995.

53. Beyrer, "Burma and Cambodia," 90–92.

54. Beyrer, "Burma and Cambodia," 92.

55. Elizabeth Reid, "A Future, If One Is Still Alive," in Jonathan Moore, ed., *Hard Choices: Moral Dilemmas in Humanitarian Intervention* (Lanham, MD: Rowman & Littlefield, 1998), 275.

56. Equality NOW, Women's Action 2.1, December 1996.

57. Jennifer Soriano, "Trafficking in Sex," < *www.shewire.com* > , quoting the Planned Parenthood Global Partners Program, February 1, 2000; and Brad Knickerbocker, "Prostitution's Pernicious Reach Grows in the US," *Christian Science Monitor* October 23, 1996. See also "Foreigners Misled into Forced Labor," *USA Today* April 3, 2000; and "After the Fall, Traffic in Flesh, Not Dreams," *New York Times* June 11, 2000.

58. Eoin O'Brien, M.D., "The Diplomatic Implications of Emerging Diseases," in Kevin M. Cahill, M.D., *Preventive Diplomacy* (New York, Basic Books, 1996), 259.

59. Chemical and Biological Arms Control Institute/Center for Strategic and International Studies, 2000, "Contagion and Conflict: Health as a Global Security Challenge," 36.

60. Jonathan B. Tucker, "The Eleventh Plague: The Politics of Biological and Chemical Weapons," reviewed in *Bulletin of Atomic Scientists* March 13, 1997.

61. Brad Roberts, "1995 and the End of the Post-Cold War Era," *Washington Quarterly* (Winter 1995).

QUESTIONS FOR DISCUSSION AND WRITING

1. Examine the introductory paragraphs. How does the writer develop an explanation of the core problem? Paragraph 1 ends with a rhetorical question and paragraph 3 begins with one. How do these questions tie the situation in Russian prisons to your concern?

2. Paragraphs 1 through 6 develop an argument, the conclusion of which is, "One of the most effective ways to treat the disease would be to insist on respect for human rights." On your own or with classmates, write out the premises and evidence that lead to this conclusion/assertion and evaluate the argument.

3. The paragraphs following this assertion develop a refutation to opposing views. What are the chief objections to the author's position that he anticipates? What strategies does he use to respond to these objections? Does the author adequately support the connection between health and human rights? Of the several examples the author uses to support his view, which do you find most effective?

4. Write an essay in which you discuss the assertion that supporting human rights in other countries is crucial to US policy. Determine whether you will support this view with ethical and emotional appeals as well as practical and logical appeals.

5. Research one of the health issues raised in this essay—diseases such as dengue fever, the HIV/AIDS epidemic, the Asian sex trade, or bioterrorism, or a more commonplace but still dangerous illness such as tuberculosis. What is the current situation with regard to the threat these diseases pose? You could consider narrowing your topic by focusing not only on a specific health issue but on a specific geographical region as well.

Drinking Poison:
The Lesson of Bhopal

TEJASWINI MORE

Tejaswini More was born in Denver, Colorado, and is completing a college degree in mathematics. She hopes to become a physician and practice with traditionally underserved populations. Her interest in mental health issues has roots in her work in neurobiologist Robert Sapolsky's laboratory and in her work at a nongovernment organization in Moscow serving battered women. She has won awards for her academic papers, including one from the Center for Research on Women and Gender at Stanford University. The essay that follows, which is documented with endnotes, developed from a discussion in her "Medical Practice in Foreign Lands" class. More is an avid runner, and she is on her university's Tae Kwon Do team. More writes for *Street Forum,* a campus newsletter focusing on issues affecting the homeless, and has written for and edited an undergraduate research journal. Her honors include academic and humanities awards and a National Goldwater Scholarship.

In a time when fears of nuclear attacks and bioterrorism increasingly populate our emotional landscape, it is hard to believe that one of today's most lethal substances is something as simple as water. More than five million people die each year from water-related diseases such as cholera, diarrhea, and dysentery; in fact most disease in the developing world is related to poor water quality. The lethality of water takes on special meaning in the small Asian nation of Bangladesh, where more than half of the country's population is now at risk of drinking arsenic-polluted groundwater. The calamity that has befallen Bangladesh ranks as the largest mass poisoning of a population in history and exceeds the scale of the accidents in Bhopal, India, in 1984, and Chernobyl, the Ukraine, in 1986.

Bangladesh's current public health disaster has its origins in the same technology that ushered in the country's so-called Green Revolution. During the 1970s and 1980s, hundreds of thousands of tubewells were sunk into underground aquifers across the country, allowing farmers to irrigate their fields year round and produce three to four crops. As the wells drained the aquifers, however, the underlying arsenic-containing bedrock was exposed to air, causing the release of arsenic into the remaining water.

Historically, Bangladesh is a country that has always been faced with the problem of potable water scarcity. The surface waters of the country have been contaminated with microorganisms, which cause a significant burden of disease and mortality. The recent discovery of arsenic in the groundwater supply adds yet another dimension to the country's already poor indices of health and threaten to disrupt its path to development in the years ahead.

Potable Water Scarcity in Bangladesh

At a distance, Bangladesh is not a country one would easily associate with potable water scarcity. More water enters Bangladesh each year as surface water inflow and rainfall than can ever be used effectively—enough to submerge every meter of the country under more than nine meters of water. The country sits astride the confluence of two of the world's greatest rivers, the Ganges and the Brahmaputra, and is penetrated by 230 rivers and tributaries. The rivers endow the soils of Bangladesh with extraordinary fertility, which permits the country to support the highest density of agricultural population in the world.

Yet to this abundance of surface water there, too, exists a sinister side. Indeed, according to a World Health Organization (WHO) report on water and sanitation programs in Bangladesh published in 1990, nearly 80 percent of the human diseases found in Bangladesh are related to unclean water.[1] How is it that water can be the source of so much sickness in Bangladesh? Many official explanations favor purely ecological factors. These analyses indicate that the apparent abundance of water that Bangladesh is famous for conceals important water shortages that prevail during the dry months of November through May. This cycle of floods and droughts, it is argued, undermines agriculture production and promotes poor health indices. Moreover, the topographical flatness of Bangladesh makes the country take on the character of a massive open drain. During floods, which inundate one-third of Bangladesh every year, water flows freely through the densely populated land, picking up and carrying along residues of dirt, germs, and unhealthy detritus. This constant and uncontrollable contact between people and

contaminated surface water has been linked to the high incidence of waterborne disease (the most common are those transmitted by the fecal-oral route: diarrhea, typhoid, viral hepatitis A,
cholera, dysentery) witnessed in Bangladesh.[2]

Yet the pervasiveness of waterborne disease in Bangladesh
cannot be seen as the sum consequence of ecological factors
alone for the problem appears to have an inherently infrastructural dimension as well. In most of rural Bangladesh, a public
sanitation system is virtually nonexistent. Due to the lack of sanitation infrastructure, people frequently use local ponds and
streams as sewers without realizing that they are increasing the
risk of disease in their community. Studies conducted by the
World Health Organization suggest that sanitation infrastructure
is at least as effective in preventing disease as improved water
supply but is often more difficult to accomplish because it requires major behavioral changes and significant household
cost.[3,9] The construction of a public sanitation system in the near
future is unlikely because the local government currently allo-
cates less than 1 percent of its annual budget to health and sanitation. In recognition of the role that sanitation plays in health
of the population of Bangladesh, UNICEF has recently adopted a
program to construct over one million new latrines from
2001–2005 (increasing coverage by an estimated 5 percent), yet
as of January 2002, 60 percent of Bangladesh's 126 million people remain without latrines or any other sanitation system.

The government's reluctance to pursue the development of
a public sanitation system is likely a consequence of
Bangladesh's small economies of scale. With a per capita gross
domestic product (GDP) of only $282 and an increasingly nega-
tive trade balance, Bangladesh ranks among the poorest nations
in the world. The predominantly agrarian economy of
Bangladesh—agriculture accounts for 30 percent of GDP—is
constantly undermined by flooding of the Ganges River that results in repeated crop and property damage. Additionally, the unstable economic and agricultural environment have, together,
produced a child malnutrition figure that is a whopping 68 percent for children under the age of five and an under five mortality rate that is reported as 113 per 1,000 live births.[4] The
malnutrition of many children and adults in Bangladesh increases their susceptibility to waterborne diseases and, in combination with the lack of adequate sanitation infrastructure,
partially explains the high incidence of waterborne diseases in
this country.

Frequently overlooked, however, is the role that industrial
pollutants discharged into the surface waters of Bangladesh play

in the country's public health crisis. Industrial wastewater is discharged into the Ganges River by a number of industries situated upstream of Bangladesh in India. India's Central Pollution Control Board has listed sixty-seven grossly polluting industries in the state of West Bengal, the Indian province adjacent to Bangladesh. The industries represented were manufacturers of refined sugar, paper, cloth, wool, cotton, batteries, fertilizers, and steel. Heavy metal assays of the river water and sediment in West Bengal and Bangladesh have found disturbing quantities of cadmium, zinc, nickel, lead, chromium, and copper. Arguments between India and Bangladesh over water sharing have become highly politicized in recent years and disputes over the extent to which India is allowed to dump its industrial waste into the Ganges remain largely unresolved.[2] India, like Bangladesh, is a developing nation struggling to balance economic development with ecological destruction. The conflict over water sharing with Bangladesh manifests the inherently economic issues that contribute to the lack of potable water in Bangladesh.

While the scarcity of potable water is a common problem throughout the developing world, the situation in Bangladesh is unique because of its particular social context. Although the country is predominantly Muslim, there are 14 million Hindus living in Bangladesh. Members of the Hindu community have views on the treatment of the Ganges River that differ significantly from the views of most journalists, activists, and government officials working with pro-environment agendas. Many Hindus in the region subscribe to the belief that the Ganges directly descends from the forehead of Lord Shiva. The Ganges' purpose on Earth, it is believed, is to purify the sins of mankind while remaining pure and unpolluted itself. Thus, despite the well known problems of surface water contamination with microorganisms, many Hindus continue to utilize the waters of the Ganges for bathing and domestic consumption. Moreover, it is a common Hindu practice to deposit cremated individuals into the Ganges. It is believed that the Ganges purifies the ashes of the dead and carries away the partially or fully cremated bodies without being adversely affected itself. Hindu priests interviewed by anthropologist K. D. Alley of Auburn University indicate that it is not material dirtiness that transforms the Ganges River, but rather the Ganges River who transforms material waste.[2] Thus, the cultural perception of the rivers that flow through Bangladesh introduces an interesting, but troubling, dilemma: belief in the fundamental purity of the surface waters of Bangladesh (from a religious standpoint) cultivates the river's denigration from a scientific viewpoint. While it is not fair to assume that the religious beliefs of Hindus in Bangladesh make them blind to the contamination of their water supply—this most certainly is not the case—it is important to realize that programs designed to alleviate the public health problems of Bangladesh face not only ecological and economic obstacles but also social hurdles that are unique to the Indian subcontinent.

Addressing the Problem of Poor Water Quality in Bangladesh: Good Intentions, Unforeseen Results

At the time of Bangladesh's independence from India in the early 1970s, the ecological, economic, and social factors that influenced water quality in Bangladesh collided to present the country with a serious health crisis. The newly formed government, struggling to define itself as well as breathe life into a poor economy constantly undermined by uncontrollable ecological forces, had neither the time nor the money to address the festering water problem. In her book *Handpumps to Health,* UNICEF's Maggie Black wrote, "The lack of even rudimentary health services, also badly damaged, and contamination of open wells and village tanks, gave rise to fears of epidemics of cholera and diarrheal disease on an uncontainable scale." In an effort to alleviate the crisis, UNICEF offered an assistance package that promoted the use of groundwater in place of the highly contaminated surface waters. Working with the Department of Public Health Engineering, in addition to local nongovernmental organizations (NGOs) such as the Grameen Bank, UNICEF began to install tube wells (tubes roughly 5 centimeters in diameter that are inserted into the ground at depths usually less than 200 meters). During the following decade, the tube wells became so popular that people who had originally refused to use the groundwater (on the basis that it was "the devil's water") began installing tubewells on their own initiative. By 1997, 10 million tubewells were installed, 900,000 of which had been funded by UNICEF. The success of groundwater cultivation, driven largely by the private sector, led UNICEF to proclaim, in its 1997 annual report that it had surpassed its goal of providing 80 percent of the population by 2000 with access to safe drinking water.[5]

There are conflicting reports about the extent to which waterborne diseases were mitigated as a direct consequence of the installation of tubewells. Reports presented by UNICEF (published in July 1990), report that despite the introduction of bacteria-free water, a drop in diarrheal disease did not occur. The report suggested that the heavy pollution and population of the waterwashed environment counteracted efforts to reduce waterborne disease via tubewells. Without sanitary latrines, it argued, such forces would continue to wreak havoc on the health of the local population.[3]

Oddly enough, a second report, published by the United Nations Foundation in October 1999, asserted that the development of tubewells successfully reduced the incidence of waterborne disease in Bangladesh. The report stated that "partly as a result of the tubewell initiative and other hygiene measures promoted by UNICEF and other donors, the infant mortality rate in Bangladesh dropped almost by half over a thirty-six year period—from 151 per thousand in 1960 to 83 per thousand in 1996. The mortality rate for children under the age of five also dropped from 247 per thousand to 113 per thousand over the same period."[6]

Although it is unclear as to whether or not the tubewells actually reduced the incidence of illnesses related to unclean water, it seems that the tubewell program initiated by UNICEF did have certain advantages. Firstly, numerous tubewells eroded the power of wealthy landowners who previously controlled water rights. Under the new system, water was available at the people's doorsteps, saving women and children from walking countless hours to open ponds and rivers. Secondly, the tubewells provided a cheap solution that took into consideration the small economies of scale of the country. Since Bangladesh was, and is, largely rural, centralised cleaning systems and piped water supplies would simply have been impractical.

Paradoxically, the water from these tubewells—although relatively free from microorganisms—has been found to contain arsenic, a naturally occurring substance that is also one of the highest-risk environmental carcinogens known. The tragic irony is that UNICEF efforts to address the poor water quality problems in Bangladesh have, in effect, led to the largest mass poisoning of a population in history. It is estimated that of a total population of 126 million, between 35 and 77 million are at risk of drinking arsenic-contaminated water. The scale of this medical and environmental disaster is beyond the accidents at Bhopal, India and Chernobyl, Ukraine.[7]

The first cases of arsenic-induced skin lesions were diagnosed in Bangladesh in 1987 and by 1993, arsenic contamination of the water in tubewells was confirmed. Based on population density measurements in 1998, the British Geological Survey estimated that the number of people in Bangladesh exposed to arsenic concentrations above 50 ug/L (five times the maximum level recommended by WHO) was about 21 million.[7]

The delay between the introduction of tubewells and the identification of arsenic in the drinking water supply is a consequence of the fact that the health effects of ingesting arsenic-contaminated drinking water appear slowly. The first signs of arsenicosis (appearing five to fifteen years after the beginning of exposure) is melanosis (small black or white marks on the body) followed by keratoses (hardening of the skin), skin lesions, and eventually skin cancer. The fact that only a small number of skin cancer cases have appeared in Bangladesh is not comforting in that the low incidence most likely reflects the typical latency of twenty years after the beginning of exposure. It is reasonable to expect marked increases in skin cancer as well as internal (bladder and lung) cancer in Bangladesh, once sufficient latency has been reached. The final stages of arsenicosis is very disfiguring—parts of the body develop gangrene and eventually fall off, giving victims the appearance of leprosy patients. The social effect of arsenicosis is, as can be expected, profound. The 1999 UNF report on arsenic poisoning in Bangladesh indicates that the hardest hit provinces of Bangladesh are treated like leper colonies. Women suffering from arsenicosis often face divorce or are unable to marry (particularly problematic in a largely Muslim society where women have few economic opportunities to support themselves) and children are forced to drop out of school to hide the problem.[6]

The problem of arsenic poisoning is also especially significant in Bangladesh because of the high levels of malnutrition. In humans, the liver methylates inorganic arsenic consumed in drinking water. The resulting metabolic products are then excreted in urine. Evidence suggests that nutrition may affect the liver's methylation efficiency of arsenic as well as the toxicity to arsenic of the body. Generally, the poor suffer the greatest from malnutrition and thus from the effects of arsenicosis as well.

Unfortunately, while there is much known about the effects of arsenicosis on health, very little is known about the extent to which it is reversible. However, preliminary epidemiological studies suggest that in its early stages, arsenicosis is reversible if clean water is supplied to patients and all exposure to arsenic is cut off.[8] The potential for minimizing the effects of arsenicosis highlights the importance of developing immediate and effective ways of introducing clean water supplies to Bangladesh.

Global Response to Arsenic Poisoning in Bangladesh

In attempting to solve Bangladesh's potable water deficiency in the early 1970s, international aid organizations ultimately created a second, more severe, problem associated with arsenic contamination of groundwater in tubewells. Although arsenic contamination of water can be reduced by fairly straightforward methods, the issue is complicated by Bangladesh's weak economy and lack of infrastructure. Nevertheless, the sheer scale of the problem and the international responsibility for the problem requires that immediate strategies to address the potable water crisis be pursued.

Currently, efforts are being focused on water quality testing   20
and identification of arsenic-contaminated wells. In a place where the composition of the underlying water table in neighboring villages (or even households!) is vastly different, there is no alternative but to test almost every one of the ten million tubewells in the country. UNICEF, in collaboration with the World Bank and local NGOs, has designed a program to address the arsenic contamination of Bangladesh which involves the blanket testing of one million tubewells in a quarter of the affected area, information and awareness campaigns, equipping zonal laboratories for water quality testing, training local staff, and providing alternative technologies to affected communities. Once certain wells are found to be contaminated with arsenic, volunteers and aid workers paint the well pump red and inform the local population to subsequently use the well only for washing. A cursory survey of 800 villages conducted by the WHO suggests that nearly half of the country's tubewells, in more than 40,000 villages, may contain arsenic levels exceeding the WHO limits by severalfold. Given these figures, some epidemiologists have surmised that nearly 24 million people are potentially at risk of developing arsenicosis. More discouraging than this, however, is the finding that wells in the Faridpur district, which were tested and found to be safe in 1995, are becoming contaminated. Despite international cooperation and funding, progress in identifying all of the poisoned tubes has been slow and some of the agencies responding to the arsenic crisis have indicated that it may likely take thirty years before all of the toxic wells are found—longer than it took to sink all ten million wells in the first place!

There are only a limited number of alternative sources of safe drinking water that have proven to be sustainable in other countries. These include shallow tubewells for zones where arsenic is undetected, arsenic-free water from deeper aquifers (>200 meters), rainwater harvesting, pond-sand filtration, and piped water supply from safe or treated sources. In the long run, it is likely that much of Bangladesh's safe water will have to come from deeper wells, and yet their construction requires a significant amount of capital which Bangladesh simply does not have. Additionally, the possibility that wells may start to bring up arsenic months or years after they are tested as safe has further dampened the initiative to sink deeper wells.

While it is possible that pond filtration and rainwater harvesting may indeed work well for certain areas of Bangladesh, there is general recognition of the fact that Bangladesh's periodic droughts make it impossible for that to be the main strategy.

Some suggested interventions also include the introduction of chemical packets that can be mixed in water and left to stand overnight. The WHO/PAHO Pan American Center of Sanitary Engineering and Environmental Sciences in Lima, Peru, (CEPIS) has developed a mixture that combines arsenic removal with disinfection that has proven to successful in Latin America. The Center for Environmental Studies at Stevens Institute of Technology in Hoboken, NJ claims to have developed a chemical-based system of arsenic removal that would cost less than $5 a year for a family. Currently, several test trials involving twenty to thirty families are currently being conducted to evaluate the efficacy of similar proposals and Khawaja Minnatullah of the World Bank indicates that "no proven affordable arsenic removal technology has been found yet."[4]

While chemical treatment of contaminated water is very cheap, difficulties arise in finding ways to properly dispose of the sludge and in training people to use such chemicals safely. Moreover, because arsenic-contaminated water appears to be crystal clear water, it could be difficult to convince people to chemically treat their water. From a public health perspective, the most viable solution to solving emergency health problems usually involves using existing technology that is familiar to the population. It has been suggested that interventions requiring modifications of existing behavior (say, for example, using a different, arsenic-free tubewell located in another area) are generally more effective than introducing interventions of a new and completely unfamiliar nature (chemical packets).

There will, ultimately, be no blanket solution that will address the water concerns of all Bangladeshis. Instead, each village must have its own plan that is tailored to its specific needs. Work on these plans, however, requires first a knowledge of which tubewells are contaminated and this task alone may very well take several decades to complete.

What Went Wrong? Lessons from Bangladesh

From the early 1980s until well into the 1990s, the international response to the crisis of poor water quality in Bangladesh was heralded as one of the most successful health campaigns ever.

The health programs initiated by UNICEF in Bangladesh ultimately led to the establishment of 10 million tubewells and, as stated in a 1997 report, "improved water resources for 80 percent of the population of Bangladesh." The health statistics were not the only dimension of the tubewell program that was eulogized. The UNICEF program developed partnerships with NGOs and local communities to mobilize the private sector into developing its own safe water resources. Thus, UNICEF was lauded for cultivating self-sufficiency in the population whose problems it was trying to address. The seemingly perfect project design effected by UNICEF begs the question: How could such a well intentioned, carefully thought out project lead to such horrific tragedy?

The factors that contributed to the creation of one of the greatest public health blunders in human history together tell a tale that beggars belief. At the time that the wells were being installed, arsenic was not recognized as a problem in water supplies and, therefore, standard water testing procedures did not include tests for arsenic. Although WHO had a guideline on arsenic as far back as 1958—0.2 mg/L—WHO favored a risk-benefit and cost-benefit approach when it came to determining whether or not chemical assays on microbe-free water supplies should be conducted in a nation or region. Denis Peach, head of groundwater at the British Geological Survey, noted in a recent issue of *The Independent* (London) that while "[it] is true that arsenic was one of the many parameters in the WHO guidelines, it was and remains common practice not to measure all of the determinants on the list for reasons of cost and/or availability of facilities."[8] UNICEF further maintains that none of the international aid agencies working in South Asia during the early 1970s was testing for arsenic, as there was no evidence of its presence in the geographical formations of the regions. The Bangladeshi government claims that it first became aware of the groundwater contamination in 1993, concluding in 1995 that the problem was pervasive and likely related to tubewells. However, according to local physician Quazi Quamruzzaman of the Dhaka Community Hospital, the government had been notified as early as 1985 that Bangladeshis being treated in West Bengal, India, were being diagnosed with arsenic poisoning. In spite of the health warnings issued by Indian community hospitals, no investigations into groundwater contamination were pursued.

The World Bank positions itself with the Bangladeshi government in indicating that it, too, never knew about the groundwater contamination with arsenic until 1993, as arsenic was never tested for before that year. However, Peter Ravenscroft, a tubewell engineer working as a consultant for the firm Mott

MacDonald's operation in Dhaka, indicated that he first found arsenic in the groundwater in the late 1980s and published his findings in the early 1990s.

It was only a decade after Ravenscroft's initial findings that the international community finally acknowledged the magnitude of the problem at hand and accepted responsibility for helping Bangladesh. In 1998, the World Bank began a three-year program to blanket test tubewells in 4,000 villages (out of a total of 68,000) to identify what fraction of the tubewells were contaminated. This was the first step in what was designed to be a fifteen year program that would, in theory, result in the complete screening of the country's ten million tubewells.

The program initiated by the World Bank, however, appears to be foundering as World Bank officials and local government officials bicker over how to spend the program's funds. As of June 2001 (the year in which the first part of the program should have been completed) only 800 villages had been screened—roughly 1 percent of the country's total villages. UNICEF's representative Shahida Azfar indicated in a conference given in May 2001 that, "to date, only 250,000 tubewells have been tested. If we keep this up, it will take us thirty years to complete the testing."

While Bangladesh waits for a solution to its potable water crisis, the waterborne diseases that it long sought to avoid have started to return at increasing rates. The issue highlights one of the central lessons to be learned from this tragedy. Perhaps the greatest flaw in the safe water program initiated in Bangladesh in the 1970s was that it was an extremely unidimensional approach to addressing the lack of potable water. The program concentrated millions of dollars worth of resources on the development of tubewells, leaving little if any money for infrastructural improvements related to sanitation development. Although UNICEF and WHO tried to introduce water-seal latrines in the 1980s, rising prices of materials worldwide meant that UNICEF had to subsidize 70 percent of the total cost. UNICEF tried to develop a financially self-supporting latrine program, but since the program was partially dependent on government funds, it was always vulnerable to the perennial budgetary shortfalls. Due to this reliance on government and household funds, the program fell through in the early 1980s and the problem of sanitation was swept aside while the development of tubewells was doggedly pursued. In retrospect, it seems that Bangladesh and UNICEF ought to have approached the problem of poor water quality in a diversified fashion—addressing the immediate medical need of clean water in addition to the problem of poor sanitation, lack of infrastructure, poverty, and malnutrition. While such a task may have been too much to bear, if there had just been an attempt to develop sanitation and water purification facilities for surface waters while concomitantly investigating new sources of microbe-free water, the current deficiency of potable water in Bangladesh would not be so massive a problem. The World Bank reports that, currently, 47 percent of the people in Bangladesh lack adequate sanitation facilities. The lack of sanitation facilities and the growing scarcity of clean water has led to a resurgence of diarrhea and other waterborne diseases—precisely the same ailments that international efforts tried to address thirty years ago. The lesson, then, that we must take from this tragedy is that we cannot expect to find a blanket solution to solve all of public health problems. Each situation requires significant forethought by and solid communication between teams of engineers, physicians, local government officials, and international organizations.

Notes

1. "Global Water Supply and Sanitation Assessment 2000 Report." *World Health Organization.* Online. Netscape Navigator. March 2, 2001. < *http://www.who.int/water_sanitation_health/Globassessment/Global1.htm* >.

2. Eaton, David J. *Water Resource Cooperation Between Nepal, India, and Bangladesh.* Lyndon B. Johnson School of Public Affairs Publishing, 1992.

3. Black, Maggie. *From Handpumps to Health.* United Nations Children's Fund, 1990.

4. "Bangladesh at a Glance" *World Bank.* Online. Netscape Navigator. March 13, 2001. < *http://www.sulstanford.edu/resources* >.

5. "Rural Water and Sanitation in Asia" *National Patriotic Health Campaign Committee.* Online. Netscape Navigator. March 3, 2001. < *http://www.chinadevelopmentbrief.com/Feb99RuralWaterAndSanitation.htm* >.

6. "Arsenic Poisoning in Bangladesh and West Bengal." *United Nations Foundation Report* October 1999.

7. "Arsenic in Drinking Water: Fact Sheet No. 210." *World Health Organization.* Online. March 2, 2001. < *http://www.who.int/inf-fs/en/fact210.htm* >.

8. Pearce, Fred. "Death in a Glass of Water." *The Independent* January 19, 2001.

9. Wolman, Abel. *Water, Health, and Society.* Bloomingfield: Indiana University Press, 1969.

10. Twort, Alan C. *Water Supply.* IWA Publishing, 2000.

QUESTIONS FOR DISCUSSION AND WRITING

1. Assess this essay in terms of academic conventions: Format, use of evidence, and clear assertions of thesis and topic sentences. What are the essay's strengths and weaknesses? What is your sense of the author's voice and tone?

2. Discuss the author's explanation about social factors in the potable water problem in Bangladesh. Do you agree that outsiders have a difficult time understanding the use of the Ganges River water, despite surface contamination, because of its religious significance for Hindus? Does the writer adequately qualify and explain this point?

3. What are the "good intentions, unforeseen results" of the UNICEF program to develop wells for drinking water?

4. According to the author, what lessons can be learned from this "public health blunder"?

The Obligation to Endure

RACHEL CARSON

Rachel Carson (1907–1964) was a biologist and writer of numerous essays and books about the environment. Her works are credited as the roots of the environmental movement of the late twentieth century. In 1932, Carson received her master's degree in zoology from Johns Hopkins University, becoming a junior aquatic biologist with the US Bureau of Fisheries in 1936. Carson's seminal work, *Silent Spring,* was published in 1962. *Silent Spring* is a work of nonfiction devoted to the effects of widespread and virtually unregulated use of pesticides in the twentieth century, most importantly the compound DDT. Though Carson suffered endless criticism from the chemical industry and others invested in DDT, *Silent Spring* prompted the US government to scrutinize the harmful effects of pesticides—leading to a nationwide ban on the manufacture of DDT in 1972. Carson died in 1964 of breast cancer and in 1980 received the highest honor awarded to civilians in the United States, the Presidential Medal of Freedom. The essay that follows was published as a chapter of *Silent Spring.*

The history of life on earth has been a history of interaction between living things and their surroundings. To a large extent, the physical form and the habits of the earth's vegetation and its animal life have been molded by the environment. Considering the whole span of earthly time, the opposite effect, in which life actually modifies its surroundings, has been relatively slight. Only within the moment of time represented by the present century has one species—man—acquired significant power to alter the nature of his world.

During the past quarter century this power has not only increased to one of disturbing magnitude but it has changed in character. The most alarming of all man's assaults upon the environment is the contamination of air, earth, rivers, and sea with dangerous and even lethal materials. This pollution is for the most part irrecoverable; the chain of evil it initiates not only in the world that must support life but in living tissues is for the most part irreversible. In this now universal contamination of the environment, chemicals are the sinister and little recognized partners of radiation in changing the very nature of the world—

the very nature of its life. Strontium 90, released through nuclear explosions into the air, comes to earth in rain or drifts down as fallout, lodges in soil, enters into the grass or corn or wheat grown there, and in time takes up its abode in the bones of a human being, there to remain until his death. Similarly, chemicals sprayed on croplands or forests or gardens lie long in soil, entering into living organisms, passing from one to another in a chain of poisoning and death. Or they pass mysteriously by underground streams until they emerge and, through the alchemy of air and sunlight, combine into new forms that kill vegetation, sicken cattle, and work unknown harm on those who drink from once pure wells. As Albert Schweitzer has said, "Man can hardly even recognize the devils of his own creation."

It took hundreds of millions of years to produce the life that now inhabits the earth—eons of time in which that developing and evolving and diversifying life reached a state of adjustment and balance with its surroundings. The environment, rigorously shaping and directing the life it supported, contained elements that were hostile as well as supporting. Certain rocks gave out dangerous radiation; even within the light of the sun, from which all life draws its energy; there were short-wave radiations with power to injure. Given time—time not in years but in millennia—life adjusts, and a balance has been reached. For time is the essential ingredient; but in the modern world there is no time.

The rapidity of change and the speed with which new situations are created follow the impetuous and heedless pace of man rather than the deliberate pace of nature. Radiation is no longer merely the background radiation of rocks, the bombardment of cosmic rays, the ultraviolet of the sun that have existed before there was any life on earth; radiation is now the unnatural creation of man's tampering with the atom. The chemicals to which life is asked to make its adjustment are no longer merely the calcium and silica and copper and all the rest of the minerals washed out of the rocks and carried in rivers to the sea; they are the synthetic creations of man's inventive mind, brewed in his laboratories, and having no counterparts in nature.

To adjust to these chemicals would require time on the scale that is nature's; it would require not merely the years of a man's life but the life of generations. And even this, were it by some miracle possible, would be futile, for the new chemicals come from our laboratories in an endless stream; almost five hundred annually find their way into actual use in the United States alone. The figure is staggering and its implications are not easily grasped—five hundred new chemicals to which the bodies of men and animals are required somehow to adapt each year, chemicals totally outside the limits of biologic experience.

Among them are many that are used in man's war against nature. Since the mid-1940s over two hundred basic chemicals have been created for use in killing insects, weeds, rodents, and other organisms described in the modern vernacular as "pests"; and they are sold under several thousand different brand names.

These sprays, dusts, and aerosols are now applied almost universally to farms, gardens, forests, and homes—nonselective chemicals that have the power to kill every insect, the "good" and the "bad," to still the song of birds and the leaping of fish in the streams, to coat the leaves with a deadly film, and to linger on in soil—all this though the intended target may be only a few weeds or insects. Can anyone believe it is possible to lay down such a barrage of poisons on the surface of the earth without making it unfit for all life? They should not be called "insecticides," but "biocides."

The whole process of spraying seems caught up in an endless spiral. Since DDT was released for civilian use, a process of escalation has been going on in which ever more toxic materials must be found. This has happened because insects, in a triumphant vindication of Darwin's principle of the survival of the fittest, have evolved super races immune to the particular insecticide used, hence a deadlier one has always to be developed—and then a deadlier one than that. It has happened also because, for reasons to be described later, destructive insects often undergo a "flareback," or resurgence, after spraying, in numbers greater than before. Thus the chemical war is never won, and all life is caught in its violent crossfire.

Along with the possibility of the extinction of mankind by nuclear war, the central problem of our age has therefore become the contamination of man's total environment with such substances of incredible potential for harm—substances that accumulate in the tissues of plants and animals and even penetrate the germ cells to shatter or alter the very material of heredity upon which the shape of the future depends.

Some would-be architects of our future look toward a time when it will be possible to alter the human germ plasm by design. But we may easily be doing so now by inadvertence, for many chemicals, like radiation, bring about gene mutations. It is ironic to think that man might determine his own future by something so seemingly trivial as the choice of an insect spray.

All this has been risked—for what? Future historians may well be amazed by our distorted sense of proportion. How could intelligent beings seek to control a few unwanted species by a

10

method that contaminated the entire environment and brought the threat of disease and death even to their own kind? Yet this is precisely what we have done. We have done it, moreover, for reasons that collapse the moment we examine them. We are told that the enormous and expanding use of pesticides is necessary to maintain farm production. Yet is our real problem not one of *overproduction?* Our farms, despite measures to remove acreages from production and to pay farmers *not* to produce, have yielded such a staggering excess of crops that the American taxpayer in 1962 is paying out more than one billion dollars a year as the total carrying cost of the surplus-food storage program. And is the situation helped when one branch of the Agriculture Department tries to reduce production while another states, as it did in 1958, "It is believed generally that reduction of crop acreages under provisions of the Soil Bank will stimulate interest in use of chemicals to obtain maximum production on the land retained in crops"?

All this is not to say there is no insect problem and no need of control. I am saying, rather, that control must be geared to realities, not to mythical situations, and that the methods employed must be such that they do not destroy us along with the insects.

The problem whose attempted solution has brought such a train of disaster in its wake is an accompaniment of our modern way of life. Long before the age of man, insects inhabited the earth—a group of extraordinarily varied and adaptable beings. Over the course of time since man's advent, a small percentage of the more than half a million species of insects have come into conflict with human welfare in two principal ways: as competitors for the food supply and as carriers of human disease.

Disease-carrying insects become important where human beings are crowded together, especially under conditions where sanitation is poor, as in times of natural disaster or war or in situations of extreme poverty and deprivation. Then control of some sort becomes necessary. It is a sobering fact, however, as we shall presently see, that the method of massive chemical control has had only limited success, and also threatens to worsen the very conditions it is intended to curb.

Under primitive agricultural conditions the farmer had few insect problems. These arose with the intensification of agriculture—the devotion of immense acreages to a single crop. Such a system set the stage for explosive increases in specific insect populations. Single-crop farming does not take advantage of the principles by which nature works; it is agriculture as an engineer might conceive it to be. Nature has introduced great variety into the landscape, but man has displayed a passion for simplifying it. Thus he undoes the built-in checks and balances by which nature holds the species within bounds. One important natural check is a limit on the amount of suitable habitat for each species. Obviously then, an insect that lives on wheat can build up its population to much higher levels on a farm devoted to wheat than on one in which wheat is intermingled with other crops to which the insect is not adapted.

The same thing happens in other situations. A generation or more ago, the towns of large areas of the United States lined their streets with the noble elm tree. Now the beauty they hopefully created is threatened with complete destruction as disease sweeps through the elms, carried by a beetle that would have only limited chance to build up large populations and to spread from tree to tree if the elms were only occasional trees in a richly diversified planting.   15

Another factor in the modern insect problem is one that must be viewed against a background of geologic and human history: the spreading of thousands of different kinds of organisms from their native homes to invade new territories. This worldwide migration has been studied and graphically described by the British ecologist Charles Elton in his recent book *The Ecology of Invasions.* During the Cretaceous Period, some hundred million years ago, flooding seas cut many land bridges between continents and living things found themselves confined in what Elton calls "colossal separate nature reserves." There, isolated from others of their kind, they developed many new species. When some of the land masses were joined again, about fifteen million years ago, these species began to move out into new territories—a movement that is not only still in progress but is now receiving considerable assistance from man.

The importation of plants is the primary agent in the modern spread of species, for animals have almost invariably gone along with the plants, quarantine being a comparatively recent and not completely effective innovation. The United States Office of Plant Introduction alone has introduced almost 200,000 species and varieties of plants from all over the world. Nearly half of the 180 or so major insect enemies of plants in the United States are accidental imports from abroad, and most of them have come as hitchhikers on plants.

In new territory, out of reach of the restraining hand of the natural enemies that kept down its numbers in its native land, an invading plant or animal is able to become enormously abundant. Thus it is no accident that our most troublesome insects are introduced species.

These invasions, both the naturally occurring and those dependent on human assistance, are likely to continue indefinitely.

Quarantine and massive chemical campaigns are only extremely expensive ways of buying time. We are faced, according to Dr. Elton, "with a life-and-death need not just to find new technological means of suppressing this plant or that animal"; instead we need the basic knowledge of animal populations and their relations to their surroundings that will "promote an even balance and damp down the explosive power of outbreaks and new invasions."

Much of the necessary knowledge is now available but we do   20
not use it. We train ecologists in our universities and even employ them in our governmental agencies but we seldom take their advice. We allow the chemical death rain to fall as though there were no alternative, whereas in fact there are many, and our ingenuity could soon discover many more if given opportunity.

Have we fallen into a mesmerized state that makes us accept as inevitable that which is inferior or detrimental, as though having lost the will or the vision to demand that which is good? Such thinking, in the words of the ecologist Paul Shepard, "idealizes life with only its head out of water, inches above the limits of toleration of the corruption of its own environment . . . Why should we tolerate a diet of weak poisons, a home in insipid surroundings, a circle of acquaintances who are not quite our enemies, the noise of motors with just enough relief to prevent insanity? Who would want to live in a world which is just not quite fatal?"

Yet such a world is pressed upon us. The crusade to create a chemically sterile, insect-free world seems to have engendered a fanatic zeal on the part of many specialists and most of the so-called control agencies. On every hand there is evidence that those engaged in spraying operations exercise a ruthless power. "The regulatory entomologists . . . function as prosecutor, judge and jury, tax assessor and collector, and sheriff to enforce their own orders," said Connecticut entomologist Neely Turner. The most flagrant abuses go unchecked in both state and federal agencies.

It is not my contention that chemical insecticides must never be used. I do contend that we have put poisonous and biologically potent chemicals indiscriminately into the hands of persons largely or wholly ignorant of their potentials for harm. We have subjected enormous numbers of people to contact with these poisons, without their consent and often without their knowledge. If the Bill of Rights contains no guarantee that a citizen shall be secure against lethal poisons distributed either by private individuals or by public officials, it is surely only because our forefathers, despite their considerable wisdom and foresight, could conceive of no such problem.

I contend, furthermore, that we have allowed these chemicals to be used with little or no advance investigation of their effect on soil, water, wildlife, and man himself. Future generations are unlikely to condone our lack of prudent concern for the integrity of the natural world that supports all life.

There is still very limited awareness of the nature of the threat. This is an era of specialists, each of whom sees his own problem and is unaware of or intolerant of the larger frame into which it fits. It is also an era dominated by industry, in which the right to make a dollar at whatever cost is seldom challenged. When the public protests, confronted with some obvious evidence of damaging results of pesticide applications, it is fed little tranquilizing pills of half truth. We urgently need an end to these false assurances, to the sugar coating of unpalatable facts. It is the public that is being asked to assume the risks that the insect controllers calculate. The public must decide whether it wishes to continue on the present road, and it can do so only when in full possession of the facts. In the words of Jean Rostand, "The obligation to endure gives us the right to know."

QUESTIONS FOR DISCUSSION AND WRITING

1. Carson is a scientist whose work has been widely read by educated generalists. Analyze the essay's stance, tone, and style with regard to the ways in which Carson makes her topic accessible to nonscientists. Include in your assessment the level of language and the choice of metaphor and sentence structure.

2. What is Carson's main argument? How does she support it? How does she respond to possible objections—for example, opponents who might suggest she wants to ban all pesticides and who would argue that she is unrealistic?

3. How does Carson's example of suburban elm trees and Dutch elm disease help connect her key points to a wide range of readers? Are there readers she might reach with that example who would be unmoved by concerns about agriculture?

4. Research Carson's other books and articles and note the reception her work received at the time it was published. You could also consider focusing on changes in policy or practice that resulted directly or indirectly from her research and publications.

The Ugly Guzzlers

DERRICK Z. JACKSON

Derrick Z. Jackson was born in Milwaukee, Wisconsin, and graduated from the University of Wisconsin at Milwaukee; he holds honorary degrees from the Episcopal Divinity School in Cambridge, Massachusetts, and from Salem State College in Salem, MA. He was a Nieman Fellow in Journalism at Harvard University and has been a *Boston Globe* columnist since 1988. In addition to being a 2001 finalist for the Pulitzer Prize for commentary, he has received numerous honors including awards for commentary from the National Association of Black Journalists and the New England Division of the American Cancer Society, the Columbia University Meyer Berger Award for coverage of New York City, and a human rights award from Curry College in Milton, MA. The essay that follows was published in July 2001.

Europe's latest stereotype of the ugly American is the lazy fat guy mowing down the trees in his personal Sherman tank. It is the paranoid ninety-pound woman whose forehead barely crests over the steering wheel of her three-ton cocoon. We are the nation of insufferable whiners about our subsidized price of petrol.

"You Americans and your giant cars," a British hiker said to us at a Swiss alpine hut. "Why do you need those things?"

"Your cars are monstrous," said a German telecommunications businessman on a train out of Frankfurt. "It's unbelievable that anyone would need a car the size you drive."

"Doesn't anyone care about the environment back in the States?" asked one of our hosts in rural northern Germany.

President Bush was held in particular scorn by nearly every 5 European we met on a recent vacation to Switzerland and Germany. His pulling out of the Kyoto accords on global warming was viewed as an arrogant declaration of who owns the White House. As the British hiker put it, "You are the United States of Oil."

The sneer we show to the world on the environment is sure to worsen before it gets better. Last month a US Department of Transportation report found that sport utility vehicles (SUVs), minivans, and pickup trucks now account for 51 percent of new vehicle sales. The report also found that those vehicles, classified as light-duty trucks, now account for more miles driven on American roads than do passenger cars.

The effects of these gas guzzlers are becoming as choking as a sheet of smog. Preliminary federal figures released last month found that in the last three years, carbon dixoide emissions from transportation have for the first time surpassed the CO_2 emissions from industrial sources. Carbon dioxide emissions are a leading contributor to global warming.

In greater Washington, DC, the percentage of SUVs has grown from 15 percent of personal vehicles to 25 percent in the last five years. The spewing of emissions from these cars that get less than twenty miles a gallon will likely force the region over its acceptable limits for air pollution. If the region goes over the limit, it cannot initiate new road and bridge projects.

Just as the size of the American house has grown even as the size of the American family has shrunk, the size of our cars has mushroomed without an excusable rationale. Detroit keeps telling us we need sport utility vehicles to roar over mountains and plow through lakes. The dream of leaving one's tire tracks on rugged landscapes has allowed automakers to charge on average 58 percent more for SUVs than for passenger cars.

But in the report from the Department of Transportation, authors Kara Maria Kockelman and Yong Zhao of the University of Texas found that sport utility vehicles are used no more than passenger cars for recreational purposes.

Years ago, the auto lobby succeeded in avoiding miles-per-gallon standards on SUVs, minivans, and pickup trucks by having them classified as cargo vehicles. But the authors of the Department of Transportation report found "no strong indication that minivans and SUV's are used as 'work' vehicles." They even found that "pickups are more popular among households than they were twenty years ago when American life was less urban, so it is not clear that pickups are performing unusual services either."

It is clear what unusual damage the giant American car is doing. The Europeans we met were quick to say they were not perfect, with a highly publicized debate this spring in northern Germany over nuclear waste. What they could not understand was the extent of America's ignorance, denial, or selfishness about a problem we could easily work on by raising fuel standards.

We are only 6 percent of the world's population, but we produce about a quarter of the world's greenhouse gases. This week, it was reported that a panel appointed by the National Academy of Sciences says that fuel efficiency can be increased. But, fitting of a panel backed by Bush, the report set no specific goals. The panel included no environmentalists, only engineers and consultants tied to the oil and auto industries.

That does not inspire much hope of a serious raising of standards. It will surely inspire more shaking of heads from our European friends. In their minds American men are going to grow fatter and women even more tiny as our cars grow from tanks into aircraft carriers. Americans seem incapable of looking themselves in the mirror and declaring how ugly they are.

QUESTIONS FOR DISCUSSION AND WRITING

1. The essay's introduction references the "ugly American" stereotype. Are you familiar with it? If so, to what is the term a reference? If not, how do you interpret the phrase?

2. How do you respond to the specific comments from Europeans, particularly the "you Americans" lead-in?

3. The author cites specific evidence—examples, facts, figures—to support the view that Americans' apparent contempt for the environment, symbolized by large cars, is causing problems on a global scale. How convincing is his evidence? Does the author's stance affect your receptivity to this evidence?

4. Write a response to the author, either agreeing with his view but offering other supporting arguments or refuting his essay and making your own point that driving SUVs and other large vehicles in suburban or urban settings is appropriate.

The Next Step for U.S. Climate Change Policy

WARWICK MCKIBBIN

Warwick McKibbin is professor of economics at the Australian National University and has published widely in professional journals as well as in popular periodicals. In addition to degrees from Australian universities, he holds a Ph.D. from Harvard University and is a nonresident senior fellow at the Brookings Institution.

PETER WILCOXEN

Peter Wilcoxen is an associate professor of economics at the University of Texas at Austin, as well as a nonresident fellow in economic studies at the Brookings Institution. The essay that follows, in addition to being published by the Brookings Institution, was included in *The Best American Political Writing 2002*.

During the recent European summit, President Bush faced criticism from his European counterparts, from protestors and from much of the world media for his stance on rejecting the Kyoto Protocol. Why is there almost universal criticism despite the fact that the Bush administration has done the world a favor by abandoning the Kyoto Protocol? The approach of fixed targets and timetables for emissions reduction at an unknown economic cost is an infeasible and undesirable approach to climate change. The Protocol never had any chance of ratification. The reason for the outcry is that rather than put in place a better alternative to Kyoto, the Bush administration has so far left a vacuum in place of a climate change response. If the administration moves quickly to put a more realistic policy on the table, then the focus of the global reaction can be shifted from outrage to reasoned debate. Abandoning the Kyoto Protocol could be the most important and positive environmental legacy of the Bush administration. The European summit was the first opportunity to act, but it was lost. The next opportunity is at the COP6(II) negotiations to be held in Bonn in July.

Being realistic means discarding a couple of notions cherished by the ideologically pure at either end of the political spectrum. The first thing to go should be the claim that climate change is not a problem. It is quite clear that human activity is raising global concentrations of carbon dioxide. While climatologists disagree about how much warming will occur and when it will happen, virtually no one seriously suggests that we can emit as much carbon dioxide as we want into the atmosphere without any adverse consequences.

The second notion to go should be the one at the other end of the spectrum: The idea that climate change is such an overwhelming problem that it must be stopped no matter what the cost. Frankly, too little is known about the damages caused by climate change and the costs of reducing emissions to draw this conclusion. To pretend that climate policy doesn't need to take costs into consideration is to guarantee that any climate change treaty will be rejected by the US Senate as well as by many other governments.

A good way to think about the climate change problem is by analogy to driving in the rain. Both involve risk: Rain increases the chance of being involved in a serious accident and carbon dioxide emissions increase the chance of a serious climate problem. The right response to risks like these is prudence: When it is raining, people drive more carefully and avoid unnecessary trips. Likewise, in the face of a potential climate problem, a sensible thing to do would be to slow the growth of carbon dioxide emissions. In neither case is it practical to escape the risk entirely. Few people would be in favor of a law prohibiting driving in the rain under any circumstances. Similarly, few people would be willing to accept sharp reductions in fossil fuel use today simply because it might cause a problem sometime in the future.

After tossing the ideological baggage overboard, what might prudent and realistic governments do about climate change? The answer is to look for a global warming policy with three key features. First, the policy should slow down carbon dioxide emissions where it is cost-effective to do so. Second, the policy should involve some mechanism for compensating those who will be hurt economically. Third, since climate change is a global problem, any solution will require a high degree of consensus both domestically and internationally. However, consensus is the operative word; it is not realistic to think that a rigid global regulatory regime for greenhouse policy can ever be implemented. Few countries want to relinquish sovereignty over setting their own policies, especially when the policies in question can have large economic effects.

We have set out such a policy in a recent Brookings Policy Brief. Our proposed permit trading system is much like the one now used to control sulphur emissions. The main difference would be that the market would include a mechanism that would prevent the price of a permit from exceeding a specified threshold. The threshold price would be set for ten years at a time. Thus emissions would be allowed to vary over time and not be fixed as under the Kyoto Protocol. There are mechanisms in the detailed proposal that allow medium term targets and a market to price these. The permits would be given freely to each citizen and to existing emitters to grandfather emissions. These would be tradable in an open market. Any additional permits that would be required to keep the price from exceeding the threshold would be sold by the government in that year. By raising the price of carbon, the net effect of the policy would be to discourage increases in emissions, and to encourage reductions where they are cost-effective, but without levying a sudden multi-billion dollar burden on fuel users. This would be a significant, realistic step toward controlling climate change.

A key feature of the policy is that it is flexible. The permit price could be adjusted as needed when better information becomes available on the seriousness of climate change and the cost of reducing emissions.

As a unilateral policy this is feasible. Success would encourage other countries to join a more coordinated system. A country could join a multilateral system by adopting the policy domestically and no international negotiations would be required. If the same permit price were chosen in all countries, the system would reach a very efficient and low-cost outcome — very similar to that from a global permit trading system but without the problems associated with international permit trading. Flexibility is crucial because it is clear from current negotiations that only a small subset of countries would agree to be initial participants in a climate change treaty.

It is time for the Bush administration to offer realistic alternatives to the Kyoto Protocol. The debate must move away from ideological battles over impractical goals and un-implementable policies to a discussion of policies that could be concrete but cost-effective steps to slow the growth of carbon dioxide emissions.

QUESTIONS FOR DISCUSSION AND WRITING

1. Summarize the authors' proposed alternative to the Kyoto Protocol. What reasons and evidence do they offer to support their proposal?

2. Where in the political/ideological spectrum do the authors locate themselves and their position? Do the authors seem credible and authoritative? Do you accept their premises and evidence as given or do you want more evidence to be convinced of their view?

3. In what ways do the authors see the issue of climate change as global and international? How does this view factor into their proposal?

4. Research climate change from a perspective that interests you: ecological, political, economic, or some other disciplinary approach. Consider writing both a documented research paper and a position paper or brief commentary on your topic for a campus or local newspaper or other public forum.

U.S. Forest Conservation May Increase Deforestation Elsewhere

PAM MAYFIELD

Pam Mayfield wrote the following report as a student intern in the Office of University Communications at Ohio State University in May 1999. The research she summarizes here was originally published in the *American Journal of Agricultural Economics* by Brent Sohngen, assistant professor of agricultural, environmental, and development economics at Ohio State University; Robert Mendelsohn, a professor of forestry at Yale University; and Roger Sedjo, a senior fellow at Resources for the Future in Washington, DC.

A new study examining the future of world timber markets suggests that forest conservation efforts in North America and Europe could lead to increased deforestation in threatened tropical forests. The study predicts the loss of one hectare (2.47 acres) of previously inaccessible forest in Asia, South America, Africa, and the former Soviet Union for every twenty hectares set aside and protected in North America and Europe. In short, the forests saved in Europe and America are replaced by the felling of trees elsewhere.

"A small amount of forest conservation here can have negative worldwide effects," said Brent Sohngen, co-author of the study and assistant professor of agricultural, environmental, and development economics at Ohio State University.

For the most part, foresters ignore timber supplies available in many of the world's tropical forests because these areas are expensive to harvest at current prices. However, Sohngen's models predict this situation could change if forest conservation in North America and Europe raises world prices. "North America currently produces 35 percent of global timber. Conserving only 5 to 10 percent of timberland in a region that supplies such a large proportion of global harvests will increase harvests elsewhere, including tropical forests that presently are inaccessible."

Many scientists are concerned about the possible ecological implications of the decline of tropical forests: The loss of biodiversity and undiscovered species, increased soil erosion, and the reduction of plants that remove CO_2 from the atmosphere. The United Nations Food and Agriculture Organization points out that as of 1990, the tropics contained 60 percent of the world's inaccessible forests—over 800 million hectares, nearly twice the area of the state of Texas.

Sohngen conducted the study with Robert Mendelsohn, a professor of forestry at Yale University, and Roger Sedjo, a senior fellow at Resources for the Future in Washington, DC. The results were published in a recent issue of the *American Journal of Agricultural Economics.* The researchers developed a variety of models that examined how worldwide demand for timber might affect the conservation of forests across the globe between 1995 and 2135. They examined both current and predicted global timber supply, demand, prices, and harvest costs. Their analyses accounted for supply and harvest differences across several geographic regions and compared regeneration and forest development costs.

Part of the researchers' model examined two possible scenarios. The first assumes that 5 percent of North American and European forests will be preserved and the second suggests 10 percent of these forests will be saved.

Both scenarios predict that these set-asides would increase worldwide timber prices by 1 to 2 percent, while increasing timber harvests in other parts of the world by 1 percent. In the 5 percent scenario, the model predicts 1.4 million hectares of previously economically inaccessible forests are harvested elsewhere, and in the 10 percent case, an additional 2 million hectares of inaccessible forests are harvested elsewhere. These additional timber harvests would likely occur in tropical areas, Sohngen said.

Sohngen said simple economics helps explain why forest conservation in North America and Europe may increase deforestation in the tropics and elsewhere. "As supply decreases through increased conservation efforts in North America, timber prices will rise, making it economically feasible to harvest trees from areas where it was previously too expensive," he said.

However, Sohngen said that the same economics that create this predicament could also play a role in solving it. Increased tropical harvests require expansion into areas of forest that have never been cut before. This demands the construction of roads and the transportation of equipment and labor into remote places. These outlays would be quite costly. However, harvesting in already developed forests throughout the world eliminates these construction costs, resulting in higher profits. This increased profit margin acts as an incentive for better management of these areas.

Sohngen pointed out, however, that government tax breaks and subsidies for timber companies often work against sound management of forest lands. Many federal governments, including that of the United States, pay for new road construction to make forests accessible. Relieving timber companies of the construction expenses enables them to harvest affordably in previously inaccessible areas.

The model shows that these access costs play a critical role in the amount of inaccessible tropical forests that are lost to timber harvesting. Low access costs predict a loss of 150 million hectares over the next fifty to seventy-five years, while high access costs lower that figure to 50 million hectares. Although none of their scenarios predicts the elimination of timber harvests in the world's tropical forests, Sohngen said he believes most of the increase in timber production will come from second- and third-growth forests and from tree plantations planted specifically for timber. In the tropics, these plantations have primarily been developed on degraded agricultural land.

Sohngen noted that their predictions only apply to forest loss due to timber harvesting, which the model suggests plays only a minor role in tropical deforestation. "Other local factors not considered by this model—such as increasing development of agriculture—may still pose a threat."

QUESTIONS FOR DISCUSSION AND WRITING

1. This selection is a report furnished by the communication office of the university where one of the researchers is on the faculty. What is the rhetorical situation? For what audience or audiences is this article intended? What is the role of a university in publicizing the research of its faculty? How do you think this selection differs from the researchers' publication of their work in an academic journal?

2. What is the central point of this article? What are the most significant findings reported? Do you find the researchers' conclusions surprising or counterintuitive? Do you find the explanation for these findings well reasoned?

3. What are the implications for global environmental issues if these findings are supported in future studies? In the larger context, what factors besides timber harvesting may play a role in deforestation?

4. Find the original research in the academic journal where it was first published, and write an essay analyzing the differences between the essay for specialists in the journal and the article for generalists included here. Consider documentation of sources, structure of the article, specialized versus general language, assumptions about the readers' knowledge, and other aspects of writing.

5. Research deforestation from an international perspective, or focus on deforestation and sustainable growth methods in one particular region or country.

Deforestation

NASA

The National Aeronautics and Space Administration (NASA) is a civilian agency of the US federal government with the mission of conducting research and developing operational programs in the areas of space, artificial satellites, and rocketry. NASA came into existence on October 1, 1958, superseding the previously established National Advisory Committee on Aeronautics (NACA), an agency that had been oriented primarily toward laboratory research. The creation of NASA was spurred by American lack of preparedness when the Soviet Union launched the first artificial satellite, Sputnik, on October 4, 1957. The images included here, and other satellite images of Earth, can be accessed from the NASA Web site in the section called Visible Earth, which is a searchable directory of images at *http.//visibleearth.nasa.gov/*. (Please see color images on pages C–5 and C–6 of the inserts.)

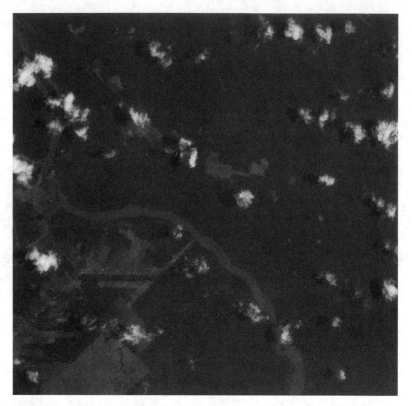

HIGH-RESOLUTION VIEW OF DEFORESTATION IN AMAZONIA

Throughout history, patterns of settlement have followed roads, rivers, and other lines of transportation. The frontiers of the twenty-first century are no exception. This high-resolution image of Amazonia shows farms cleared from the jungle spreading out on either side of a narrow dirt road. Above and to the right of the river that bisects the image is almost unbroken forest. The river, a tributary of the Amazon, is colored brown by the large amount of sediment it carries, possibly the result of deforestation upstream.

The image was acquired for the *Large Scale Biosphere-Atmosphere Experiment in Amazonia (LBA)* by the IKONOS satellite, which is owned and operated by Space Imaging Corporation. Centered near 10° south, 62° West, the image has a resolution of about eight meters per pixel, reduced from IKONOS' four-meter maximum color resolution. The LBA is an intensive field campaign in which scientists are studying the environment of Amazonia, the role of Amazonia in global climate, and the effects of human-caused change in the region.

(ROBERT SIMMON/NASA)

DEFORESTATION IN BRAZIL

This image shows the extent of deforestation in the state of Rondonia, Brazil. Acquired by the Advance Spaceborne Thermal Emission and Reflection Radiometer (ASTER) on August 24, 2000, the false-color image combines near-infrared, red, and green light. Tropical rainforest appears bright red, while pale red and brown areas represent cleared land. Black and gray areas have probably been recently burned. The Jiparana River appears blue.

With a maximum spatial resolution of fifteen meters, ASTER does not produce imagery as detailed as the IKONOS satellite, which has a maximum resolution of one meter. Compare this image with IKONOS data from the same area. The somewhat lower resolution ASTER data is not as detailed, but provides a better overview, and ASTER can acquire data over a particular region more often than IKONOS. (NASA/GODDARD SPACE FLIGHT CENTER)

QUESTIONS FOR DISCUSSION AND WRITING

1. Study each image, making sure to study the color versions in the color plate section. What is your impression of the extent and process of deforestation? Do you respond similarly to each image? If not, what accounts for your different impressions?

2. Compare and contrast the presentation of each approach to documenting deforestation. Which image would you use if you wanted to convey the beauty of the Amazon? Which would you use if you wanted to raise the alarm about deforestation?

3. Discuss the argument each image makes and the image the two make when presented together.

Chapter Six: Connections

1. What parallels do you draw between global health issues, as articulated in "A Plane Ride Away," and global political and economic issues?

2. What are the implications of America's "gas guzzling" cars beyond the perception of other societies regarding American attitudes?

3. Research Web sites and other images of the Amazon and other areas where deforestation is a concern. How do point of view and method of visual documentation affect your response to the images? Are they consistent or divergent?

4. Compare approaches to the problems of deforestation and climate change policy as discussed in this chapter.

5. Consider the concerns raised in this chapter in view of globalization, discussed in Chapter Four.

6. Consider some of the values and beliefs presented in the Appendix. What values, for good or for ill, may be driving contemporary health and environment issues?

Chapter Six: End-of-Chapter Assignments

1. Based on your own research or as a group project for your class, develop a PowerPoint presentation or Web site to inform others, such as campus or community groups or local schools, about an environmental or health issue of concern locally or globally.

2. Research the Kyoto agreement—its drawbacks and benefits—and related legislation designed to address air pollution and emissions.
3. Research hybrid vehicles, solar energy, or other alternative energy sources. What are the obstacles to successful development and implementation? Which are available now but underutilized?
4. Investigate political aspects of oil production and policy, such as worldwide boycotts, wilderness drilling, or military interventions.
5. Research pharmaceutical companies' provisions for catastrophe in arranging stockpiles of valuable medicines (i.e., antibiotics, insulin, vaccines). Alternatively, research drug company funding of medical research, particularly of the AIDS vaccine and treatment.
6. Research the current status of public health or defense policy with regard to the threat of bioterrorism or infectious diseases. You could focus on specific concerns, such as smallpox, bubonic plague, or anthrax, or on more esoteric illnesses and vaccine development.
7. Research models of successfully managed growth or resource management, tree farming, and the like. Consider controversial policies such as allowing fires to burn out in national and state parks such as Yosemite National Park.
8. Compare and contrast Web sites from different perspectives such as World Trade Organization and Amazonia. Suggestions are included at the end of this chapter and in previous chapters.

Chapter Six: Web Sites for Further Exploration

World Health Organization
http://www.who.int/en/
International Committee of the Red Cross
http://www.icrc.org/
International Federation of Red Cross and Red Crescent Societies
http://www.ifrc.org/
Doctors Without Borders
http://www.doctorswithoutborders.org/
National Institute of Health (US)
http://www.nih.gov/
Institut Pasteur
http://www.pasteur.fr/english.html
Contradictions of the Enlightenment: Darwin, Freud, Einstein, and Modern Art (includes interesting readings on medicine and early papers on medical discoveries)
http://www.fordham.edu/halsall/mod/modsbook36.html

European Environment Agency
http://www.eea.eu.int/
National Council for Science and the Environment
http://www.NCSEonline.org/
Amazon Forest
http://www.amazonia.org/
The Green Lane (Canada)
http://www.ec.gc.ca/
Earth Observatory, NASA site (images and texts)
http://earthobservatory.nasa.gov/
Rachel Carson
http://www.rachelcarson.org/
Environmental News Network
http://www.enn.com/news/
http://www.enn.com/aboutenn/

7

CONFLICT: IMAGES
OF THE OTHER

INTRODUCTION

Author Sam Keen writes, "In all propaganda, the face of the enemy is designed to provide a focus for most of our hatred. He is the other. The outsider. The alien. He is not human. If we can only kill him, we will be rid of all within and without ourselves that is evil." Before we make war, Keen has noted, we make an idea of the enemy.

In this chapter we examine a number of ways in which we develop an image of the other, and the other develops an image of us. As Keen further notes, there are universal images or archetypes, ways of imagining and defining the other that transcend culture, time, and place. These images become concrete in a range of media that cross the disciplines of history, psychology, philosophy, myth, literature, and visual rhetoric.

People are drawn to concrete images that provide clarity and certitude rather than ambiguity. Political psychologists have noted that in wartime, when sides are well defined, mental health improves and suicide rates go down. As a political cartoonist states, it is simply easier to take a side. In times of war and conflict, we tend to dichotomize, or divide the world into good and evil, us and them, friend and foe. We then endow the enemy we have identified with qualities of evil and depravity. In American history that role has been fulfilled, for the dominant culture, by American Indians, by immigrants and people of color, and by wartime enemies. Americans, too, have been portrayed as the alien and the hostile enemy by other societies, often in ways that are uncomfortable and inflammatory from Americans' perspective.

The texts and images in this chapter include background reading on the process of depicting or creating the enemy and primary sources including a short story, examples of visual propaganda, presidential rhetoric characterizing the enemy, and reflective essays on persistent cultural scapegoating and on the contemporary relationship between former Cold War foes.

We begin with the selection from Sam Keen, "Apparitions of the Hostile Imagination." An archetype is a universal, recurrent type or theme, and the word is apropos here given Keen's psychological approach. The term is both a shorthand process of identifying others and a system that fulfills one's needs to identify with his or her own group.

The process of losing all identification with the other is ironically portrayed in Mark Twain's short story, "The War Prayer." He sets the scene in a town full of patriotic fervor preparing, with a sermon in church as encouragement, to smite their enemies and cause devastation, pain, and death. No one, not even a messenger from God, can help them to cross the psychological divide and empathize with their enemies, although Twain likely hoped the audience of his short story would get his point. The process of developing an image of the other side unfolds in American President Franklin Delano Roosevelt's speech after the attack on Pearl Harbor, a highly formal, but highly connotative speech formally requesting from Congress a declaration of war. Although subtle in its approach, this speech nevertheless initiated a process of developing an identification of the enemy that became pervasive for the duration of World War II.

Other examples of war rhetoric, in a different medium, follow the Roosevelt address. A propaganda poster from World War II provides a prime example of dehumanizing and stereotyping the enemy. In "DANGER!," images of both German and Japanese enemies confront us. Americans have also been the object of concern in visual rhetoric. In addition to extreme representations common in war-era propaganda materials, more mundane characterizations follow, as depicted in the nineteenth-century woodcut of a carousing America. We then turn from images of the enemy to an article appearing in Online *Pravda* that asks whether old enemies, Russians and Americans, are now friends or enemies. After decades of the Cold War and nuclear brinksmanship, that the question is even asked today indicates a remarkable shift in the post-Cold War world.

Themes from Keen and other readings in this chapter, such as hostile projection and stereotyping, inform the following selection by *Newsweek's* Mortimer Zuckerman. In "A Shameful Contagion," Zuckerman analyzes the most recent iteration of anti-Semitism to surface in Europe, the image of the Jews and Israel as the enemy. As Zuckerman argues, "Fascism came and went; Communism came and went; anti-Semitism came and stayed."

Following 9/11 and the war in Afghanistan, remarkably disturbing texts and images have surfaced, and a postcard from the Afghanistan/Pakistan border region, obtained in early 2002, provides one example—a startling image of a child, with Osama bin Laden as his inspiration, taking up arms against a formidable enemy. Echoing a mechanistic view of American forces, this postcard represents the enemy not as human beings but as a rain of machinery and ordnance assaulting their small but determined foes. As troubling as this image may be, we are unlikely to expect that it echoes scenes from American history, but the next selection, a photograph of a very young Civil War soldier, shifts our perspective of the postcard and provides a different context for us to consider.

Visual imagery can serve a need to create solidarity among one's own group as well as to reinforce negative stereotypes of the enemy, both processes common in political murals. The tradition of political murals goes back many years in Northern Ireland; initially more the preserve of Protestant loyalists, Irish Republicans and nationalists have also expressed their political views of themselves and the other side through murals, particularly in Belfast. The selections here represent different points of view and different stages in the conflict. Mural subjects include depictions of paramilitary groups, a Catholic view of the Orange Order Protestant group and the police's role in enforcing their rights to march, and an assessment of prospects for peace following the 1998 Good Friday Accords that lay the groundwork for peace. We close the chapter with an essay reporting on efforts toward conflict resolution in Northern Ireland, "Living with Terrorism: Northern Ireland Shares Lessons," by journalist Kathleen LaCamera. Describing a process of reflection, one minister notes, "It takes a long time to engage with critical reflection—and some are happier with the old stereotypes." He and others describe a process of working one-on-one, building relationships, and building bridges.

As you read and view these selections, consider how they make their arguments and what viewpoints they represent. Consider also how you might use these selections as a starting point to think critically and write reflectively as you continue to view important issues from alternative perspectives and develop your own informed viewpoints. Finally, consider using the Web sites provided in this book and on its companion Web site to extend your knowledge, develop tools for research, and enhance your critical thinking.

Apparitions of the Hostile Imagination

SAM KEEN

Sam Keen was born in 1931 and educated at Ursinus College (BA), Harvard Divinity School (S.T.B. and Th. M), and Princeton University (M.A. and Ph.D.). He has been a professor of philosophy and religion at a number of institutions and has been a contributing editor of *Psychology Today*. More recently he has worked as a lecturer, seminar leader, and consultant. Exploring philosophical, religious, and psychological topics, Keen is the author of numerous books, including *Apology for Wonder* (1969), *The Passionate Life: Stages of Loving* (1983), *Fire in the Belly: On Being a Man* (1991), and *Learning to Fly: Trapeze—Reflections on Fear, Trust, and the Joy of Letting Go* (1999); he also co-produced an award-winning PBS documentary, *Faces of the Enemy* (1987). His work was the subject of a PBS special by Bill Moyers. Keen, who currently lives in northern California, writes on his Web site that "The practice of philosophy is a way of life that results from falling in love with questions—the great mythic questions that can never be given definitive answers." The selection below is from his book *Faces of the Enemy: Reflections of the Hostile Imagination* (1986).

Look carefully at the face of the enemy. The lips are curled downward. The eyes are fanatical and far away. The flesh is contorted and molded into the shape of monster or beast. Nothing suggests this man ever laughs, is torn by doubts, or shaken by tears. He feels no tenderness or pain. Clearly he is unlike us. We need have no sympathy, no guilt, when we destroy him.

In all propaganda, the face of the enemy is designed to provide a focus for our hatred. He is the other. The outsider. The alien. He is not human. If we can only kill him, we will be rid of all within and without ourselves that is evil.

How are these faces of the enemy created? And why is the repertoire of images so universal?

No one knows for certain when warfare became an abiding human habit. Some archaeologists believe there was a pre-Neolithic Eden peopled by peaceful hunters and gatherers, and that greed and systematic violence arose only when the agricultural revolution created sufficient surplus wealth to tempt some men to steal what others had produced. The best evidence we have suggests that warfare is no more than 13,000 years old. According to Sue Mansfield, our earliest human artifacts from the Paleolithic period testify to hunting, art, myth, and ritual, but give no pictures of men engaged in battle[1]

Once invented, warfare became a nearly universal practice. But there are enough exceptions to establish the crucial point on which hope rests its delicate case: Enemy making and warfare are social creations rather than biological imperatives. The peaceful peoples, such as the Hopi, the Tasaday, the Mbuti Pygmies, the K'ung! Bushmen of the Kalahari, the Copper Eskimo, the Amish, and others, show us that human beings are capable of creating sophisticated cultures without the use of systematic violence, without a warrior class and a psyche organized around defending the tribe against an enemy. According to Geoffrey Gorer,

> The most significant common traits in these peaceful societies are that they all manifest enormous gusto for concrete physical pleasures—eating, drinking, sex, laughter—and that they all make very little distinction between the ideal characters of men and women, particularly that they have no ideal of brave, aggressive masculinity. . . . They do not have heroes or martyrs to emulate or cowards or traitors to despise; their religious life lacks significant personalized gods and devils; a happy, hard-working and productive life is within the reach of all.[2]

The parable of the gentle tribes teaches us that there is nothing in our genes or in the essential human condition that makes warfare an inevitable human destiny. Moreover, says Ashley Montagu,

> Throughout the two million years of man's evolution the highest premium has been placed on cooperation, not merely intragroup cooperation, but also intergroup cooperation, or else there would be no human beings today.[3]

For the moment, let us note this thread of hope as we turn to the study of the more common human condition of consensual paranoia and the world created by the hostile imagination. In times past and present (and, we hope, future), there have existed people governed more by the spirit of Eros than the dark hand of Thanatos.

Sadly, the majority of tribes and nations create a sense of social solidarity and membership in part by systematically creating enemies. The corporate identity of most peoples depends on dividing the world into a basic antagonism:

Us	versus	Them
Insiders	versus	Outsiders
The tribe	versus	The enemy

In other words, paranoia, far from being an occasional individual pathology, is the normal human condition. It is considered both normal and admirable, the essence of tribal loyalty and patriotism, to direct vitriolic hatred toward strangers we hardly know and to reserve love for those familiar to us. The habit of directing our hostility outward toward those who are unknown to us is as characteristic of human beings as our capacity for reason, wonder, or tool making. In fact, it is most often *Homo hostilis* who directs the energies of *Homo sapiens* and *Homo faber.* Our hostility regularly perverts reason into rationalization and propaganda, and makes our creativity serve the forces of destruction by making swords rather than plowshares.

The hostile imagination begins with a simple but crippling   10
assumption: what is strange or unknown is dangerous and intends us evil. The unknown is untrustworthy. The Latin word *hostis* originally meant a stranger, one not connected to us by kin or ties of blood.

Around the basic antagonism between insiders and strangers the tribal mind forms an entire myth of conflict. The mythic mind, which still governs modern politics, is obsessively dualistic. It splits everything into polar opposites. The basic distinction between insiders and outsiders is parlayed into a paranoid ethic and metaphysic in which reality is seen as a morality play, a conflict between

The tribes	versus	The enemy
Good	versus	Evil
The Sacred	versus	The profane

One primary function of this paranoid metaphysic of *Homo hostilis* is to justify the killing of outsiders and to rationalize warfare. Myth, besides telling us who we are, where we came from, and what is our destiny, sanctions the killing of strangers who are considered nonhuman and profane. Myth makes killing or dying in war a sacred act performed in the service of some god or immortal ideal. Thus, the creation of propaganda is as old as the hostile imagination. Truth is the first sacrifice we make in order to belong to any exclusive group.

The object of warfare is to destroy or kill the enemy. But who is this enemy? Almost all works on war refer to the enemy obliquely. A strange silence pervades political, military, and popular thought on this matter. Our reluctance to think clearly about the enemy appears to be an unconscious conspiracy. We systematically blur distinctions and insist that the enemy remain faceless, because we are able to perpetuate the horror of war, to be the authors of unthinkable suffering only when we blind ourselves to what we are doing. Traditionally we have maintained this practice of unthinking by creating dehumanizing stereotypes of the objects of our violence and reserving our rational thought for determining the weapons, strategies, and tactics we will use in destroying "them."

Laurens Van der Post recounts how one mechanism of dehumanization worked in a Japanese prison camp during World War II:

> The Japanese showed a sudden reluctance to meet our eyes in the course of our daily contacts. We knew that they were taking precautions to ensure that not a single glimpse of one's obvious and defenseless humanity should slip through their defenses and contradict the caricature some demoniac *a priori* image had made of us within them. The nearer the storm came the more intense the working of this mechanism became. I had seen its most striking manifestation in the eyes of a Japanese officer who, with a condemned Ambonese soldier before him, had had to lean forward and brush the long black hair from the back of the neck over the head and eyes of the condemned man before he could draw his sword and cut off the man's head. Before the blow fell he had been compelled to look straight ahead over the doomed head seeing neither it nor us who stood, raggedly, in a long line in front of him.[4]

As a rule, human beings do not kill other human beings. Before we enter into warfare or genocide, we first dehumanize those we mean to "eliminate." Before the Japanese performed medical experiments on human guinea pigs in World War II, they named them *maruta*—logs of wood. The hostile imagination systematically destroys our natural tendency to identify with others of our species. *Homo hostilis* cripples imagination by forcing it to serve the limited purposes of hatred and propaganda. A full-bodied imagination would lead us to the recognition that those we are fighting against are like ourselves. They hurt when struck, fear death, love their children, hate going to war, and are filled with feelings of doubt and impotence.

The purpose of propaganda is to paralyze thought, to prevent discrimination, and to condition individuals to act as a mass. The modern warfare state removes the individuality of those who serve it by forcing them into uniform, and systematically destroys the complexities of those against whom it fights. "The" enemy is always singular, a limbolike category, to which we may assign any threat about which we do not wish to think clearly. The paranoid mind wraps the enemy in a fog. When war begins, clarity and charity are exiled for the duration. It is not a person we kill, but an idea. The art of propaganda is to create a portrait that incarnates the idea of what we wish to destroy so we will react rather than think, and automatically focus our free-floating hostility, indistinct frustrations, and unnamed fears. The elements from which the portrait is assembled are standard curses and routine insults that have been in use since the beginning of recorded history.

When Western countries go to war against Asians, they usually portray them as faceless hordes. A US Army film made during World War II characterized Japanese soldiers as "alike as photoprints from the same negative." We have habitually portrayed Asians as so different from ourselves that they place a low value on life. The old image of Genghis Khan and the Mongol hordes still haunts us and is retooled and pressed into service when needed. American forces in Korea found themselves swamped by an "ochre horde," a yellow tide of faceless masses, cruel and nerveless subhumans, the incomprehensible and the inscrutable Chinese, the human sea. Less than a generation later we were to face the same archetypically degraded enemy, now labeled "gooks," "dinks," "slopes," in Vietnam.

Front-line soldiers frequently report that when they come 15
on an enemy dead and examine his personal effects—letters from home, pictures of loved ones—the propaganda image fades and it becomes difficult or impossible to kill again. Who can forget the moving scene in *All Quiet on the Western Front* when the German soldier is forced to spend the night in a foxhole with a Frenchman he has bayoneted?

The enemy is not merely flesh and blood but devil, demon, agent of the dark forces. Nor is warfare, ancient or modern, waged only on the historical field of battle. Behind the scenes of World War II, no less than in the Trojan Wars, competing gods directed the action of mortal warriors.

God and country may be quite separable in theory, but in day-to-day politics and religion they are fused. God sanctifies *our* social order, *our* way of life, *our* values, *our* territory. Thus, warfare is applied theology. Probe the rhetoric used to justify war, and you will find that every war is a "just" war, a crusade, a battle between the forces of good and evil. Warfare is a religio-political ritual in which the sacred blood of our heroes is sacrificed to hallow our ground and to destroy the enemies of God. Battle is the corporate ordeal through which the heroic nation justifies its claim, and refutes its enemies' claim, to be the chosen people of God, the bearers of an historical destiny, the representatives of the sacred.

That there is a seamless joining of religion and politics should be obvious from the way the rhetoric of warfare has been borrowed from theologians. Satan was regularly used by theologians and inquisitors to discredit their opponents. Catholic theologians said Luther's heresy should be dismissed because the voice of the devil was speaking through him. And Luther used the same rhetoric against the rebelling peasants, declaring them to be "the agents of the devil," and their revolt a prelude to the destruction of the world. He states as clearly as any other sacred warrior the terrible self-righteousness of holy war in which carnage becomes a devotion.

The most terrible of all the moral paradoxes, the Gordian knot that must be unraveled if history is to continue, is that we create evil out of our highest ideals and most noble aspirations. We so need to be heroic, to be on the side of God, to eliminate evil, to clean up the world, to be victorious over death, that we visit destruction and death on all who stand in the way of our heroic historical destiny. We scapegoat and create absolute enemies, not because we are intrinsically cruel, but because focusing our anger on an outside target, striking at strangers, brings our tribe or nation together and allows us to be a part of a close and loving in-group. We create surplus evil because we need to belong.

It is within this context that the iconography of political propaganda must be understood. Whatever a society considers bad, wrong, taboo, profane, dirty, desecrated, inhumane, impure, will make up the epithets assigned to the enemy. The enemy will be accused of whatever is forbidden—from sadism to cannibalism. Study the face of the enemy and you will discover the political equivalent of Dante's circles of hell, the geography of evil, the shape of the shadow we deny.

Notes

1. Sue Mansfield, *The Gestalts of War* (New York: Dial Press, 1982).

2. Geoffrey Gorer, "Man Has No Killer Instinct," in Ashley Montagu, ed., *Man and Aggression* (London: Oxford Univ. Press, 1968), 34.

3. Ashley Montagu, "The New Litany of Innate Depravity," in *Man and Aggression,* 15.

4. Laurens Van der Post, *Merry Christmas, Mr. Lawrence* (New York: Quill, 1983), 153.

QUESTIONS FOR DISCUSSION AND WRITING

1. What is the main point of this selection? What are the core assertions? Do you find the reasons and evidence the author gives persuasive? Which support is most effective?

2. Discuss the "basic antagonisms" Keen discusses. Is this categorization supported by the discussion that follows?

3. Keen suggests we believe that "what is strange or unknown is dangerous and intends us evil." Discuss this assertion in view of both Keen's examples and contemporary politics.

4. Keen writes, "God and country may be quite separable in theory, but in day-to-day politics and religion they are fused." Do you agree with this view? Do you think it is true of diverse cultures and societies? Does this assertion explain part of the process of making enemies?

5. Keen argues that the enemy, or the other, is the focus for our hatred. Do you accept a psychological explanation or do you believe this process can be attributed to other factors?

6. Research the nature of propaganda and consider whether Keen's analysis and discussion are supported by other scholars and writers.

The War Prayer

MARK TWAIN

Mark Twain is the pseudonym of Samuel Clemens (1835–1910), one of the most prominent writers in American literature. He was born and raised in Missouri. Twain held numerous jobs—printer, riverboat pilot, gold prospector—before discovering success as a writer with the publication of *The Celebrated Jumping Frog of Calaveras County and Other Sketches* (1867) and *The Innocents Abroad* (1869). Twain established his reputation as a humorist through his classic novels *The Adventures of Tom Sawyer* (1876) *and The Adventures of Huckleberry Finn* (1885); the latter work can still evoke controversy. Twain had long been a critic of American society, but in his later years he grew more pessimistic, as the ironic story that follows, written in 1904–1905, well illustrates.

It was a time of great and exalting excitement. The country was up in arms, the war was on, in every breast burned the holy fire of patriotism; the drums were beating, the bands playing, the toy pistols popping, the bunched firecrackers hissing and spluttering; on every hand and far down the receding and fading spread of roofs and balconies a fluttering wilderness of flags flashed in the sun; daily the young volunteers marched down the wide avenue gay and fine in their new uniforms, the proud fathers and mothers and sisters and sweethearts cheering them with voices choked with happy emotion as they swung by; nightly the packed mass meetings listened, panting, to patriot oratory which stirred the deepest deeps of their hearts, and which they interrupted at briefest intervals with cyclones of applause, the tears running down their cheeks the while; in the churches the pastors preached devotion to flag and country, and invoked the God of Battles, beseeching His aid in our good cause in outpouring of fervid eloquence which moved every listener. It was indeed a glad and gracious time, and the half dozen rash spirits that ventured to disapprove of the war and cast a doubt upon its righteousness straightway got such a stern and angry warning that for their personal safety's sake they quickly shrank out of sight and offended no more in that way.

Sunday morning came—next day the battalions would leave for the front; the church was filled; the volunteers were there, their young faces alight with martial dreams—visions of the stern advance, the gathering momentum, the rushing charge, the flashing sabers, the flight of the foe, the tumult, the enveloping smoke, the fierce pursuit, the surrender—then home from the war, bronzed heroes, welcomed, adored, submerged in golden seas of glory! With the volunteers sat their dear ones, proud, happy, and envied by the neighbors and friends who had no sons and brothers to send forth to the field of honor, there to win for the flag, or, failing, die the noblest of noble deaths. The service proceeded; a war chapter from the Old Testament was read; the first prayer was said; it was followed by an organ burst that shook the building, and with one impulse the house rose, with glowing eyes and beating hearts, and poured out that tremendous invocation—

> "God the all-terrible!   Thou who ordainest,
> Thunder thy clarion and lightning thy sword!"

Then came the "long" prayer. None could remember the like of it for passionate pleading and moving and beautiful language. The burden of its supplication was, that an ever-merciful and benignant Father of us all would watch over our noble young soldiers, and aid, comfort, and encourage them in their patriotic work; bless them, shield them in the day of battle and the hour of peril, bear them in His mighty hand, make them strong and confident, invincible in the bloody onset; help them to crush the foe, grant to them and to their flag and country imperishable honor and glory—

An aged stranger entered and moved with slow and noiseless step up the main aisle, his eyes fixed upon the minister, his long body clothed in a robe that reached to his feet, his head bare, his white hair descending in frothy cataract to his shoulders, his seamy face unnaturally pale, pale even to ghastliness. With all eyes following him and wondering, he made his silent way; without pausing, he ascended to the preacher's side and stood there, waiting. With shut lids the preacher, unconscious of his presence, continued his moving prayer, and at last finished it with the words, uttered in fervent appeal, "Bless our arms, grant us the victory, O Lord our God, Father and Protector of our land and flag!"

The stranger touched his arm, motioned him to step aside—which the startled minister did—and took his place. During some moments he surveyed the spellbound audience with solemn eyes, in which burned an uncanny light; then in a deep voice he said:

"I come from the Throne—bearing a message from Almighty God!" The words smote the house with a shock; if the stranger perceived it he gave no attention. "He has heard the prayer of His servant your shepherd, and will grant it if such shall be your desire after I, His messenger, shall have explained to you its import—that is to say, its full import. For it is like unto many of the prayers of men, in that it asks for more than he who utters it is aware of—except he pause and think.

"God's servant and yours has prayed his prayer. Has he paused and taken thought? Is it one prayer? No, it is two—one uttered, the other not. Both have reached the ear of Him Who heareth all supplications, the spoken and the unspoken. Ponder this—keep it in mind. If you would beseech a blessing upon yourself, beware! lest without intent you invoke a curse upon a neighbor at the same time. If you pray for the blessing of rain upon your crop which needs it, by that act you are possibly praying for a curse upon some neighbor's crop which may not need rain and can be injured by it.

"You have heard your servant's prayer—the uttered part of it. I am commissioned of God to put into words the other part of it—that part which the pastor—and also you in your hearts—fervently prayed silently. And ignorantly and unthinkingly? God grant that it was so! You heard these words: "Grant us the victory, O Lord our God!" That is sufficient. The *whole* of the uttered prayer is compact into those pregnant words. Elaborations were not necessary. When you have prayed for victory you have prayed for many unmentioned results which follow victory—*must* follow it, cannot help but follow it. Upon the listening spirit of God the Father fell also the unspoken part of the prayer. He commandeth me to put it into words. Listen!

"O Lord our Father, our young patriots, idols of our hearts, go forth to battle—be Thou near them! With them—in spirit—we also go forth from the sweet peace of our beloved firesides to smite the foe. O Lord our God, help us to tear their soldiers to bloody shreds with our shells; help us to cover their smiling fields with the pale forms of their patriot dead; help us to drown the thunder of the guns with the shrieks of their wounded, writhing in pain; help us to lay waste their humble homes with a hurricane of fire; help us to wring the hearts of their unoffending widows with unavailing grief; help us to turn them out roofless with their little children to wander unfriended the wastes of their desolated land in rags and hunger and thirst, sports of the sun flames of summer and the icy winds of winter, broken in spirit, worn with travail, imploring Thee for the refuge of the grave and denied it—for our sakes who adore Thee, Lord, blast their hopes, blight their lives, protract their bitter pilgrimage, make heavy their steps, water their way with their tears, stain the white snow with the blood of their wounded feet! We ask it, in the spirit of love, of Him Who is the Source of Love, and Who is the ever-faithful refuge and friend of all that are sore beset and seek His aid with humble and contrite hearts. Amen."

(After a pause) "Ye have prayed it: if ye still desire it, speak! The messenger of the Most High waits."

It was believed afterward that the man was a lunatic, because there was no sense in what he said.

QUESTIONS FOR DISCUSSION AND WRITING

1. Identify the author's purpose in writing this story. How effective is his approach in achieving this purpose?
2. Have a class member read the opening paragraph out loud. Does hearing this paragraph read aloud alter your impression or reaction to the story?
3. What tone and stance develop in the first two to three paragraphs? At what point do you sense that Twain is developing irony? How did you come to that conclusion (i.e., inflated language or imagery)? Cite specific examples that contribute to this effect and discuss how they achieve their aim.
4. Whose point of view does the messenger represent? What about the preacher and the congregation? With whom do you think the author identifies, and what creates this impression? How does Twain attempt to help his readers identify with "the other"? Do you think the audience for this story would respond differently than the congregation?
5. Write a letter to the preacher in the story, agreeing or disagreeing with his position. Alternatively, write a letter to Twain arguing for the cause of a "just war."
6. Write an analysis of this story, integrating some principle from outside research or a secondary source such as Sam Keen, or analyzing the ways in which language develops the story's irony.

Pearl Harbor Address

FRANKLIN D. ROOSEVELT

Franklin Delano Roosevelt (1882–1945) was the thirty-second president of the United States and the only president ever elected to four consecutive terms in office. He won election to the New York Senate in 1910. President Woodrow Wilson appointed him Assistant Secretary of the Navy and he was the Democratic nominee for vice president in 1920. In 1921 he was stricken with poliomyelitis and worked hard to regain use of his legs. In 1928 Roosevelt became governor of New York. He was elected president in November 1932, subsequently guiding America through the Great Depression and World War II, ironically dying just three weeks before the Nazi surrender. Roosevelt gave the address that follows the day after the Japanese attack on the American fleet at Pearl Harbor, Hawaii.

To the Congress of the United States: Yesterday, December 7, 1941—a date which will live in infamy—the United States of America was suddenly and deliberately attacked by naval and air forces of the Empire of Japan.

The United States was at peace with that nation and, at the solicitation of Japan, was still in conversation with its government and its emperor looking toward the maintenance of peace in the Pacific. Indeed, one hour after Japanese air squadrons had commenced bombing in Oahu, the Japanese ambassador to the United States and his colleague delivered to the secretary of state a formal reply to a recent American message. While this reply stated that it seemed useless to continue the existing diplomatic negotiations, it contained no threat or hint of war or armed attack.

It will be recorded that the distance of Hawaii from Japan makes it obvious that the attack was deliberately planned many days or even weeks ago. During the intervening time the Japanese government had deliberately sought to deceive the United States by false statements and expressions of hope for continued peace.

The attack yesterday on the Hawaiian Islands has caused severe damage to American naval and military forces. I regret to tell you that very many American lives have been lost. In addition American ships have been reported torpedoed on the high seas between San Francisco and Honolulu.

Yesterday the Japanese government also launched an attack against Malaya. 5

Last night Japanese forces attacked Hong Kong.

Last night Japanese forces attacked Guam.

Last night Japanese forces attacked the Philippine Islands.

Last night the Japanese attacked Wake Island.

This morning the Japanese attacked Midway Island.

Japan has, therefore, undertaken a surprise offensive ex- 10 tending throughout the Pacific area. The facts of yesterday speak for themselves. The people of the United States have already formed their opinions and well understand the implications to the very life and safety of our nation.

As Commander-in-Chief of the Army and Navy I have directed that all measures be taken for our defense.

Always will we remember the character of the onslaught against us.

No matter how long it may take us to overcome this premeditated invasion, the American people in their righteous might will win through to absolute victory.

I believe I interpret the will of the Congress and of the peo- 15 ple when I assert that we will not only defend ourselves to the uttermost but will make very certain that this form of treachery shall never endanger us again.

Hostilities exist. There is no blinking at the fact that our people, our territory, and our interests are in grave danger.

With confidence in our armed forces—with the unbounded determination of our people—we will gain the inevitable triumph—so help us God.

I ask that the Congress declare that since the unprovoked and dastardly attack by Japan on Sunday, December 7, 1941, a state of war has existed between the United States and the Japanese Empire.

QUESTIONS FOR DISCUSSION AND WRITING

1. Roosevelt develops a logical argument for the conclusion that ends the speech, a request for the declaration of war. Identify the steps in the logic and the premises that lead to this conclusion.

2. Examine closely the language in this speech. How does the language evolve over the speech (e.g., in naming the enemy)? How does the impression of the enemy develop through terms such as "suddenly and deliberately attacked" and "treachery"?

3. Write an essay analyzing the persuasive appeals of this speech. You could focus on a certain type of appeal, such as appeals to ethos or logos or subtle appeals to emotion.

4. Argue that typecasting the enemy was a necessary task for Roosevelt to provide for the defense of the nation. Alternatively, argue that this speech began a process that inevitably led to dehumanizing the enemy to the extent that nuclear weapons became an option.

Images of the Other: Carousing American and WARNING! Our Homes Are in Danger NOW!

Carousing American

This woodblock print from the Edo period, c. 1861, by Yoshi-tora, portrays an American sailor with a prostitute holding a bottle, presumably of alcohol. Americans and other nation-alities populated the entertainment district of Yokohama, a situation this image captures.

A bearded American holds a stemmed glass while his companion, a Japanese courtesan, holds a large bottle. Hundreds of courtesans lived in Miyozaki, the entertainment district of Yokohama; few other women lived in the port city in the first years after its opening to international trade. Drinking was a major pastime for the foreign merchants and sailors there, whether at private parties such as those in the Gankirō in Miyozaki, or in the "grog shops," which numbered 24 by 1865.[1] Public drunkenness was not uncommon among the men of many nationalities who came to Yokohama, and their drinking was frequently portrayed in Yokohama prints. (FREER GALLERY OF ART & ARTHUR M. SACKLER GALLERY/SMITHSONIAN INSTITUTION)

[1]Paske-Smith, *Western Barbarians,* 277.

World War II Poster: Warning! Our Homes Are in Danger Now!

This poster from World War II is one of many printed and distributed during the war era. See discussion in Chapter One regarding persuasive appeals and visual rhetoric for background on strategies of persuasion. This poster is in the National Archives and Records Administration collection.

(NATIONAL ARCHIVES AND RECORDS ADMINISTRATION)

QUESTIONS FOR DISCUSSION AND WRITING

1. Identify the elements in each image that contribute to the overall effect. Analyze any appeals to ethos, pathos, and logos in each image. Which appeals do you find most effective?

2. How is "the other" characterized in each image? Which character evokes the strongest emotional reaction and how was that response elicited?

3. In Warning!, how does the representation of American homes and their relative size affect the poster's emotional appeals?

4. What point of view does the Japanese woodblock print convey? Consider researching images of Americans or Europeans from Asian perspectives. What themes emerge?

5. Based on your response to Question 1, select a poster and write an essay analyzing its persuasive appeals.

6. Analyze a number of propaganda posters and determine what common themes or strategies emerge. Do they tend to rely on certain types of appeals? Is the stereotyping consistent? Are certain emotions, such as fear, evoked more than others, such as pride in and identification with one's country?

Russia and USA: Friends or Enemies?

DMITRY LITVINOVICH

Except for periods of time during which it was shut down, *Pravda* has been published for almost eighty years. From 1912 until 1991 it was a publication of the Communist Party and essentially a state newspaper. After the dissolution of the USSR it changed hands several times. The Internet newspaper Online *Pravda* was launched in January 1999 and describes the approach of the print and online versions as follows: "The newspaper *Pravda* analyzes events from the point of view of the party's interests, whereas Online *Pravda* takes a pro-Russian approach to forming its policy." The article that follows was published in Online *Pravda* on November 15, 2001.

Recently, it has become very fashionable to carry out polls connected with different events.

The Public Opinion fund regularly runs polls on the following subject: In your opinion, is the US a friendly or an unfriendly state toward Russia? As usual, there are three variants of answer: a friendly one, an unfriendly one, and "it is difficult to answer."

Polls were carried out in February, September, and November of this year. The dynamics are very interesting. In February, 52 percent of people expressed their negative attitude to America, while in September, only 46 percent held a negative attitude. The percentage of people positively relating to the US was 32 and 38 percent, respectively. The percentage of people who could not determine their attitude was 15 percent in February and 16 percent in September.

The September 11 events have influenced the results of the polls. Russians who know the reality of the explosion of an apartment building sympathized with the Americans. However, many people noticed that we had not heard any words of sympathy from the United States when there were terrorist explosions in Moscow and Volgodonsk.

The poll carried out this November showed a little more optimistic result, though the difference from the September results was not big. The negative attitude toward the United States was still 43 percent of the people (in September, it was 46 percent). This was equal to the amount of people who responded positively (while in September, their number made 38 percent).

Therefore, a conclusion can be made that there are more 5
pluses than minuses in the relations between Russia and the US
However, it would be too early to speak about global warming in
the bilateral relations. We have been enemies for a very long
time, so we cannot become friends in a moment. And besides,
an instinctive pragmatism does not allow us to believe in the
Americans' sincerity.

QUESTIONS FOR DISCUSSION AND WRITING

1. This brief essay, appearing in Online *Pravda,* a counterpart of
   the Russian newspaper, discusses results from a series of
   opinion polls taken in Russia about the United States. From
   what you read here, does the methodology of the polls seem
   sound? Based on these polls, the author draws several conclusions. Do they seem warranted from the data? Are some
   inferences more well-supported than others? How is the
   essay structured? Does that structure seem similar to opinion
   pieces in American media?

2. The author notes that Russia and the United States have been
   historical enemies and that although there are "more pluses
   than minuses" in the relationship, one cannot yet speak of
   "global warming." Do you think most Americans would share
   this view? What do you make of the reference to Russians'
   "instinctive pragmatism"? Is it an aspect of the Russian character with which you are familiar? What do you think it
   means for Russian-US relations?

3. Look up Online *Pravda* and research current topics in Russian-
   US relations. Consider posting comments in response to one
   or several of the articles you review, and read postings from
   Russia or other countries. How do your responses on the
   topic vary? Write an analysis of your findings.

4. What effect do you believe the Russia-US split over the Iraq
   war has had on Russian attitudes toward the United States?
   Consider researching this topic in the forums or commentary
   and articles in Online *Pravda.*

5. Research the Cold War between the USSR and the United
   States. Consider focusing on some aspect of this period of
   time, such as arms control, Cold War rhetoric, McCarthyism, or
   espionage. Consider searching some of the documents of this
   era that have been declassified and may be available online.

A Shameful Contagion

MORTIMER ZUCKERMAN

Mortimer Zuckerman, a publisher and real estate developer, was born in 1937 in Quebec, Canada, and graduated with high honors from McGill University. He holds an LLM degree from Harvard Law School and an MBA from Wharton School of Business at the University of Pennsylvania. He became an American citizen in 1977. Zuckerman is the publisher and editor-in-chief of *U.S. News and World Report* and publisher of the *New York Daily News.* He serves on the Advisory Board of the Graduate School of Journalism at the University of California at Berkeley and the Board of the International Crisis Group; he is also a member of the Council on Foreign Relations and the International Institute of Strategic Studies. Zuckerman was awarded the French government's prestigious Commandeur de L'Ordre des Arts et des Lettres. The essay that follows was published as an editorial on October 7, 2002, in *U.S. News and World Report.*

Europe is sick again. The memory of six million murdered Jews, it seems, is no longer inoculation against the virus of anti-Semitism. It has taken hold, on the supposedly liberal left as well as the xenophobic right, all too long unchecked by feeble political leadership with one eye on the vengeful sentiments of millions of anti-Zionist immigrants from North Africa and the Middle East. The historic anti-Semitism denying individual Jews the right to live as equal members of society has horribly coalesced with a new version of anti-Semitism that denies the collective expression of the Jewish people, namely Israel, to live as an equal member of the family of nations. From Kiev in the East to Bilbao and Barcelona in Spain, and Rome in the South, from Marseilles to Paris to Berlin in the West, the poison is at work. Somehow anti-Semitism in Europe has outdone every other ideology and prejudice in its power and durability. Fascism came and went; Communism came and went; anti-Semitism came and stayed. And now it has been revitalized.

"Fire and Broken Glass"

Some of the manifestations of the campaign are spelled out in a report by the Lawyers Committee for Human Rights aptly titled "Fire and Broken Glass." The summary of evil deeds can only sketch the daily nightmare. Jews, and people presumed to be Jewish, are assaulted across the region. Attackers, shouting racist slogans, throw stones at schoolchildren, at worshippers leaving religious services, at rabbis. Jewish homes, schools, and synagogues are firebombed. Windows are smashed. Scores of Jewish cemeteries are desecrated with anti-Jewish slogans and threats and Nazi symbols on walls and monuments. In Belgium, thugs beat up the chief rabbi. In Britain, the left-wing journal *New Statesman* depicts a large Star of David stabbing the Union Jack. In London, a young student reading Psalms is stabbed twenty-seven times on a city bus. A mural in a Scottish church depicts a crucified Jesus surrounded by Israeli soldiers. In Italy, *La Stampa* publishes a Page 1 cartoon of a tank emblazoned with the Jewish star pointing its gun at the baby Jesus, who pleads, "Surely, they don't want to kill me again." In France, where there have been hundreds of acts of violence, walls in Jewish neighborhoods have been defaced with slogans proclaiming, "Jews to the gas chambers." In Germany, the Free Democratic Party has unofficially adopted anti-Semitism as a campaign technique to attract Germany's sizable Muslim minority. A former German defense minister blames the power of the Jews for all the perceived ills of American foreign policy. German Jews are advised not to wear anything in public that will identify them as Jewish because their safety cannot be guaranteed. A listing of such incidents could fill, and fill again, this entire magazine—even though they represent just a fraction of the total number of such crimes, their racial origin concealed in routine statistics of ordinary assault and vandalism.

All it takes for evil to flourish, as Edmund Burke reminded us, is for good men to remain silent. That, alas, has been the pattern. When things were getting out of hand a year ago, the French government finally made a forthright stand, and it had an effect. (Kudos to Harvard University President Lawrence Summers, who recently spoke out forcefully against anti-Semitic trends in US academia.) Many public officials in Europe make racist, anti-Jewish statements but too often escape rebuke. Many Europeans are shocked by the re-emergence of hatred of Jews, but the most common reaction has been complacency. Israel seems to be absorbing Europe's lingering anti-Jewish feelings, which are easier for many to express as anti-Zionism than anti-Semitism.

How do they do this? By applying two of the oldest anti-Semitic techniques: The double standard and moral equivalency. The double standard is manifest in the way Jews and the Jewish state are judged in a way no other people would be. With venom unsurpassed in modern dialogue, Europe demands that Israel acts as if it has to win the "moral man of the year" award just to defend itself. Israel is attacked for any deviation, no matter how trivial, as if responding to those that seek its destruction is a moral failure. This pernicious, and intellectually dishonest, double standard has the effect of implicitly denying Israel the right to the same measures of self-defense that any other state would exert. When Israelis take steps to assert their collective rights of self-defense in the face of unprecedented terrorist attacks against innocent Israeli civilians, they encounter an almost unanimous condemnation from the European establishment and the European media. European detractors turn every Israeli act of defense into its current euphemism: Crimes against humanity. The Europeans took the election of Ariel Sharon as a license to view every act of self-defense as an aggression. They forgot what produced Sharon's election, namely the terrorism that Yasser Arafat launched in September 2000 against the most left-wing government in Israeli history—a government that had just made the most far-reaching proposals to settle the conflict.

What provoked Europe's latest hostility was Israel's incursion into the West Bank, which was in response to the unprecedented campaign of terror, culminating in the Netanya Passover bombing in which 29 Israelis perished and more than 140 were injured. If any other country in the world were bleeding from terrorism at the same rate as Israel, would there be any question of its right to defend itself? To deny Israel's right to defend itself, of course, is to deny the right of the Jews to a state that can perform the minimal function of protecting its own citizens.

The European double standard toward Israel takes many forms. Witness the eagerness with which so many in Europe diminished, and even dismissed, Israel's previously unimaginable concessions at Camp David, swallowing the Palestinian version of events there, despite a forceful American repudiation of that spin. Witness the almost hysterical reaction in Europe to a nonexistent massacre in Jenin, even as it failed to pay attention to the cumulative massacres of civilians in Israel. The *Guardian* newspaper in London betrayed its historic association with the founding of Israel with the outrageous editorial utterance that Jenin was every bit as bad as 9/11. Witness Europe's virtual acquiescence in the World Conference Against Racism held in South Africa, where Israel, the only democracy in the region with a program of civil rights and full Arab participation in government, was accused of genocide, ethnic cleansing, racism, and apartheid, while the vicious racism of the Middle East and Africa was ignored.

5

Paradox Upon Paradox

The traditional attacks from the right based on national, religious, or ethnic reasons have been surpassed by the more driving force of the extreme left, which invokes political or universal reasons, like human rights, antiglobalism, and socialism. Ever obsessed by anti-Americanism, they have seized on the Middle East crisis as a way to attack the United States and Israel as being unfeeling toward the poor of the world. For them, the Palestinians have become the poster child for Third World victimization. Indeed, the Israeli-Palestinian dispute is portrayed as an extended human-interest story told exclusively from the Palestinian point of view. Unmentioned is the fact that there is not a single democratic state in the entire region, that there would not be a single Israeli soldier in any Palestinian city or any checkpoint were Jews not the daily targets of terror. Ignoring the corrupt, authoritarian regime in Palestine, the critics from the left attack Israel on universalist issues, arguing that Israel is an occupying power in the West Bank oppressing the Palestinians. They pay not the slightest heed to the fact that Israel is there because the Arabs made war. Never do they acknowledge that the Palestinians could have had their own state just two years ago, and perhaps be flourishing in peace now, if they had not been incited to still more insensate violence. The paradoxes are dizzying—and malign. Israel, a country victimized by terrorism, stands accused of perpetrating terrorism, the Jews described as Nazis, and their Arab tormentors cast in the role of helpless Jews.

Next, of course, is the moral-equivalency trap. When Israel responds to terrorism, Europe treats it as if the response and the terrorism are morally equal; as if there were no difference between the arsonist and the firefighter; as if Israel's response, which seeks to minimize civilian casualties, is equal to the terrorism, which seeks to maximize civilian casualties; as if the premeditated campaign of suicide murder were a sane response to an extraordinarily generous proposal that would have provided Palestinians with a state—a proposal many in Palestine now fervently wish their corrupt and vicious leadership had embraced.

Of course, the point of the double standard and moral equivalency is to create the impression that Israel is an illegitimate state, among the world's worst human-rights violators, and thus legitimize the extinction of a state the Arabs have never accepted. The insight of Amos Oz, a liberal Israeli writer, is pertinent. He is haunted, he says, by the observation that before the Holocaust, European graffiti read "Jews to Palestine," only to be transformed in modern times into "Jews out of Palestine." The message to Jews, notes Oz, is, "Don't be here and don't be there. That is, *Don't be.*"

Europe seems to be unconscious of the virulence of the 10 campaign of lies against Israelis in Palestine and throughout the Middle East, where the fact of the Holocaust is routinely described by media and governments as a Jewish invention, and where teachers foment a hatred of Israel and fail even to acknowledge its existence in history texts and maps in the schools subsidized by Europeans!

The unprecedented and unbridled hatred embodied by jihad, sanctioned by authoritarian Arab states, is, of course, a device to divert their populations from the failures of their own societies. But Europe, the killing fields of so many Jews, should know better. It should be the first to understand that Jews, of all people, have the right to defend, even overdefend themselves from the consequences of hate. Europe has a historic duty to redeem the crimes committed on its soil by first recognizing and then repudiating the persecution Jews face today and vigorously defending the collective right of the Jewish state to defend itself from its legions of hate-blinded enemies.

Anything less defames the glories of a European civilization dedicated to the dignity of man, freedom, honor, and decency.

QUESTIONS FOR DISCUSSION AND WRITING

1. Identify the core point of this essay and the evidence used to support that point. Analyze the ways in which the essay's introduction provides a context for this assertion. For example, analyze the parallel structure and repetition of the last two sentences of paragraph 1.

2. Evaluate the extent and range in paragraph 3 and the juxtaposition of this list with the Edmund Burke reference. How does the arrangement reinforce Burke's point?

3. Zuckerman sets up his explanation for the spread of anti-Semitism with a rhetorical question, paragraph 5, and a two-part response over the next several paragraphs. Evaluate the effectiveness of this arrangement and other assert-support structures in the essay. How do these organizational strategies guide the reader through his argument?

4. Does Zuckerman respond to opposing or alternative views? If so, identify that response and evaluate its merit. On balance, are you persuaded by his essay or not? Explain your response.

5. Write an essay evaluating Zuckerman's argument, perhaps focusing on language, use of example, use of reasoning, and organizational strategies.

Islamist Postcard

This postcard is part of a collection acquired by New Zealand journalist Theodore White in April 2002 in Afghanistan and Pakistan. The collection includes a number of postcards with various poses and motifs and school texts used in the Taliban-run schools.

(HOOVER INSTITUTION ARCHIVES)

QUESTIONS FOR DISCUSSION AND WRITING

1. Identify and analyze the elements of the postcard. To whom is the postcard intended to appeal? What is the argument? What action should follow the argument? What are the persuasive appeals? Be especially mindful of appeals to ethos.

2. What is your response to seeing a young boy juxtaposed with guns? Would your response be different if these postcards were from the Afghan-Russian war era rather than post–9/11?

3. Research the role of the child-warrior in history, considering both declared wars and those undeclared and considered guerilla warfare. Consider researching the plight of child soldiers in contemporary tribal conflict.

4. Write an analytical essay focusing on the persuasive appeals of this postcard.

Callow, Brave, and True: A Gospel of Civil War Youth

JAY S. HOAR

Jay S. Hoar has traveled extensively researching, lecturing, and interviewing Civil War veterans and their families. He has taught in Maine high schools (1960–1964), at Maine Maritime Academy in Castine (1964–1967), and at the University of Maine at Farmington. He has also published *The South's Last Boys in Grey* (1986), biographies of veterans of the Confederate army in the Civil War or War Between the States. The photograph that follows is of David Wood, age ten, and is from *Callow, Brave, and True* (1999), a collection of biographies of more than forty-five of the youngest soldiers to serve in the Civil War.

Tintype courtesy Richard H. Wood

David Wood at the time of his enlistment in the Union Army

(JAY S. HOAR)

QUESTIONS FOR DISCUSSION AND WRITING

1. How does your viewing of the Islamist postcard in this chapter affect your attitude toward this photograph?

2. How does viewing this photograph, in turn, affect your assessment of the Islamist postcard? Do you have a different attitude about seeing the child with a gun in the postcard after viewing this photograph?

3. The Civil War was fought on American soil and between Americans. What comparisons and contrasts can you draw, if any, with the current geopolitical climate?

4. Research the role of children in the American Civil War, including both combat and noncombat roles and drawing from both sides in the conflict.

5. Research the changing concept of childhood through the ages. You might want to focus on a particular era or society—for example, Native American youth, Anglo Colonial-era children, or the child-soldiers in a contemporary conflict.

Belfast Murals:
Northern Ireland

Murals from both sides of the Northern Ireland conflict have charted the course of this conflict for many years. While the Protestant-Catholic and British-Irish conflicts in this region have deep historical roots, violence has escalated over the past thirty years, a period known as "The Troubles." The violence frequently escalates during the July "Marching Season," which prominently features the Orange Order, a Protestant organization that attempts to recreate its historical marching route that now takes it through Catholic neighborhoods. In 1998, the Good Friday Accords were instrumental in bringing about a peace process still underway, and hopes for peace have pervaded more recent murals. Multiple factions operate on both sides of this conflict, but the most prominent are Loyalists, who want to keep the Six Counties of Northern Ireland tied to Britain; and the Republicans or Nationalists, who want Northern Ireland to become part of the Republic of Ireland in the south. Both sides have also been associated with paramilitary groups.

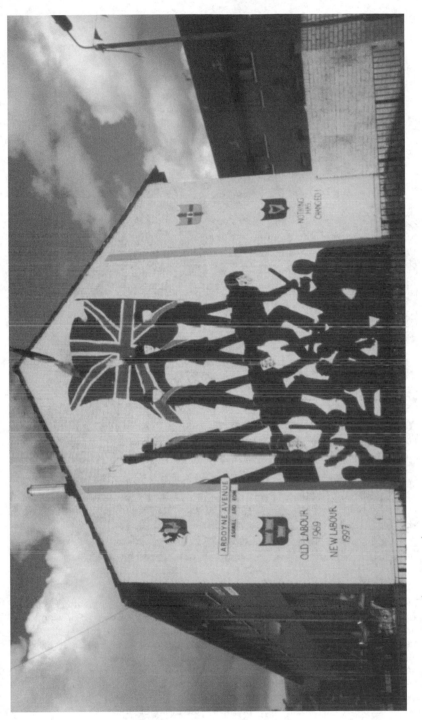

Anti-Orange Marches Mural

Later, the issue of Orange Order marches figures prominently in a number of murals. For example, one, painted in Ardoyne Avenue, North Belfast, in August 1997, depicted the nationalist population as being trampled down by the Royal Ulster Constabulary (RUC), who hold up their riot shields to allow Orange Order marchers to proceed. Location and Date: Ardoyne Avenue, Belfast, 1997 (WJ ROLSTON)

Pro-Agreement Mural

The Good Friday Agreement of 1998 has begun to figure in murals, with demands that the promises of that Agreement for the nationalist population be delivered. For example, a mural painted on Garvaghy Road, Portadown in July 1998 quotes one such promise—"freedom from sectarian harassment"—and juxtaposes this with the threat of unwanted Orange Order marches in the area. Three dancers, signifying Irish culture, are dwarfed by a looming Orange Order member who holds a petrol bomb; the flames from the bottle are red, white, and blue, the British colours. Prophetically, this mural was completed two days before three young nationalist children were burnt to death in Ballymoney, County Antrim, by loyalists protesting the failure of Orange Order marchers to proceed along the Garvaghy Road. Location and Date: Garvaghy Road, Portadown, July 1998. (WJ ROLSTON)

Ireland/Mural-1

A Protestant young man and child climb onto a railing in north Belfast, Northern Ireland, in front of a large Loyalist mural painted on the side of a building Wednesday, October 24, 2001. Decommissioning of IRA weapons has started in an attempt to further the peace process. (AP/WIDE WORLD PHOTO)

Ireland/Mural 2

A man passes an Ulster Defense Association mural in the mainly Protestant area of east Belfast, Northern Ireland, Friday, Oct. 12, 2001. Cease-fires in Northern Ireland called by two outlawed anti-Catholic groups no longer exist, Britain said Friday in a move that could stoke more Protestant violence. (AP/WIDE WORLD PHOTO)

QUESTIONS FOR DISCUSSION AND WRITING

1. Review the images. What are the elements of each image? What appeals does each make? Are there common strategies or themes?

2. What are the pros and cons of using murals to communicate political ideas?

3. In what ways are images of "us and them" being created in these murals? What is the image of each side conveyed in the mural and in the whole composition of the photograph?

4. Research other Belfast murals on the Web and analyze them in view of the Keen reading in this chapter.

5. In small groups, design a mural that conveys a political point or idea, perhaps one related to recent political changes such as the "war on terrorism" and the US response to terrorism in its domestic policies. Present your design to others in the class and explain why you designed it as you did.

6. Research the history of this conflict, focusing on its roots, on the Irish independence movement in the early twentieth century, or on the recent history of "The Troubles" and the Good Friday Accords.

Living with Terrorism: Northern Ireland Shares Lessons

KATHLEEN LACAMERA

Kathleen LaCamera is a minister and television producer as well as a United Methodist News Service correspondent based in England. In the article that follows she reports on the efforts at critical reflection and attempts to build bridges between the two communities hurt by thirty years of violence in the Northern Ireland conflict known as "The Troubles."

BELFAST, Northern Ireland (UMNS)—Beryl Kelly knows all about the human toll of "collateral damage."

Fifteen years ago, the Methodist laywoman was caught in an ambush as she was getting her car out of the garage for a family outing. The blast from a nearby rocket launcher tore through her inner ear, leaving her unconscious and bleeding. Years later, she is still being treated for increasing pain and hearing problems.

But Kelly was not the object of the attack. The Irish Republican Army (IRA), a paramilitary group, was trying to hit a "military" target—British army troops on patrol. Kelly was what is sometimes called "collateral damage," a civilian who had the bad luck to be in the wrong place at the wrong time.

Despite this and other experiences along Belfast's volatile Springfield Road, Kelly resisted the bitterness that drove many Protestants to move away or turn against their Catholic neighbors. Her neighbors were a godsend, not the enemy, according to this mother of five.

"When a pipe bomb would go off, or there was trouble out in front of the house, my neighbors would lift my children over the back hedge and let them sleep in their houses," she said. "My children loved it because they had bunk beds."

Ask Kelly what lessons she has learned in thirty-plus years of living with the terrorism and violence of "The Troubles" and "Helping each other was the key to it all," she told United Methodist News Service. "We never asked whether anyone was Catholic or Protestant. We all just saw a need and we met it."

During the last three decades, nearly four thousand people have died in the conflict that has pitted Catholic against

Protestant in Northern Ireland and spawned paramilitary or terrorist groups on both sides of the religious divide. A fragile peace process struggles to move conflict on from military to political solutions. But terrorism continues to be part of the fabric of life in Northern Ireland.

"If we had only listened thirty years ago," reflected the Rev. Harold Good, president of the Irish Methodist Conference and member of Northern Ireland's Human Rights Commission. "Even the best people in our churches have said we should just go in there with force and sort it all out. But it's not that simple. . . . We've learned there is no military solution to our problem."

Catholic Brendan Bradley lost a younger brother, an older sister, an uncle, a nephew, and a cousin in The Troubles, killed by people on all sides of the conflict. Bradley now spends most of his time at the Survivors of Trauma Center that he helped to found in North Belfast. Outside the center, there is the frequent sound of police surveillance helicopters keeping an eye on one of Belfast's most violent areas. Inside, the center offers everything from one-to-one advice and counseling to after-school programs for neighborhood children.

As Bradley sat helping an eight-year-old boy with math 10 homework, he explained that in his experience, two wrongs never make a right. When responding to terrorism a bit of "righteousness" and a whole lot of "wrongness" is a righteousness that is too costly, said Bradley.

In the days following the death of his seventeen-year-old brother, Francis, in 1975, Bradley was told that two people would be murdered as revenge for Francis' death. "I said, 'I don't want that,' but was told it wasn't my decision."

Reflecting on the US terrorist attacks, Bradley said he understands why Americans must respond to the "bully." But he also hoped the mistakes and suffering of Catholic and Protestants across Northern Ireland could serve as a warning against a response motivated by revenge.

"Revenge won't help. How much do you need to feel better? Ten bodies? Two hundred bodies? Two thousand? A whole country? What will sort you out? It's like alcohol."

For Methodists and for many others in Northern Ireland, the interfaith Corrymeela community and its sister organization, the Mediation Network, have been a valuable resource for conflict resolution. Doug Baker, an American working for the network, said the terrorists who attacked the United States must be held accountable, but also must be understood.

"Nothing justifies this [attack on the US], but there are things   15
that might make it more understandable. . . . If you want to rid the
world of terrorism, put as much energy into removing the motivation for it, rather than just investing in mechanisms that prevent it."

Trevor Williams, head of Corrymeela, was even more blunt.
"When Paul instructed us to love our enemies it wasn't just good
for them, it was good for us as well."

Williams maintained that the people who can teach us the
most about ourselves are our enemies. "As a Protestant, I need
Catholics to help me understand who I am. . . . I need them to
tell me why they are angry with me."

In the eastern part of Belfast, where shipyards that once
provided employment are silent and the appeal of hardline
Protestant paramilitaries is great, the Rev. Gary Mason is the pastor of the East Belfast Mission. His Methodist church is not only
a worshipping congregation, but also a mission reaching out to
people with employment, youth, family, and community services throughout the area.

Here, Williams' directive to "love your enemies" would
stick hard in the throats of those who feel abandoned and isolated. Mason recalled that following the attacks on the World
Trade Center and the Pentagon, there was a period of reflection
in his community

"People looked at the United States and said, 'We don't want to   20
end up like this.' " But he noted with regret the mood did not last long
in a place where violence has been the norm for so many years.

Not far from Mason's church, a high-ranking commander in
one of the Protestant paramilitaries told United Methodist News
Service that he "couldn't believe his eyes" when he watched
what was happening in New York. "I'm deeply hurt by this kind
of terrorism," he said.

He advised Americans to take military action that, by necessity, would be "ruthless and cruel."

"You have to fight terror with terror," he said, and then
added, "You can't defeat a terrorist. This will be a long war—it's
about suffering."

Noting the widely differing views on conflict resolution in   25
his own small community, Mason has learned a peaceful future
is built one relationship at a time. His advice to people in the
United States is to begin building bridges of understanding with
people in their own communities.

"Bring facilitators into your churches; get Christians and
Muslims together to hear each others' stories and pain. . . . Ultimately, there has to be a listening and a learning process."

The need for listening and critical reflection is something that has not come easily to a place where every death fuels the need for more war to avenge it. Methodist minister and theologian Johnston McMaster of the Irish School of Ecumenics described the reflection process as extremely painful and something that only three decades of violence finally pushed the people of Northern Ireland to undertake.

"It takes a long time to engage with critical reflection—and some are happier to live with the old stereotypes," he explained. "I don't condone evil, but we must look at what makes an angry young man that will plant a bomb or drive an airplane into a building."

Bertie Laverty is a Catholic woman whose own journey of critical reflection has led her to put a human face on the Protestants she used to see only as "the enemy." Laverty is the project coordinator for Fourth Spring, a joint Catholic-Protestant community center. The Springfield Methodist Church, where the center is based, is one of four ecumenical partners in the project.

Laverty had never met a Protestant until she went to university. In the exclusively Catholic neighbourhood where she grew up, young men, even her own father, were routinely shoved around and beaten by police. She admitted that if she had been a boy, she would have joined the IRA. "When a policeman was killed, my friends and I would celebrate," she recalled. 30

She now spends her days building bridges between segregated communities in West Belfast. She counts both Catholics and Protestants among her friends. Recently she found out that the wife of one of her Protestant friends was among those killed by a bomb planted by Republican terrorists years ago. Protestants were people she said she cared little about back then.

Laverty said she sees the world differently now, and although she understands what drives people in the Catholic Nationalist community to terrorism, she does not condone it. Instead, she has found a place to address the problems that motivate terrorism, working on a one-to-one basis with mothers, fathers, children, youth, and others who live and work along the Springfield Road.

QUESTIONS FOR DISCUSSION AND WRITING

1. How does the use of personal narrative affect the article's persuasiveness?

2. Does the author appear to take sides on the Protestant-Catholic conflict, or rather to maintain a relatively neutral stance? What in the text supports your view? What point does the author make about collateral damage and the statistics of violence?

3. What are the divergent views on violence and conflict resolution expressed in this article? Based on this text, do you have a sense of which approach seems most likely to succeed?

4. Research the history of the conflict in Northern Ireland, focusing on some particular aspect, such as the Good Friday Accords, the role of paramilitary groups, or changes in policing. Alternatively, research the Forgiveness Project and its work with survivors of violence in Northern Ireland.

Chapter Seven: Connections

1. Using your discussion of this chapter's readings as a starting point, discuss the ways in which a dehumanized image in some of the selections supports the principles of creating an image of the enemy discussed by Keen

2. What principles from Keen apply to the images in the political murals in this chapter or elsewhere? What might Mark Twain say about the political and religious conflict in Northern Ireland?

3. What are the similarities, and differences, between murals as political statements and the posters and photographs you have viewed in this chapter and elsewhere?

4. Keen writes, "Truth is the first sacrifice we make in order to belong to any exclusive group." What evidence of this premise have you found in this and previous chapters?

5. Compare and contrast the images of the enemy in President Roosevelt's speech and in President Bush's (see Chapter Eight).

6. Keen discusses ways in which the enemy is characterized and dehumanized. Can you imagine a way in which the youngster in the Islamist photograph might be demonized? What about the American Civil War child soldier?

7. How does the Russians' ability to identify with the United States after the 9/11 attacks support points made in the Keen essay? How does Americans' lack of empathy for the terrorist attacks in Russia support other findings from the Keen essay?

8. With classmates, develop a "war prayer" about the two sides in the American Revolutionary War or another conflict or current political situation such as the "war on terror."

9. Compare and contrast this chapter's views about conceptualizing "the other" with the selections in another chapter.

Chapter Seven: End-of-Chapter Assignments

1. Investigate tourism in formerly communist states and develop your understanding of the rhetorical shift from the socialist agenda to a more capitalistic stance. In addition to Russia, consider smaller countries in Africa and Asia.

2. Research propaganda, particularly visual propaganda. You could focus on a particular genre or type of propaganda. Or, consider focusing on materials with a particular theme—preserving materials for the war effort at home, for example, or fear tactics and emotional appeals.

3. Research conflicts between peoples one might consider to be related ethnically. Examples include North and South Korea, Sierra Leone, the Congo, Kashmir, Rwanda, Northern Ireland, People's Republic of China and Taiwan, and Eastern European states.

4. Using the extensive databases online with materials on the Northern Ireland political situation, research the history of this conflict, the Orange Order, the Irish Republican Army, Marching Season, or the extensive Belfast murals.

5. Research the British point of view in the American Revolutionary War. Try to find primary sources such as letters, pamphlets, and broadsides that argue for the Loyalist point of view.

6. Research some aspect of the Norman Conquest or the Battle of Hastings that interests you. For example, if you are interested in health issues, research the state of medicine, in society at large or on the battlefield; or investigate the legal process involving people from two cultures and languages meeting in court.

7. Follow the news and consider participating in a discussion on some of the international Web sites listed at the end of this chapter from countries with whom the United States has been in conflict.

8. Analyze appeals to ethos and pathos in an image or text from a time of war or conflict, such as a propaganda poster. You can find a number of them online at the National Archives Web site, *www.NARA.org*, or in a variety of other Internet sources. Use the principles discussed in Keen on by another write to support your analysis.

9. With peers, develop a Web site focusing on providing information and the positive exchange of ideas and information across cultures. The site could include links to other Web sites and space for posting information or discussion comments. Make an effort to welcome posts from international participants. Consider inviting participants from specific overseas schools, perhaps with your instructor's help in contacting them.

10. Through your campus community service center or on your own, get in touch with a local community agency whose mission is to promote intercultural or global understanding. Some examples include Amnesty International, Global Exchange, Global Routes, and Eastern European Service Agency. For a service learning or community writing experience, you could consider two options. You could volunteer to do some projects for the agency and write about your experiences in a reflective essay or journal, or you could arrange to do writing for the agency such as newsletters, grant proposals, brochures, or press releases for some of your course writing assignments.

Chapter Seven: Web Sites for Further Exploration

Institute for War and Peace Reporting
http://www.iwpr.net/home_index_new.html
Newseum—Freedom Forum, International Media Issues
http://www.freedomforum.org/
Antiwar
http://www.antiwar.com/
The Anti-Defamation League
http://www.adl.org/
Middle East Peace Gateway
http://www.mideastweb.org/index.html
Ireland—Conflict Archive on the Web: CAIN (Northern Ireland conflict)
http://cain.ulst.ac.uk/index.html
Irish News
http://www.Ireland.com
http://www.Irishnews.com
Online *Pravda* (in English)
http://english.pravda.ru/
Russian Newspapers
http://www.moscowtimes.ru/

http://www.russianobserver.com/

Cold War Museum

http://www.coldwar.org

Cold War International History Project: Document Library

http://cwihp.si.edu/csihplib.nsf

Hoover Institution Archives and Library

http://www-hoover.stanford.edu/hila

US National Archives and Record Administration (NARA)

http://www.archives.gov/

Consider the following Web sites for additional research: Irish Hub

http://larkspirit.com/general/irishhub.html

Inter Press Service Global Gateway, the Alternative News Link (a subscription-based news service, but brief summaries are accessible)

http://www.ips.org/index.htm

8

A POST–9/11 WORLD

INTRODUCTION

The story of 9/11 is in many respects one of images: Planes exploding into towers, New Yorkers running from disintegrating buildings; firefighters and rescue workers running into them; flags flying amid smoldering debris and across freeways, cities, and neighborhoods. Images of the immediate aftermath include those from overseas: Thousands in public squares around the world observing America's loss in solidarity and prayer; widely played images of some crowds "dancing in the streets"; Yasser Arafat donating blood; mug shots of the event's perpetrators broadcast continuously; a smoldering Pentagon; and, some time later, two beacons of light representing the lost towers.

This chapter rests on the premise that most readers are familiar with the more prominent and graphic of these images. Its goal rather is to present for analysis and discussion several perspectives on 9/11 and its aftermath. The selections in this chapter include speeches by principal actors in the events; analysis by scholars, writers, and commentators; and some of the images that surfaced following the events. A goal of this chapter, as with the rest of this book, is to encourage analysis as well as reflection and to encourage readers to apply a critical eye to different perspectives on a remarkably sensitive and evocative topic. Another goal is to provide both primary sources and background readings and to encourage connections among the layers of the complex, difficult topics in an effort to deepen our understanding of the stark images that have come to represent it in our collective consciousness.

We begin this chapter with *New York Times* writer Natalie Angier's reflection on Americans' response to this act in "Of Altruism, Heroism, and Nature's Gifts in the Face of Terror." Angier discusses both the specific acts of courage and selflessness and the theoretical social and biological perspectives that attempt to explain the kinds of altruistic behavior that characterized response to the tragedy.

We then turn to the speech of a new, untested president who took office following a controversial and divisive election. President George W. Bush's September 20, 2001, address to a joint session of Congress, to the nation, and to the world articulated America's response to this attack.

Next is the text of Osama bin Laden's statement following the attacks, broadcast on the al Jazeera network and world-wide. In this statement bin Laden, considered the architect of the 9/11 and other terrorist acts that preceded it, as well as the leader of the al Qaeda terrorist network, lays out his rationale for these acts, links them to other causes, and appeals to God's authority to justify and strengthen his position. In exploring what motivates those who would willingly die as they bring destruction to others, some have pointed to religious beliefs and the reward expected in an afterlife. Sam Keen's discussion (see Chapter Seven) may provide a helpful basis for understanding the process of creating and destroying an enemy.

In addition to the abundance of graphic photographic images pervading the media post–9/11, editorial cartoons developed images to make their points succinctly but cautiously, particularly in the immediate aftermath of the attacks. Consistent with the written discourse, the artistic renderings on this topic responded to diverse perspectives. The two cartoons here, published in Los Angeles and Tehran, capture both the historical context with which many Americans tried to understand the event—a comparison with Pearl Harbor—and the concern overseas about a potentially heavy-handed American reaction to the event.

We then turn to a brief essay by a frequent commentator on Middle Eastern and international affairs, Thomas Friedman, Pulitzer Prize-winning writer for the *New York Times*. In this selection from November 27, 2001, entitled "The Real War," Friedman argues, "We're not fighting to eradicate terrorism. Terrorism is just a tool. We're fighting to defeat an ideology: Religious totalitarianism, a view of the world that my faith must reign supreme and can be affirmed and held passionately only if all others are negated." His hope is that Islam will reinterpret the past and its core texts and come to accept "plurality and modernism" as Judaism and Christianity have after centuries of struggle.

Salman Rushdie, the writer given a death sentence in Iran for writing a novel clerics said disrespected Islam, contradicts the careful statements of world leaders disassociating the 9/11 attacks from Islam per se and blaming a violent subgroup of Muslims or Islamists instead. In his essay "Yes, This Is about Islam," Rushdie calls for the voices of moderate Islam and for the reconciliation of Islam with modernity and with secular humanist principles.

Although bin Laden and others have claimed to be acting at least in part on behalf of the Palestinian cause, the editor of *Palestinian Report* expresses some reservations about this linkage. In his essay "Unresolved Palestinian Problem Remains a Magnet," Ghassan Khatib notes that allying with the Palestinian situation is designed to evoke support for bin Laden's cause among Muslims and Arabs. Despite highly publicized images of Palestinians ostensibly rejoicing following the 9/11 attacks, Khatib notes that fundamentalists, not ordinary Palestinian citizens, were doing so; nevertheless, he argues that the Palestinian authority should distinguish itself from the "world pariahs of the Taliban and bin Laden" and at the same time express wariness over use of force against Afghan civilians. He argues that the legitimacy of the Palestinian cause is itself rooted in international law and not dependent on linkage to some other political cause.

The next selection features two controversial and widely distributed photographs. The first photograph, by photographer Jan Bauer, captures a young girl with fake explosives around her waist in the manner of a suicide bomber, marching with her father in front of a sign in a pro-Palestinian demonstration. The second photograph offers a concrete image of the literal removal of Saddam Hussein's regime in Iraq.

The chapter ends with what some might consider a quintessentially American response, reminiscent of Scarlett O'Hara in *Gone with the Wind*. Among the many flyers, flags, and "United We Stand" posters papering American towns and cities, we find patriotic posters with another theme: Go shopping. The final selection from the San Francisco government Web site features a popular design by artist Craig Frazer. The poster, "America: Open for Business," was widely distributed through chambers of commerce and is still visible at numerous shops and locales.

As you read these selections and integrate them with your own experience, observations, beliefs about, understanding of, and reflections on this core event in American history, you will, as Aristotle might assert, be engaging your whole being, emotions, and judgment as well as critical and analytical capabilities. It is neither desirable nor even possible to dismiss completely your personal and emotional reactions to these events. As a student and a scholar, your work entails examining these events with your critical faculties and in light of your own experience and background. This chapter in particular is one in which you may find that you can benefit from collaborating with peers in making meaning of the experiences, words, and images explored here.

Of Altruism, Heroism, and Nature's Gifts in the Face of Terror

NATALIE ANGIER

Natalie Marie Angier, born in 1958 in New York, was educated at the University of Michigan and Barnard College, where she received a BA in 1978. She is a Pulitzer Prize-winning American journalist and science writer who has written on a range of topics from molecular biology to female physiology. Currently science writer for the *New York Times,* she has published a number of books including *Natural Obsessions: The Search for the Oncogene* (1988; published as *Natural Obsessions: Striving to Unlock the Deepest Secrets of the Cancer Cell,* in 1999), *The Beauty of the Beastly: New Views on the Nature of Life* (1995), and *Woman: An Intimate Geography* (1999). Her awards include the Pulitzer Prize (1991), Lewis Thomas Prize, Rockefeller University (1990), and the journalism award of the American Association for the Advancement of Science (1992). The following essay appeared in the *New York Times* on September 18, 2001.

For the wordless, formless, expectant citizens of tomorrow, here are some postcards of all that matters today:

Minutes after terrorists slam jet planes into the towers of the World Trade Center, streams of harrowed humanity crowd the emergency stairwells, heading in two directions. While terrified employees scramble down, toward exit doors and survival, hundreds of New York firefighters, each laden with seventy to one hundred pounds of lifesaving gear, charge upward, never to be seen again.

As the last of four hijacked planes advances toward an unknown but surely populated destination, passengers huddle together and plot resistance against their captors, an act that may explain why the plane fails to reach its target, crashing instead into an empty field outside Pittsburgh.

Hearing of the tragedy whose dimensions cannot be charted or absorbed, tens of thousands of people across the nation storm their local hospitals and blood banks, begging for the chance to give blood, something of themselves to the hearts of the wounded—and the heart of us all—beating against the void.

Altruism and heroism. If not for these twin radiant badges ⁵
of our humanity, there would be no us, and we know it. And so,
when their vile opposite threatened to choke us into submission
last Tuesday, we rallied them in quantities so great we surprised
even ourselves.

Nothing and nobody can fully explain the source of the emotional genius that has been everywhere on display. Politicians
have cast it as evidence of the indomitable spirit of a rock-solid
America; pastors have given credit to a more celestial source.
And while biologists in no way claim to have discovered the key
to human nobility, they do have their own spin on the subject.
The altruistic impulse, they say, is a nondenominational gift, the
birthright and defining characteristic of the human species.

As they see it, the roots of altruistic behavior far predate
Homo sapiens, and that is why it seems to flow forth so readily
once tapped. Recent studies that model group dynamics suggest
that a spirit of cooperation will arise in nature under a wide variety of circumstances.

"There's a general trend in evolutionary biology toward recognizing that very often the best way to compete is to cooperate," said Dr. Barbara Smuts, a professor of anthropology at the
University of Michigan, who has published papers on the evolution of altruism. "And that, to me, is a source of some solace
and comfort."

Moreover, most biologists concur that the human capacity
for language and memory allows altruistic behavior—the desire
to give, and to sacrifice for the sake of others—to flourish in measure far beyond the cooperative spirit seen in other species.

With language, they say, people can learn of individuals they ¹⁰
have never met and feel compassion for their suffering, and
honor and even emulate their heroic deeds. They can also warn
one another of any selfish cheaters or malign tricksters lurking
in their midst.

"In a large crowd, we know who the good guys are, and we
can talk about, and ostracize, the bad ones," said Dr. Craig
Packer, a professor of ecology and evolution at the University of
Minnesota. "People are very concerned about their reputation,
and that, too, can inspire us to be good."

Oh, better than good.

"There's a grandness in the human species that is so striking, and so profoundly different from what we see in other animals," he added. "We are an amalgamation of families working
together. This is what civilization is derived from."

At the same time, said biologists, the very conditions
that encourage heroics and selflessness can be the source of

profound barbarism as well. "Moral behavior is often a within-group phenomenon," said Dr. David Sloan Wilson, a professor of biology at the State University of New York at Binghamton." Altruism is practiced within your group, and often turned off toward members of other groups."

The desire to understand the nature of altruism has occupied   15
evolutionary thinkers since Charles Darwin, who was fascinated by the apparent existence of altruism among social insects. In ant and bee colonies, sterile female workers labor ceaselessly for their queen, and will even die for her when the nest is threatened. How could such seeming selflessness evolve, when it is exactly those individuals that are behaving altruistically that fail to breed and thereby pass their selfless genes along?

By a similar token, human soldiers who go to war often are at the beginning of their reproductive potential, and many are killed before getting the chance to have children. Why don't the stay-at-homes simply outbreed the do-gooders and thus bury the altruistic impulse along with the casualties of combat?

The question of altruism was at least partly solved when the British evolutionary theorist William Hamilton formulated the idea of inclusive fitness: The notion that individuals can enhance their reproductive success not merely by having young of their own, but by caring for their genetic relatives as well. Among social bees and ants, it turns out, the sister workers are more closely related to one another than parents normally are to their offspring; thus it behooves the workers to care more about current and potential sisters than to fret over their sterile selves.

The concept of inclusive fitness explains many brave acts observed in nature. Dr. Richard Wrangham, a primatologist at Harvard, cites the example of the red colobus monkey. When they are being hunted by chimpanzees, the male monkeys are "amazingly brave," Dr. Wrangham said. "As the biggest and strongest members of their group, they undoubtedly could escape quicker than the others." Instead, the males jump to the front, confronting the chimpanzee hunters while the mothers and offspring jump to safety. Often, the much bigger chimpanzees pull the colobus soldiers off by their tails and slam them to their deaths.

Their courageousness can be explained by the fact that colobus monkeys live in multimale, multifemale groups in which the males are almost always related. So in protecting the young monkeys, the adult males are defending their kin.

Yet, as biologists are learning, there is more to cooperation   20
and generosity than an investment in one's nepotistic patch of DNA. Lately, they have accrued evidence that something like

group selection encourages the evolution of traits beneficial to a group, even when members of the group are not related.

In computer simulation studies, Dr. Smuts and her colleagues modeled two types of group-living agents that would behave like herbivores: one that would selfishly consume all the food in a given patch before moving on, and another that would consume resources modestly rather than greedily, thus allowing local plant food to regenerate.

Researchers had assumed that cooperators could collaborate with genetically unrelated cooperators only if they had the cognitive capacity to know goodness when they saw it.

But the data suggested otherwise. "These models showed that under a wide range of simulated environmental conditions you could get selection for prudent, cooperative behavior," Dr. Smuts said, even in the absence of cognition or kinship. "If you happened by chance to get good guys together, they remained together because they created a mutually beneficial environment."

This sort of win-win principle, she said, could explain all sorts of symbiotic arrangements, even among different species— like the tendency of baboons and impalas to associate together because they use each other's warning calls.

Add to this basic mechanistic selection for cooperation the human capacity to recognize and reward behaviors that strengthen the group—the tribe, the state, the church, the platoon—and selflessness thrives and multiplies. So, too, does the need for group identity. Classic so-called minimal group experiments have shown that when people are gathered together and assigned membership in arbitrary groups, called, say, the Greens and the Reds, before long the members begin expressing amity for their fellow Greens or Reds and animosity toward those of the wrong "color."

"Ancestral life frequently consisted of intergroup conflict," Dr. Wilson of SUNY said. "It's part of our mental heritage."

Yet he does not see conflict as inevitable. "It's been shown pretty well that where people place the boundary between us and them is extremely flexible and strategic," he said. "It's possible to widen the moral circle, and I'm optimistic enough to believe it can be done on a worldwide scale."

Ultimately, though, scientists acknowledge that the evolutionary framework for self-sacrificing acts is overlaid by individual choice. And it is there, when individual firefighters or office workers or airplane passengers choose the altruistic path that science gives way to wonder.

Dr. James J. Moore, a professor of anthropology at the University of California at San Diego, said he had studied many species, including many different primates. "We're the nicest species I know," he said. "To see those guys risking their lives, climbing over rubble on the chance of finding one person alive, well, you wouldn't find baboons doing that." The horrors of last week notwithstanding, he said, "the overall picture to come out about human nature is wonderful."

"For every 50 people making bomb threats now to mosques," he said, "there are 500,000 people around the world behaving just the way we hoped they would, with empathy and expressions of grief. We are amazingly civilized." 30

True, death-defying acts of heroism may be the province of the few. For the rest of us, simple humanity will do.

QUESTIONS FOR DISCUSSION AND WRITING

1. According to the author, in what ways do altruism and heroism define humanity? Does the author develop this view?
2. Examine the overall structure of the essay, with its opener discussing 9/11, an explanation of human behavior, and the conclusion that ties it back to the topic of 9/11. How does this structure affect coherence and unity in the essay?
3. Outline the biologists' view of altruism and cooperation. How convincing is this view? Does this view enrich, or detract from, the merit of altruistic behavior? Do you agree with the author's assertion about the role of individual choice in altruistic behavior?
4. Research social psychological theories about altruistic behavior, perhaps following up on one of the authors or arguments cited in this essay.
5. Write an essay on self-sacrifice that explores Angier's view and perhaps considers additional sources.

Address to Joint Session of Congress, September 20, 2001

GEORGE W. BUSH

George Walker Bush (1946–) became the 43rd president of the United States of America in 2001 in one of the closest elections in American history, defeating Democratic Vice President Albert Gore by only five electoral votes. The election results were contested for several weeks until December 12, 2000, when the US Supreme Court ruled in favor of Bush in the case *Bush v. Gore*. Bush was inaugurated on January 20, 2001. Bush was born in Connecticut and grew up in Midland and Houston, Texas. His father, George H. W. Bush, was the 41st president of the United States. His brother Jeb Bush has served as governor of Florida, the site of the contested election results. Bush received a BA in 1968 from Yale University and an MBA from Harvard Business School. Bush enlisted in the Texas Air National Guard during the Vietnam War and served as an F-102 pilot until he was grounded after failing to appear for a mandatory physical exam and drug test. He worked in the oil industry, formed a partnership to purchase the Texas Rangers baseball team, and in 1994 was elected governor of Texas over incumbent Ann Richards, serving with leadership described as bipartisan. He identifies himself as born-again Christian. Following the September 11 attacks, President Bush held the highest approval ratings in history; high approval ratings are historically common for wartime presidents, when both leaders and everyday citizens tend to rally around the president. The following speech is Bush's address to a joint session of Congress on September 20, 2001.

Mr. Speaker, Mr. president pro tempore, members of Congress, and fellow Americans:

In the normal course of events, presidents come to this chamber to report on the state of the Union. Tonight, no such report is needed. It has already been delivered by the American people.

We have seen it in the courage of passengers, who rushed terrorists to save others on the ground—passengers like an exceptional man named Todd Beamer. And would you please help me to welcome his wife, Lisa Beamer, here tonight. (Applause.)

We have seen the state of our Union in the endurance of rescuers, working past exhaustion. We have seen the unfurling of flags, the lighting of candles, the giving of blood, the saying of prayers—in English, Hebrew, and Arabic. We have seen the decency of a loving and giving people who have made the grief of strangers their own.

My fellow citizens, for the last nine days, the entire world has seen for itself the state of our Union—and it is strong. (Applause.)

Tonight we are a country awakened to danger and called to defend freedom. Our grief has turned to anger, and anger to resolution. Whether we bring our enemies to justice, or bring justice to our enemies, justice will be done. (Applause.)

I thank the Congress for its leadership at such an important time. All of America was touched on the evening of the tragedy to see Republicans and Democrats joined together on the steps of this Capitol, singing "God Bless America." And you did more than sing; you acted, by delivering $40 billion to rebuild our communities and meet the needs of our military.

Speaker Hastert, Minority Leader Gephardt, Majority Leader Daschle, and Senator Lott, I thank you for your friendship, for your leadership, and for your service to our country. (Applause.)

And on behalf of the American people, I thank the world for its outpouring of support. America will never forget the sounds of our national anthem playing at Buckingham Palace, on the streets of Paris, and at Berlin's Brandenburg Gate.

We will not forget South Korean children gathering to pray outside our embassy in Seoul, or the prayers of sympathy offered at a mosque in Cairo. We will not forget moments of silence and days of mourning in Australia and Africa and Latin America.

Nor will we forget the citizens of 80 other nations who died with our own: Dozens of Pakistanis; more than 130 Israelis; more than 250 citizens of India; men and women from El Salvador, Iran, Mexico, and Japan; and hundreds of British citizens. America has no truer friend than Great Britain. (Applause.) Once again, we are joined together in a great cause—so honored the British prime minister has crossed an ocean to show his unity of purpose with America. Thank you for coming, friend. (Applause.)

On September 11, enemies of freedom committed an act of war against our country. Americans have known wars—but for the past 136 years, they have been wars on foreign soil, except for one Sunday in 1941. Americans have known the casualties of war—but not at the center of a great city on a peaceful morning.

Americans have known surprise attacks—but never before on thousands of civilians. All of this was brought upon us in a single day—and night fell on a different world, a world where freedom itself is under attack.

Americans have many questions tonight. Americans are asking: Who attacked our country? The evidence we have gathered all points to a collection of loosely affiliated terrorist organizations known as al Qaeda. They are the same murderers indicted for bombing American embassies in Tanzania and Kenya, and responsible for bombing the USS *Cole*.

Al Qaeda is to terror what the Mafia is to crime. But its goal is not making money; its goal is remaking the world—and imposing its radical beliefs on people everywhere.

The terrorists practice a fringe form of Islamic extremism that has been rejected by Muslim scholars and the vast majority of Muslim clerics—a fringe movement that perverts the peaceful teachings of Islam. The terrorists' directive commands them to kill Christians and Jews, to kill all Americans, and make no distinction among military and civilians, including women and children.

This group and its leader—a person named Osama bin Laden—are linked to many other organizations in different countries, including the Egyptian Islamic Jihad and the Islamic Movement of Uzbekistan. There are thousands of these terrorists in more than sixty countries. They are recruited from their own nations and neighborhoods and brought to camps in places like Afghanistan, where they are trained in the tactics of terror. They are sent back to their homes or sent to hide in countries around the world to plot evil and destruction.

The leadership of al Qaeda has great influence in Afghanistan and supports the Taliban regime in controlling most of that country. In Afghanistan, we see al Qaeda's vision for the world.

Afghanistan's people have been brutalized—many are starving and many have fled. Women are not allowed to attend school. You can be jailed for owning a television. Religion can be practiced only as their leaders dictate. A man can be jailed in Afghanistan if his beard is not long enough.

The United States respects the people of Afghanistan—after all, we are currently its largest source of humanitarian aid—but we condemn the Taliban regime. (Applause.) It is not only repressing its own people; it is threatening people everywhere by sponsoring and sheltering and supplying terrorists. By aiding and abetting murder, the Taliban regime is committing murder.

And tonight, the United States of America makes the following demands on the Taliban: Deliver to United States authorities all the leaders of al Qaeda who hide in your land. (Applause.) Release all foreign nationals, including American citizens, you have unjustly imprisoned. Protect foreign journalists, diplomats, and aid workers in your country. Close immediately and permanently every terrorist training camp in Afghanistan, and hand over every terrorist, and every person in their support structure, to appropriate authorities. (Applause.) Give the United States full access to terrorist training camps, so we can make sure they are no longer operating.

These demands are not open to negotiation or discussion. 20 (Applause.) The Taliban must act, and act immediately. They will hand over the terrorists, or they will share in their fate.

I also want to speak tonight directly to Muslims throughout the world. We respect your faith. It's practiced freely by many millions of Americans, and by millions more in countries that America counts as friends. Its teachings are good and peaceful, and those who commit evil in the name of Allah blaspheme the name of Allah. (Applause.) The terrorists are traitors to their own faith, trying, in effect, to hijack Islam itself. The enemy of America is not our many Muslim friends; it is not our many Arab friends. Our enemy is a radical network of terrorists, and every government that supports them. (Applause.)

Our war on terror begins with al Qaeda, but it does not end there. It will not end until every terrorist group of global reach has been found, stopped, and defeated. (Applause.)

Americans are asking, why do they hate us? They hate what we see right here in this chamber—a democratically elected government. Their leaders are self-appointed. They hate our freedoms—our freedom of religion, our freedom of speech, our freedom to vote and assemble and disagree with each other.

They want to overthrow existing governments in many Muslim countries, such as Egypt, Saudi Arabia, and Jordan. They want to drive Israel out of the Middle East. They want to drive Christians and Jews out of vast regions of Asia and Africa.

These terrorists kill not merely to end lives, but to disrupt 25 and end a way of life. With every atrocity, they hope that America grows fearful, retreating from the world and forsaking our friends. They stand against us, because we stand in their way.

We are not deceived by their pretenses to piety. We have seen their kind before. They are the heirs of all the murderous ideologies of the twentieth century. By sacrificing human life to serve their radical visions—by abandoning every value except the will to power—they follow in the path of fascism, and Nazism, and totalitarianism. And they will follow that path all the way, to where it ends: In history's unmarked grave of discarded lies. (Applause.)

Americans are asking: How will we fight and win this war? We will direct every resource at our command—every means of diplomacy, every tool of intelligence, every instrument of law enforcement, every financial influence, and every necessary weapon of war—to the disruption and to the defeat of the global terror network.

This war will not be like the war against Iraq a decade ago, with a decisive liberation of territory and a swift conclusion. It will not look like the air war above Kosovo two years ago, where no ground troops were used and not a single American was lost in combat.

Our response involves far more than instant retaliation and isolated strikes. Americans should not expect one battle, but a lengthy campaign, unlike any other we have ever seen. It may include dramatic strikes, visible on TV, and covert operations, secret even in success. We will starve terrorists of funding, turn them one against another, drive them from place to place, until there is no refuge or no rest. And we will pursue nations that provide aid or safe haven to terrorism. Every nation, in every region, now has a decision to make. Either you are with us, or you are with the terrorists. (Applause.) From this day forward, any nation that continues to harbor or support terrorism will be regarded by the United States as a hostile regime.

Our nation has been put on notice: We are not immune   30
from attack. We will take defensive measures against terrorism to protect Americans. Today, dozens of federal departments and agencies, as well as state and local governments, have responsibilities affecting homeland security. These efforts must be coordinated at the highest level. So tonight I announce the creation of a Cabinet-level position reporting directly to me—the Office of Homeland Security.

And tonight I also announce a distinguished American to lead this effort, to strengthen American security: A military veteran, an effective governor, a true patriot, a trusted friend—Pennsylvania's Tom Ridge. (Applause.) He will lead, oversee, and coordinate a comprehensive national strategy to safeguard our country against terrorism, and respond to any attacks that may come.

These measures are essential. But the only way to defeat terrorism as a threat to our way of life is to stop it, eliminate it, and destroy it where it grows. (Applause.)

Many will be involved in this effort, from FBI agents to intelligence operatives to the reservists we have called to active duty. All deserve our thanks, and all have our prayers. And tonight, a few miles from the damaged Pentagon, I have a message for our military: Be ready. I've called the Armed Forces to alert, and there is a reason. The hour is coming when America will act, and you will make us proud. (Applause.)

This is not, however, just America's fight. And what is at stake is not just America's freedom. This is the world's fight. This is civilization's fight. This is the fight of all who believe in progress and pluralism, tolerance and freedom.

We ask every nation to join us. We will ask, and we will need, the help of police forces, intelligence services, and banking systems around the world. The United States is grateful that many nations and many international organizations have already responded—with sympathy and with support. Nations from Latin America, to Asia, to Africa, to Europe, to the Islamic world. Perhaps the NATO charter reflects best the attitude of the world: An attack on one is an attack on all.

The civilized world is rallying to America's side. They understand that if this terror goes unpunished, their own cities, their own citizens may be next. Terror, unanswered, can not only bring down buildings, it can threaten the stability of legitimate governments. And you know what—we're not going to allow it. (Applause.)

Americans are asking: What is expected of us? I ask you to live your lives, and hug your children. I know many citizens have fears tonight, and I ask you to be calm and resolute, even in the face of a continuing threat.

I ask you to uphold the values of America, and remember why so many have come here. We are in a fight for our principles, and our first responsibility is to live by them. No one should be singled out for unfair treatment or unkind words because of their ethnic background or religious faith. (Applause.)

I ask you to continue to support the victims of this tragedy with your contributions. Those who want to give can go to a central source of information, *libertyunites.org,* to find the names of groups providing direct help in New York, Pennsylvania, and Virginia.

The thousands of FBI agents who are now at work in this investigation may need your cooperation, and I ask you to give it.

I ask for your patience, with the delays and inconveniences that may accompany tighter security; and for your patience in what will be a long struggle.

I ask your continued participation and confidence in the American economy. Terrorists attacked a symbol of American prosperity. They did not touch its source. America is successful because of the hard work and creativity and enterprise of our people. These were the true strengths of our economy before September 11, and they are our strengths today. (Applause.)

And, finally, please continue praying for the victims of terror and their families, for those in uniform, and for our great country. Prayer has comforted us in sorrow, and will help strengthen us for the journey ahead.

Tonight I thank my fellow Americans for what you have already done and for what you will do. And ladies and gentlemen of the Congress, I thank you, their representatives, for what you have already done and for what we will do together.

Tonight, we face new and sudden national challenges. We   45
will come together to improve air safety, to dramatically expand the number of air marshals on domestic flights, and take new measures to prevent hijacking. We will come together to promote stability and keep our airlines flying, with direct assistance during this emergency. (Applause.)

We will come together to give law enforcement the additional tools it needs to track down terror here at home. (Applause.) We will come together to strengthen our intelligence capabilities to know the plans of terrorists before they act, and find them before they strike. (Applause.)

We will come together to take active steps that strengthen America's economy and put our people back to work.

Tonight we welcome two leaders who embody the extraordinary spirit of all New Yorkers: Governor George Pataki and Mayor Rudolph Giuliani. (Applause.) As a symbol of America's resolve, my administration will work with Congress, and these two leaders, to show the world that we will rebuild New York City. (Applause.)

After all that has just passed—all the lives taken, and all the possibilities and hopes that died with them—it is natural to wonder if America's future is one of fear. Some speak of an age of terror. I know there are struggles ahead, and dangers to face. But this country will define our times, not be defined by them. As long as the United States of America is determined and strong, this will not be an age of terror; this will be an age of liberty, here and across the world. (Applause.)

Great harm has been done to us. We have suffered great   50
loss. And in our grief and anger we have found our mission and our moment. Freedom and fear are at war. The advance of human freedom—the great achievement of our time, and the great hope of every time—now depends on us. Our nation—this generation—will lift a dark threat of violence from our people and our future. We will rally the world to this cause by our efforts,

by our courage. We will not tire, we will not falter, and we will not fail. (Applause.)

It is my hope that in the months and years ahead, life will return almost to normal. We'll go back to our lives and routines, and that is good. Even grief recedes with time and grace. But our resolve must not pass. Each of us will remember what happened that day, and to whom it happened. We'll remember the moment the news came—where we were and what we were doing. Some will remember an image of a fire, or a story of rescue. Some will carry memories of a face and a voice gone forever.

And I will carry this: It is the police shield of a man named George Howard, who died at the World Trade Center trying to save others. It was given to me by his mom, Arlene, as a proud memorial to her son. This is my reminder of lives that ended and a task that does not end. (Applause.)

I will not forget this wound to our country or those who inflicted it. I will not yield; I will not rest; I will not relent in waging this struggle for freedom and security for the American people.

The course of this conflict is not known, yet its outcome is certain. Freedom and fear, justice and cruelty, have always been at war, and we know that God is not neutral between them. (Applause.)

Fellow citizens, we'll meet violence with patient justice—assured of the rightness of our cause, and confident of the victories to come. In all that lies before us, may God grant us wisdom, and may He watch over the United States of America. 55

Thank you. (Applause.)

QUESTIONS FOR DISCUSSION AND WRITING

1. Identify the immediate and extended audiences for this speech. What elements of the speech seem targeted to different audiences? How does Bush meet the multiple rhetorical demands of the audience and purpose for this text?

2. After reading or listening to this whole speech, go over the text again and analyze the ways in which appeals to authority and common values, emotions, and logic contribute to the speech's effectiveness. How does Bush unite Americans and allies? How does he characterize and develop the idea of the enemy? How does he differentiate between friends and enemies of the Muslim faith?

3. Evaluate how the structure of the speech contributes to persuasion. Consider overall structure—introduction, body, conclusion—and sentence-level strategies, such as repetition, parallel construction, and short sentences.

4. Write an essay in which you analyze the persuasive appeals in this speech. Consider focusing on stylistic issues, such as anaphora (sentence-opener repetition), parallelism, and diction; or on logic, such as structure of argument and logical fallacies.

Statement, October 7, 2001

OSAMA BIN LADEN

Osama Bin Laden (1957–), is the Saudi-born head of the al Qaeda terrorist organization. Bin Laden is one of 52 children of Muhammad Bin Laden, a wealthy businessman with ties to Saudi Arabia's royal family. Osama Bin Laden had prepared to succeed his father in the construction business by studying business in college, but he eventually became interested in supporting the Mujahideen, a group of guerrilla fighters that organized in Afghanistan after the Soviet invasion in 1979. Bin Laden established the Maktab al-Khidamat organization in the early 1980s, whose purpose was to send money, weapons, and soldiers to support the defense of Afghanistan. In 1988, Bin Laden founded al Qaeda with former members of Maktab al-Khidamat. During the Gulf war, bin Laden was a major critic of the American presence in Saudi Arabia and he relocated to Sudan in 1991. Bin Laden orchestrated and financed several major terrorist attacks in the 1990s, moving to Afghanistan in 1998 after the Taliban regime took control of that country. In 1998, bin Laden and his colleague Ayman Zawahiri issued a fatwa under the name World Islamic Front for Jihad against Jews and Crusaders. The edict declared that Muslims should kill Americans and American allies wherever possible. As the apparent mastermind of the September 11 attacks and numerous international terrorist attacks, bin Laden tops the FBI's "Most Wanted" list along with several of his deputies. The selection that follows is a transcript of bin Laden's reaction to reports of the 9/11 attacks.

I bear witness that there is no God but Allah and that Mohammad is his messenger.

There is America, hit by God in one of its softest spots. Its greatest buildings were destroyed, thank God for that. There is America, full of fear from its north to its south, from its west to its east. Thank God for that.

What America is tasting now is something insignificant compared to what we have tasted for scores of years. Our nation [the Islamic world] has been tasting this humiliation and this degradation for more than eighty years. Its sons are killed, its blood is shed, its sanctuaries are attacked, and no one hears and no one heeds.

When God blessed one of the groups of Islam, vanguards of Islam, they destroyed America. I pray to God to elevate their status and bless them.

Millions of innocent children are being killed as I speak. 5
They are being killed in Iraq without committing any sins, and we don't hear condemnation or a fatwa [religious decree] from the rulers. In these days, Israeli tanks infest Palestine—in Jenin, Ramallah, Rafah, Beit Jalla, and other places in the land of Islam, and we don't hear anyone raising his voice or moving a limb.

When the sword comes down [on America], after eighty years, hypocrisy rears its ugly head. They deplore and they lament for those killers, who have abused the blood, honor, and sanctuaries of Muslims. The least that can be said about those people is that they are debauched. They have followed injustice. They supported the butcher over the victim, the oppressor over the innocent child. May God show them His wrath and give them what they deserve.

I say that the situation is clear and obvious. After this event, after the senior officials have spoken in America, starting with the head of infidels worldwide, Bush, and those with him. They have come out in force with their men and have turned even the countries that belong to Islam to this treachery, and they want to wag their tail at God, to fight Islam, to suppress people in the name of terrorism.

When people at the ends of the earth, Japan, were killed by their hundreds of thousands, young and old, it was not considered a war crime, it is something that has justification. Millions of children in Iraq is something that has justification. But when they lose dozens of people in Nairobi and Dar es Salaam [capitals of Kenya and Tanzania, where US embassies were bombed in 1998], Iraq was struck and Afghanistan was struck. Hypocrisy stood in force behind the head of infidels worldwide, behind the cowards of this age, America and those who are with it.

These events have divided the whole world into two sides. The side of believers and the side of infidels, may God keep you away from them. Every Muslim has to rush to make his religion victorious. The winds of faith have come. The winds of change have come to eradicate oppression from the island of Muhammad, peace be upon him.

To America, I say only a few words to it and its people. I swear by God, who has elevated the skies without pillars, neither America nor the people who live in it will dream of security before we live it in Palestine, and not before all the infidel armies leave the land of Muhammad, peace be upon him.

God is great, may pride be with Islam. May peace and God's mercy be upon you.

QUESTIONS FOR DISCUSSION AND WRITING

1. Discuss your emotional as well as rational responses to this text. How do you think these responses affect your analysis of the text?
2. Appeals to ethos generally attempt to establish the authority of the author. Analyze the appeals to ethos in this text. How often, and for what apparent purpose, does bin Laden reference God? In what ways might bin Laden use these references to establish authority?
3. What rationale does bin Laden give for action against America? What arguments does he make by analogy and how effective do you find them? What are the stated goals?
4. Analyze the logic of the speech, including any logical fallacies such as either–or fallacies or ad hominem attacks.
5. Analyze appeals to pathos in this text. Keeping in mind that this text is in translation, do you find language or references designed to evoke emotional response? Cite specific examples and the response they seem designed to elicit.
6. Building on these discussion questions, write an essay analyzing some aspect of this text, such as ethical or emotional appeals.

Editorial Cartoons: Post–9/11

Numerous editorial cartoons addressed the events of 9/11, generally in a somber rather than humorous manner. The cartoons that follow were identified by student writer Percy Ballard in a research paper analyzing the ways in which editorial cartoons grappled with 9/11 in the United States and abroad. Two of the cartoons he found and analyzed are included here, one published in the United States and one published in Iran. For additional examples of editorial and political cartoons, search online and also consider traditionally published collections updated annually.

A DAY OF INFAMY

(COPLEY NEWS SERVICE)

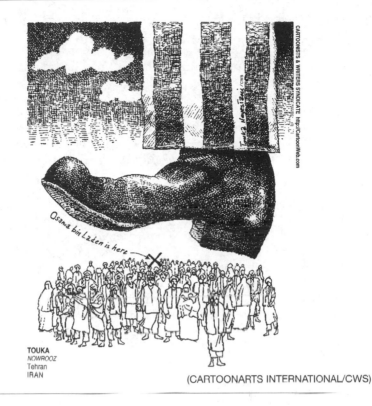

TOUKA
NOWROOZ
Tehran
IRAN

(CARTOONARTS INTERNATIONAL/CWS)

QUESTIONS FOR DISCUSSION AND WRITING

1. Discuss the visual reference and analogy to Pearl Harbor and the argument that the first figure makes. Do you find the comparison persuasive? Analyze the logic of the cartoon's persuasive appeals and discuss what rebuttal to the cartoon's arguments opponents might make.

2. Identify the rhetorical situation—audience and purpose—of the second figure and the stance you would expect the author and primary audience would have. Then, put the argument of this cartoon into your own words, sorting out premises and conclusions. As in Question 1, analyze the persuasive appeals and logic for the argument.

3. Analyze the ways in which each cartoon reflects and invokes its primary audience's values and emotions. Do you think the cartoons are equally effective in making a point?

4. In groups or pairs, draft a cartoon that makes a point about a topic raised in this chapter or another political or social issue. Then explain to the rest of your class what your argument is and what appeals you used to make your cartoon persuasive.

The Real War

THOMAS L. FRIEDMAN

Thomas L. Friedman (1953–) is a journalist for the *New York Times* specializing in the Middle East and a three-time winner of the Pulitzer Prize. Friedman earned a BA in Mediterranean studies from Brandeis University in 1975 and a Master of Philosophy degree in Modern Middle East studies from Oxford in 1978. From 1979 to 1984, Friedman reported from war-torn Beirut, Lebanon, leaving after a mortar attack on his neighborhood. Friedman went on to Jerusalem, where until 1988 he served as Israel bureau chief. Although of Jewish-American heritage, Friedman is considered an unbiased and critical investigator of the Middle East conflict. Friedman's books include *From Beirut to Jerusalem* (1983), which chronicles his ten years in the Middle East and his transformation from an admirer of Israeli policy to its public detractor; the book concludes with Friedman's observation that the Arab-Israeli conflict requires international intervention. He also published *The Lexus and the Olive Tree* (2000), which has been translated into twenty languages. The following essay was published in the *New York Times* on November 27, 2001.

If 9/11 was indeed the onset of World War III, we have to understand what this war is about. We're not fighting to eradicate "terrorism." Terrorism is just a tool. We're fighting to defeat an ideology: Religious totalitarianism. World War II and the cold war were fought to defeat secular totalitarianism—Nazism and Communism—and World War III is a battle against religious totalitarianism, a view of the world that my faith must reign supreme and can be affirmed and held passionately only if all others are negated. That's bin Ladenism. But unlike Nazism, religious totalitarianism can't be fought by armies alone. It has to be fought in schools, mosques, churches, and synagogues, and can be defeated only with the help of imams, rabbis, and priests.

The generals we need to fight this war are people like Rabbi David Hartman, from the Shalom Hartman Institute in Jerusalem. What first attracted me to Rabbi Hartman when I reported from Jerusalem was his contention that unless Jews reinterpreted their faith in a way that embraced modernity, without weakening religious passion and in a way that affirmed that God speaks multiple languages and is not exhausted by just one faith, they would have no future in the land of Israel. And what also impressed me was that he knew where the battlefield was. He set up his own schools in Israel to compete with fundamentalist Jews, Muslims, and Christians, who used their schools to preach exclusivist religious visions.

After recently visiting the Islamic madrasa in Pakistan where many Taliban leaders were educated, and seeing the fundamentalist religious education the young boys there were being given, I telephoned Rabbi Hartman and asked: How do we battle religious totalitarianism?

He answered: "All faiths that come out of the biblical tradition—Judaism, Christianity, and Islam—have the tendency to believe that they have the exclusive truth. When the Taliban wiped out the Buddhist statues, that's what they were saying. But others have said it too. The opposite of religious totalitarianism is an ideology of pluralism—an ideology that embraces religious diversity and the idea that my faith can be nurtured without claiming exclusive truth. America is the Mecca of that ideology, and that is what bin Laden hates and that is why America had to be destroyed."

The future of the world may well be decided by how we fight this war. Can Islam, Christianity, and Judaism know that God speaks Arabic on Fridays, Hebrew on Saturdays and Latin on Sundays, and that he welcomes different human beings approaching him through their own history, out of their language and cultural heritage? "Is single-minded fanaticism a necessity for passion and religious survival, or can we have a multilingual view of God—a notion that God is not exhausted by just one religious path?" asked Rabbi Hartman.

Many Jews and Christians have already argued that the answer to that question is yes, and some have gone back to their sacred texts to reinterpret their traditions to embrace modernity and pluralism, and to create space for secularism and alternative faiths. Others—Christian and Jewish fundamentalists—have rejected this notion, and that is what the battle is about within their faiths.

What is different about Islam is that while there have been a few attempts at such a reformation, none have flowered or found the support of a Muslim state. We patronize Islam, and mislead ourselves, by repeating the mantra that Islam is a faith with no serious problems accepting the secular West, modernity, and pluralism, and the only problem is a few bin Ladens.

Although there is a deep moral impulse in Islam for justice, charity, and compassion, Islam has not developed a dominant religious philosophy that allows equal recognition of alternative faith communities. Bin Laden reflects the most extreme version of that exclusivity, and he hit us in the face with it on 9/11.

Christianity and Judaism struggled with this issue for centuries, but a similar internal struggle within Islam to re-examine its texts and articulate a path for how one can accept pluralism and modernity—and still be a passionate, devout Muslim—has not surfaced in any serious way. One hopes that now that the world spotlight has been put on this issue, mainstream Muslims too will realize that their future in this integrated, globalized world depends on their ability to reinterpret their past.

QUESTIONS FOR DISCUSSION AND WRITING

1. What is the real war Friedman describes? How does it relate to World War II and the cold war? Why do you think he uses the term "war"?

2. How does Friedman's endorsement of Judaism's and Christianity's need to reinterpret their religious texts to allow for "plurality and diversity" affect his credibility in calling for Islam to do so?

3. Would you agree with Rabbi Hartman that one's "faith can be nurtured without claiming exclusive truth"? Does Friedman offer ways to implement this view?

4. Do you think Friedman's position is persuasive? If not, on what other bases might he argue that Islam should accept plurality and diversity?

5. Friedman uses the metaphor of war in this essay. Rewrite his argument using a different metaphor.

6. This essay originally appeared as a commentary in the *New York Times*. Write a response to Friedman as a letter to the editor agreeing with his stance, pointing out alternative views, or refuting his views.

Yes, This Is about Islam

SALMAN RUSHDIE

Salman Rushdie is an essayist and author of fiction born in Bombay, India, in 1947 to a middle-class Muslim family that later relocated to Pakistan; he attended school in England at age fourteen and later graduated from Kings College at Cambridge University. His narrative style is often associated with magical realism, a literary technique that does not follow ordinary physical rules or normal patterns of cause and effect. An author of numerous short stories, Rushdie has received critical acclaim for *Midnight's Children* (1981) and *Shame* (1983); in 1989, his publication of *The Satanic Verses* prompted the Ayatollah Khomeini of Iran to issue a fatwa (religious edict) in response to Rushdie's blasphemous depiction of the prophet Muhammad, calling on all Muslims to kill Rushdie and those who helped publish his book. After Rushdie's Japanese translator was murdered in 1991, Rushdie went into hiding. In 1998, the Iranian government promised not to carry out Rushdie's death sentence, but the fatwa remains in force; the bounty on Rushdie has increased to nearly $3 million, and Rushdie remains in hiding under private security while he continues to write and publish. Other books include *In Good Faith* (1990), *Imaginary Homelands: Essays and Criticism* (1991), *Wizard of Oz* (1992), *East, West* (1994), *The Moor's Last Sigh* (1995), *Mirror Work: 50 Years of Indian Writing 1947–1997*, with Elizabeth West (1997), *The Ground Beneath Her Feet* (1999), and *Fury* (2001). The essay that follows was published in the *New York Times* on November 2, 2001.

"This isn't about Islam." The world's leaders have been repeating this mantra for weeks, partly in the virtuous hope of deterring reprisal attacks on innocent Muslims living in the West, partly because if the United States is to maintain its coalition against terror it can't afford to suggest that Islam and terrorism are in any way related.

The trouble with this necessary disclaimer is that it isn't true. If this isn't about Islam, why the worldwide Muslim demonstrations in support of Osama bin Laden and al Qaeda? Why did those 10,000 men armed with swords and axes mass on the

Pakistan-Afghanistan frontier, answering some mullah's call to jihad? Why are the war's first British casualties three Muslim men who died fighting on the Taliban side?

Why the routine anti-Semitism of the much-repeated Islamic slander that "the Jews" arranged the hits on the World Trade Center and the Pentagon, with the oddly self-deprecating explanation offered by the Taliban leadership, among others, that Muslims could not have the technological know-how or organizational sophistication to pull off such a feat? Why does Imran Khan, the Pakistani ex-sports star-turned-politician, demand to be shown the evidence of al Qaeda's guilt while apparently turning a deaf ear to the self-incriminating statements of al Qaeda's own spokesmen (there will be a rain of aircraft from the skies, Muslims in the West are warned not to live or work in tall buildings)? Why all the talk about American military infidels desecrating the sacred soil of Saudi Arabia if some sort of definition of what is sacred is not at the heart of the present discontents?

Of course this is "about Islam." The question is, what exactly does that mean? After all, most religious belief isn't very theological. Most Muslims are not profound Koranic analysts. For a vast number of "believing" Muslim men, "Islam" stands, in a jumbled, half-examined way, not only for the fear of God—the fear more than the love, one suspects—but also for a cluster of customs, opinions, and prejudices that include their dietary practices; the sequestration or near-sequestration of "their" women; the sermons delivered by their mullahs of choice; a loathing of modern society in general, riddled as it is with music, godlessness, and sex; and a more particularized loathing (and fear) of the prospect that their own immediate surroundings could be taken over—"Westoxicated"—by the liberal Western-style way of life.

Highly motivated organizations of Muslim men (oh, for the voices of Muslim women to be heard!) have been engaged over the last thirty years or so in growing radical political movements out of this mulch of "belief." These Islamists—we must get used to this word, "Islamists," meaning those who are engaged upon such political projects, and learn to distinguish it from the more general and politically neutral "Muslim"—include the Muslim Brotherhood in Egypt, the blood-soaked combatants of the Islamic Salvation Front and Armed Islamic Group in Algeria, the Shiite revolutionaries of Iran, and the Taliban. Poverty is their great helper, and the fruit of their efforts is paranoia. This paranoid Islam, which blames outsiders, "infidels," for all the ills of

Muslim societies, and whose proposed remedy is the closing of those societies to the rival project of modernity, is presently the fastest growing version of Islam in the world.

This is not wholly to go along with Samuel Huntington's thesis about the clash of civilizations, for the simple reason that the Islamists' project is turned not only against the West and "the Jews," but also against their fellow Islamists. Whatever the public rhetoric, there's little love lost between the Taliban and Iranian regimes. Dissensions between Muslim nations run at least as deep, if not deeper, than those nations' resentment of the West. Nevertheless, it would be absurd to deny that this self-exculpatory, paranoiac Islam is an ideology with widespread appeal.

Twenty years ago, when I was writing a novel about power struggles in a fictionalized Pakistan, it was already de rigueur in the Muslim world to blame all its troubles on the West and, in particular, the United States. Then as now, some of these criticisms were well-founded; no room here to rehearse the geopolitics of the cold war and America's frequently damaging foreign policy "tilts," to use the Kissinger term, toward (or away from) this or that temporarily useful (or disapproved-of) nation-state, or America's role in the installation and deposition of sundry unsavory leaders and regimes. But I wanted then to ask a question that is no less important now: Suppose we say that the ills of our societies are not primarily America's fault, that we are to blame for our own failings? How would we understand them then? Might we not, by accepting our own responsibility for our problems, begin to learn to solve them for ourselves?

Many Muslims, as well as secularist analysts with roots in the Muslim world, are beginning to ask such questions now. In recent weeks Muslim voices have everywhere been raised against the obscurantist hijacking of their religion. Yesterday's hotheads (among them Yusuf Islam, aka Cat Stevens) are improbably repackaging themselves as today's pussycats.

An Iraqi writer quotes an earlier Iraqi satirist: "The disease that is in us, is from us." A British Muslim writes, "Islam has become its own enemy." A Lebanese friend, returning from Beirut, tells me that in the aftermath of the attacks on September 11, public criticism of Islamism has become much more outspoken. Many commentators have spoken of the need for a Reformation in the Muslim world.

I'm reminded of the way noncommunist socialists used to distance themselves from the tyrannical socialism of the Soviets; nevertheless, the first stirrings of this counterproject are of great significance. If Islam is to be reconciled with modernity, these voices must be encouraged until they swell into a roar. Many of them speak of another Islam, their personal, private faith.

The restoration of religion to the sphere of the personal, its depoliticization, is the nettle that all Muslim societies must grasp in order to become modern. The only aspect of modernity interesting to the terrorists is technology, which they see as a weapon that can be turned on its makers. If terrorism is to be defeated, the world of Islam must take on board the secularist-humanist principles on which the modern is based, and without which Muslim countries' freedom will remain a distant dream.

QUESTIONS FOR DISCUSSION AND WRITING

1. Rushdie frames his essay as a response to statements that 9/11 was not "about Islam." Does he rebut these points clearly? Do his examples in paragraphs 2 and 3 adequately refute this opposing view?

2. Rushdie asserts that if Muslim nations accept responsibility for their problems rather than blaming the West, they could then learn to solve their own problems. Are you persuaded of this point based on the reasons and evidence he gives?

3. Rushdie concludes by arguing for the return of religion "to the sphere of the personal" of Muslim societies that are trying to become modern. Does he support the assumption that Muslim societies would wish to become modern? If not, do you nevertheless accept that premise?

4. Write a response to Rushdie that argues with his view and supports those who assert that 9/11 was not "about Islam." Be sure to support your views and to deal with Rushdie's most persuasive points in your refutation.

Unsolved Palestinian Problem Remains a Magnet

GHASSAN KHATIB

Ghassan Khatib was born in Nablus, Palestine, in 1954 and currently serves as minister of labor in the Palestine National Authority. He was a member of the Madrid Peace Delegation in 1991 and was involved in the Washington negotiations from 1991 to 1993. He was appointed minister of labor in 2002. Khatib was a lecturer at Birzeit University's Cultural Studies Program. Khatib holds an MA in Development Studies from Manchester University and a BA in Economics and Business Administration from Birzeit University. He is pursuing a doctorate in middle east politics at the University of Durham. In 1971, Khatib joined the Palestinian People's Party and was elected as a member in its political office in 2000. He was detained by Israel on several occasions, the most recent of which was in 1990. He is director of the Jerusalem Media and Communications Center (JMCC), a nongovernmental organization that conducts public opinion polls and provides media support to journalists in the occupied Palestinian territories. A long-time advocate of Palestinian-Israeli dialogue, Khatib is the co-founder and director of *BitterLemons.org*, a Palestinian Israeli Internet based political magazine. He serves on the editorial board of the *Israel-Palestine Journal*, a political journal offering Palestinian and Israeli perspectives. The article that follows was published in *The Palestine Report*, an online newsmagazine, which has been published in Jerusalem for nearly 15 years and is available at < *http://www.palestinereport.org* >.

When Osama bin Laden put the Palestinian cause at the core of the speech he delivered to the world and released immediately after the outbreak of American and British hostilities against Afghanistan, he was deliberately attempting to extract legitimacy from the Muslim and Arab public by linking his cause to that of Palestinians and exploiting their frustration.

Given that, one can extrapolate that the Palestinian cause is the most legitimate and credible in the region. Ten years ago, when Iraqi President Saddam Hussein was on the verge of offensives from the American-led coalition, he also linked his cause with that of Palestinians, saying he would end his occupation of Kuwait only when Israel ended its occupation of the West Bank and Gaza Strip.

Even US President George Bush and the American administration seem to feel that they must do something in support of the Palestinian people and cause if they want to succeed in ensuring Arab backing for an anti-terrorism coalition.

While Saddam's linkage strategy was at that time very appealing to the Arabs and more so to the Palestinian people and leadership, bin Laden's today is not. While bin Laden's words may have spoken to the current frustrations of Palestinians, comparisons being made between Palestinian feelings towards Iraq and Afghanistan are otherwise, inaccurate and overblown.

There are many reasons for the sympathy and solidarity between Palestinians and Iraqis, not only in that both are Arabs and Muslims and culturally similar but, more importantly, that they share geographical proximity. Iraq, too, has sent armies to fight with Palestinians in every war in Palestine since the beginning of the Palestinian problem.   5

Afghanistan, however, is completely different. First, Afghanis are not Arabs and are distant from Palestine and the Palestinians. Second, most Palestinians did not accept the attack on American civilians on September 11 as justifiable and—although they also do not justify the use of force and violence by Americans against the Afghanis—they do not strongly identify with the Taliban and bin Laden, except for feelings of common humanity and a sort of desperation that finally someone is speaking about their cause. In addition, Palestinian society maintains a secular majority that does not identify strongly with the Taliban ideology and regime.

That is why, in spite of the appeal of Osama bin Laden, the ordinary Palestinian public has not expressed a great deal of enthusiasm in support of bin Laden or his alleged actions. Those Palestinians who express this strongly are Palestinian Islamic fundamentalists who identify with bin Laden on an ideological basis. That explains the fact that the only place where demonstrations in support of bin Laden took place was in and around the Islamic University in Gaza, which is a main stronghold for Hamas and Islamic Jihad.

To put these demonstrations in context, some members of Hamas and Islamic Jihad have been looking for ways to challenge Palestinian President Yasser Arafat's decision to cease fire.

Tying Palestinians to bin Laden, they found a chance to exploit and undermine the power of the Palestinian Authority by leading a demonstration in solidarity with the Taliban and bin Laden.

Arafat, too, responded with political interests in mind. He has not been able to pressure Hamas to cooperate with his unpopular cease fire and found that now was the time to increase pressure on the opposition. Arafat believed that the majority of the Palestinian public would understand attempts to prevent Hamas aligning Palestinians with the Taliban and bin Laden. That is why it seemed politically feasible to move against Hamas or other factions' demonstrations in support of bin Laden, while he was not at all able to move against Hamas when it was violating his cease fire orders. In the end, the public was shocked at the level of brutality used by the Palestinian police in handling the demonstrations and the press was disturbed by the measures taken to prevent it from covering these events.

These events only further confirm previous analysis of the nature and the extent of control Arafat has on the Palestinian territories. Again, Arafat's ability to "control" depends on whether his public supports his demands. When Arafat wants to enforce something that enjoys the understanding and support of the majority of his people, then he has control and can be effective. But when he is implementing a cause that is unpopular and is imposed upon him, he cannot be "in control" because he will not be able to impose his will, even by force.

The Palestinian Authority, as it works to avoid a political trap linking the Palestinian struggle with the world pariahs of bin Laden and the Taliban, is absolutely unjustified in the brutality with which it handled the demonstration in Gaza that ended in several deaths. And this is not the only problem in the Palestinian Authority's performance in this crisis. The Palestinian Authority also prevented the foreign and local media from covering the demonstration (which only backfired, because it left the media with the false impression that perhaps there were many attempts to demonstrate in support of bin Laden that were not reported on due to the blackout policy of the Palestinian Authority).

The Palestinian Authority made another major mistake by not delivering a clear and strong official response to bin Laden's statement, one that reconfirmed its condemnation of the September 11 attacks, and at the same time expressed wariness over the use of force against innocent Afghani civilians. That statement should have distinguished the Palestinian cause from that of the Taliban and responded to bin Laden's linkage attempt to tie the two inextricably.

As long as there is an illegitimate Israeli occupation on the Palestinian territories, as long as the refugee problem of four million Palestinians is not solved and as long as East Jerusalem and al Aqsa mosque remain under the control of the Israeli occupiers, we will continue to see attempts to make use of the legitimacy of the Palestinian cause—whether they are right or wrong, or coming from Bush or bin Laden. The Palestinian people, however, root the legitimacy of their cause in human rights and international law, specifically United Nations Security Council 242, which calls for an end to the Israeli occupation. Until the Palestinian problem is resolved, it will be difficult, if not impossible, to use the principles of human rights and international law in other conflicts in the region.

QUESTIONS FOR DISCUSSION AND WRITING

1. Much of the political rhetoric about the Middle East references the Palestinian cause. How does this author explain the linkage of Palestinians to various causes? How does he both compare and contrast Palestinian issues with those claiming solidarity with them? What do others have to gain by claiming this solidarity? What justification do they seek?

2. Evaluate the logical appeals in the first two paragraphs. Does the author clearly state the case? How do paragraphs 7 through 9 respond to internationally televised images of Palestinians "dancing in the streets" after the 9/11 attacks? Why would the author need to address this point, relative to his purpose in this text?

3. According to the author, Palestinians root their cause in human rights and international law. How persuasive is this authority? Do you have a sense of why, then, their cause has not been resolved?

4. The author discusses a "political trap." What is this trap and how might Yasser Arafat get around it? What other political traps are you aware of with regard to contemporary politics?

5. Discuss the persuasive appeals in this essay. In a topic frequently discussed in heated terms, to what degree to you believe this author has based his argument on appeals to logos rather than pathos and ethos?

6. Write an essay analyzing Khatib's argumentation, with particular attention to form and structure.

Child "Suicide Bomber" and Saddam Statue

In the selections that follow, we see images that traveled the globe through Internet, broadcast, and print media. AP photographer Jan Bauer took the first photograph at a pro-Palestinian rally in Germany; the image evoked outrage in some quarters. The second image is a graphic portrayal of the literal as well as figurative downfall of Saddam Hussein.

As you critically analyze these images, consider the extent to which each image makes an argument.

Man, at pro-Palestinian demonstration in Germany, carries his daughter, who is wearing a mock suicide terrorist explosive belt.   (AP/WIDE WORLD PHOTOS)

(AP/WIDE WORLD PHOTOS)

QUESTIONS FOR DISCUSSION AND WRITING

1. Analyze the composition of each image—the elements, the setting and people, the foreground and background. Where is your eye drawn? What captures your attention? What recedes in the background?

2. Analyze each image's appeals to logic, emotion, and values and beliefs. What is the argument each image makes? What is the supporting evidence for the argument? What logical fallacies do you find? What emotions does each image evoke? How does such an appeal persuade the viewer?

3. Write an essay analyzing the persuasiveness of one of these images. Alternatively, research other images of 9/11 and its aftermath and analyze one image or a pair of images.

America: Open for Business

CRAIG FRAZER

This poster was sponsored by San Francisco city government in response to the economic downturn following the 9/11 attacks. The poster has been popular throughout business and shopping areas and was widely distributed throughout the San Francisco Bay Area following 9/11, in some cases being hand-delivered by the mayor and city supervisors. This design, by artist Craig Frazer, ingeniously combines motifs such as a patriotic flag and a symbol of business and consumerism.

(CRAIG FRAZIER STUDIO)

QUESTIONS FOR DISCUSSION AND WRITING

1. Analyze the poster's elements, composition, argument, and appeals. What is its message? How persuasively does it convey that message? What are the pros and cons of emphasizing shopping in this poster?
2. How do the composition, design, symbolism, and argument compare with other posters in this book or ones you have seen in your community?
3. How do you think societies unfriendly to the United States might interpret this image?
4. Research and if possible collect or copy samples of patriotic posters from your community or distributed on the Internet and bring them to class to analyze themes, arguments, and appeals. Consider using a Google image search to find similar images.

Chapter Eight: Connections

1. Discuss Friedman's theme as outlined in "The Real War" in view of Huntington's and Said's essays in Chapter Three.
2. Outline Rushdie's and Friedman's arguments and identify common themes and opposing views.
3. Compare and contrast appeals to ethos and pathos in the speeches of Bush and bin Laden.
4. Search the Web for editorial cartoons on the topic of 9/11 and its aftermath. Analyze the argument of each image and the appeals it uses to persuade the audience.
5. In view of the Keen reading in the previous chapter, what kinds of typecasting and dichotomizing do you find in the selections in this chapter or in other texts and images on the topic of the September 11 attacks?
6. Compare and contrast the images in this chapter with the photographs in Chapter Seven.
7. Set up a classroom dialogue on the topic of 9/11 in which different students take on the roles of Zuckerman (Chapter Seven), Friedman, Rushdie, Huntington, and Said. Assign a moderator and have the rest of the class follow the discussion and analyze the positions and views expressed in this discussion.

8. Discuss the underlying themes of Chapter Seven and this chapter with regard to the wars in Afghanistan and Iraq.

9. Compare and contrast the images of children in this text and discuss the issues raised by these images.

Chapter Eight: End-of-Chapter Assignments

1. Using the speeches of Roosevelt (Chapter Seven) and Bush (this chapter) as a starting point, research presidential rhetoric in times of crisis. Analyze rhetorical situations—audience and purpose—and strategies presidents use to unite Americans and characterize the enemy.

2. Read Eric Hoffer's *The True Believer* and apply the principles he discusses to one of the mass movements of the twentieth century.

3. Drawing from Keen and other sources you identify, such as Paul Fussell's book *Wartime* or the writing of Amin Malouf, write an essay in which you explore ways in which stereotyping pervades the images and texts post–9/11.

4. Research the practice of racial profiling and its effectiveness or ineffectiveness as a means of law enforcement.

5. Research Camp Xray, the detention center at Guantanamo Bay, Cuba, for captives held on suspicion of involvement in terrorist acts, and the relevant legal principles and public policy such as the 1949 Geneva Conventions and international definitions of prisoners of war.

6. Read one of linguist George Lakoff's essays on image and metaphor (available online) and apply the principles he outlines to the video, photographic images, posters, and editorial cartoons circulated on and after September 11.

7. Drawing from discussion in Connections, write an essay analyzing persuasive appeals, such as appeals to ethos, in the Bush and bin Laden speeches included here.

8. In pairs or groups, devise an editorial cartoon about a contemporary political or social situation and then present and explain your image to the rest of the class.

9. Research the psychology or science of image processing, with a focus on recent work that explores how perceiving traumatic images can "rewire" the brain's processing.

10. Research the ways in which the 9/11 attacks have provoked trauma reactions and the types of treatment that have been developed to work with trauma survivors.

11. Research the effects of war and trauma on children and efforts to treat them, such as art and play therapy. Consider, for example, Northern Ireland, Rwanda, and Sierra Leone.
12. Research the ways in which survivors of war and trauma, such as Vietnam veterans and civilians, survivors of the Cambodian killing fields, child and adult veterans of conflict in Africa, and Central American war and conflict survivors, have been affected by trauma and how adult survivors have been faring in the years since.

Chapter Eight: Web Sites for Further Exploration

University of Michigan Documents Center, America's War Against Terrorism
World Trade Center/Pentagon Terrorism and the Aftermath
http://www.lib.umich.edu/govdocs/usterror.html
Cable News Network (US)
http://www.cnn.com
British Broadcasting Co. Web Site
http://www.bbc.com
Al Jazeera Web Site
http://www.cursor.org/aljazeera.htm
Opinion Pages
http://www.opinion-pages.org/index.html
CIA World Factbook Site
http://www.cia.gov/cia/publications/factbook/geos/bk.html
CIA Electronic Reading Room
http://foia.state.gov/
George Lakoff, "Metaphors of Terror" (Article)
http://www.press.uchicago.edu/News/911lakoff.html
Translation Web Site
http://tarjim.ajeeb.com/ajeeb/default.asp?lang=1
Palestine Report
http://www.jmcc.org/media/reportonline/report.html
The Middle East Media Research Institute
http://www.memri.org/

APPENDIX:
PRECEDENTS
AND TRADITIONS

TEXTS

The Golden Rule across Religions

Ten Commandments of Moses

What Is Buddhism?

Mahatma Gandhi, "Satyragraha"

Charter of the United Nations

United States Bill of Rights

The Seneca Falls Declaration (1848)

ONLINE RESOURCES

The Bible Online
http://bible.com/bible_read.html

The Koran Online
http://etext.lib.virginia.edu/koran.html

The Works of Aristotle Online
http://www.gustavus.edu/oncampus/academics/philosophy/aris.html

The Works of Confucius Online
http://www.gustavus.edu/oncampus/academics/philosophy/confucius.html

The Character of an Old English Puritan, or Nonconformist
http://www.cet.com/~mtr/GereeChar.html

The US Declaration of Independence
*http://www.archives.gov/exhibit_hall/charters_of_freedom/
declaration/declaration_transcription.html*

Karl Marx, *Das Kapital,* Online (in English)
http://csf.colorado.edu/psn/marx/Archive/1867-C1/

THE GOLDEN RULE ACROSS RELIGIONS

The Golden Rule or the ethic of reciprocity is found in the scriptures
of nearly every religion. It is often regarded as the most concise and
general principle of ethics. It is a condensation in one principle of all
longer lists of ordinances such as the Decalogue.

Bahá'í Faith

> *And if thine eyes be turned towards justice, choose thou for thy neigh-
> bour that which thou choosest for thyself.*
>
> Epistle to the Son of the Wolf, 30

Hindu Faith

> *This is the sum of duty: Do naught to others which if done to thee
> would cause thee pain.*
>
> The Mahabharata

Jewish Faith

> *What is hateful to you, do not to your fellow men. That is the entire
> Law; all the rest is commentary.*
>
> The Talmud

Zoroastrian Faith

> *Whatever is disagreeable to yourself do not do unto others.*
>
> Shayast-na-Shayast 13:29

Buddhist Faith

Hurt not others with that which pains yourself.

Udana-Varga

Christian Faith

All things whatsoever ye would that men should do to you, do ye even so to them: for this is the law and the prophets.

The Gospel of Matthew 7:12; The Gospel of Luke 6:31

Muslim Faith

No one of you is a believer until he desires for his brother that which he desires for himself.

Hadith

And yet some other sources:

Do not do unto others what angers you if done to you by others.

Isocrates 436-338 BCE

An it harm none, do what thou wilt.

Wiccan Rede

Tzu-kung asked, "Is there a single word which can be a guide to conduct throughout one's life?" The Master said, "It is perhaps the word shu. Do not impose on others what you yourself do not desire."

Analects 15.24

Refraining from doing what we blame in others.

By Thales
As quoted in Diogenes Laertius, Vol. 1, p. 39.
(submitted by Gaylen Bunker)

Christianity: Thou shalt love thy neighbor as thyself.

Summations by the author of this article did not include the following comparable statement of Jesus Christ in the New Testament, King James version, which says a bit more that what the author is representing under Christianity.

It is found in the book of Matthew, Chapter 7, verse 12, and says:

Therefore all things whatsoever ye would that men should do to you, do ye even so to them: for this is the law and the prophets.

You shall love your neighbor as yourself.

Judaism and Christianity. Bible, *Leviticus 19.18*

Whatever you wish that men would do to you, do so to them.

> Christianity. Bible, *Matthew 7.12*

Not one of you is a believer until he loves for his brother what he loves for himself.

> Islam. Forty Hadith of *an-Nawawi 13*

A man should wander about treating all creatures as he himself would be treated.

> Jainism. *Sutrakritanga 1.11.33*

Try your best to treat others as you would wish to be treated yourself, and you will find that this is the shortest way to benevolence.

> Confucianism. *Mencius VII.A.4*

One should not behave towards others in a way which is disagreeable to oneself. This is the essence of morality. All other activities are due to selfish desire.

> Hinduism. *Mahabharata, Anusasana Parva* 113.8

Tsukung asked, Is there one word that can serve as a principle of conduct for life? Confucius replied, It is the word shu—reciprocity: Do not do to others what you do not want them to do to you.

> Confucianism. *Analects 15.23*

Leviticus 19.18: *Quoted by Jesus in* Matthew 22.36-40. Mencius VII.A.4 *and* Analects 15.23: *cf.* Analects 6.28.2, *p. 975.*

Comparing oneself to others in such terms as Just as I am so are they, just as they are so am I, he should neither kill nor cause others to kill.

> Buddhism. *Sutta Nipata 705*

One going to take a pointed stick to pinch a baby bird should first try it on himself to feel how it hurts.

> African Traditional Religions. *Yoruba Proverb* (Nigeria)

One who you think should be hit is none else but you. One who you think should be governed is none else but you. One who you think should be tortured is none else but you. One who you think should be enslaved is none else but you. One who you think should be killed is none else but you. A sage is ingenuous and leads his life after comprehending the parity of the killed and the killer. Therefore, neither does he cause violence to others nor does he make others do so.

> Jainism. *Acarangasutra 5.101-2*

The Ariyan disciple thus reflects, Here am I, fond of my life, not wanting to die, fond of pleasure and averse from pain. Suppose someone should rob me of my life . . . it would not be a thing pleasing and delightful to me. If I, in my turn, should rob of his life one fond of his life, not wanting to die, one fond of pleasure and averse from pain, it would not be a thing pleasing or delightful to him. For a state that is not pleasant or delightful to me must also be to him also; and a state that is not pleasing or delightful to me, how could I inflict that upon another?

As a result of such reflection he himself abstains from taking the life of creatures and he encourages others so to abstain, and speaks in praise of so abstaining.

> Buddhism. *Samyutta Nikaya v.353*

A certain heathen came to Shammai and said to him, Make me a proselyte, on condition that you teach me the whole Torah while I stand on one foot. Thereupon he repulsed him with the rod which was in his hand. When he went to Hillel, he said to him, What is hateful to you, do not do to your neighbor: that is the whole Torah; all the rest of it is commentary; go and learn.

Judaism. Talmud, *Shabbat 31a*

Teacher, which is the great commandment in the law? Jesus said to him, You shall love the Lord your God with all your heart, and with all your soul, and with all your mind. This is the great and first commandment. And a second is like it, You shall love your neighbor as yourself.

Christianity. Bible, *Matthew 22.36–40*

TEN COMMANDMENTS OF MOSES

Deuteronomy 5:6–21

(6) I am the Lord your God, who brought you out of Egypt, out of the land of slavery.

(7) You shall have no other gods before me.

(8) You shall not make for yourself an idol in the form of anything in heaven above or on the earth beneath or in the waters below. (9) You shall not bow down to them or worship them; for I, the Lord your God, am a jealous God, punishing the children for the sin of the fathers to the third and fourth generation of those who hate me, (10) but showing love to thousands who love me and keep my commandments.

(11) You shall not misuse the name of the Lord your God, for the Lord will not hold anyone guiltless, who misuses his name.

(12) Observe the Sabbath day by keeping it holy, as the Lord your God has commanded you. (13) Six days you shall labor and do all your work, (14) but the seventh day is a Sabbath to the Lord your God. On it you shall not do any work, neither you, nor your son or daughter, nor your manservant or maidservant, nor your ox, your donkey or any of your animals, nor the alien within your gates, so that your manservant and maidservant may rest as you do.

(15) Remember that you were slaves in Egypt and that the Lord your Godbrought you out of there with a mighty hand and an outstretched arm. Therefore the Lord your God has commanded you to observe the Sabbath day.

(16) Honor your father and your mother, as the Lord your God has commanded you, so that you may live long and that it may go well with you in the land the Lord your God is giving you.

(17) You shall not murder.

(18) You shall not commit adultery.

(19) You shall not steal.

(20) You shall not give false testimony against your neighbor.

(21) You shall not covet your neighbor's wife. You shall not set your desire on your neighbor's house or land, his manservant or maidservant, his ox or donkey, or anything that belongs to your neighbor.

WHAT IS BUDDHISM?

Buddhism has alternately been called a religion, a philosophy, an ideology, and a way of life. As with all the other great spiritual traditions that have withstood the test of time, Buddhism offers many different paths for people with different kinds of sensibilities, needs, and capacities.

There are several ways of understanding differences within Buddhism.

The Spread of Buddhism into Different Cultures
Buddhism began in Northern India six hundred years before the Christian era. Over a period of about one thousand years, Buddhism spread north into Tibet; south into Sri Lanka; southeast into Laos, Cambodia, and Vietnam; east into Burma, China, Korea, and Japan. As Buddhism spread it adapted to these "host" cultures and in each case was shaped and influenced in flavor and style by pre-existing rituals and cosmologies. Thus, we speak of Tibetan Buddhism or Japanese Buddhism or Korean Buddhism. And within each cultural sphere, many different paths, lineages, and sects have emerged.

Core Teachings
There are immutable core teachings expounded by the historical Buddha, Shakyamuni, that create a collective wellspring for all forms

of Buddhism. Specifically, these are the Four Noble Truths and the Eightfold Path. Yet these basic teachings have themselves been subject to interpretation and again have various flavors within different Buddhist cultures.

There is No One Buddhism
There has never been, nor is there now, a central authority in Buddhism. There is no equivalent to the Holy Father of the Roman Church or to anything that resembles papal law. With no supreme arbiter, the diversification of Buddhism has flourished. This also means that there is no one Buddhism. There are many Buddhisms. So when we try to answer the question, "What is Buddhism?" we can only try our best to present the most inclusive and pan-Buddhist answers. And yet, it will serve you well to remember that the vast array of traditions, combined with the absence of a singular authority, means that in general, thinking in terms of "right and wrong" answers and "good and bad" answers is not a very useful approach.

Diversity of View and Understanding
This diversity of view and understanding may offer a refreshing alternative to doctrinal rigidity. It can also yield some very sloppy and indulgent versions of what "Buddhism means to me." But to maintain respect for differences, keep in mind some of the historic distinctions that exist within all religions and within all cultures. Some people approach spiritual belief systems in order to comfort themselves and to soften the inevitable harsh blows of life—illness, loss, death, grief. For many people, the communal activity of ritual—congregations or sanghas—itself offers a powerful experience of transcending the claustrophobic boundaries of the individual self in order to participate in a larger, more generous, bountiful experience. This can also be easily accomplished through collective singing or chanting, which is such a common feature of religions around the world. There is the way lay people engage in religion versus the lifestyle and commitments made by monastics. There are mystics and maverick masters, enlightened householders, dutiful abbots, and those whose spiritual aspirations demand to know what this life is all about.

The Three Main Vehicles
Today in the West, through Western converts to Buddhism and Asian immigrant communities, we have an unprecedented opportunity to experience every kind of Buddhism, and furthermore, to bring to our understanding an educated, historical perspective of the whole sweep of Buddhist activity. For an introduction to Buddhism, we offer the most generalized, commonly accepted, main "yanas" or vehicles of the Buddha's teachings which have come to be known as Theravada, Mahayana, and Vajrayana.

Theravada, Mahayana, and Vajrayana
There is a longstanding debate about whether these different yanas were all taught by the Buddha himself or were introduced later on and, for reasons of "skillful means," attributed to the historical Buddha.

All three, however, share a common foundation encapsulated in the Buddha's first teaching, the Four Noble Truths, which he delivered at the Deer Park in Sarnath. The first Truth starts with the point that suffering is an undeniable part of this world of birth and death. Because of this emphasis on suffering, Buddhism has wrongly been confused with nihilism and pessimism. But the Buddha focused on suffering in the same way that a doctor focuses on disease: only by addressing the problem can a solution be found. This solution lies in the remaining three Noble Truths: that suffering has a cause, which is craving based on ignorance; that suffering can be ended by eliminating its cause; and that the cause can be eliminated through developing the path of virtue, concentration, and discernment.

The discernment developed in meditation is central to the path, in that it sees through the illusory notion of self-identity that grows out of craving and ignorance, thus leading to repeated suffering and stress. Buddhism points out that any experience we might identify as our "self" is impermanent, continually in flux, coming into existence and passing away, conditioned from one moment to the next by interrelated, empty phenomena. If we do not abandon our sense of self-identity, we are bound to suffer pain and alienation, as our "self" inevitably falls subject to circumstances outside our control.

To gain freedom from this predicament, we must first develop a healthy sense of self based on being harmless and compassionate, both to ourselves and to others. Then, through meditation, we enter the present moment by dropping our memories of the past and fantasies about the future. Observing the present, we see that our "self" is simply an internal dialogue of incessant chatter. As this chatter grows still, a point is reached in which "self," "other," and "present" are transcended. That is where liberation is found.

MAHATMA GANDHI, "SATYAGRAHA"

I have drawn the distinction between passive resistance as understood and practised in the West and satyagraha before I had evolved the doctrine of the latter to its full logical and spiritual extent. I often used "passive resistance" and "satyagraha" as synonymous terms: but as the doctrine of satyagraha developed, the expression "passive resistance" ceases even to be synonymous, as passive resistance has admitted of violence as in the case of suffragettes and has been universally acknowledged to be a weapon of the weak. Moreover passive resistance does not necessarily involve complete adherence to truth under every circumstance. Therefore it is different from satyagraha in three essentials: Satyagraha is a weapon of the strong; it admits of no violence under any circumstance whatever; and it ever insists upon truth. I think I have now made the distinction perfectly clear.

(From a letter, January 25, 1920)

In the application of satyagraha, I discovered, in the earliest stages, that pursuit of Truth did not admit of violence being inflicted on one's opponent, but that he must be weaned from error by patience and sympathy. For, what appears to be truth to the one may appear to be error to the other. And patience means self-suffering. So the doctrine came to mean vindication of Truth, not by infliction of suffering on the opponent but one's own self.

Satyagraha and its offshoots, noncooperation and civil resistance, are nothing but new names for the law of suffering.

With satya combined with ahimsa, you can bring the world to your feet. Satyagraha in its essence is nothing but the introduction of truth and gentleness in the political (i.e., the national life).

Satyagraha is utter self-effacement, greatest humiliation, greatest patience, and brightest faith. It is its own reward.

Satyagraha is a relentless search for truth and a determination to reach truth.

It is a force that works silently and apparently slowly. In reality, there is no force in the world that is so direct or so swift in working.

Satyagraha literally means insistence on truth. This insistence arms the votary with matchless power. This power or force is connoted by the word satyagraha. Satyagraha, to be genuine, may be offered against parents, against one's wife or one's children, against rulers, against fellow-citizens, even against the whole world.

Such a universal force necessarily makes no distinction between kinsmen and strangers, young and old, man and woman, friend and foe. The force to be so applied can never be physical. There is in it no room for violence. The only force of universal aplication can, therefore, be that of ahimsa or love. In other words, it is soul-force.

Love does not burn others, it burns itself. Therefore, a satyagrahi (i.e., a civil resister) will joyfully suffer even unto death.

It follows, therefore, that a civil resister, whilst he will strain every nerve to compass the end of the existing rule, will do no intentional injury in thought, word, or deed to the person of a single Englishman. This necessarily brief explanation of satyagraha will perhaps enable the reader to understand and appreciate the following rules:

As an individual:

1. A satyagrahi (i.e., a civil resister) will harbour no anger.

2. He will suffer the anger of the opponent.

3. In so doing he will put up with assaults from the opponent, never retaliate; but he will not submit, out of fear of punishment or the like, to any order given in in anger.

4. When any person in authority seeks to arrest a civil resister, he will voluntarily submit to the arrest, and he will
   not resist the attachment or removal of his own property,
   if any, when it is sought to be confiscated by authorities.

5. If a civil resister has any property in his possession as a
   trustee, he will refuse to surrender it, even though in defending it he might lose his life. He will, however, never retaliate.

6. Nonretaliation excludes swearing and cursing.

7. Therefore a civil resister wil never insult his opponent,
   and therefore also not take part in many of the newly
   coined cries which are contrary to the spirit of ahimsa.

8. A civil resister will not salute the Union Jack, nor will he
   insult it or officials, English or Indian.

9. In the course of the struggle if anyone insults an official or
   commits an assault upon him, a civil resister will protect
   such official or officials from the insult or attack even at
   the risk of his life.

(Young India, February 27, 1930)

The movement of nonviolent noncooperation has nothing in common
with the historical struggles for freedom in the West. It is not based on
brute force or hatred. It does not aim at destroying the tyrant. It is a
movement of self-purification. It therefore seeks to convert the tyrant. It
may fail because India was not ready for mass nonviolence. But it would
be wrong to judge the movement by false standards. My own opinion is
that the movement has in no ways failed. It has found an abiding place
in India's struggle for freedom.

Although noncooperation is one of the main weapons in the armoury of satyagraha, it should not be forgotten that it is after all only a
means to secure the cooperation of the opponent consistently with truth
and justice. The essence of nonviolent technique is that it seeks to liqui-
date antagonisms but not the antagonists themselves. In nonviolent
fight you have, to a certain measure, to conform to the tradition and conventions of the system you are pitted against. Avoidance of all relationship with the opposing power, therefore, can never be a satyagrahi's
object but transformation or purification of that relationship.

Civil disobedience is the inherent right of a citizen. He dare not give
it up without ceasing to be a man. Civil disobedience is never followed
by anarchy. Criminal disobedience can lead to it. Every state puts down
criminal disobedience by force. It perishes if it does not.

A satyagrahi obeys the laws of society intelligently and of his own
free will, because he considers it to be his sacred duty to do so. It is only
when a person has thus obeyed the laws of society scrupulously that he

is in a position to judge as to which particular laws are good and just and which unjust and iniquitous. Only then does the right accrue to him of civil disobedience of certain laws in well-defined circumstances.

Fasting is a potent weapon in the satyagraha armoury. It cannot be taken by everyone. Mere physical capacity to take it is no qualification for it. It is of no use without a living faith in God. It should never be a mechanical effort or a mere imitation. It must come from the depth of one's soul. It is, therefore, always rare.

I believe that every man and woman should learn the art of self-defence in this age. This is done through arms in the West. Every adult man is conscripted for army training for a definite period. The training for satyagraha is meant for all, irrespective of age or sex. The more important part of the training here is mental, not physical. There can be no compulsion in mental training.

CHARTER OF THE UNITED NATIONS

Preamble

We the Peoples of the United Nations Determined

to save succeeding generations from the scourge of war, which twice in our lifetime has brought untold sorrow to mankind, and

to reaffirm faith in fundamental human rights, in the dignity and worth of the human person, in the equal rights of men and women and of nations large and small, and

to establish conditions under which justice and respect for the obligations arising from treaties and other sources of international law can be maintained, and

to promote social progress and better standards of life in larger freedom,

And for these Ends

to practice tolerance and live together in peace with one another as good neighbors, and

to unite our strength to maintain international peace and security, and

to ensure by the acceptance of principles and the institution of methods, that armed force shall not be used, save in the common interest, and

to employ international machinery for the promotion of the economic and social advancement of all peoples,

Have Resolved to Combine our Efforts to Accomplish these Aims

Accordingly, our respective Governments, through representatives assembled in the city of San Francisco, who have exhibited their full powers found to be in good and due form, have agreed to the present Charter of the United Nations and do hereby establish an international organization to be known as the United Nations.

UNITED STATES BILL OF RIGHTS

Amendment I

Congress shall make no law respecting an establishment of religion, or prohibiting the free exercise thereof; or abridging the freedom of speech, or of the press; or the right of the people peaceably to assemble, and to petition the government for a redress of grievances.

Amendment II

A well-regulated militia, being necessary to the security of a free state, the right of the people to keep and bear arms, shall not be infringed.

Amendment III

No soldier shall, in time of peace be quartered in any house, without the consent of the owner, nor in time of war, but in a manner to be prescribed by law.

Amendment IV

The right of the people to be secure in their persons, houses, papers, and effects, against unreasonable searches and seizures, shall not be violated, and no warrants shall issue, but upon probable cause, supported by oath or affirmation, and particularly describing the place to be searched, and the persons or things to be seized.

Amendment V

No person shall be held to answer for a capital, or otherwise infamous crime, unless on a presentment or indictment of a grand jury, except in cases arising in the land or naval forces, or in the militia, when in actual service in time of war or public danger; nor shall any person be subject for the same offense to be twice put in jeopardy of life or limb; nor shall be compelled in any criminal case to be a witness against himself, nor be deprived of life, liberty, or property, without due process of law; nor shall private property be taken for public use, without just compensation.

Amendment VI

In all criminal prosecutions, the accused shall enjoy the right to a speedy and public trial, by an impartial jury of the state and district wherein the crime shall have been committed, which district shall have been previously ascertained by law, and to be informed of the nature and cause of the accusation; to be confronted with the witnesses against him; to have compulsory process for obtaining witnesses in his favor, and to have the assistance of counsel for his defense.

Amendment VII

In suits at common law, where the value in controversy shall exceed twenty dollars, the right of trial by jury shall be preserved, and no fact tried by a jury, shall be otherwise reexamined in any court of the United States, than according to the rules of the common law.

Amendment VIII

Excessive bail shall not be required, nor excessive fines imposed, nor cruel and unusual punishments inflicted.

Amendment IX

The enumeration in the Constitution, of certain rights, shall not be construed to deny or disparage others retained by the people.

Amendment X

The powers not delegated to the United States by the Constitution, nor prohibited by it to the states, are reserved to the states respectively, or to the people.

THE SENECA FALLS DECLARATION (1848)/ ELIZABETH CADY STANTON

1. Declaration of Sentiments

When, in the course of human events, it becomes necessary for one portion of the family of man to assume among the people of the earth a position different from that which they have hitherto occupied, but one to which the laws of nature and of nature's God entitle them, a decent respect to the opinions of mankind requires that they should declare the causes that impel them to such a course.

We hold these truths to be self-evident: that all men and women are created equal; that they are endowed by their Creator with certain inalienable rights; that among these are life, liberty, and the pursuit of happiness; that to secure these rights governments are instituted, deriving their just powers from the consent of the governed. Whenever any form of government becomes destructive of these ends, it is the right of those who suffer from it to refuse allegiance to it, and to insist upon the institution of a new government, laying its foundation on such principles, and organizing its powers in such form, as to them shall seem most likely to effect their safety and happiness. Prudence, indeed, will dictate that governments long established should not be changed for light and transient causes; and accordingly all experience hath shown that mankind are more disposed to suffer, while evils are sufferable, than to right themselves by abolishing the forms to which they are accustomed. But when a long train of abuses and usurpations, pursuing invariably the same object, evinces a design to reduce them under absolute despotism, it is their duty to throw off such government, and to provide new guards for their future security. Such has been the patient sufferance of the women under this government, and such is now the necessity which constrains them to demand the equal station to which they are entitled. The history of mankind is a history of repeated injuries and usurpations on the part of man toward woman, having in direct object the establishment of an absolute tyranny over her. To prove this, let facts be submitted to a candid world.

He has never permitted her to exercise her inalienable right to the elective franchise.

He has compelled her to submit to laws, in the formation of which she had no voice.

He has withheld from her rights which are given to the most ignorant and degraded men—both natives and foreigners.

Having deprived her of this first right of a citizen, the elective franchise, thereby leaving her without representation in the halls of legislation, he has oppressed her on all sides.

He has made her, if married, in the eye of the law, civilly dead. He has taken from her all right in property, even to the wages she earns.

He has made her, morally, an irresponsible being, as she can commit many crimes with impunity, provided they be done in the presence of her husband.

In the covenant of marriage, she is compelled to promise obedience to her husband, he becoming, to all intents and purposes, her master—the law giving him power to deprive her of her liberty, and to administer chastisement.

He has so framed the laws of divorce, as to what shall be the proper causes, and in case of separation, to whom the guardianship of the children shall be given, as to be wholly regardless of the happiness of women—the law, in all cases, going upon a false supposition of the supremacy of man, and giving all power into his hands.

After depriving her of all rights as a married woman, if single, and the owner of property, he has taxed her to support a government which recognizes her only when her property can be made profitable to it.

He has monopolized nearly all the profitable employments, and from those she is permitted to follow, she receives but a scanty remuneration. He closes against her all the avenues to wealth and distinction which he considers most honorable to himself. As a teacher of theology, medicine, or law, she is not known.

He has denied her the facilities for obtaining a thorough education, all colleges being closed against her.

He allows her in Church, as well as State, but a subordinate position, claiming Apostolic authority for her exclusion from the ministry, and, with some exceptions, from any public participation in the affairs of the Church.

He has created a false public sentiment by giving to the world a different code of morals for men and women, by which moral delinquencies which exclude women from society, are not only tolerated, but deemed of little account in man.

He has usurped the prerogative of Jehovah himself, claiming it as his right to assign for her a sphere of action, when that belongs to her conscience and to her God.

He has endeavored, in every way that he could, to destroy her confidence in her own powers, to lessen her self-respect and to make her willing to lead a dependent and abject life.

Now, in view of this entire disfranchisement of one-half the people of this country, their social and religious degradation—in view of the unjust laws above mentioned, and because women do feel themselves aggrieved, oppressed, and fraudulently deprived of their most sacred rights, we insist that they have immediate admission to all the rights and privileges which belong to them as citizens of the United States.

In entering upon the great work before us, we anticipate no small amount of misconception, misrepresentation, and ridicule; but we shall use every instrumentality within our power to effect our object. We shall employ agents, circulate tracts, petition the State and National legislatures, and endeavor to enlist the pulpit and the press in our behalf. We hope this Convention will be followed by a series of Conventions embracing every part of the country.

2. Resolutions

WHEREAS, The great precept of nature is conceded to be, that "man shall pursue his own true and substantial happiness." Blackstone in his Commentaries remarks, that this law of Nature being coeval with mankind, and dictated by God himself, is of course superior in obligation to any other. It is binding over all the globe, in all countries and at all times; no human laws are of any validity if contrary to this, and such of them as are valid, derive all their force, and all their validity, and all their authority, mediately and immediately, from this original; therefore,

Resolved, That such laws as conflict, in any way with the true and substantial happiness of woman, are contrary to the great precept of nature and of no validity, for this is "superior in obligation to any other."

Resolved, That all laws which prevent woman from occupying such a station in society as her conscience shall dictate, or which place her in a position inferior to that of man, are contrary to the great precept of nature, and therefore of no force or authority.

Resolved, That woman is man's equal—was intended to be so by the Creator, and the highest good of the race demands that she should be recognized as such.

Resolved, That the women of this country ought to be enlightened in regard to the laws under which they live, that they may no longer publish their degradation by declaring themselves satisfied with their present position, nor their ignorance, by asserting that they have all the rights they want.

Resolved. That inasmuch as man, while claiming for himself intellectual superiority, does accord to woman moral superiority, it is pre-eminently his duty to encourage her to speak and teach, as she has an opportunity, in all religious assemblies.

Resolved, That the same amount of virtue, delicacy, and refinement of behavior that is required of woman in the social state, should also be required of man, and the same transgressions should be visited with equal severity on both man and woman.

Resolved, That the objection of indelicacy and impropriety, which is so often brought against woman when she addresses a public audience, comes with a very ill-grace from those who encourage, by their attendance, her appearance on the stage, in the concert or in feats of the circus.

Resolved, That woman has too long rested satisfied in the circumscribed limits which corrupt customs and a perverted application of the Scriptures have marked out for her, and that it is time she should move in the enlarged sphere which her great Creator has assigned her.

Resolved, That it is the duty of the women of this country to secure to themselves their sacred right to the elective franchise.

Resolved, That the equality of human rights results necessarily from the fact of the identity of the race in capabilities and responsibilities.

Resolved, therefore, That, being invested by the creator with the same capabilities, and the same consciousness of responsibility for their exercise, it is demonstrably the right and duty of woman, equally with man, to promote every righteous cause by every righteous means; and especially in regard to the great subjects of morals and religion, it is self-evidently her right to participate with her brother in teaching them, both in private and in public, by writing and by speaking, by any instrumentalities proper to be used, and in any assemblies proper to be held; and this being a self-evident truth growing out of the divinely implanted principles of human nature, any custom or authority adverse to it, whether modern or wearing the hoary sanction of antiquity, is to be regarded as a self-evident falsehood, and at war with mankind.

Resolved, That the speedy success of our cause depends upon the zealous and untiring efforts of both men and women, for the overthrow of the monopoly of the pulpit, and for the securing to women an equal participation with men in the various trades, professions, and commerce.

CREDIT LIST

INDEX